OXFORD STUDIES IN THE ABRAHAMIC RELIGIONS

General Editors

Adam J. Silverstein   Guy G. Stroumsa

OXFORD STUDIES IN THE ABRAHAMIC RELIGIONS

This series consists of scholarly monographs and other volumes at the cutting edge of the study of Abrahamic Religions. The increase in intellectual interest in the comparative approach to Judaism, Christianity, and Islam reflects the striking surge in the importance of religious traditions and patterns of thought and behaviour in the twenty-first century, at the global level. While this importance is easy to detect, it remains to be identified clearly and analysed from a comparative perspective. Our existing scholarly apparatus is not always adequate in attempting to understand precisely the nature of similarities and differences between the monotheistic religions, and the transformations of their 'family resemblances' in different cultural and historical contexts.

The works in the series are devoted to the study of how 'Abrahamic' traditions mix, blend, disintegrate, rebuild, clash, and impact upon one another, usually in polemical contexts, but also, often, in odd, yet persistent ways of interaction, reflecting the symbiosis between them.

TITLES IN THE SERIES INCLUDE:

The Making of the Abrahamic Religions in Late Antiquity
Guy G. Stroumsa

Judaism, Sufism, and the Pietists of Medieval Egypt
A Study of Abraham Maimonides and His Times
Elisha Russ-Fishbane

Purity, Community, and Ritual in Early Christian Literature
Moshe Blidstein

Islam and Its Past

Jahiliyya, Late Antiquity, and the Qurʾan

Edited by
CAROL BAKHOS AND
MICHAEL COOK

OXFORD
UNIVERSITY PRESS

OXFORD
UNIVERSITY PRESS

Great Clarendon Street, Oxford, OX2 6DP,
United Kingdom

Oxford University Press is a department of the University of Oxford.
It furthers the University's objective of excellence in research, scholarship, and education by publishing worldwide. Oxford is a registered trade mark of Oxford University Press in the UK and in certain other countries

First Edition published in 2017
Impression: 1

Published in the United States of America by Oxford University Press
198 Madison Avenue, New York, NY 10016, United States of America

British Library Cataloguing in Publication Data
Data available

Library of Congress Control Number: 2016960748

ISBN 978–0–19–874849–6

Printed and bound by
CPI Group (UK) Ltd, Croydon, CR0 4YY

In memoriam
Patricia Crone
1945–2015

Table of Contents

List of Contributors ix

Introduction 1
Carol Bakhos and Michael Cook

1. Reflections on the State of the Art in Western Qur'anic Studies 4
Devin Stewart

2. Processes of Literary Growth and Editorial Expansion in Two Medinan Surahs 69
Nicolai Sinai

3. 'O Believers, Be Not as Those Who Hurt Moses': Q 33:69 and Its Exegesis 120
Joseph Witztum

4. Pagan Arabs as God-fearers 140
Patricia Crone

5. Locating the Qur'an and Early Islam in the 'Epistemic Space' of Late Antiquity 165
Angelika Neuwirth

6. Were there Prophets in the Jahiliyya? 186
Gerald Hawting

7. Early Medieval Christian and Muslim Attitudes to Pagan Law: A Comparison 213
Michael Cook

8. Remarks on Monotheism in Ancient South Arabia 247
Iwona Gajda

Index 257

List of Contributors

Carol Bakhos is Professor of Late Antique Judaism and Study of Religion at the University of California, Los Angeles.

Michael Cook is Professor of Near Eastern Studies at Princeton University.

Patricia Crone was formerly Andrew W. Mellon Professor at the Institute for Advanced Study, Princeton.

Iwona Gajda is a researcher at the Centre National de la Recherche Scientifique (CNRS), Paris.

Gerald Hawting is Emeritus Professor at the School of Oriental and African Studies, London.

Angelika Neuwirth is Professor of Arabic Studies at the Freie Universität Berlin.

Nicolai Sinai is Associate Professor of Islamic Studies at the Oriental Institute, Oxford, and Fellow of Pembroke College, Oxford.

Devin Stewart is Professor of Arabic and Islamic Studies and MESAS Chair at Emory University.

Joseph Witztum is a member of the Department of Arabic Language and Literature at the Hebrew University of Jerusalem.

Introduction

Carol Bakhos and Michael Cook

This volume has its origin in a conference held at the UCLA G. E. von Grunebaum Center for Near Eastern Studies in October 2013. The theme of the conference was 'Islam and its Past: Jahiliyya and Late Antiquity in the Qur'an and Tradition', and the occasion for it was the conferment of the Levi della Vida Award on Patricia Crone. It was a happy occasion for all, despite the fact that at the time the honoree was already ill with terminal cancer and died less than two years later. In preparing the volume for publication we have retained the title of the conference, but have modified the subtitle to reflect the content of the volume more precisely.

This volume is not, however, a publication of all and only the talks given at that conference. Of the six talks given there, four appear here in a revised form, namely those of Joseph Witztum, Patricia Crone, Gerald Hawting, and Michael Cook. At the same time four articles that were not presented at the conference are included as chapters in this volume, namely those of Devin Stewart, Nicolai Sinai, Angelika Neuwirth, and Iwona Gajda.

All the chapters in this volume are concerned directly or indirectly with the Islamic revelation, and for the most part this means the Qur'an.

In his 'Reflections on the State of the Art in Western Qur'anic Studies' (Chapter 1), Devin Stewart provides a wide-ranging survey of the development and current state of qur'anic studies in the Western academy. He shows how interest in the field has recently grown, how the ways in which it is cultivated have changed, how it has ramified, and how difficult it now is for any one scholar to keep abreast of it. This survey is placed first in the volume not only because it can serve outsiders as a coherent introduction to the field as a whole, but also because it can draw the attention of specialists at work in one valley to what is currently going on in other valleys.

The next two contributions are research articles that aptly illustrate two of the trends in the scholarship surveyed by Stewart. In 'Processes of Literary Growth and Editorial Expansion in Two Medinan Surahs' (Chapter 2), Nicolai

Sinai reconstructs the redactional history of the opening passages of Q 5, dealing with dietary prohibitions and the performance of ablution before prayer, and Q 9, concerning warfare against the 'Associators' (*mushrikūn*). Sinai thus devotes his chapter to what one might call the internal archaeology of the text. If we start from the Qurʾan as we have it in our hands, how far and by what means can we convincingly reconstruct the earlier history of the text? What makes for a definite inference, a plausible inference, and an inference so vague as not to be worth making? The chapter sets out guidelines and criteria for research of this kind, and applies them to the study of the particular passages from the Qurʾan referred to above. Given that such methods were developed in scholarship on the text of the Bible as much as a century-and-a-half ago, and have since been applied well beyond the point of exhaustion in that field, one might have thought that specialists on the Qurʾan would already have done most of what can be done with them. Mercifully for the next generation of scholars, Sinai's chapter shows that in the study of the Qurʾan the point of exhaustion for such methods still lies far in the future.

In '"O Believers, Be Not as Those Who Hurt Moses": Q 33:69 and its Exegesis' (Chapter 3), Joseph Witztum, by contrast, probes what one might call the external archaeology of the text. If we start from a knowledge of the content of the Bible as refracted in Jewish and Christian tradition down to the eve of the rise of Islam, what can we do to better understand what the Qurʾan is saying, what it is not saying, and what it is doing in saying or not saying it? Given that the relevant sources in Hebrew, Aramaic, Syriac, and Greek were mostly published long ago, and that a quorum of scholars of earlier generations were able to use these and the Islamic sources conjointly, one might again have expected the point of exhaustion to have been reached some time ago. Here again Witztum's chapter, with its focus on one particular puzzle in one particular verse, shows that we are still a very long way from the point of exhaustion. This too is a pleasant discovery, and good news for the next generation.

The two chapters that follow are concerned less with what is going on inside the Qurʾan and more with situating it in a wider field. Patricia Crone's chapter, 'Pagan Arabs as God-fearers' (Chapter 4), is part of an exploration of the milieu in which the Meccan component of the Qurʾan made its appearance. The general question is what we can say about that milieu by combining a careful reading of the relevant parts of the Qurʾan with what we know about the religious trends of Late Antiquity in Arabia and elsewhere. More specifically, the issue is what we can learn in this way about the manner in which the 'polytheists' of the Qurʾan related to the Jewish and Christian traditions: were they Godfearers in the sense familiar from the study of ancient Judaism? Angelika Neuwirth's chapter, 'Locating the Qurʾan and Early Islam in the "Epistemic Space" of Late Antiquity' (Chapter 5), is a broader approach to the questions that arise if we resolutely consider the Qurʾan as a text of Late

Antiquity—not just looking at those features of it that could be seen as normal in that context, but also identifying what is innovative about it against the Late Antique background. Here the focus is on the 'believers' rather than the 'polytheists'. In particular, the chapter is a call for a broader and more sustained focus on the variety of typological strategies creatively employed by the Qurʾan in putting material drawn from the Bible at the service of the community of believers.

The last three chapters do not have the Qurʾan as their prime focus, though the first two certainly have something to say about it, and the last has implications for it. The three chapters engage in different ways with notions of monotheism in pre-Islamic Arabia. In 'Were There Prophets in the Jahiliyya?' (Chapter 6) Gerald Hawting brings together Islamic traditions about prophets in Arabia in the generations immediately preceding Muhammad, and analyses the conflicting ideological pressures that may lie behind these reports. Michael Cook's 'Early Medieval Christian and Muslim Attitudes to Pagan Law: A Comparison' (Chapter 7) compares and contrasts medieval Christian and Islamic ideas about the acceptability or otherwise of pagan law under the monotheist dispensation, and again seeks to identify the motivations involved.

Finally, in 'Remarks on Monotheism in Ancient South Arabia' (Chapter 8), Iwona Gajda discusses a pre-Islamic Arabian monotheism that is attested epigraphically, and thus known to us independently of the Islamic tradition. Its relevance to the understanding of the formation of Islam derives not least from this independence: as in the case of Sozomen's account of the Saracens who returned to the observance of the Hebrew customs and laws, we do not have to ask ourselves whether we are looking at a phenomenon of real life or an artifact of Islamic thought.

We live in a time when the study of the Qurʾan has been making a remarkable comeback after spending a generation on the back-burner. This volume will give the interested reader a broad survey of what has been happening in the field and concrete illustrations of some of the more innovative lines of research that have recently been pursued. Our only regret is that Patricia Crone, whose substantial contribution to this efflorescence is represented in this volume, is no longer here to see its completion.

Carol Bakhos and Michael Cook

1

Reflections on the State of the Art in Western Qurʾanic Studies

Devin Stewart

In 2013, a Malaysian court ruled that it was illegal for non-Muslims to use the word 'Allah' in the Malay language to refer to God. The motivation behind this was a desire to create a sharp divide between what is Islamic and what is Christian on the grounds that the two are essentially and categorically different, and therefore must be kept apart. On the other end of the spectrum, the works of Lühling and Luxenberg argue that the Qurʾan was originally a Christian text that has been misread, doctored, and obscured over the centuries. In their view, the attention of modern scholars to the text can retrieve the underlying Christian messages. The proper framework for interpretation of the Qurʾan is the subject of heated debate at present, both in popular culture and in academe, and the most strident voices are at these two poles. While there have been many important developments in qur'anic studies over the past three decades, it is fair to say that a major thrust of the debate is the significant divide over this very question: whether one considers the Qurʾan part of the biblical tradition or not.

If this debate were not so pervasive, and if the views on either side were not so entrenched, one might be tempted to dismiss it as a tempest in a tea-pot, a squabble that is fairly easy to resolve once one examines the evidence. A reasonable assessment of the material in the Qurʾan shows that it draws on three main traditions: Jewish tradition, Christian tradition, and pre-Islamic pagan traditions of the Arabian Peninsula and the surrounding region. It is undeniable that the Qurʾan is related intimately to biblical tradition, not only because biblical characters and concepts appear frequently there, but also because the Qurʾan presents itself as such, stressing that the only true god is identical with the God of biblical tradition, and that Islam's sacred text confirms the Torah and the Gospel that went before it. This relationship is not limited to Christian tradition, as many current writings, including

Luxenberg's work, appear to argue; Jewish tradition is equally if not more important as background of the Qurʾan. In addition, the influence of pre-Islamic Arabian religion, often ignored by authors on both sides of this ideological divide, cannot be denied. Many of the conventional features of the Qurʾan's surahs show affinities with oracular and other forms used by the *kuhhān*, the religious specialists of pre-Islamic Arabia.

While they are certainly correct in suggesting that the Qurʾan is related to Christian texts and Christian traditions, an idea that is not new, the recent proponents of Christian influence are guilty in general of skewing the evidence in a certain manner. Some writings in the 'Syriacist' trend seem intent on proving that the Qurʾan is at base a Christian document, or that it is derivative of Christianity. In a number of cases, these works identify Christian precursors of various passages or elements of the qurʾanic text. In doing so, they often ignore the particular uses that Christian stories and concepts are put to in the Qurʾan and the ways in which they are modified and adapted to the Qurʾan's structures and rhetorical strategies; they seem to be denying the Qurʾan's originality. In some cases they appear to be using the Qurʾan as evidence in a debate that is internal to Christian theology. Again, this issue appears to me to be resolvable with ease. A reasonable survey of the Qurʾan reveals that the elements of biblical tradition, whether Jewish or Christian, are modified and adapted to an original framework that is distinct from those of the Hebrew Bible and the New Testament.

This debate is also based on a stark dichotomy of method. The proponents of Christian influence argue that one must eschew Islamic tradition in analysing the Qurʾan. They portray those who resort to the *sīrah* of the Prophet and *tafsīr* in order to understand the qurʾanic text as naïve empiricists who are merely reproducing Islamic salvation history rather than engaging in critical investigation.[1] The preferable alternative, they argue, is to treat the Qurʾan as part of the preceding, biblical tradition and to detect affinities between passages of the Qurʾan and earlier Christian—and to a lesser extent, Jewish—texts. The other camp, which includes many, but not all, scholars in the Arab world, Iran, Pakistan, India, Indonesia, and elsewhere, argue that reliance on material outside the Islamic tradition will lead to incorrect and misleading results. One must avoid outside sources and rely on *tafsīr, ḥadīth, sīrah*, and

[1] This dichotomy is presented with various degrees of sophistication and nuance, but it appears to be a standard feature of the introductions to many recent works on the Qurʾan. See the introductions to the following works, among others: Stephen J. Shoemaker, *The Death of a Prophet: The End of Muhammad's Life and the Beginnings of Islam* (Philadelphia: University of Pennsylvania Press, 2012); Gabriel S. Reynolds, 'Introduction: Qurʾānic Studies and its Controversies', in Gabriel S. Reynolds, ed., *The Qurʾān in its Historical Context* (London: Routledge, 2008), 1–25; Gabriel S. Reynolds, *The Qurʾan and its Biblical Subtext* (London: Routledge, 2010); Emran El Badawi, *The Qurʾān and the Aramaic Gospel Traditions* (London: Routledge, 2014); Carlos Segovia, *The Quranic Noah and the Making of the Islamic Prophet: Study of Intertextuality and Religious Identity Formation in Late Antiquity* (Berlin: De Gruyter, 2015).

the Islamic tradition. The dichotomy is of course false. There is no reason not to use sources from both the biblical tradition and from Islamic tradition to understand the Qur'an—indeed, one might argue that they overlap to begin with, and one may use one's discretion to distinguish which statements are relevant to the text. In addition, these are not the only possible methodological stances one might take, and there are additional connections that one might emphasize instead, such as pre-Islamic Arabian tradition or ancient Near Eastern religious practices. This debate has been productive in some areas, but ideological divides, narrow and incomplete views of the history of qur'anic studies, and narrow specialization have hindered constructive conversations and progress.

A QUANTUM LEAP

The good news is that the field of qur'anic studies is booming at present, after remaining a relatively quiet corner of Arabic and Islamic studies for the middle decades of the twentieth century. The bad news is that the feverish activity has produced no grand consensus—on any aspect of the discipline, really. Far from it—the questions about the Qur'an and early Islamic history that scholars writing in the 1960s had felt were settled and well understood have now all been called into question and are the subject of the most disparate views. Qur'anic studies are experiencing growing pains, and they appear somewhat chaotic, even to insiders. It is an opportune moment to step back and to assess the discipline, taking into account its historical trajectory and long-term trends. Because of the confusion surrounding some of the trends in the discipline, it may be useful to provide some background concerning the history of the field that will help interpret current developments, many of which are represented by the contributions to this volume. It would seem to be an appropriate time to observe the field from afar and with some historical sense and to describe its contours, assess its accomplishments, and discuss the challenges that it faces.

PERIODIZATION AND FOCUS

The history of western qur'anic studies may be divided into five rough periods:

I. twelfth to sixteenth century;
II. sixteenth to nineteenth century;
III. nineteenth century to Second World War;
IV. mid-twentieth century;
V. late twentieth century to the present.

In addition, one may distinguish three large fields of enquiry in qur'anic studies. The first field is the investigation of text of the Qur'an in order to determine its 'original' or 'intended' meaning, to determine its sources, the history of its revelation, and the history of its recording and transmission. The second field is the investigation of how the Qur'an has been understood and used over the centuries in exegesis and other texts, a type of reader-response criticism. The third is the appreciation of the Qur'an as literature without strict attention to the concerns of either of the preceding two approaches, or adherence to their assumptions or modes of argument. In general, the first has dominated Western scholarship, except for a hiatus in the mid-twentieth century. The second and third were largely ignored in Western scholarship until the twentieth century.

Christian and Jewish scholars have long been interested in the Qur'an as part of their polemical exchanges with Muslim scholars in the course of prolonged political confrontations and their long-term goals of proselytizing to the Muslims and of preventing the slow erosion of Eastern Christian populations through conversion to Islam. In the medieval period, they argued that the Prophet was a renegade, heretical Christian—this explained why the Qur'an resembled the Bible in some respects but did not accord with it in many respects. It also allowed them to view Islam as a derivative, unoriginal, and defective religion. One accomplishment of this period was the first serious translation of the Qur'an into Latin by Robert of Ketton in 1143, *Lex Mahumet pseudoprophete*.

A new phase of interest in Arabic and Islam was ushered in in the sixteenth century with the advent of accomplished scholars who sought to understand scripture through linguistic analysis, not only of Hebrew and Greek, the primary biblical languages, but also of other languages that played a role in the history of Jewish and Christian texts, such as Aramaic, Syriac, Armenian, Ethiopic, and so on. There was a decided increase in the quality of Arabic philology. This period witnessed the establishment of the Maronite College in Rome in 1584, which produced several prominent Arabists, including Gabriel Sionita (Jibrāʾīl al-Ṣahyūnī) and Victor Sciallac (Naṣrallāh Shalaq al-ʿĀqūrī), who served as important teachers and resources for European scholars. François Savary de Brèves (1560–1627) created Arabic fonts and set up an Arabic printing press in Rome. He tried but failed to found a school for Oriental languages in Paris, and he got stipends for Gabriel Sionita and Victor Sciallac to teach Arabic and work on Arabic materials. This period saw the establishment of professorships in Arabic in major European universities and the activities of Arabists such as Joseph Justus Scaliger (1540–1609) in Paris, and Thomas Erpenius (1584–1624), Jacob Golius (1596–1667), and Albert Schultens (1686–1750) in Leiden. Erpenius' 1614 Arabic grammar would be used until the nineteenth century. Golius wrote the first major European dictionary of Arabic, the *Lexicon Arabico-Latinum* (Leiden, 1653), which would only be superseded by Freytag's Arabic-Latin *Lexicon* in the nineteenth century. Ludovigo Maracci (1612–1700) published a new Latin Qur'an translation as *Alcorani Textus Universus Arabicè et Latinè* at Padua in 1698. Catholic and Protestant scholars, working separately but along parallel lines, produced polyglot Bibles, grammars, and commentaries, the ultimate goal of which was to provide a scientifically sound assessment and analysis of scripture. While many of these scholars explicitly stated their desire to spread the Christian faith in the world, one senses that they were also motivated by a fundamental fascination with language and with the complexities of textual transmission that was in some sense ecumenical. This fascination led them to investigate areas that had not been the focus of sustained interest to their predecessors, including Arabic and Islamic religious texts.

The third period stretches from the early nineteenth century to the Second World War and likewise coincided with European advances in Arabic philology in general, including the foundation in 1795 of a school of Oriental languages in Paris. Antoine Sylvestre de Sacy (1758–1838) taught Arabic there and soon became the head of the school; he taught entire generations of important Orientalists. His students included a number of German and Austrian students who became the most important scholars of Arabic and Islamic studies in the following generation, such as Georg Wilhelm Friedrich Freytag (1788–1861), whose most important achievement was the *Lexicon Arabico-Latinum* (Halle, 1830–1837), an expanded and improved version of Golius' dictionary. Austrian and German scholars took the lead in studies related to the Qurʾan in particular. In 1834, the German Orientalist Gustav Flügel (1802–1870) published an edition of the Qurʾan followed by a concordance of the Qurʾan, *Concordantiae Corani arabicae* (1842). Heinrich Ferdinand Wüstenfeld (1808–1889) produced *Das Leben Muhammeds nach Muhammed Ibn Ishak* in 1858–1860. Aloys Sprenger (1813–1893) published an edition of al-Suyūṭī's *al-Itqān fī ʿulūm al-Qurʾān*, an important comprehensive traditional source on the qur'anic sciences in Calcutta in 1856. It is the scholarship of this period that set the stage for modern qur'anic studies.

THE OLD BIBLICISTS, OR THE BEGINNINGS OF MODERN WESTERN QURʾANIC STUDIES

The modern Western investigation of the Qurʾan may be dated to 1833, when Abraham Geiger, the founder of Reform Judaism, published *Was hat Mohammed aus dem Judenthume aufgenommen?* ('What Did Muhammad Take Over from Judaism?'). In this work he showed that many of the narratives and references in the text to biblical figures did not derive directly from the

Bible, but rather from para-biblical texts such as midrashic commentaries on Genesis and Exodus. This mode of scholarship would be continued by others in the nineteenth and early twentieth centuries—because European scholars were well-versed in biblical traditions and, in a number of cases, had been trained in biblical studies, it was only natural for them to identify the connections between particular elements of the Qurʾan and Jewish and Christian texts, whether from the Bible or from various apocryphal texts. Abraham Geiger identified specific elements of Jewish tradition that appeared in the Qurʾan. Other scholars took up the goal of identifying and explaining such material in the nineteenth and early twentieth centuries, including Schapiro, Hirschfeld, and others, culminating in the work of Heinrich Speyer on the Jewish material in the Qurʾan, which was published in 1931.[2]

This mode of scholarship was interrupted by the flight of Jewish scholars from Germany in the years leading up to the Second World War. The critical mass of qur'anic scholars was dispersed, and continuity was broken. Josef Horovitz, Fritz [S.D.] Goitein, and others who were involved to some extent in qurʾanic studies in their youth ended up elsewhere, and many ended up contributing primarily to other fields of Arabic, Islamic, and Middle Eastern studies.[3]

During this period, there developed a controversy between two groups of scholars, one of which claimed that Jewish tradition exerted the predominant influence on the Qurʾan, while the members of the other group claimed that Christian tradition exerted the predominant influence. On the Jewish side was of course Abraham Geiger himself, but his work was extended by Hartwig Hirschfeld, Israel Schapiro, Josef Horovitz, Charles Cutler Torrey, Heinrich Speyer, and others, such as Avraham Katsch. On the Christian side were scholars such as Julius Wellhausen, Richard Bell, Karl Ahrens, Tor Andrae, and others. Scholars on the Christian side emphasized not only the material having to do with obvious Christian elements such as the stories of Jesus, Mary, and John the Baptist, but also the apocalyptic content of the Qurʾan,

[2] Abraham Geiger, *Was hat Mohammed aus dem Judenthume aufgenommen?* (Bonn: Baaden, 1833); Hartwig Hirschfeld, *Jüdische Elemente im Koran: ein Beitrag zur Koranforschung* (Berlin: Selbstverlag, 1878); Hartwig Hirschfeld, *Beiträge zur Erklärung des Koran* (Leipzig: Schulze, 1886); Hirschfeld, *New Researches into the Composition and the Exegesis of the Qoran* (London: Royal Asiatic Society, 1902); Israel Schapiro, *Die aggadische Elemente im Erzählender Teil des Korans* (Leipzig: Fock, 1907); Josef Horovitz, *Koranische Untersuchungen* (Berlin: De Gruyter, 1926); Josef Horovitz, 'Bemerkungen zur Geschichte und Terminologie des islamischen Kultus', *Der Islam* 15–16 (1926–1927): 249–63; Heinrich Speyer, *Die biblischen Erzählungen im Qoran* (Gräfenheinichen: Schulze, 1931); F. Rosenthal, 'The History of Heinrich Speyer's *Die biblischen Erzählungen im Qoran*', in D. Hartwig, W. Homolka, M. Marx, and A. Neuwirth, eds, *Im vollen Licht der Geschichte: Die Wissenschaft des Judentums und die Anfänge der kritischen Koranforschung* (Würzburg: Ergon, 2008), 113–16.

[3] Fritz Goitein, *Das Gebet im Qorān*, doctoral dissertation Universität Frankfurt am Main, 1923.

which was seen to accord with the *Book of Revelation* more than with Jewish traditions, and what they saw as Christian interpretations of Old Testament figures such as Moses. This debate was productive, in that it spurred the participants on either side to identify additional connections and to refine their arguments. The truth, however, is that it is misleading to present the matter as a dichotomy. (This is an endemic failing of qurʾanic studies until the present day.)

As mentioned above, a survey of the Qurʾan suggests that it draws on three great traditions: Jewish tradition, Christian tradition, and the pagan religious tradition of Arabia and the surrounding regions. All three traditions have contributed to the Qurʾan to a large degree, and the whole combines these various elements into an original framework. The decided advantage of Western scholars was that they knew biblical tradition well and had studied the other Semitic languages, and so they naturally had expertise with regard to Jewish and Christian material.

The study of pagan influence remained much less developed, but it was not ignored entirely. The major publication on this topic was that of Julius Wellhausen, *Reste arabischen Heidentums*, first published in 1887, with a second edition in 1897. There were some other studies from this period, such as Henry Lammens's *Le culte des bétyles et les processions religieuses chez les Arabes préislamiques*, but very little attention was paid to it until the work of Toufic Fahd much later.[4] Until recently, the pre-Islamic pagan religious influence on the Qurʾan has been underemphasized. Indeed, some scholars have argued that it did not constitute a strong religious tradition at all, including W. Montgomery Watt, who describes the pre-Islamic Arabs' religion as 'tribal humanism'. This view is belied by the text of the Qurʾan itself, which stresses that the pagan opponents of the prophets do not want to give up the religion of their forefathers, which suggests that they have a high degree of reverence for their traditional beliefs and consider it a fully fledged religion.

The first European attempt to write a critical introduction to the Qurʾan in general was *Einleitung in den Koran*, published by Gustav Weil (1808–1889) in 1844; a second, revised edition was published in 1878. He wrote this work after writing a work on Muhammad. He divided it into three parts, the first treating the biography of Muhammad, the second the Qurʾan, and the third Islam. The section on the Qurʾan focuses primarily on the chronology of the

[4] Henry Lammens, *Le culte des bétyles et les processions religieuses chez les Arabes préislamiques. Bulletin de l'Institut Français d'Archéologie Orientale* 17 (Cairo: Institut français d'archéologie orientale, 1920); Toufic Fahd, *La divination arabe: études religieuses, sociologiques et folkloriques sur le milieu natif de l'islam* (Leiden: Brill, 1966); Fahd, *Le Panthéon de l'Arabie centrale à la veille de l'hégire* (Paris: P. Geuthner, 1968).

text, proposing a division into four periods—Early Meccan, Middle Meccan, Late Meccan, and Medinan—that would remain influential.[5]

In 1858, in a move that would have a profound effect on the future of qur'anic studies, the French Académie des Inscriptions announced a competition for a work on the history of the Qur'an, inviting submissions from all around Europe. The competition ended in a three-way tie: the prize was divided equally between the German Theodor Nöldeke, the Austrian Aloys Sprenger, and the Italian Michele Amari (1806–1889). Amari's work seems never to have been published. The other two would become major works of qur'anic studies for the next century, with Nöldeke's work overshadowing that of Sprenger.

Nöldeke had completed his dissertation *De origine et compositione Surarum qoranicarum ipsiusque Qorani* at Göttingen in 1856. When he heard of the contest he immediately repaired to Berlin to consult additional manuscripts and to expand his dissertation. After winning the prize, he published the expanded work as *Geschichte des Qorans* (Göttingen, 1860). This work became a standard textbook for the following generations, as Nöldeke, his direct students, and others continued to conduct research in the same areas. A new edition of his work, expanded into three volumes, was published between 1909 and 1938. Nöldeke's student Friedrich Schwally (1863–1919) published the first volume of the new edition—*Über den Ursprung des Qorans* (On the Origin of the Qur'an)—in 1909. The second volume—*Die Sammlung des Qorans* (The Collection of the Qur'an)—was published in 1919, just after Schwally had passed away. Gotthelf Bergsträsser worked for years on the third volume—*Die Geschichte des Korantextes* (The History of the Qur'anic Text)—but when he died in a mountaineering accident in 1933, the work was completed by Otto Pretzl and published in 1938. The work for which Aloys Sprenger was awarded the prize was published in 1861–65 as *Das Leben und die Lehre des Mohammad, nach bisher größtenteils unbenutzten Quellen*, in 3 volumes; a second, revised edition was published in 1869.[6]

Both of these works owed a tremendous debt to *al-Itqān fī ʿulūm al-Qurʾān* by Jalāl al-Dīn al-Suyūṭī (d. 911/1505). This work summarized the results of hundreds of works in the tradition of medieval Islamics and perhaps more than any other single work made it possible for Nöldeke and Sprenger to write their own treatises. This explains to a certain extent the degree of agreement

[5] Gustav Weil, *Einleitung in den Koran* (Bielefeld: Belhagen und Klasing, 1844); 2nd edn (Beilefeld: Belhagen und Klasing, 1878).

[6] *Das Leben und die Lehre des Mohammad, nach bisher größtenteils unbenutzten Quellen*, in 3 vols, 1st edn (Berlin: Nicolai, 1861–65); 2nd edn., (Berlin: Nicolai, 1869). Hartmut Bobzin, 'Theodor Nöldekes *Biographische Blätter* aus dem Jahr 1917', in Werner Arnold and Hartmut Bobzin, eds, '*Sprich doch mit deinen Knechten aramäisch, wir verstehen es!' 60 Beiträge zur Semitistik. Festschrift für Otto Jastrow zum 60. Geburtstag* (Wiesbaden: Harrassowitz, 2002), 90–104, esp. 94–5.

between their views and those of medieval Muslim scholars. Nevertheless, both scholars made acute observations and had considerable critical acumen. Nöldeke's *Geschichte*, expanded by his successors, became the definitive work in the field. His scholarship was made available, in small part, to the English-speaking world by Richard Bell, and to the Francophone world by Régis Blachère in their introductions to the Qurʾan.[7] Unfortunately, the full work was not available to a wider audience until its translation into Arabic in 2004 and into English in 2013.[8] Many scholars of qurʾanic studies have adopted Nöldeke's periodization as correct, and many studies have been based on this periodization.

In the work of many major scholars of the period, the study of the Qurʾan was closely related to investigations of the life of Muhammad and early Islamic history. Both Weil and Sprenger wrote biographies of the Prophet, and Nöldeke and his successors also paid attention to the Prophet's lifetime. They used Ibn Hishām's *Sīrah* extensively, as well as *ḥadīth* material. Their approach was not uncritical, but Goldziher's criticism of *Ḥadīth* in *Muhammedanische Studien* later convinced scholars of the Qurʾan that the standard *ḥadīth* collections were even less reliable than they had thought.[9]

This strand of nineteenth-century German scholarship led directly to a plan on the part of Bergsträsser to complete a critical edition of the Qurʾan. He began to collect manuscripts in order to undertake the project, and he described his goals and plans. When he died in 1933, his student Anton Spitaler inherited the manuscripts but never undertook the work. Several scholars were inspired by Nöldeke's work to produce translations of the Qurʾan in which the surahs were rearranged in chronological order. The first attempt was that of John Medows Rodwell (1808–1900), who produced an English translation that arranged the surahs in chronological order in 1861. Later important translations that adopted a similar rearrangement were Richard Bell's English translation in 1937–1939, and Régis Blachère's French translation in 1947. In 2016, Sami Aldeeb Abu Sahlieh published an edition and French translation of the Qurʾan in which the surahs of both the edition and the translation are arranged in supposed chronological order.[10]

[7] Régis Blachère, *Introduction au Coran* (Paris: Maisonneuve, 1947); Richard Bell, *Introduction to the Qurʾān* (Edinburgh: Edinburgh University Press, 1953).

[8] Arabic translation by Georges Tamer (Beirut: Konrad-Adenauer, 2004); English translation by Wolfgang Behn (Leiden: Brill, 2013).

[9] Gustav Weil, *Mohammed der Prophet, sein Leben und seine Lehre: aus handschriftlichen Quellen und dem Koran geschöpft und dargestellt* (Stuttgart: Metzler, 1843); Aloys Sprenger, *Das Leben und die Lehre des Mohammad, nach bisher größtenteils unbenutzten Quellen*, 3 vols, 1st edn (Berlin: Nicolai, 1861–65); Ignaz Goldziher, *Muhammedanische Studien*, 2 vols (Halle: Max Niemeyer, 1888–1889).

[10] Richard Bell, *The Qurʾān. Translated, with a Critical Re-arrangement of the Surahs*, 2 vols (Edinburgh: Edinburgh University Press, 1937–9); Régis Blachère, *Le Coran. Traduction selon un essai de reclassement des sourates* (Paris: G.-P. Maisonneuve, 1949); Sami Aldeeb Abu Sahlieh,

An important scholar of qurʾanic studies from the period between the two world wars was Arthur Jeffery (1892–1959), an Australian who was trained in Semitic languages and had spent years in Cairo, but taught in New York at Columbia University and Union Theological Seminary. In 1937, he published *Materials for the History of the Text of the Qurʾān*, among a number of other works on the text of the Qurʾan.[11]

The *Geschichte des Qorans*—even in its expanded version—did not treat all topics within qurʾanic studies. Nöldeke was of course aware of such matters, but had made a conscious choice to separate them out of his work. The main topics he dealt with were the internal chronology of the text, the process by which the text had been gathered together, and the subsequent textual history of the Qurʾan. These were treated in three sections of his original text, and these three sections became the basis of the three-volume elaboration of his work. Following the method of Gustav Weil, and drawing on the medieval Islamic scholarship, he divided the *surah*s of the Qurʾan into four periods: Early Meccan, Middle Meccan, Late Meccan, and Medinan. This necessarily involved an investigation of early Islamic sources, the biography of the Prophet, the history of the early Muslim community, and qurʾanic style. Nöldeke's work omitted discussion of the Jewish and Christian texts that were related to the Qurʾan, topics which he left to other scholars to develop.

Another major topic addressed by a groundbreaking investigation during this period was *tafsīr* or qur'anic exegesis.[12] Ignaz Goldziher's *Die Richtungen der Islamischen Koranauslegung* may be viewed as the counterpart of Nöldeke's *Geschichte des Qorans* for the field of *tafsīr*. This important work provided an excellent overview of the various modes of Islamic commentary on the Qurʾan, including traditional, dogmatic, mystical, sectarian, and modern exegesis, something that had not been addressed in earlier Western scholarship. It also included a discussion of the early stages of qur'anic exegesis, and an insightful discussion of al-Ṭabarī's *Jāmiʿ al-bayān fī taʾwīl āy al-Qurʾān* after that work had been introduced to Western scholarship by Otto Loth in 1881.[13]

During this period a critical tradition of scholarship was established, primarily in Germany and Austria, but with influence in England, France, and elsewhere. There was a critical mass of scholars in relatively close contact with

Le Coran: texte arabe et traduction française, 2nd edn (Ochettaz: Aldeeb, 2016); Abu Sahlieh, *Al-Qurʾān al-karīm bi-l-tasalsul al-tāʾrīkhī* (Ochettaz: Aldeeb, 2015).

[11] Arthur Jeffery, *Materials for the History of the Text of the Qurʾān: The Old Codices* (Leiden: Brill, 1937); Arthur Jeffery, 'The Mystic Letters of the Qurʾan', *The Moslem World* 14 (1924): 247–60; Arthur Jeffery, 'Abū 'Ubayd on the Verses Missing from the Qurʾān', *Muslim World* 28 (1938): 61–5; Arthur Jeffery, *The Foreign Vocabulary of the Qurʾan* (Baroda: Oriental Institute, 1938); Arthur Jeffery, *The Qurʾān as Scripture* (New York: R.F. Moore, 1952).

[12] Ignaz Goldziher, *Die Richtungen der Islamischen Koranauslegung* (Leiden: Brill, 1920).

[13] Otto Loth, 'Ṭabaris Korankommentar', *Zeitschrift der Deutschen Morgenländischen Gesellschaft* 35 (1881): 588–628.

each other, including a number of the best Arabists of the time, and they were interested in many of the same problems and consciously built on the studies of their predecessors. The three main fronts along which this scholarship advanced are represented by Speyer's *Die biblische Erzählungen im Koran*, Nöldeke's *Geschichte des Qorans*, and Goldziher's *Die Richtungen der islamischen Koranauslegung*, that is, the biblical sources of the Qurʾan, the history of the qur'anic text, and commentaries on the Qurʾan. This continuity was interrupted by a number of factors, including especially the rise of the Nazi regime, which led to the flight of Jewish scholars from Germany and Austria, as well as the Second World War, which made communication between different national communities of scholars difficult. The untimely death of Bergsträsser in 1933 in a mountaineering accident did not help. Because of the small numbers of scholars involved in the project of Oriental studies in general, and in qurʾanic studies in particular, the field could not weather the disturbances very well. Two of the main strands of investigation of this period, represented by the legacies of Speyer and Nöldeke, respectively, nearly came to a halt.

THE INTERRUPTION

The fourth period stretches from before the Second World War to the later twentieth century. The fifth period began in the late twentieth century and continues today. The truth is that qurʾanic studies experienced significant continuity during the third period, lost it in the fourth, and has regained it in the fifth. Individual scholars continued to work on the Qurʾan: Richard Bell and Montgomery Watt in England, Régis Blachère in France, Arthur Jeffery in the United States, Rudi Paret in Germany, and a handful of other scholars. However, there was no central locus for study of the Qurʾan, and many scholars worked on the Qurʾan only as a sideline. Most of these scholars did not produce a steady stream of students who would carry on research in the field. Some topics were mostly ignored, including especially the history of the text and the relationship between the Qurʾan and Jewish and Christian texts.

One important factor behind this neglect was concern with inter-religious dialogue, which was evident in the work of several leading scholars, especially W. Montgomery Watt, who was a minister in the Scottish Episcopalian Church and extremely concerned about relations between Christians and Muslims. It was seen as expedient and responsible to avoid certain topics that could be perceived as offensive by Muslims, and these included anything that might suggest that the Qurʾan was based on or borrowed from earlier texts or that the Prophet himself authored or edited the text. The influential *Introduction to the Qurʾan* of Richard Bell was edited and published in a new edition by Watt, and little attention was given to the Jewish and Christian texts that were clearly related to the Qurʾan. Along with the concern for dialogue came a desire to treat the Qurʾan as Muslims treated it—to take seriously the fact that the Qurʾan was a religious community's sacred text. Works by Arthur Jeffery, William Graham, and others studied the Qurʾan as a sacred text.[14] Certain questions that had the potential to muddy the waters of inter-religious understanding, such as the question of Jewish and Christian sources of the Qurʾan and the textual criticism of the received scripture, were ignored.

Certain topics gained new emphasis, such as the psychology of the Prophet Muhammad, his prophetic experience, and his historical persona, perhaps in response to the Historical Jesus movement in New Testament studies. Such studies were first written in the 1930s, and again were perhaps inspired by an urge to promote good relations with Muslims by avoiding controversial topics. It cannot be a coincidence that Johann Fück wrote about the originality of the Prophet Muhammad after spending the years 1930–1935 teaching in Dhaka. Tor Andrae, Harris Birkeland, Rudi Paret, and others wrote on the psychology of the Prophet as well.[15]

A number of scholars in religious studies who were interested in the Qurʾan turned to studies of *Tafsīr*. Such studies were favoured because they took the Qurʾan seriously as sacred text, the foundational text of a religious community. They also sidestepped potentially sensitive issues, such as those of the sources of the Qurʾan and the historical criticism of the text, avoiding claims that the Qurʾan borrowed from Jewish and Christian traditions or that Muhammad was the author of the text. This shift in focus gave scholars more leeway to present critical assessments, because it was easier to suggest that al-Ṭabarī or al-Suyūṭī missed something than to suggest that the Qurʾan itself was less than perfect. In some fashion, then, the turn to *tafsīr* went along with the attention to Christian–Muslim dialogue, since it was undertaken partly in a conscious effort to avoid offending Muslims' sensibilities couched in reverence for the Prophet and for the received text of the Qurʾan. The study of *tafsīr* was therefore adopted as a kinder, nicer sort of Orientalism. This approach led to advances

[14] Jeffery, *The Qurʾan as Scripture*; William Graham wrote several studies on the Qurʾan, including 'The Earliest Meaning of Qurʾān', *Der Islam* 23–4 (1984): 361–77, *ḥadīth qudsī*, as well as *Divine Word and Prophetic Word in Early Islam* (Oxford: Oxford University Press, 1977), and *Beyond the Written Word: Oral Aspects of Scripture in the History of Religion* (Cambridge: Cambridge University Press, 1987).

[15] Johann Fück, 'Die Originalität des arabischen Propheten', *Zeitschrift der Deutschen Morgenländischen Gesellschaft* 90 (1936): 509–25; Tor Andrae, *Muhammad, Sein Leben und Sein Glaube* (Göttingen: Vandenhoeck & Ruprecht, 1932); Harris Birkeland, *'The Lord Guideth': Studies on Primitive Islam* (Oslo: H. Aschehoug, 1956); Rudi Paret, *Mohammed und der Koran: Verkündigung und Geschichte des arabischen Propheten* (Stuttgart: Kohlhammer, 1957).

in understanding of the modes of *tafsīr* and in the scholarly apparatus surrounding the Qur'an.

Focus on *tafsīr* and the genres of work that had grown up around the Qur'an in pre-modern Islamic scholarship thus sidestepped the thorny issue of appearing to critique the Qur'an or the Prophet directly. Scholars who did this work include Andrew Rippin, who wrote dozens of studies of *tafsīr* and other genres of medieval Islamic qur'anic studies that grew up around the sacred text, Jane McAuliffe, particularly in her work *Qur'anic Christians*, and Brannon Wheeler in his book on *Moses in the Quran and Islamic Exegesis.*[16] There was of course nothing inherently wrong with studies of this kind, but some of this work implied that this was actually the best or preferred mode of doing qur'anic studies, when it actually avoided studiously certain topics that merited serious investigation. The result was that the work of the Old Biblicists on the connections between the Qur'an and the Bible that had reached a high point in the work of Heinrich Speyer was neglected and not continued. The effect was made much graver simply by the fact that there were so few hands working in the field.

The psychology of the Prophet was undertaken by Johann Fück, Rudi Paret, W. Montgomery Watt, Harris Birkeland, and others. In general these studies took a less sceptical and critical approach towards Islamic sources and had the advantage of accepting—or at least not flying in the face of—traditional Muslim understandings of the biography of the Prophet and the fulfilment of his prophetic role.

Moreover, in this period the historical context was placed in the background and attention focused on the text synchronically. One type of work to do this included discussions of the Qur'an's major themes. Prominent publications in this area were those of Isutzu, Fazlur Rahman, and Jacques Jomier on qur'anic themes.[17] A similar approach has been undertaken by scholars who address the Qur'an as literature.[18]

[16] See bibliography for a list of Rippin's work. Jane D. McAuliffe, *Qur'ānic Christian: An Analysis of Classical and Modern Exegesis* (Cambridge: Cambridge University Press, 1991); Brannon M. Wheeler, *Moses in the Quran and Islamic Exegesis* (London: Routledge, 2002).

[17] Toshihiko Izutsu, *God and Man in the Qur'an* (Tokyo: Keio University, 1964); Toshihiko Izutsu, *Ethico-Religious Concepts in the Qur'an* (Montreal: McGill University Press, 1966); Fazlur Rahman, *Major Themes of the Qur'ān* (Minneapolis: Bibliotheca Islamica, 1980); Jacques Jomier, *Les grands thèmes du Coran* (Paris: Le Centurion, 1978), translated into English as *The Great Themes of the Qur'ān* (London: SCM Press, 1997).

[18] Andrew Rippin, 'The Qur'ān as Literature: Perils, Pitfalls and Prospects', *British Society for Middle Eastern Studies Bulletin* 10 (1983): 38–47.

Significant progress was made during this period in the field of *tafsīr*, but the pace of publication has quickened considerably in the last few decades. Significant advances have been made in the understanding of commentators such as al-Ṭabarī, al-Jubbāʾī, al-Thaʿlabī, al-Ṭabrisī, al-Zamakhsharī, al-Biqāʿī, and others.[19] A number of studies have been devoted to modern *tafsīr*, which remains a very productive genre of Islamic letters.[20] However, we are still far from having a grand, synthetic history of *tafsīr*, and Goldziher's work remains the best overview of *tafsīr* in general. In the meantime, hundreds of commentaries that were unavailable to Goldziher have been published, providing much new material for analysis, and hundreds of studies have been published in Arabic and other Islamic languages on qurʾanic commentary.

THE COMPOSITION OF THE QURʾAN AND *FORMGESCHICHTE*

The history of qurʾanic studies has repeatedly witnessed the publication of an innovative hypothesis that is either poorly understood or entirely ignored. Sometimes it sparks some interest until a damning review appears, but is then consigned to the dustbins of oblivion. The result is a series of one-sided conversations in which scholars do not respond directly to one another and in the end fail to build on each other's advances or even to engage in a productive debate. This phenomenon is illustrated well by the work of Richard Bell and John Wansbrough, two scholars in qurʾanic studies who attempted to apply the methods of *Formgeschichte* ('Form-History'), particularly as developed by scholars of the New Testament, chief among which was Rudolf Bultmann, who sought to explain the process by which the pre-existing texts that formed the synoptic gospels came together. Richard Bell produced a translation of the Qurʾan that not only rearranged the surahs according to their historical order but also aimed to reveal all the additions, interpolations, and editorial joins in the text. His vision of how this process occurred is quite complicated, and he supposed, in addition, that some originally separate texts that happened to be recorded on the face and the obverse of a single page or

[19] Claude Gilliot, *Exégèse, langue, et théologie en Islam* (Paris: Librairie Philosophique J. Vrin, 1990); Daniel Gimaret, *Une Lecture mutazilite du Coran* (Louvain: Peeters, 1994); Bruce Fudge, *al-Ṭabrisī and the Craft of Commentary* (London: Routledge, 2011); Andrew J. Lane, *A Traditional Muʿtazilite Commentary: The Kashshāf of Jār Allāh al-Zamakhsharī* (Leiden: Brill, 2006); Walid A. Saleh, *The Formation of the Classical Tafsīr Tradition: The Qurʾān Commentary of al-Thaʿlabī (d. 427/1035)* (Leiden: Brill, 2004); Walid A. Saleh, *In Defense of the Bible: A Critical Edition and an Introduction to al-Biqāʿī* (Leiden: Brill, 2008).

[20] Johanna Pink, *Sunnitischer Tafsir in der modernen islamischen Welt: akademische Traditionen, Popularisierung und nationalstaatliche Interessen* (Leiden: Brill, 2011).

folio of parchment ended up joined together in one surah. Much of the logic behind these assessments of the historical redaction of surahs is set forth in his commentary, which was published long after in two volumes.[21] Later scholarship has not addressed many of his proposals, but there is a general sense that they involve excessive suggestions of later manipulation of the text. The only scholarly treatment of specific claims by Bell of which I am aware is that of Robinson, who argues that a number of Bell's suggestions would disrupt or go against the integral unity of the text that was obviously intended.[22]

In 1977 and 1978, John Wansbrough published *Quranic Studies* and *The Sectarian Milieu*. These works certainly provoked a response in the field, but the debate that they stirred up has not been particularly productive until recently, in part because other scholars in the field did not share Wansbrough's approach and concerns, but also because Wansbrough's work was poorly understood. Wansbrough was something of a hermetic writer: he did not explain or justify his overall approach and did not state the assumptions on which it was based. He also rigorously avoided writing introductions and conclusions that would have made his ideas more accessible to the reader. As it is, one must do some detective work to figure out his method and argument. The fundamental aspect of Wansbrough's work that he fails to explain is that it is an attempt to apply the theories of Rudolf Bultmann regarding the New Testament to qurʾanic material. His *Quranic Studies* corresponds to Bultmann's *Die synoptische Tradition* (1921), and his *Sectarian Milieu* corresponds to Bultmann's *Das Urchristentum im Rahmen der antiken Religionen* (1949). In the first work, he explains how the Qurʾan was put together from independent 'prophetic logia' circulating in the community, as Bultmann does for the synoptic Gospels, the gospels of Matthew, Mark, and Luke. In the second, just as Bultmann endeavoured to explain how the early Christian community was influenced by the major religious traditions of the surrounding communities, Judaism and Hellenistic religion, Wansbrough endeavoured to demonstrate how nascent Islam was influenced by Judaism and Christianity. When the works came out, they were criticized for throwing out or radically rejecting much of the material from Islamic tradition, for claiming that the Qurʾan was probably collected and canonized outside the Arabian Peninsula, perhaps in Iraq, and for setting the date of canonization long after the time of the Prophet, as much as two centuries or more. What few scholars realized, however, whether they were supporters or distractors, was that Wansbrough's work was based on unsupported assumptions: that the process of collection and

[21] Richard Bell, *The Qurʾān. Translated, with a Critical Re-arrangement of the Surahs*, 2 vols. (Edinburgh: Edinburgh University Press, 1937–9); Bell, *A Commentary on the Qurʾan*, 2 vols, C. E. Bosworth and M. E. J. Richardson, eds (Manchester: University of Manchester Press, 1991).

[22] Neal Robinson, *Discovering the Qurʾan: A Contemporary Approach to a Veiled Text* (London: SCM, 1996), 94–96, 177, 184, 187.

canonization of the Qur'an recapitulated that of the New Testament and that this process occurred as the proponents of *Formgeschichte*, especially Bultmann, had imagined it. The idea is not preposterous, but neither is it obviously correct. A serious response to the works would be a careful comparison of the collection and canonization of the Qur'an to that of the New Testament.[23]

CONTEMPORARY QUR'ANIC STUDIES

Qur'anic studies have experienced an explosion of interest over the last three decades. Heightened interest has led to institutional changes that cannot simply be reversed, even if the current excitement dies down in the near future. Academic positions for specialists in Islam have been created. The *Journal of Qur'anic Studies* was founded in 1999 at the School of Oriental and African Studies in London, and associated biennial conferences have been held there regularly since then. *The Encyclopaedia of the Quran*, a major summation of Western scholarship to date, was published in 2001–2006. Since 2007, the German Berlin-Brandenburgische Akademie der Wissenschaften has funded a massive, long-term project, the Corpus Coranicum, to collect and document qur'anic manuscripts and other texts related to the contents of the Qur'an. They have published online commentaries of the surahs of the Qur'an, at the same time generating a number of works of qur'anic scholarship by Angelika Neuwirth, Nicolai Sinai, and others. The German government has also embarked on a mission to train teachers of Islamic religion, a move that is having an effect of encouraging the production of even more Qur'anic scholarship. The International Qur'anic Studies Association was founded several years ago and has been holding regular annual conferences in the United States since 2013. It will soon begin publication of a new journal, *Journal of the International Qur'anic Studies Association*, as well as a book series; an online *Review of Qur'anic Research* and a regular blog are already in place. IQSA began holding biennial international conferences of qur'anic studies in 2015, with an inaugural conference in Jakarta, Indonesia. The Institute of Ismaili Studies in London has promoted qur'anic scholarship through a number of international conferences and workshops, and it has been publishing a series of books focusing on the Qur'an and *tafsīr*. In addition, Routledge in London and Brill in Leiden both have book series devoted to qur'anic studies, not to mention

[23] See Josef Van Ess, 'Rezension zu Wansbrough, *Qur'anic Studies*', *Bibliotheca Orientalis* 35 (1978): 349–53; Angelika Neuwirth, 'Rezension zu Wansbrough, *Qur'anic Studies*', *Die Welt des Islams* 23–24 (1984): 539–42; Devin J. Stewart, 'Wansbrough, Bultmann, and the Theory of Variant Traditions in the Qur'ān', 17–51, in Angelika Neuwirth and Michael Sells, eds, *Qur'ānic Studies Today* (London: Routledge, 2016).

the publication of major works in Germany, France, and Italy. In 2015, HarperCollins published a *Study Qur'an*, which includes a new translation of Islam's sacred text along with a substantial selection of English translations from commentaries from the pre-modern Islamic tradition. The newly constituted field of qur'anic studies is becoming more regular, integrated, and ensconced in institutions than ever before. Dozens of recent doctoral dissertations focus on the Qur'an, and the number of young scholars whose main academic focus is some aspect of the Qur'an is quite astounding in comparison to the situation just twenty years ago. The field as a whole is much larger than it has been at any point in history.

Qur'anic studies are becoming more and more like biblical studies, something that has distinct advantages and disadvantages. New scholars in the field should have an easier time getting trained and learning about the traditions of the field, important reference works, and important debates in the history of qur'anic scholarship. At the same time, there has been an explosion in publication that will make it increasingly difficult to cover the field. As in biblical studies, one will have to wade through a morass of mediocre publications to find significant advances in scholarship, and this problem is bound to worsen as time goes on. As in biblical studies, many concerned citizens with various pious impulses, political axes to grind, or far-fetched theories, but without rigorous training, will feel compelled to write works on the Qur'an. Because of the tremendous demand by publishers for works on the Qur'an, specialists in Judaism and Christianity, as well as specialists in various fields of Islamic studies such as Sufism, history, and philosophy, have been attracted to the Qur'an. It is becoming quite difficult to keep abreast of all the new publications in qur'anic studies, something that will work towards the creation of distinct subspecialties in the field. At present, these are by no means as finely distinguished as the subfields of biblical studies, but one can already see a great divide between the qur'anic manuscript and material culture specialists on the one hand and specialists in literary and philological aspects of qur'anic studies on the other.

The new wave of interest in qur'anic studies has produced scholarship of many types, concentrating on many specific areas of research. Among the most influential trends, I would like to single out nine for analysis. For convenience, I have termed these trends: New Biblicism, Allohistory, Late Antiquarianism, New Textualism, Ring Theory, Feminist Criticism, Prophetic Typology, Oral Performance, and Canonization.

THE NEW BIBLICISTS

In 2000, an anonymous author using the pseudonym Cristoph Luxenberg published a book in German that claimed to 'decipher' the Qur'an. This work argues for Christian influence on the Qur'an, which is not at all surprising, but in order to do so adopts a radical thesis, that the Qur'an was originally couched in a 'mixed' language, an Arabic-Aramaic creole. Recognition of this nature of qur'anic language, Luxenberg claims, allows one to decipher difficult or puzzling passages in the text, revealing their true, original meaning. The work seems to have hit a nerve. It was widely read and created a flurry of reactions both among scholars and among the wider public.

Luxenberg's work has continued to be the basis of debate and contention until the present. Luxenberg published a second edition of his work in 2004, a third in 2007, and an English translation also in 2007. The new editions and the translation looked more handsome and added a few more footnotes and entries in the bibliography, but they did not remove, modify, or defend more adequately any of the specific propositions Luxenberg had made earlier. They remained essentially the same as the first edition.[24]

The critical reaction to this work was often not very well reasoned, but at least it was large. On the one hand, some scholars lauded the work as the first serious application of biblical criticism to the Qur'an and as a rigorous philological exercise. This is of course not true. The author's method is based on the adoption of a radical, improbable assumption and a mechanical resort to Syriac dictionaries rather than expert philological analysis. On the other hand, many Islamicists denounced the work as shoddy scholarship that failed to cite the relevant studies in the field and did not adhere to the standard modes of Arabic and Islamic studies. For a number of these scholars, it rankled that an amateur wrote such a book as this, and they sought to defend their turf from the outsider. Most such defences focused on the method and approach of Luxenberg rather than on his concrete propositions about the text of the Qur'an.[25] It should be remembered, however, that amateurs may come up with important results, whether by serendipity or diligent, deliberate work. After all, the architect Michael Ventris, who deciphered Linear B in 1952 after years of determined analysis, was also an amateur, and no one suggests that his accomplishments were anything less than brilliant. In addition, one must keep in mind that someone using a flawed methodology might stumble upon an important result and that attacking the method does not necessarily disprove the result. Moreover, one must admit as well that most of the scholars who write on the Qur'an are not at base specialists on the Qur'an (or Syriac and Aramaic), but actually were trained in other subfields of Arabic and Islamic

[24] Christoph Luxenberg, *Die syro-aramäische Lesart des Koran. Ein Beitrag zur Entschlüsselung der Koransprache* (Berlin: Das Arabische Buch, 2000); *The Syro-Aramaic Reading of the Koran: A Contribution to the Decoding of the Language of the Koran* (Berlin: Hans Schiler, 2007).

[25] Christoph Burgmer, ed., *Streit um den Koran—Die Luxenberg-Debatte, Standpunkte und Hintergründe* (Berlin: Hans Schiler, 2004).

studies and so are also amateurs with respect to qur'anic scholarship. It is true that some of them are better Arabists than Luxenberg, but the difference between them might be one of degree rather than one of category.

On the face of it, a number of Luxenberg's general ideas are quite plausible. That the Qurʾan shows traces of Christian influence is so obvious as to be irrefutable. Qurʾanic language, at least in certain passages, includes Aramaic or Syriac lexical items, such as the word *ṭūr*, which refers to Mount Sinai and which clearly derives from the Aramaic or Syriac word *ṭōr* 'mountain', distinguishing it from other mountains mentioned in the text, which are termed *jabal, jibāl*, using the ordinary Arabic word for mountain. It cannot derive from the Hebrew word for mountain, *har*, which is quite different. Other examples, such as the word *yamm* 'sea', are not so clear, for they could derive either from Hebrew directly or from Aramaic or Syriac. In addition, certain passages of the Qurʾan are closely related to Christian texts: the beginning section of *Sūrat Maryam*, for example, is closely related to the beginning of the Gospel of Luke, the beginning of *Sūrat al-Kahf* is related to the Christian saints' story of the Seven Sleepers of Ephesus, and the story of the fall of Iblīs, recounted several times in the Qurʾan, is related to a similar account in the *Life of Adam and Eve*. It is also possible that the language of some of these qur'anic passages reflects the language of the underlying texts, whether transmitted orally or textually. A similar argument has been made with regard to the Aramaic linguistic features that can be detected in the Greek of the Gospels, and it has met with wide acceptance. Most early Christian texts, whether canonical or non-canonical, were originally composed in Greek but had been translated before the advent of Islam into many languages, including Syriac, Armenian, Georgian, and Ethiopic, but of these it appears that Syriac would have been most accessible to Arabs in and around North and Central Arabia, given that the native Christian populations of the Levant and most of Iraq would have been speaking some form of Aramaic and that their main church language would have been Syriac.

However, Luxenberg's claim that the Qurʾan was written in a mixed Arabic-Aramaic language seems preposterous, given the lack of historical evidence for such a language. All that one might be able to claim responsibly is that there were groups of Arabic speakers who had adopted Christianity before Islam who must have had Syriac as their liturgical language and Arabic as their spoken language, a situation that exists till this day in Christian communities in the Levant. Such speakers in the community would have had control of both idioms, and terms from the liturgical language may have come into use in popular speech. To claim that there was a mixed language goes beyond the limits of the evidence. It is even unclear whether the Bible, or parts of it, had been translated into Arabic by these Christian groups before the advent of Islam.

Perhaps most importantly, almost all of the concrete proposals of Luxenberg are demonstrably wrong, and the mechanical procedure he describes as his method, involving successive rounds of consultation of Syriac dictionaries, based on the assumption that any problematic passage must have an underlying text that is Syriac/Aramaic, does not inspire confidence. A very small number of his suggested emendations make sense and are worth serious consideration, about three or four out of hundreds. Some of his remarks concerning the script of the Qurʾan are also worth consideration, such as the claim that a *yāʾ* in the script could represent the vowel -*ā*-, which is clearly true but seems to have little to do with Syriac. Even the parts of Luxenberg's work that make plausible points could be presented and argued much more clearly.

One consequence of the controversy over Luxenberg's work was that the earlier work of Günther Lüling was resurrected and discussed. In this work, a 1971 dissertation, Lüling argued that one can retrieve a Christian hymnal with strophic, poetic hymns, if one examines the Qurʾan carefully, and that this material was systematically altered by later Muslims to obscure the fact. In some ways, Lühling's work was similar methodologically to that of Luxenberg, particularly in stressing Christian influence and the alteration of the text.[26] Like Luxenberg's work, though, Lüling's work proved more interesting ideologically than textually. Most of his specific suggestions about the text seem unreasonable. Luxenberg has continued to write additional pieces and articles that adopt the same method as that used in his book, such as an essay on Christmas in the Qurʾan.[27]

Luxenberg's work spurred scholars of the Qurʾan to focus on Syriac language and religious literature, and some observers have referred to 'the Syriac turn' in qurʾanic studies. Some scholars such as Sidney Griffith had already been doing this work, but a sea-change was brought about, to such an extent that it had a major effect on the teaching of Syriac in academic institutions in Europe and North America. The chief works that were produced by this sort of attention to Syriac have been written by Gabriel Said Reynolds, Holger Zellentin, Emran El-Badawi, and Joseph Witztum (whose 2011 dissertation, *The Syriac Milieu of the Qurʾan: The Recasting of Biblical Narratives*, has not yet been published). The studies of Reynolds, El-Badawi, and Witztum all attempt to explain biblical material in the qur'anic text by examining material from the Christian tradition written in Syriac. Zellentin's work takes a more circumspect approach, arguing that the Christian text of the *Didascalia* reveals something of the legal context that is evident in

[26] Günter Lüling, *Über den Ur-Qur'an. Ansätze zur Rekonstruktion vorislamischer christlicher Strophenlieder im Qurʾan* (Erlangen: Lüling, 1974); 3rd corrected edn published in 2004; Lüling, *A Challenge to Islam for Reformation. The Rediscovery and Reliable Reconstruction of a Comprehensive Pre-Islamic Christian Hymnal Hidden in the Koran under Earliest Islamic Reinterpretations* (New Delhi: Motilal Banarsidass Publishers, 2003).

[27] Cristoph Luxenberg, 'Noël dans le Coran', in Anne-Marie Delcambre and Joseph Bosshard, eds, *Enquêtes sur l'Islam: en hommage à Antoine Moussali* (Paris: Éditions Desclée de Brouwer, 2004), 117–38; Luxenberg, 'Weihnachten im Koran', 35–41, in *Streit um den Koran.*

the qur'anic text.[28] The emphasis on Syriac is certainly evident in recent work, but the type of scholarship being produced is not entirely new. I would rather connect it with the earlier work in the tradition of Geiger, Speyer, and others. It is merely that in the argument over the dominant influence on Islam, the pendulum has swung sharply towards the Christian side rather than the Jewish side. For this reason I would label such scholarship as partaking in 'New Biblicism', recognizing its relationship to earlier scholarship, rather than Syriacism. The 'New' recognizes that this resumption of research has been taken up after a considerable hiatus. There are a few recent studies coming out of a similar background but that stress connections with Jewish texts, such as that of Carlos Segovia.[29]

These recent studies have produced some tangible results. Several studies have pointed out the close relationship between the narrative of Dhū al-Qarnayn in *Sūrat al-Kahf* and the *Neshāna*, the Syriac Alexander Legend.[30] Zellentin argues that Christian discussions of the law reveal many of the background assumptions behind the qurʾanic discussion of the law. There are also similarities between the discussion of the qurʾanic abrogation of Jewish law by Jesus and Christian discussions of the same topic. One result convincingly argued by El-Badawi is that qur'anic statements that priests and rabbis of the Christians and Jews overstep their bounds and claim authority that they do not have draw on anti-clerical views expressed in Christian literature. These explorations of Christian, Syriac connections are undertaken in a more level-headed manner than the works of Lühling and Luxenberg, but they also run the risk of reading more into the text than is actually there. Any number of passages of the Qur'an show obvious connections with the Bible or biblical tradition, but it is difficult to show that the biblical elements that are evident in the text indeed come through later Syriac translations of the Bible,

[28] Sidney Griffith, 'Christian Lore and the Arabic Qurʾān: "The Companions of the Cave" in *Surat al-Kahf* and Syriac Christian Tradition', in Gabriel S. Reynolds, ed., *The Qurʾān in its Historical Context* (London: Routledge, 2008), 109–37; Gabriel S. Reynolds, *The Qurʾan and Its Biblical Subtext* (London: Routledge, 2010); Emran El-Badawi, *The Qurʾān and the Aramaic Gospel Traditions* (London: Routledge, 2014); Holger Michael Zellentin, *The Qurʾān's Legal Culture: The Didascalia Apostolorum as a Point of Departure* (Tübingen: Mohr Siebek, 2013); Joseph Witztum, 'The Foundations of the House (Q 2:127)', *Bulletin of the School of Oriental and African Studies* 72.1 (2009): 25–40; Joseph Witztum, *The Syriac Milieu of the Qurʾān: The Recasting of Biblical Narratives*. Ph.D. dissertation, Princeton University, 2011; Joseph Witztum, 'Joseph among the Ishmaelites: Q 12 in Light of Syriac Sources', in Gabriel S. Reynolds, ed., *New Perspectives on the Qurʾān: The Qurʾān in its Historical Context 2* (London: Routledge, 2011), 425–48.

[29] Carlos A. Segovia, *The Quranic Noah and the Making of the Islamic Prophet: Study of Intertextuality and Religious Identity Formation in Late Antiquity* (Berlin: De Gruyter, 2015).

[30] Tommaso Tesei, 'The Chronological Problems of the Qurʾān: The Case of the Story of Ḏū l-Qarnayn (Q 18:83–102)', *Rivista degli Studi Orientali* 84 (2011): 457–66; TommasoTesei, 'The Prophecy of Ḏū-l-Qarnayn and the Origins of the Qurʾānic Corpus', *Miscellanea Arabica* (2013–14): 273–90; Kevin Van Bladel, 'The Alexander Legend in the Qurʾān 18:83–102', in *The Qurʾān in its Historical Context* (London: Routledge, 2010), 175–213.

commentaries, sermons, and other works, and not through Jewish sources or sources in other languages.

The New Biblicists on the whole argue that pre-modern commentaries on the Qurʾan and related material that purport to explain the text be viewed with suspicion when one is seeking to investigate qur'anic origins, in large part because Muslim believers often cite such material as incontrovertible arguments simply because they accept such sources as authoritative and beyond question. There are certainly reasons to exercise caution when using the Islamic commentarial tradition as means to get at the sense of the Qurʾan during the time of the Prophet or its original meaning. In eschewing it, the New Biblicists are reacting to a large extent to arguments on the basis of authority that are uttered by modern commentators on the text: a particular verse must be interpreted in X fashion because al-Ṭabarī, or al-Zamakhsharī, or al-Bayḍāwī says so. In many cases, traditional interpretations, including ones that are widely accepted or influential, may be shown to have little basis in the text. In other cases, it can be demonstrated that the commentators, as a whole, fail to detect an interpretation that appears obvious for other reasons, including parallel information from biblical texts.

There is some reason to agree with this procedure. For example, the term *kawthar* (108:1) is widely attested in qur'anic commentaries and related works to be a proper noun, the name of a river or pool in which the believers cleanse themselves before entering paradise. This interpretation has absolutely no support from the text itself or the context in which it appears, and it seems to be completely arbitrary: commentators attached a celestial meaning to the word because it is unusual and mellifluous. Similarly, the reference to *awtād* in *Sūrat al-Fajr* (Q 89) is taken literally to refer to 'tent-pegs', the ordinary meaning of that word, which does not seem substantial enough to merit consideration in the context. This is then interpreted as an Arab tribal idiom that refers to a great chief by stating that he has many tent-pegs, and by extension many tents and a large clan. Alternatively, commentators suggested that Pharaoh executed the Hebrew children by throwing them on stakes. Given that the reference to Pharaoh occurs in a list of the impressive ruins of bygone nations, it seems reasonable to throw out the 'tent-peg' or 'stake' interpretations as clearly wrong, and instead to argue that the *awtād* refer to the pyramids, on account of their characteristic shape.[31] This interpretation has the advantage of making perfect sense in the context, and it is corroborated by yet other passages that refer to the visible ruins of past civilizations.

The general result of this examination is that it is perfectly reasonable to jettison some interpretations found in *tafsīr*, even dominant or influential

[31] Aharon Ben-Shemesh, 'Some Suggestions to Qurʾan Translators', *Arabica* 16 (1969): 81–3, and 'Some Suggestions to Qur'an Translators', *Arabica* 17 (1970): 199–204.

ones. However, it must be admitted that, even in these cases, the *tafsīrs* on occasion provide alternative interpretations more in line with what we have argued is the correct interpretation. In addition, the New Biblicists in many cases ignore the utility of *tafsīr* for the study of reader reception or Muslim modes of interpretation. Again, this is a reaction not simply to the invocation of authority on the part of modern Muslims, but primarily to the history of Western qurʾanic scholarship itself, which focused on *tafsīr* and other topics in the mid-twentieth century and ignored investigations of biblical parallels.

The New Biblicists not only argue against adopting the traditional framework for the interpretation of the Qurʾan but also argue that Western scholarship on the Qurʾan in general, particularly in the latter half of the twentieth century, has uncritically adopted the same procedure and assumptions to a large extent. In doing this, they set up a dichotomy between such naïve studies that take as their basis the Islamic traditional framework and the biography of the Prophet, and critical studies that take as their basis the assumption that the Qurʾan can be understood best through comparison with biblical texts. It should be obvious that these are not in any sense direct opposites or extremes and so can only be viewed as a dichotomy in a very imprecise sense.

In addition, *tafsīrs* also present grammatical and lexical analyses as well as potentially relevant information about Arabic language, expressions, usages, and rhetoric that may help the modern scholar in interpreting particular passages. It is possible to argue that there is considerable continuity between the Arabic of the Qurʾan and the Arabic available for examination in the classical period, whether poetry attributed to figures of the pre-Islamic and early Islamic periods, or proverbs, orations, lexical citations, or other pieces of information about usage, which exegetes such as al-Ṭabarī group under the rubric of *kalām al-ʿarab*. These matters of general usage of the language which, we know from other cases, can be passed down over centuries and remain more or less intact, differ from *asbāb al-nuzūl*, which purport to record historical events, circumstances, and verbatim conversations that occurred centuries earlier. In most cases, these accounts are likely, or at least potentially created in order to explain a particular verse or passage, and were based on the text rather than being independent explanations of the passage, with the result that using them to interpret the text involves circular reasoning. I would argue, though, that the *asbāb al-nuzūl* accounts often convey an accurate assessment of the formal and functional features of the text, and so nevertheless may be quite valuable for interpreting it.

At present, this constructed opposition between the New Biblicists and their putative opponents, including traditional Muslim scholarship as well as Western scholarship that draws on the traditional sources, is a major characteristic of the field. It is important to realize that the New Biblicists, through their own reasoning, have set aside large swaths of qur'anic studies as unimportant. Use of biblical texts applies most directly to those qur'anic texts that involve explicitly biblical characters and contexts. Other texts, such as those that are related to pre-Islamic pagan religions or that treat extra-biblical themes, would presumably not be as susceptible to these methods. And if the New Biblicists argue that the background of the Qur'an is entirely biblical, then they are certainly mistaken.

Another possible criticism of the New Biblicists' view is that *tafsīr*, *sīrah*, and the other genres of Muslim discourse surrounding the Qur'an are not in fact divorced from biblical tradition. The *Sīrah* of Ibn Hishām shows many connections with biblical tradition, itself being in effect the Islamic gospel, devoted to the life and mission of the Prophet Muhammad. *Tafsīr* and *ḥadīth* present myriad quotations and paraphrases of biblical material, and the *Isrā'īliyyāt*, though rejected as a legitimate source for understanding the Qur'an, had early on been incorporated into the tradition of Islamic commentaries on the Qur'an and so would continue to be preserved and commented on in later exegeses. Recent studies have revealed that some scholars in thepre-modern Islamic tradition drew actively on biblical tradition in attempting to understand the Qur'an. It was long known that early commentators drew freely on Jewish and Christian tradition, but it was thought that this stopped by the tenth century, and that such material was categorically condemned as '*Isrā'īliyyāt*'. Indeed, many later scholars such as Ibn Kathīr and Ibn Taymiyyah strictly forbade resort to sources from 'outside' Islam and had harsh remarks for Muslims scholars who were willing to use them. However, direct recourse to biblical material, aside from that which had early on become incorporated into Islamic exegeses of the Qur'an, was undertaken by a number of later scholars, despite the general ban. Significant engagement with the Bible is seen in the work of exceptional later scholars such as al-Ḥārallī (d. 637/1239) and al-Biqā'ī (d. 885/1480). Al-Ḥārallī makes insightful remarks about the analogical uses of biblical stories in the Qur'an, and al-Biqā'ī wrote a substantial work on the Hebrew Bible, defending its use in qur'anic exegesis.

In one respect, the New Biblicists may be said to have made an advance over Geiger and the Old Biblicists. Geiger and others claimed that the Prophet merely borrowed material from the Bible or biblical tradition for inclusion in the Qur'an. When there was a clear discrepancy between the qur'anic version of a biblical story and the 'original' story, they were quick to suggest that the Prophet had merely misunderstood the original, or that it had got garbled in transmission. The New Biblicists for the most part recognize that the Qur'an is not merely borrowing biblical material but rather engaging in a creative commentary or rewriting of the biblical texts. Still, this recognition is not kept in mind thoroughly in scholarship of this trend. The result of much recent scholarship is to show that what appeared to be innovations in the

Qurʾan—elements of biblical stories that differed from Genesis, Exodus, and so on—had actually developed already in later Jewish or Christian texts. Important questions remain concerning the particular function the biblical narratives serve in their modified versions in the Qurʾan: what explains the form in which they appear, and what function do the changed stories serve in their current context, or, what effect do the modified stories have on the Qurʾan's audience?

THE EXTRA-PENINSULISTS, OR THE ALLOHISTORIANS

In 1977, the same year when Wansbrough's *Quranic Studies* appeared, another book appeared that proposed a radically new thesis: *Hagarism*, by Michael Cook and Patricia Crone. In my view, this book is the result of a thought experiment. Since it is generally accepted that the traditional Islamic sources regarding the mission of the Prophet and the early history of the Islamic community are biased and problematic, Cook and Crone set forth to determine what the history of Islam would look like if one based it on contemporary sources in Greek, Syriac, and so on instead of the usual Arabic sources. The result was an ingenious alternative history to the usual account. The book was criticized heavily, both by those who could accept no criticism of the traditional account and by scholars who, while not entirely trusting of early Islamic sources, were not prepared to reject them to such an extent. The debates over *Hagarism* died down over the next few decades, but the fervour over Luxenberg's work resurrected them, and there are now several groups of scholars dedicated to pursuing the lines of research begun by *Hagarism*. Many engage as well in New Biblicism to some extent. One group includes a number of German scholars such as Karl-Heinz Ohlig, Markus Gross, and Gerard Puin, who have founded an institute called 'Inara' (Enlightenment) and who have been publishing edited volumes from the early 2000s until the present. They have written a number of studies that support the general ideas behind the views of Luxenberg. Israeli scholars Nevo and Koren have also been engaging in similarly sceptical scholarship. Stephen Shoemaker identifies the publication of *Hagarism* as a watershed moment in the history of Islamic studies, claiming that it clarified the line between naïve traditionalist scholarship and critical, revisionist scholarship. His recent book *The Death of the Prophet* may be viewed as an extension of *Hagarism*.[32]

[32] Stephen J. Shoemaker, *The Death of a Prophet.*

The influence of *Hagarism* has been combined to some extent with that of Wansbrough's works and, more recently, with that of Luxenberg to produce a number of historical analyses of the rise of Islam.[33] Chief among the facts that emerge from an examination of these 'outside' sources, and a chief basis of *Hagarism*, is the fact that these texts do not refer to invading 'Muslims' but rather use other terms such as *mhaggraye*, apparently from Arabic *muhājirūn*, or *ṭayyāye* 'Arabs'—an appellation deriving from the name of the Ṭayy tribe. This has led to a supposition, taken up in many studies in various ways, that Islam had not been formed by the time of the invasion and was not its impetus. Rather, the motivation for the invasion was political—it was essentially an Arab invasion, and the Empire once established somehow took on an Islamic character over time, a view espoused by Koren and Nevo. Other, alternative explanations, such as that of Fred Donner, portray the invaders as members of a religious movement, but one that was originally quite different from Islam. Donner, drawing on the Qur'an, which refers to the followers of the nascent movement not as Muslims but as Mu'minūn, 'Believers', calls this movement that of 'the Believers', which again was later transformed into Islam by some historical process.[34]

Another aspect that is shared by many of these studies is a focus on Jerusalem. Stephen Shoemaker has argued that the invasions focused on Jerusalem, adding the idea that the Prophet Muhammad was still alive and led the invasions himself.[35] Koren, Nevo, and others claim in addition that the name Muhammad is not attested until a late date—throwing out the traditional evidence completely and relying on physical details and evidence, such as a Persian coin that uses Muhammad apparently as a title rather than a proper name.[36]

There are two general problems with much of this scholarship. One is the assumption that outsiders' views are on the whole more accurate and reliable than accounts from within the tradition, on the grounds that insiders generally skew accounts of themselves in order to present their tradition in a positive light, and so on. While all scholars are aware of the potential for skewed, exaggerated views involved in salvation history, and even for significant cover-ups, repressions, and back-projections, many of the scholars who write these

[33] Many scholars seem to be unaware that this is an incongruous combination. Wansbrough was committed to a postmodern theoretical framework that elided questions of origins and explicitly avoided hard conclusions. Michael Cook and Patricia Crone were more decidedly positivistic in their assumptions than he was, which led, ironically, to a current of scholarship that reified conclusions that Wansbrough himself was reluctant to formulate.

[34] Fred M. Donner, *Muhammad and the Believers: At the Origins of Islam* (Cambridge, Massachusetts: Harvard University Press, 2010).

[35] Stephen J. Shoemaker, *The Death of a Prophet*.

[36] Yehuda D. Nevo and Judith Koren, *Crossroads to Islam: The Origins of the Arab Religion and the Arab State* (Amherst, New York: Prometheus Books, 2000). Other adherents to this trend are Karl Ohlig, Markus Gross, and other members of the Inara Institute.

studies forget that outside sources are by no means neutral and objective, especially when there has been a history of antagonism between the two groups. In fact, they tend to distort history even more than the accounts of insiders, who are in some ways more constrained by their internal interlocutors and tradition. In addition, they simply have more limited access to raw information of the other tradition. So, Shāfiʿīs describing the history of Ḥanafī jurisprudence, Sunnis describing the history of Shiism, Ashʿarīs writing the history of Muʿtazilī theology, Protestants writing the history of the Catholic popes, Jews writing the history of Christianity—all would tend to distort the material more rather than less than the insiders.

The second point is that many of these studies are very critical of the tradition, demanding a high degree of certainty for acceptance of evidence that is found in traditional accounts, thus throwing out that evidence very easily, but then constructing an alternative narrative that is highly speculative and imaginative and not based on a strict assessment of the probability of the evidence.

Nevertheless, this trend in scholarship has produced some positive results. One is the assembly and analysis of many texts that were earlier ignored, written in languages other than Arabic. In *Seeing Islam as Others Saw it,* Robert Hoyland has compiled a large number of texts, from outside of the Islamic tradition and in a number of languages, which describe the invasion of the Middle East and the establishment of the Islamic Empire.[37] In addition, these studies corroborate other indications that a major ideological shift occurred in early Islamic history, as Islam moved from a small, sectarian movement to a major religion that was ensconced in an imperial apparatus. The shift served to differentiate Islam more starkly from, and to assert its superiority over, Judaism and Christianity, whereas there are many indications that, before the shift, a more ecumenical stance was possible.

THE LATE ANTIQUARIANS

Overlapping to various extents with the New Biblicists and also with the Allohistorians are a group I have dubbed the Late Antiquarians, whose chief characteristic is their fondness for the term 'Late Antique'. The term appears to have arisen first among classicists. As used by Peter Brown and others, it was to some extent a marketing tool, a way to argue that studying Christian topics in

[37] Robert G. Hoyland, *Seeing Islam as Others Saw It: A Survey and Evaluation of Christian, Jewish and Zoroastrian Writings on Early Islam* (Princeton: Darwin Press, 1997).

the centuries before Islam was somehow making grander statements about human history than a label like fifth-century Christian Egypt would suggest. Using it with force was a way to undertake something very important—to bring focus to bear on what had been something of a no-man's land—the historical period between ancient Near Eastern history, which ended with Alexander the Great, and the rise of Islam in the seventh century CE, and, from the point of view of classics in particular, a way to assert that something interesting happened after the fall of the Roman Empire to the barbarian onslaught.[38]

Because of the way in which academic departments had divided up the world, the history of this particular time, like that of the geographical area of Afghanistan, had been falling through the cracks. In Islamic studies, scholars used the term to signal a concerted attempt to connect Islamic material directly with what preceded it, as opposed to the usual procedure, which was to treat the beginning of Islamic history as a radical break with the past. The training of Islamic historians, which generally ignored Greek, Latin, Middle Persian, Coptic, Aramaic, and other ancient languages and concentrated on Arabic, often made that break difficult to overcome. For several decades now, scholars have been attempting to write more synthetic studies that consider the rise of Islam together with the developments of the preceding centuries. In the 1990s, Lawrence Conrad began editing a series of books—Studies in Late Antiquity and Early Islam.[39] Various conferences were held with the terms Late Antiquity and Islam in their titles. Typical works in this vein include Garth Fowden's recent books *From Empire to Commonwealth* and *Before and After Muhammad*.[40]

Adoption of the 'late antique' in qur'anic studies serves several purposes simultaneously. First, it indicates that the Qur'an draws on Jewish, Christian, and pagan or syncretist traditions, without stressing the influence of any one tradition to the exclusion of the others. Secondly, it avoids the claim of direct textual borrowing or the indiscriminate lifting of materials from Jewish or Christian texts, suggesting instead that the Qur'an drew on a body of material in general circulation in the cultures of the Near East at the time. Thirdly, it sets the Qur'an on an equal footing with the Hebrew Bible and

[38] Peter Brown, *The World of Late Antiquity, 150–750 A.D.* (New York: Harcourt Brace Jovanovich, 1971).

[39] These included, for example: Averil Cameron and G. R. D. King, eds, *The Byzantine and Early Islamic Near East II: Land Use and Settlement Patterns*, Papers of the Second Workshop on Late Antiquity and Early Islam (Princeton: The Darwin Press, 1994); Averil Cameron, ed., *The Byzantine and Early Islamic Near East III: States, Resources and Armies*, Papers of the Third Workshop on Late Antiquity and Early Islam. Studies in Late Antiquity and Early Islam 1, vol. 3 (Princeton: The Darwin Press, 1995).

[40] Garth Fowden, *From Empire to Commonwealth: Consequences of Monotheism in Late Antiquity* (Princeton: Princeton University Press, 1993); *Before and After Muhammad: The First Millennium Refocused* (Princeton: Princeton University Press, 2014).

the New Testament, avoiding the implication that the Qurʾan is a derivative document that can be understood by determining its underlying 'sources' but that will necessarily remain a pale reflection of the other scriptures. Rather, it as a highly original work that engages the figures, stories, and concepts of the biblical tradition—and other Near Eastern traditions—and responds to them in a dynamic, complex fashion. The most important scholarly invocations and justifications of this view have been in the recent work of Angelika Neuwirth.[41]

THE SHEEPSKINNERS, OR THE NEW TEXTUALISTS

The history of the qur'anic text was one of the main foci of Gustav Weil's and Theodor Nöldeke's studies of the Qurʾan. This topic was an abiding interest of medieval Muslim scholars of qurʾanic studies, and Weil and Nöldeke drew on their work. The traditional division of the surahs of the Qurʾan into Meccan and Medinan surahs was a historical critical operation, the focus of which was not geographical but rather chronological. Also related to historical criticism of the text were lists of the order of the surahs, lists of the surahs found in the qurʾanic codices of Companions such as Ibn Masʿūd and Ubayy, and the genre of *asbāb al-nuzūl* (the occasions of revelation), which explained the historical circumstances in response to which certain surahs or shorter passages had been revealed.

The history of the Qurʾan's text is another area in which scholarship has resumed investigation of a topic that lay moribund for many decades. The Corpus Coranicum project has in essence resurrected the project of Gotthelf Bergsträsser of completing a critical edition of the Qurʾan. The tradition of Nöldeke survived in a tenuous line, through Bergsträsser's student Anton Spitaler, who wrote a work on the verse-counting traditions in pre-modern Islamic literature early on in his career[42] but subsequently turned his attention to non-qurʾanic topics. It is through Spitaler's students Angelika Neuwirth and Stefan Wild that the tradition maintained some kind of continuity. Rudi Paret did not focus specifically on the history of the text, but his greatest achievement was his *Kommentar und Konkordanz*, which he published as a companion volume to his translation of the Qurʾan. This work provides a commentary on the Qurʾan giving the main points that have been discussed in Western scholarship and weighing in on the various debates concerning them. He also

[41] Angelika Neuwirth, *Der Koran als Text der Spätantike: Ein europäischer Zugang* (Berlin: Verlag der Weltreligionen, 2010), and *Scripture, Poetry and the Making of a Community* (Oxford: Oxford University Press, 2014).

[42] Anton Spitaler, *Die Verszählung des Koran im islamischer Überlieferung* (Munich: Bayerischen Akademie der Wissenschaften, 1935).

provides detailed lists of *Belegen*, 'parallel attestations', which allow the reader to see quickly how similar phrases have been used throughout the Qurʾan.[43] Two other important contributions were Angelika Neuwirth's *Studien zur Komposition der mekkanischen Suren* (1981) and Tilman Nagel's *Medinensische Einschübe in mekkanischen Suren* (1995). Neuwirth's work is a detailed examination of the form of the Meccan surahs with particular attention to rhyme, rhythm, and strophic structure. It is primarily what she would call a 'literary' analysis, looking at the text directly first, without paying attention to outside sources, but it makes a number of arguments about the history of the text, particularly regarding form, style, and rhyme, among which is the observation that, even within the Meccan period, the variety of end-rhymes decreases over time. Tilman Nagel's work focuses on a topic that had been dealt with by medieval scholars, passages that appear to be interpolations into existing surahs because they break the flow of the original surah, sometimes changing the end-rhyme, other times maintaining the same end-rhyme but producing incongruously long verses, and so on. His work undertakes a critical examination of this traditional material, agreeing overall with many of the conclusions of the medieval scholars.[44]

Nöldeke's chronology of the Qurʾan's surahs has come under question, but it has not been superseded. Scholars have pointed out that the system is inherently imperfect because of the existence of interpolations. Even if surahs can be assigned to a particular period, it is not really possible to determine an exact chronological order. It has also been noted that there is a danger of circular reasoning, because our chronology is based on an understanding of historical events, and knowledge of historical events connected with the history of the early community may have been due to speculation on the basis of the qurʾanic text that later became incorporated into the *Sīrah* of the Prophet and other texts. Gabriel Reynolds and Emmanuelle Stefanidis have written appraisals of Nöldeke's chronology.[45] Overall, though, Nöldeke's chronology at least in outline has been corroborated by stylistic analysis of the text. Behnam Sadeghi confirms a similar chronology based on the quantitative analysis of stylistic features.[46]

Progress is being made also on the history of the text. From the Arab world, collections of qurʾanic variants based on a wider collection of sources than

[43] Rudi Paret, *Der Koran, Kommentar und Konkordanz* (Stuttgart: Kohlhammer, 1971).

[44] Angelika Neuwirth, *Studien zur Komposition der mekkanischen Suren* (Berlin: De Gruyter, 1981); Tilman Nagel, *Medinensische Einschübe in mekkanischen Suren* (Göttingen: Vandenhoeck & Ruprecht, 1995).

[45] Gabriel S. Reynolds, 'Le problème de la chronologie du Coran', *Arabica* 58 (2011): 477–502; Emmanuelle Stefanidis, 'The Qurʾan Made Linear: A Study of the *Geschichte des Qorâns*' Chronological Reordering', *Journal of Qurʾanic Studies* 10:2 (2008): 1–22.

[46] Behnam Sadeghi, 'The Chronology of the Qurʾān: A Stylometric Research Program', *Arabica* 58 (2011): 210–99.

those that were available in the early twentieth century have been published, and these resources have made it easier to examine the full gamut of variants preserved in Islamic literature. Aḥmad Mukhtār ʿUmar and ʿAbd al-ʿĀl Sālim Makram published an encyclopaedia of qurʾanic variants in eight volumes in 1988, and ʿAbd al-Laṭīf al-Khaṭīb published an even larger encyclopaedia of qurʾanic variants in eleven volumes in 2002.[47] Works by Christopher Melchert, Mustafa Shah, Shady Nasser, Michael Cook, and others have focused on the study of the *qirāʾāt* in Islamic literature.[48]

François Déroche has often impressed upon lecture audiences the tremendous expense involved in producing an early copy of the Qurʾan by showing them an image of a flock of sheep. Rag-paper or pulp-paper was not introduced to the Middle East until the late eighth century, and early Qurʾan manuscripts were made of parchment. In order to make a full, handsome copy of the Qurʾan, a patron would have had to slaughter scores and scores of sheep to obtain the skins, and then pay for the laborious process of turning those sheepskins into high-quality parchment. The production of Qurʾans was therefore relatively limited and centralized, something that would change with the advent of pulp-paper, which was much more easily produced and much cheaper. The investigation of early qurʾanic manuscripts is perhaps the only area of scholarship regarding which no one can deny that real progress has been made over the past few decades.

It is probably in the field of qurʾanic codicology that the most important concrete advances have been made. Several decades ago, the period from the death of the Prophet until the time of Ibn Mujāhid was something like a black box. All that scholars could do was to repeat the traditional account with suitable suspicion and to agree that the collection of the Qurʾan occurred at some point between the time of the prophet and several centuries later. Now the chronological window has narrowed considerably, and a better framework has been put in place for dating fragments of early Qurʾan manuscripts according to their script, format, paper, ornamentation, and other physical characteristics, including Qurʾans produced under Umayyad patronage. And these results, unlike many of the results reached in other subfields of qurʾanic studies, tend to build on and corroborate each other, rather than being met with general

[47] Aḥmad Mukhtār ʿUmar and ʿAbd al-ʿĀl Sālim Makram, *Muʿjam al-qirāʾāt al-qurʾāniyya*, 2nd edn, 8 vols (Kuwait: Maṭbaʿat Jāmiʿat al-Kuwayt, 1988); ʿAbd al-Laṭīf al-Khaṭīb, *Muʿjam al-qirāʾāt* (Damascus: Dār Saʿd al-Dīn, 2002).

[48] Christopher Melchert, 'Ibn Mujāhid and the Establishment of the Seven Qurʾānic Readings', *Studia Islamica* 91 (2000): 5–22; Michael Cook, 'The Stemma of the Regional Codices of the Koran', *Graeco-Arabica* 9–10 (2004): 89–104; Mustafa Shah, 'The Early Arabic Grammarians' Contribution to the Collection and Authentication of the Qurʾanic Readings: The Prelude to Ibn Mujāhid's *Kitāb al-Sabʿa*', *Journal of Qurʾanic Studies* 6.1 (2004): 72–102; Shady Hekmat Nasser, *The Transmission of the Variant Readings of the Qurʾān: The Problem of Tawātur and the Emergence of Shawādhdh* (Leiden: Brill, 2013).

applause by likeminded researchers and radical doubt and rejection by their opponents.

The advances have been made through the determined analysis of early fragmentary copies of the Qurʾan, many of which had been sitting in European libraries such as the British Museum Library and the Bibliothèque Nationale de France for centuries but had been ignored because scholars had only been interested in complete manuscripts. A great deal of this type of work has been undertaken by François Déroche.[49] Other important studies of such manuscripts have been published by Yasin Dutton, Intisar Rabb, and Alba Fedeli.[50] Some of the most important texts for the earliest history belong to a spectacular find of manuscripts in the walls of the Great Mosque in Ṣanʿāʾ, Yemen. Of the manuscripts found in that cache, scholars are particularly interested in what has come to be called the Ṣanʿāʾ Palimpsest. An already quite old copy of the Qurʾan was written on parchment that had been washed off, and the text underneath, an even earlier copy of the Qurʾan, is visible. A number of scholars have been working on this text, including Behnam Sadeghi and Mohsen Goudarzi, Elisabeth Puin, and Asma Hilali.[51] Keith Small has published a study using manuscripts to examine the history of qurʾanic variants.[52] Several points have arisen from this scholarship. The most important is that some qurʾanic manuscripts are datable to a period earlier than what scholars had imagined. Many fragments date from the Umayyad period, and a few may be as early as the seventh century. In addition, there are discrepancies between

[49] See the work of François Déroche, *Les manuscrits du Coran*, 2 vols (Paris: Bibliothèque Nationale, 1983–1985), *La transmission écrite du Coran dans les débuts de l'islam. Le codex Parisino-pétropolitanus* (Leiden: Brill, 2009) and *Qurʾans of the Umayyads: A Preliminary Overview* (Leiden: Brill, 2013).

[50] Yasin Dutton, 'Red Dots, Green Dots, Yellow Dots & Blue: Some Reflections on the Vocalisation of Early Qurʾānic Manuscripts'—Part I, *Journal of Qurʾānic Studies* 1 (1999): 115–40; Part II, *Journal of Qurʾānic Studies* 2 (2000): 1–24; Yasin Dutton, 'An Early Muṣḥaf according to the Reading of Ibn ʿĀmir', *Journal of Qurʾanic Studies* 3 (2001): 71–90, 'Some Notes on the British Library's Oldest Qurʾān Manuscript (Or. 2165)', *Journal of Qurʾanic Studies* 6 (2004): 43–71, and 'An Umayyad Fragment of the Qurʾan and Its Dating', *Journal of Qurʾanic Studies* 10 (2008): 157–87; Intisar A. Rabb, 'Non-Canonical Readings of the Qurʾān: Recognition and Authenticity (the Ḥimṣī Reading)', *Journal of Qurʾanic Studies* 8 (2007): 84–127; Alba Fedeli. 'Early Qurʾānic Manuscripts, Their Text, and the Alphonse Mingana Papers Held in the Department of Special Collections of the University of Birmingham'. Dissertation, University of Birmingham, 2015.

[51] Behnam Sadeghi and Mohsen Goudarzi, 'Ṣanʿāʾ 1 and the Origins of the Qurʾān', *Der Islam* 87 (2012): 1–129; Elisabeth Puin, 'Ein früher Koranpalimpsest aus Ṣanʿāʾ (DAM 01-27.1)', in Markus Gross and Karl-Heinz Ohlig, eds, *Schlaglichter: Die beiden ersten islamischen Jahrhunderte* (Berlin: Hans Schiler, 2008), 462–93; Asma Hilali, 'Le Palimpseste de Ṣanʿāʾ et la canonisation du Coran: nouveaux éléments', *Cahiers Glotz* 21 (2010): 443–8; Asma Hilali, 'Was the Ṣanʿāʾ Qurʾan Palimpsest a Work in Progress?', in David Hollenberg, Christoph Rauch, and Sabine Schmidtke, eds, *The Yemeni Manuscript Tradition* (Leiden: Brill, 2014), 12–27.

[52] Keith E. Small, *Textual Criticism and Qurʾan Manuscripts* (Lanham, Maryland: Lexington Books, 2011).

the sets of readings recorded in later Islamic works and the information provided by manuscripts. The exact dates are in dispute, and in particular the results of carbon-dating analysis are being debated; in some cases, it appears to be giving a date that is too early. This might be caused by the fact that carbon dating of parchment should give the date when the sheep was slaughtered and not when the manuscript was recorded. In addition, the calibration used for carbon dating may not be accurate for the area of the Middle East.

SOURCES OF THE QUR'AN

A number of topics that were ignored for decades in qur'anic studies have been taken up recently with new vigour. Among the most important of these is the question of pre-existing texts and traditions that are related to the text of the Qur'an. This has been an express question addressed by the Corpus Coranicum project, though they have cast the net very widely. Rather than speaking of 'sources' of the Qur'an and 'borrowing', they have used the term 'intertexts', which leaves the exact relationship between them and the Qur'an much more open. In addition to the resort to Syriac texts mentioned above, other scholars have been investigating Ethiopic connections.[53]

On the Jewish side of the spectrum, activity has been somewhat less fervent. Angelika Neuwirth has pointed to a number of coincidences between qur'anic passages and the Psalms. Adam Silverstein has discussed the qur'anic portrayal of Haman. Segovia has pointed to parabiblical texts connected with the portrayal of Noah.[54]

A related question is that of Jewish Christians. Scholars have suggested that the particular view of Christ and the modifications of Jewish law that appear in the Qur'an result from a tradition of Jewish Christianity. The concept of Jewish Christianity arose in studies of the early Christian community and

[53] Manfred Kropp, 'Beyond Single Words: Mâ'ida, Shayṭân, jibt and ṭaghût. Mechanisms of transmission into the Ethiopic (Gəʿəz) Bible and the Qur'ān', in Gabriel S. Reynolds, ed., *The Qur'ān in its Historical Context* (London: Routledge, 2008), 204–16.

[54] Angelika Neuwirth, 'Die Psalmen im Koran neugelesen (Ps 104 und 136)', in Dirk Hartwig, Walter Homolka, Michael Marx, and Angelika Neuwirth, eds, *'Im vollen Licht der Geschichte': Die Wissenschaft des Judentums und die Anfänge der kritischen Koranforschung* (Würzburg: Ergon, 2008), 157–90; Angelika Neuwirth, 'Zeit und Ewigkeit in den Psalmen und im Koran', in Reinhard G. Kratz and Hermann Spieckermann, eds, *Zeit und Ewigkeit als Raum göttlichen Handelns* (Berlin: De Gruyter, 2009), 319–42; Adam Silverstein, 'Hāmān's Transition from the Jāhiliyya to Islam', *Jerusalem Studies in Arabic and Islam* 34 (2008): 285–308, and 'The Quranic Pharaoh', in Gabriel S. Reynolds, ed., *New Perspectives in the Qur'ān: The Qur'an in Historical Context* (London: Routledge, 2011), 467–77; Segovia, *The Quranic Noah*.

the process by which Christians broke away from the Jewish community.[55] In addition, Christian writers in the centuries before Islam periodically denounced Judaizing Christians who were living in their midst. Several studies of Jewish Christianity, including the recent study of Zellentin, have been written suggesting that the modifications of Jewish and Christian doctrine evident in the Qur'an were influenced by that tradition.[56] It remains debated whether Jewish Christians existed as a social group in or around Arabia and whether they could have exerted an influence on Islam and the Qur'an. Patricia Crone wrote a study that presents the state of the questions regarding this topic.[57]

Advances in Arabian archaeology and the study of South Arabian inscriptions have lead to some work related to the Qur'an and pre-Islamic Arabia.[58] A substantial work that attempts to investigate the rise of Islam in the context of pre-Islamic Arabian religion, taking up the trend of scholarship established by Wellhausen and Toufic Fahd, is Aziz al-Azmeh's 2014 book *The Emergence of Islam in Late Antiquity: Allah and His People*.[59] In recent years Patricia Crone published a number of studies investigating the religion of the pre-Islamic pagans based primarily on consideration of the text of the Qur'an itself.[60]

LANGUAGE AND STYLE

Yet another area that has been taken up after a hiatus is that of the language and style of the text. Nöldeke and others made important observations about

[55] Daniel Boyarin, *Border Lines: The Partition of Judaeo-Christianity* (Philadelphia: University of Pennsylvania, 2004); Daniel Boyarin, 'Rethinking Jewish Christianity: An Argument for Dismantling a Dubious Category (to which is Appended a Correction of my Border Lines)', *Jewish Quarterly Review* 99 (2009): 7–36.

[56] Zellentin, *Didascalia.*

[57] Patricia Crone, 'Islam, Judeo-Christianity and Byzantine Iconoclasm', *Jerusalem Studies in Arabic and Islam* 2 (1980): 59–95; Patricia Crone, 'Jewish Christianity and the Qur'ān', *Journal of Near Eastern Studies* 74 (2015): 225–53 and 75 (2016): 1–21 (also collected in her *Collected Studies in Three Volumes*, Leiden: Brill, 2016, vol. 1).

[58] See Iwona Gajda's chapter in this volume; Christian Julien Robin, 'Les signes de la prophétie en Arabie à l'époque de Muhammad (fin du VIe et début du VIIe siècle de l'ère chrétienne)', 433–76 in Stella Georgoudi, Renée Koch Piettre and Francis Schmidt, eds, *La raison des signes: presages, rites, destin dans les societies de la Méditerranée ancienne* (Leiden: Brill, 2012); François de Blois, 'Islam in Its Arabian Context', 615–23 in Angelika Neuwirth, Nicolai Sinai, and Michael Marx, eds, *The Qur'ān in Context: Historical and Literary Investigations into the Qur'ānic Milieu* (Leiden: Brill, 2010).

[59] Aziz al-Azmeh, *The Emergence of Islam in Late Antiquity: Allah and His People* (Cambridge: Cambridge University Press, 2014).

[60] Patricia Crone, 'The Religion of the Qur'ānic Pagans: God and the Lesser Deities', *Arabica* 57 (2010): 151–200; Patricia Crone, 'The Qur'ānic *Mushrikūn* and the Resurrection, part I', *Bulletin of the School of Oriental and African Studies* 75/3 (2012): 445–72; part II, *Bulletin of the School of Oriental and African Studies* 75/3 (2012): 1–20.

qurʾanic language, and an important discussion of qurʾanic style by Gustav Richter was published posthumously in 1940.[61] Neuwirth's studies address many issues of style and text.[62] As mentioned above, Rudi Paret's *Kommentar und Konkordanz*, a companion volume to his German translation of the Qurʾan, provided an important resource, by explaining many turns of phrase in the Qurʾan and particularly by regularly providing the *Beilege* for specific verses—parallel phrases in other parts of the Qurʾan. Mustansir Mir's work on *Verbal Idioms in the Qurʾan* also represented a significant contribution, a concrete tool for investigations of Qurʾanic language. Arthur Jeffery's *Foreign Vocabulary of the Qurʾan* and several dictionaries of qur'anic Arabic have been published recently, including that of Martin Zammit and that of Abdel Haleem and El Said Badawi, not to mention dozens of handbooks and companions to the Qurʾan and the *Encyclopaedia of the Qurʾan.*[63]

Of the types of high language that were used by the pre-Islamic Arabs, three stand out as being potentially important for understanding of the qurʾanic text: poetry, oratory, and *sajʿ*, especially as used in 'religious' texts such as omens, oracles, and supplications. Much pagan material may have been expressed in all three forms. Western scholars, like their medieval Muslim counterparts, have tended to focus on poetry more than the other types of writing. In modern studies, some advances are being made with regard to poetry and *sajʿ*, but not, as far as I am aware, with regard to oratory.

The Orientalists of the nineteenth century seem to have been much more interested in qurʾanic rhyme and rhythm than modern scholars, many of whom ignore rhyme completely in their analyses. In 1812, Hammer-Purgstall published rhyming translations of the last forty surahs of the Qurʾan, surahs 75–114, labelling this an experiment or attempt (*Probe*).[64] Friedrich Rückert (1788–1866), who learned Persian under his guidance in Vienna in 1818–19, produced the most sustained and celebrated attempt to render the rhyme of the Qurʾan into another language. Learned in dozens of languages, both Asian and European, and widely recognized as a gifted poet and translator, he was no stranger to daunting translation tasks, for he famously rendered the *Maqāmāt* of al-Ḥarīrī (d. 516/1122) into German rhymed prose, publishing the work in 1826 and 1837. He translated most of the Qurʾan, publishing parts piecemeal

[61] Gustav Richter, *Der Sprachstil des Koran, aus dem Nachlass von Dr. G. Richer herausgegeben*, ed. Otto Spies (Leipzig: Harrassowitz, 1940).

[62] See Angelika Neuwirth, *Der Koran als Text der Spätantike* and Angelika Neuwirth, *Scripture*, for an overview of this work.

[63] Mustansir Mir, *Verbal Idioms in the Qurʾan*; Arthur Jeffery, *Foreign Vocabulary of the Qurʾan*; Martin R. Zammit, *A Comparative Lexical Study of Qurʾānic Arabic* (Leiden: Brill, 2002); El Said Badawi and Muhammad Abdel Haleem, *Dictionary of Qurʾanic Usage* (Leiden: Brill, 2005).

[64] Joseph von Hammer-Purgstall, 'Die letzten vierzig Suren des Korans als eine Probe einer gereimten Uebersetzung desselben', in *Fundgruben des Orients*, vol. 2 (Vienna: Anton Schmid, 1811–12), 25–46.

throughout his career; his collected work on the Qur'an was published posthumously in 1888. The published translation covers all of the surahs of the Qur'an, including many complete surahs but leaving gaps, especially in the longer surahs.[65] Martin Klamroth (1855–1918), a Lutheran missionary who resided in Dar as-Salam in East Africa from 1903 to 1913, published rhyming translations of the fifty earliest surahs, according to Nöldeke's chronology in the late nineteenth century.[66] Shawkat Toorawa has translated many surahs of the Qur'an into rhyming English versions in an effort to include this feature of the original text that is regularly jettisoned.[67] In a recent article, Bruce Lawrence has discussed the effect of taking rhyme and rhythm into account when translating the Qur'an into English.[68] Thomas McElwain has produced a rhyming translation of the entire Qur'an, along with rhyming commentary, as part of a larger project to produce rhyming translations of Scriptures.[69] These translations have tried to capture the importance of rhyme and rhythm in the Qur'an.

Attempts to address rhyme in the Qur'an include a number of observations already in Nöldeke's *Geschichte*. A very important work with regard to rhyme is that of David Heinrich Müller, who argued that the Qur'an exhibits strophic poetry, and in this follows biblical poetry and the poetic structures of Babylonian myth. Unfortunately, his work was roundly rejected, for the most part on weak grounds: that his so-called strophes are not entirely regular. He recognized, however, that qur'anic texts shared important features with biblical poetry, something about which his views were correct, but this has not been taken up since then. A number of his other observations about poetic form involve the clever transitions between 'strophes', which he calls *continuatio*, and the formal feature of the *inclusio*, a literary device in which the final verse contains material that recalls the opening verse or line, thereby bracketing the strophe or passage. Karl Vollers's *Volkssprache und Schriftsprache im alten Arabien* addressed rhyme directly, analysing it as a crucial feature of the text and arguing that the rhyme suggested that the Qur'an's

[65] Friedrich Rückert, *Die Verwandlungen des Ebu Said von Serûg oder die Makâmen des Hariri, in freier Nachbildung, Teil 1* (Stuttgart und Tübingen: Johann Friedrich Cotta, 1826); complete edn in 2 vols (Stuttgart und Tübingen: Johann Friedrich Cotta, 1837); Friedrich Rückert, *Der Koran*, ed. August Müller (Franfurt am Main: J. D. Sauerländer, 1888).

[66] Martin Klamroth, *Die fünfzig ältesten Suren des Korans. In gereimter deutscher Übersetzung* (Hamburg: Herold'sche Buchhandlung, 1890).

[67] Shawkat M. Toorawa, '"The Inimitable Rose", Being Qur'ānic *saj'* from *Sūrat al-Ḍuḥâ* to *Sūrat al-Nâs* (Q. 93–114) in English Rhyming Prose', *Journal of Qur'ānic Studies* 8.2 (2006): 143–53; Shawkat M. Toorawa, 'Referencing the Qur'ān: A Proposal, with Illustrative Translations and Discussion', *Journal of Qur'ānic Studies* 9.1 (2007): 139–47.

[68] Bruce B. Lawrence, 'Approximating *saj'* in English Renditions of the Qur'ān: A Close Reading of Sura 93 (*al-Ḍuḥā*) and the *basmala*', *Journal of Qur'ānic Studies* 7.1 (2005): 64–80.

[69] Thomas McElwain, *The Beloved and I*, 5th edn (Adams and McElwain, 2014). This work is to be appreciated more for the sentiment that produced it than for the author's skill in rendering the text.

language had colloquial features. His work was not accepted by other scholars, who were surely correct in rejecting the thesis that the Qurʾan was written in colloquial Arabic. However, again, he had some insights that were worth preserving and following up. This strand of scholarship was largely ignored in the middle of the twentieth century. The next important publication was that of Friedrun R. Müller, *Untersuchungen zur Reimprosa im Koran*, in 1969. This work does not present an overview of *sajʿ* in the Qurʾan, but it discusses several important aspects of *sajʿ*, including changes in ordinary word order for the sake of rhyme and also changes in the forms of verse-final words for the sake of rhyme. An extremely important work was published by Angelika Neuwirth in 1981, *Studien zur Komposition der mekkanischen Suren*, which undertakes a painstaking formal analysis of the Meccan surahs.[70]

Traditional Islamic scholarship generally used poetry as a source for *shawāhid* for rare words, and Western scholars did the same. Only a few scholars have used poetry to make other points regarding concepts, forms, and other rhetorical features of the text. Recently, Thomas Bauer has used poetic examples to make a point about the use of *kull* 'all, each, every' in the Qurʾan.[71] Angelika Neuwirth has compared the qurʾanic descriptions of the ruins of earlier peoples with the *aṭlāl* scene in the classical *qaṣīdah*, and has shown how qurʾanic passages ridicule the pre-Islamic concept of ostentatious spending that is idealized in poetry.[72] Ghassan El-Masri is undertaking a fascinating project connecting poetic themes with those of the Qurʾan, a glimpse of which is presented in a recent study.[73] Also coming at the Qurʾan from poetry, Michael Sells has made several studies of the aesthetics of sound patterns in qurʾanic surahs, in addition to translating many surahs and passages of the Qurʾan.[74] Shawkat Toorawa has also

70 David Heinrich Müller, *Die Propheten in ihrer ursprünglichen Form. Die Grundgesetze der ursemitischen Poesie, erschlossen und nachgewiesen in Bibel, Keilschriften und Koran, und in ihren Wirkungen erkannt in den Chören der griechischen Tragädie*, 2 vols (Vienna: A. Hölder, 1896); Karl Vollers, *Volkssprache und Schriftsprache im alten Arabien* (Strassburg: Karl J. Trübner, 1906); Friedrun R. Müller, *Untersuchungen zur Reimprosa im Koran* (Bonn: Selbstverlag des Orientalischen Seminars der Universität, 1969); Neuwirth, *Komposition*.

71 Thomas Bauer, 'The Relevance of Early Arabic Poetry for Qurʾanic Studies including Observations on *Kull* and on 22:27, 26:225, and 52:31', in Angelika Neuwirth, Nicolai Sinai, and Michael Marx, eds, *The Qurʾan in Context: Historical and Literary Investigations into the Qurʾan* (Leiden: Brill, 2010), 699–732.

72 Neuwirth, *Der Koran als Text der Spätantike*, 672–722.

73 Ghassan El-Masri, 'Ma'sal: What the Ṭalal Would Tell Us', in Michael Sells and Angelika Neuwirth, eds, *Quranic Studies Today* (London: Routledge, 2016), 249–61.

74 Michael Sells, 'Sound, Spirit and Gender in Surat al-Qadr', *Journal of the American Oriental Society* 111 (1991): 239–59; Michael Sells, 'Sound and Meaning in Surat al-Qariʿa', *Arabica* 40 (1993): 403–30; Michael Sells, 'A Literary Approach to the Hymnic Surahs in the Qurʾan: Spirit, Gender and Aural Intertextuality', in Issa Boullata, ed., *Literary Structures of Religious Meaning in the Qurʾan* (Richmond: Curzon, 2000), 3–25.

published, in addition to rhyming translations of qurʾanic surahs, discussions of the functions of rhyme in Sūrat Maryam and other passages of the Qurʾan.[75]

In an important study, *Ancient West Arabian*, Chaim Rabin argued that a grammatical system derived from Eastern or Central Arabia and used as a high literary koine for poetry was imposed on the text of the Qurʾan.[76] Consideration of qur'anic language suggests to me that it is related more closely to that of sooth-saying and oratory than to that of poetry. Nöldeke, Wellhausen, Fahd, and others had already called attention to qurʾanic texts that resembled pre-Islamic *sajʿ*. Several studies have recently been published on the series of oaths that appear at the opening of many qur'anic surahs, by Lamya Kandil and Angelika Neuwirth.[77] Devin J. Stewart has also published a number of studies of the prosody of the Qurʾan, emphasizing the role of *sajʿ* in the Qurʾan and arguing that *sajʿ* is a type of accent or stress poetry, in which the feet or beats of parallel cola are provided by word-accent. Examination of the qurʾanic text shows that end-rhyme has far-reaching consequences for qurʾanic style, word-order, the forms of words, and the construction of qurʾanic verses. Stewart has published a study of forms in the Qurʾan that may be connected with omens and other types of oracular speech.[78]

The preceding discussions explain a large percentage of the qurʾanic studies being done today, but they are by no means exhaustive. The following presents several areas of research that are being pursued at present, in most cases separately from the types of studies mentioned above, and often with little reference to work outside that particular subfield. These ideas are relatively new.

[75] Shawkat M. Toorawa, 'Hapless Hapaxes and Luckless Rhymes: The Qurʾan as Literature', *Religion and Literature* 41.2 (summer 2009): 221–7; Shawkat M. Toorawa, 'Sūrat Maryam (Q. 19): Lexicon, Lexical Echoes, English Translation', *Journal of Qurʾanic Studies*, 13.1 (2011): 25–78.

[76] Chaim Rabin, *Ancient West Arabian* (London: Taylor's Foreign Press, 1951).

[77] Lamya Kandil, 'Die Schwüre in den mekkanischen Suren', in Stefan Wild, ed., *The Qurʾan as Text* (Leiden: Brill, 1996), 41–57; Angelika Neuwirth, *Scripture, Poetry, and the Making of a Community*, 104–12.

[78] See the work of Devin J. Stewart: '*Sajʿ* in the Qurʾan: Prosody and Structure', *Journal of Arabic Literature* 21 (1990): 101–39; 'Poetic License in the Qur'an: Ibn al-Ṣāʾigh al-Ḥanafī's *Iḥkām al-Rāy fī Aḥkām al-Āy*', *Journal of Qurʾanic Studies* 11.1 (2009): 1–54; 'The Mysterious Letters and Other Formal Features of the Qurʾan in Light of Greek and Babylonian Oracular Texts', in Gabriel S. Reynolds, ed., *New Perspectives in the Qurʾān: The Qurʾan in Context* (London: Routledge, 2011), 321–46; 'Divine Epithets and the *Dibacchius*: *Clausulae* and Qurʾanic Rhythm', *Journal of Qurʾanic Studies* 15.2 (2013): 22–64; 'Poetic License and the Qurʾanic Names of Hell: The Treatment of Cognate Substitution in al-Raghib al-Isfahani's Qurʾanic Lexicon', in Stephen Burge, ed., *The Meaning of the Word* (London: I.B. Tauris, 2015), 195–253.

THE STRUCTURE OF LONG SURAHS AND RING-THEORY

It is recognized in the traditional Muslim accounts of revelation that the Qurʾan was revealed piecemeal, and the traditional genre of *asbāb al-nuzūl* ('the occasions of revelation') suggests that some revelations consisted of short passages that were later fitted into much longer surahs. Examination of the text shows that many short surahs such as *Sūrat al-Tīn*, *Sūrat al-Zilzāl*, or *Sūrat al-Qāriʿah* were revealed in one piece and exhibit tight unity. A number of medium-length surahs such as *Sūrat al-Qamar* also appear to have been constructed as integral wholes. Many Orientalists from the nineteenth and twentieth centuries had cast doubt on the fundamental unity of the long Medinan surahs, and some described surahs such as *Sūrat al-Baqarah* or *Sūrat Āl ʿImrān* as hopeless jumbles of disparate texts discussing widely varying ideas. In response to this, another topic that has received considerable attention in Western scholarship is the textual unity and structure of individual surahs, particularly long surahs, such as *Sūrat al-Baqarah* (Q 2), *Sūrat al-Māʾidah* (Q 5), and so on, which pose a serious challenge to those who subscribe to the fundamental unity of the surah. Mustansir Mir has made accessible in English the theories of the modern commentators Ḥamīduddīn Farāhī (1860–1930) and Amīn Aḥsan Iṣlāḥī (1904–1997).[79] Iṣlāḥī and Farāhī are two modern scholars from the Indian subcontinent who endeavoured to show that all of the Qurʾan's surahs exhibit compositional unity by arguing that they each revolve around a central theme. Their analyses are based on the idea that the Qurʾan is undergirded by a particular cosmic structure reflecting the metaphysics of the universe, something that is not a concern of modern Western qur'anic scholarship—however interesting their ideas may be. Mustansir Mir has discussed this approach in several publications, including a book discussing the theory of *naẓm* in Iṣlāḥī's commentary *Tadabbur-i Qurʾān*, which drew on the work *Niẓām al-Qurʾān* of Farāhī.[80] Other scholars have endeavoured to explain the structure and unity of the longer surahs, but without stressing the idea of a central theme so strongly.[81]

[79] Amīn Aḥsan Iṣlāḥī, *Tadabbur-i Qurʾān* (Lahore: Faran Foundation, 1967–80).

[80] Mustansir Mir, *Coherence in the Qurʾan: A Study of Iṣlāḥī's Concept of Naẓm in Tadabbur-i Qurʾān* (Indianapolis: American Trust Publications, 1986); Mustansir Mir, 'The *Sūra* as a Unity: A Twentieth-Century Development in Qurʾān Exegesis', in G. R. Hawting and Abdul-Kader A. Shareef, eds, *Approaches to the Qurʾan* (London: Routledge, 1993), 211–24.

[81] A. H. Mathias Zahniser, 'Major Transitions and Thematic Borders in Two Long Sūras: al-Baqara and al-Nisāʾ', in Issa J. Boullata, ed., *Literary Structures of Religious Meaning in the Qurʾān* (Richmond: Curzon, 2000), 26–55; Nevin Reda El-Tahry, *Textual Integrity and Coherence in the Qurʾan*, doctoral dissertation, Toronto, 2010; and Neal Robinson, 'Hands Outstretched: Towards a Re-reading of *Sūrat al-Māʾida*', *Journal of Qurʾanic Studies* 3.1 (2001): 1–19; Muḥammad ʿAbdullāh Drāz, *al-Nabaʾ al-ʿaẓīm: naẓarāt jadīda fi al-Qurʾān, taqdīm ʿAbd al-ʿAzīz al-Maṭʿanī* (Cairo: Dār al-Qalam, 2008); David E. Smith, 'The Structure

Another tactic, besides the identification of a central theme of each surah, has been termed 'Semitic rhetoric' or 'ring theory'. Not to be confused with 'string theory', it is a view that many literary and other texts are essentially chiastic in structure. That is, they may be considered to adopt a mirror-like structure—ABB'A'—or what proponents term a 'concentric' structure—ABCB'A'. This is held to be true of the Arabic *qaṣīdah* and, according to this set of scholars, many qurʾanic surahs.

The function of the concentric structure is to stress the importance of the central section. Ring-theory was developed in the study of ancient works such as the Iliad and has been described in a lucid and synthetic study by Mary Douglas.[82] It was taken up in the late twentieth century by scholars in biblical studies, who began calling it 'Semitic rhetoric'. This is a most unfortunate choice of terminology. Though it is obviously related to rhetoric, the term as these scholars use it refers first and foremost to structure. However one defines it, actual Semitic rhetoric has a vast content, including most of the rhetorical figures known from the Greek and Latin traditions, and perhaps a good many that are not known in those traditions. It is certainly not limited to the one figure of the chiasm; to use it with this restrictive meaning is to slight Semites throughout history. This theory of Semitic rhetoric has been imported from biblical studies to qur'anic studies, and the chief proponent of the theory has been the Belgian scholar Michel Cuypers. His main work, *Le Festin. Une lecture de la sourate al-Mâ'ida* was published in 2007 and translated into English in 2009. In 2012, he published a work devoted to the composition of the Qurʾan and to Semitic rhetoric, in which he presented his general approach. In 2014, he published his analysis of the 33 final surahs of the Qurʾan using the same principles.[83] A number of other scholars are currently applying this method to various surahs of the Qurʾan: Raymond Farrin has applied it to *Sūrat al-Baqarah*, and Matthias Zahniser has applied it to a number of surahs as well.[84]

Like the string theorists in physics, the ring-theorists believe that they have discovered a key that will unlock untold secrets of the Qurʾan—but that boils

of Surat al-Baqarah', *Muslim World* 91.1–2 (2001): 121–36; Raymond K. Farrin, 'Surat al-Baqara: A Structural Analysis', *Muslim World* 100.1 (2010): 17–32.

[82] Mary Douglas, *Thinking in Circles: An Essay on Ring Composition* (New Haven: Yale University Press, 2007).

[83] Michel Cuypers, *Le Festin. Une lecture de la sourate al-Mâ'ida* (Paris: Lethielleux, 2007); English translation as *The Banquet: A Reading of the Fifth Sura of the Qurʾan* (Convivium Press, Miami, 2009); Michel Cuypers, *La Composition du Coran: Naẓm al-Qurʾān, rhétorique sémitique* (Paris: Gabalda, 2012); Michel Cuypers, *Une apocalypse coranique. Une lecture des trente-trois dernières sourates du Coran* (Pendé, France: Gabalda, 2014).

[84] Raymond K. Farrin, *Structure and Qurʾanic Interpretation: A Study of Symmetry and Coherence in Islam's Holy Text* (Ashland, Oregon: White Cloud Press, 2014). Carl Ernst, *How to Read the Qurʾan: A New Guide, with Select Translations* (Chapel Hill, North Carolina: University of North Carolina Press, 2011), 163–6, analyses *Sūrat al-Mumtaḥanah* (Q 60) as a ring composition.

down to the idea that the surahs of the Qurʾan conform to a sort of deep structure that can be revealed by determined vocabulary and structural analysis. Cuypers and others who apply this theory to the Qurʾan claim to be doing 'rhetorical analysis'; while it is certain that they are analysing certain aspects of qurʾanic rhetoric, it seems to me that they are neglecting a great deal. These scholars are engaged in a structural analysis that sets out to discover chiasms of various types in the text. It should be admitted that they were not the first to discover chiastic structures in the text. Neal Robinson pointed to a number of chiastic structures already in his analysis of *Sūrat al-Māʾidah*. The general principle that a 'concentric' structure such as ABCB'A' serves to focus attention on, or highlight the importance of, the central element C appears generally reasonable. The problem comes when the signs of structure are tenuous and when the claimed chiastic structures stretch over dozens, scores, or even hundreds of verses. Then there is something utterly unreasonable about the assumption that all or nearly all of the Qurʾan's surahs, rather than only some surahs, or even just some parts of some surahs, are based on these chiastic structures. Indeed, Cuypers's analyses often ignore obvious features of the text such as end-rhyme, which would make one hesitate to break a verse at mid-point, something that he does quite frequently. Moreover, identifying a chiastic structure, even if it is an evident feature of the text and not a structure forced upon the text, does not magically reveal what the message, or even the rhetoric, of the surah is. Rather, the operation purports, by identifying this deep psycho-linguistic structure, to reveal the workings of the Semitic mind.

FEMINIST CRITICISM

Another area of critical activity which was not at all a focus of interest in qurʾanic studies in the nineteenth and early twentieth centuries is feminist readings of the Qurʾan. This scholarship overlaps to a large extent with scholarship on the status of women in Islamic religion and cultures in general, which has become a large and variegated field. Barbara Stowasser and Laila Ahmed wrote useful overviews of the material related to women in Islam's basic texts. Since their works, a number of works have been written that attempt to approach the Qurʾan, qurʾanic commentary, and Islamic law from such a point of view.[85] The best known of these works in English are

[85] Leila Ahmed, *Women and Gender in Islam: Historical Roots of a Modern Debate* (New Haven: Yale University Press, 1992); Barbara Freyer Stowasser, *Women in the Qurʾan, Traditions, and Interpretation* (Oxford: Oxford University Press, 1994).

by Amina Wadud and Asma Barlas, both of whom undertake feminist readings of the Qurʾan.[86] Other scholars who have participated in this trend include Riffat Hassan, Aziza al-Hibri, Kecia Ali, Karen Bauer, and others, who touch on qur'anic topics while addressing qur'anic commentary, Islamic law, and related topics.[87] Karen Bauer's book is particularly effective in providing an overview of the historical interpretation, both pre-modern and modern, of qur'anic verses having to do with gender hierarchy, by interpreters of various schools and ideological commitments, without running rough-shod over the evidence in order to make a political point.

The degree to which these works are successful depends on one's point of view. Feminist criticism is candidly political, and one might judge it a success if it convinces readers that certain feminist political positions are supported by the Qurʾan, or at least are compatible with one or more plausible readings of the sacred text. One could also argue, to the contrary, that an excellent feminist reading of the Qurʾan is one that will not dwindle to nothing if contemporary political concerns are removed from the equation. In other words, in order for such works to stand the test of time and to contribute to qur'anic studies in general, they must reveal something substantial about the text of the Qurʾan and the history of its interpretation and not merely about the goals of the authors.

There are some obvious places to begin in constructing a feminist reading of the Qurʾan. First, there are frequent merisms that list males and females as complementary parts of a whole: believing men and believing women, and so on, which suggests that men and women are essentially equal, each forming half of humanity (and probably of genies as well, by the way). Secondly, the Qurʾan stresses the radical independence of the soul, and does not differentiate between male and female souls, or between the judgement of male and female souls. Thirdly, one text of the Qurʾan that is reminiscent of Plato describes man and woman as having been created from one soul; the implication is that

[86] Amina Wadud, *Quran and Woman: Rereading the Sacred Text from a Woman's Perspective* (Oxford: Oxford University Press, 1999) [first published in Malaysia in 1992]; Asma Barlas, *'Believing Women' in Islam: Unreading Patriarchal Interpretations of the Qurʾan* (Austin: University of Texas Press, 2002).

[87] Aziza al-Hibri, 'A Study of Islamic Herstory: Or How Did We Ever Get Into This Mess?', *Women and Islam: Women's Studies International Forum Magazines* 5 (1982): 207–19; Riffat Hassan, 'Made from Adam's Rib: The Woman's Creation Question', *Al-Mushir Theological Journal of the Christian Study Centre* (Rawalpindi, Pakistan) (Autumn 1985): 124–56; Ayesha S. Chaudury, 'I Wanted One Thing and God Wanted Another . . . : The Dilemma of the Prophetic Example and the Qurʾanic Injunction on Wife-Beating', *Journal of Religious Ethics* 39.3 (2011): 416–39; Ayesha S. Chaudury, 'The Ethics of Marital Discipline in Pre-Modern Qurʾanic Exegesis', *Journal of the Society of Christian Ethics,* 30 (2) (2010): 123–30; Kecia Ali, *Sexual Ethics and Islam: Feminist Reflections on Qurʾan, Hadith, and Jurisprudence* (Oxford: Oneworld, 2006); Kecia Ali, *Marriage and Slavery in Early Islam* (Cambridge, MA: Harvard University Press, 2010); Karen Bauer, *Gender Hierarchy in the Qurʾān: Medieval Interpretations, Modern Responses* (Cambridge: Cambridge University Press, 2015).

each forms half of the primordial human soul, without any sense of hierarchy. Fourthly, the story of Adam and Eve in the Qurʾan takes an unmistakably feminist turn that cannot be construed as accidental. Eve was not created from Adam's rib. Adam and Eve are equally responsible for eating the forbidden fruit and are equally punished. Eve did not eat the fruit first, she did not trick Adam into eating the fruit, and the message that husbands should never listen to their wives or that women are not to be trusted and lead men into disaster is intentionally removed from the story. Fifthly, the Qurʾan repeatedly critiques the Arab tribal practice of female infanticide and mocks the men in the audience for prizing male children over female children. Sixthly and perhaps most radically, the insistence on God's essential otherness implies that God has no gender, because He cannot be compared to His creation. One cannot therefore justify patriarchy on an analogy with God's control of the world. Feminist critics have addressed many of these aspects of the Qurʾan.

In addition, feminist criticism has also addressed the qur'anic texts that are most problematic for feminists. The verse that informs husbands that they may beat their wives when they are refractory (*fa'ḍribūhunna*) and reports that men are in charge of women (*al-rijāl qawwāmūn ʿalā al-nisāʾ*) (Q 4:34); and the verses about veiling (Q 24:31; 33:55, 59). Some studies, such as the recent work of Karen Bauer, have shown that the first of these verses, in any case, was already considered problematic by medieval commentators, who sought to soften the meaning conveyed by various hermeneutic means: qualifying the severity of the 'beating' involved, arguing that the verb *ḍaraba, yaḍribu* had a different sense altogether, limiting the circumstances under which beating would be allowed, and so on.

In many cases, feminist critics have endeavoured to argue that while Muslim societies have been patriarchal, the Qurʾan itself does not justify this. Instead, extra-qur'anic sources, particularly *ḥadīth* and Islamic law, have been used to justify patriarchy, and commentaries on the Qurʾan have made it so that it is difficult to avoid viewing the qur'anic text through a patriarchal lens. In a number of cases, this is demonstrably true. So, for example, the story that Eve was formed from Adam's rib, which occurs in Genesis and was purposefully excluded from the Qurʾan because its implications were ideologically rejected, occurs widely in *tafsīr*. Along with the story occurs the additional account that women are essentially crooked because Eve was formed from a crooked rib of Adam. I would argue that this misogynistic interpretation explicitly goes against the Qurʾan's intended meaning of the story of Eve. However, the implication that the Qurʾan is not at all patriarchal and that all patriarchal readings of the text are the fault of later men or later cultures is clearly untenable as well.

Recently, Ayesha Hidayatullah has examined a number of the works of the most prominent feminist interpreters of the Qurʾan and identified three hermeneutical techniques that they have most often used, labelling these:

historical contextualization, intratextual reading, and evocation of the *tawhidic* paradigm. She has discussed the underlying assumptions behind their epistemological approaches and voiced some cautious criticisms of their works. Her work is a sign of a certain maturity of this subfield of Islamic studies and a capacity for reflection and critique.[88]

TYPOLOGY

Sprenger, Horovitz, Bell, and other scholars pointed out the importance of 'punishment stories' in the Qurʾan and called attention to the regular patterns regarding the interactions of prophets with their peoples in the past that they presented. This strand of scholarship has been continued in recent decades in the works of Wansbrough, Alford Welch, and David Marshall. However, a shift of sorts has occurred with regard to the analysis of these and other biblical accounts that makes use of the term typology. Horovitz, Bell, and Watt wrote that certain oddities in the qurʾanic story of Noah and the flood, for example, were the result of back-projection, in which the Prophet inserted his own experience into the narrative, but more recently, the claim is that the earlier narratives are intended from the outset to serve as models for understanding and interpreting the Prophet's experience, the unfolding of his prophetic mission, and his complex dealings with his audience. Michael Zwettler's characterization of the logical connection between the example narrative and the Prophet's own time is preferable: 'the qurʾanic accounts of prior messengers and prophets... are expressly intended to be understood as *typological prefigurements* or *prepresentations* of which the person and career of Muhammad, Prophet and Messenger of God, provide the corresponding *recapitulation* and *fulfillment*—the *antitype*'.[89] The main point for the study of the Qurʾan is that many surahs, especially those that include punishment stories and other similar biblical narratives, regularly make analogical arguments, of various degrees of transparency, about the contemporary situation of the Prophet and his community.

Heribert Busse published a typological study of rulers in the Qurʾan. Zwettler published a typological interpretation of *Sūrat al-sshuʿarāʾ* (Q 26) in 1990, and Devin J. Stewart published a typological interpretation of *Sūrat al-Qamar* (Q 54) in 2000. Recently, Sidney Griffith has presented an excellent general discussion of qurʾanic typology in his book on the Bible in Arabic.

[88] Ayesha Hidayatullah, *Feminist Edges of the Qurʾan* (Oxford: Oxford University Press, 2014).

[89] Bell, *Introduction*, 127–8; Bell and Watt, *Introduction*, 133–4; Zwettler, 'Mantic Manifesto', 97.

Angelika Neuwirth also discusses typology in *Der Koran als Text der Spätantike*, and typology promises to be an area of strong research interest in the future.[90]

ORALITY AND THE CANONIZATION OF THE QUR'AN

One question that remains unsettled is that of the oral nature of the text. Scholars have long noted that the Qur'an includes repeated phrases and structures, and also that many of the repetitions occur with variation. These varied repetitions were treated by medieval Muslim scholars in works titled *al-Ashbāh wa'l-naẓā'ir* or *al-Wujūh wa'l-naẓā'ir*. As mentioned above, Rudi Paret provides many lists of these repeated parallel attestations (*Belegen*) in his *Kommentar und Konkordanz.* Michael Zwettler, who wrote an important work on the oral composition of Arabic poetry, suggests in his study of *Sūrat al-Shuʿarā'* (Q 26) that the surahs of the Qur'an have some of the features of oral performance. Alford Welch suggests that the punishment stories of the Qur'an, which include repeated patterns or repeated but gradually cumulative structures, show signs of oral composition, which would explain the discrepancies between the various versions of the stories. The folklorist Alan Dundes also wrote a work on the oral nature of the Qur'an, noting the typical motifs known from folk traditions that also appear in the Qur'an. Recently Andrew Bannister has written a study of oral composition in the Qur'an. Using a computer program, and covering a small set of texts, he shows what was already clear, that there is a large amount of repetition of particular phrases in the Qur'an. He concludes that the Qur'an does indeed have passages that show the evidence of oral composition. The resulting view of the composition of the Qur'an is seen as corroborating, in a sense, the traditional account of the Qur'an's transmission in Muslim sources, which argue that unbroken oral transmission has preserved the original text

[90] Heribert Busse, 'Herrschertypen im Koran', in Ulrich Haarmann and Peter Bachmann, eds, *Die Islamische Welt zwischen Mittelalter und Neuzeit: Festschrift für Hans Robert Roemer zu 65 Geburtstag* (Wiesbaden: F. Steiner, 1979), 56–80; Michael Zwettler, 'A Mantic Manifesto: The Sūra of "The Poets" and the Qurānic Foundations of Prophetic Authority', in James L. Kugel, ed., *Poetry and Prophecy: The Beginnings of a Literary Tradition* (Ithaca: Cornell University Press, 1990), 75–119, 205–31; Devin J. Stewart, 'Understanding the Koran in English: Notes on Translation, Form, and Prophetic Typology', in Zeinab Ibrahim, Nagwa Kasabgy, and Sabiha Aydelott, eds, *Diversity in Language: Contrastive Studies in English and Arabic Theoretical and Applied Linguistics* (Cairo: American University in Cairo Press, 2000), 31–48; Sidney H. Griffith, *The Qur'an in Arabic: The Scriptures of 'the People of the Book' in the Language of Islam* (Princeton: Princeton University Press, 2013), 54–96; Neuwirth, *Der Koran als Text der Spätantike*, 573–80.

intact—and this despite the evidence, recognized fully by Islamic sources, that significant variants exist. The possibility remains, however, that the matter of composition and that of subsequent transmission are quite disparate issues.

Following models of the construction of the synoptic Gospels proposed by Dibelius, Bultmann, and the proponents of *Formgeschichte*, Wansbrough's *Quranic Studies* argues that repetition with variation results from the incorporation into the Qurʾan of variant traditions that were circulating independently in pre-qurʾanic society. Recently Carlos Segovia has applied Wansbrough's approach to the qurʾanic accounts of Noah. I have critiqued this view as untenable on account of evidence of the overall rhetorical strategy and structure of the macroform—that is, of the surahs in which the variant passages occur. Wansbrough uses the versions of the story of Shuʿayb in the Qurʾan as the decisive factor in determining the shape of the microform—the individual passages presenting the story of Shuʿayb. Joseph Witztum has also critiqued Wansbrough's theory of variant traditions, on similar grounds. A number of scholars, including Alford Welch, Fred Donner, and Devin Stewart have suggested that the variation of such stories was shaped by the occasional nature of the surahs, however one conceives of that process.

Several scholars have described the Qurʾan as providing evidence for a process of development and canonization, drawing on theories of canonization in Christian biblical studies. Angelika Neuwirth, Nicolai Sinai, and the biblical scholar Karl-Friedrich Pohlmann have argued that variant texts show development over time and tell us something about changes in the community that produced them. Neuwirth stresses the liturgical context especially. Taking up one of the major concerns of Rudolph Bultmann, that of *Gemeindebildung*, 'the formation of the community', and drawing on biblical canonical criticism, she has detected in the historical stages of the Qurʾan's composition different stages in the liturgical practice of the early Muslim community. She has addressed in particular qurʾanic accounts of creation, of Mary (Q 3 and 19), and of Moses. Nicolai Sinai has addressed particular accounts of Abraham in a similar fashion. This strand of scholarship is likely to be important in the future. I have suggested that qurʾanic studies scholars might benefit from New Testament redaction criticism, such as the work of Willi Marxen, which stresses the role of the editor in crafting arguments and stressing particular points in the last stages of composition of the text, in addition to form criticism and canonical criticism.

THE QURʾAN AS A COLLECTIVE WORK

The Orientalists of the nineteenth-century spoke of the Prophet Muhammad as the author of the Qurʾan, and on occasion discussed who his informants might have been and whether they were Jews or Christians. One idea that has arisen recently in qurʾanic studies is that the Qurʾan is actually the collective product of a group, and not of a single author. It is a record of debates, polemics, discussions, and dialogue among the Prophet and various groups of interlocutors, including Jews, Christians, pagans, and believers in and opponents of the Prophet. Both Claude Gilliot and Angelika Neuwirth have discussed this polyphonic characteristic of the Qurʾan, and it goes along with the idea that the Qurʾan provides information about the development of the religious community, including especially for Neuwirth the liturgical structure of the community. A number of other scholars have addressed this aspect of the Qurʾan by focusing on polemics and debates in the text, including Mun'im Sirry, *Scriptural Polemics*, and Mehdi Azaiez, *Le contre-discours coranique*.[91] Another important study of debate in the Qurʾan, but this time coming from the perspective of logic and the construction of arguments, is Rosalind Gwynne's *Logic, Rhetoric and Legal Reasoning in the Qurʾān: God's Arguments*.[92]

LOOKING TO THE FUTURE

While the field has certainly experienced a revival, several old problems have not been overcome, and systematic advances in the understanding of the Qurʾan are proceeding more slowly than one might imagine, given the amount of attention being focused on the work. For instance, there are scores of English translations of the Qurʾan. Most of the translators are not particularly expert wielders of English prose; many are not excellent Arabists; and few have been specialists in qurʾanic studies. Arberry, for example, was an accomplished translator, a good Arabist, and wrote beautiful English, but none of his scholarly work was devoted to the Qurʾan. Tarif Khalidi is a good Arabist and an English stylist, but he is not a scholar of the Qurʾan either. The exceptions are Richard Bell, Abdel Haleem, and Alan Jones in English, Régis Blachère in French, and Rudi Paret in German. This just goes to show that the long and industrious history of translation has not produced the scholarly advances that it could have. Producing an improved translation involves solving some of the outstanding problems of qur'anic interpretation, and translators who are not fully aware of the history of the various controversies surrounding the interpretation of cruxes in the sacred text are necessarily at a disadvantage.

[91] Munʾim Sirry, *Scriptural Polemics: The Qurʾan and Other Religions* (Oxford: Oxford University Press, 2014); Mehdi Azaiez, *Le contre-discours coranique* (Berlin: De Gruyter, 2015).

[92] Rosalind Gwynne, *Logic, Rhetoric and Legal Reasoning in the Qurʾān: God's Arguments* (New York: Routledge/Curzon, 2004).

Many modern writers on qur'anic matters are not versed in the German tradition of qur'anic studies going back to Abraham Geiger and continuing until the present. It is becoming easier for someone who does not read German to gain access to this secondary literature. Abraham Geiger's work has been translated into English. Ignaz Goldziher's *Richtungen der Koranauslegung* and Nöldeke's *Geschichte des Qorans* have been translated into English and Arabic. The entries in the *Encyclopaedia of the Qur'an* incorporate many of the important results of the German tradition of scholarship. However, many important German studies from the late nineteenth century until the present are not available in translation, including the works of Horovitz, Speyer, and others, and many writers on qur'anic matters, like writers in biblical studies, are re-inventing the wheel. Scholars write new essays addressing the biblical material in the Qur'an without having examined the work of Heinrich Speyer, a comprehensive statement on the topic that built on and extended the work of his predecessors.

Emphasis on connections with Jewish and Christian influence and relations remains a key feature of European scholarship on the Qur'an. One reason for this is that the European scholars who wrote on the Qur'an had exposure to and expertise in Jewish and Christian traditions. A number of them had training in biblical studies before entering the field of qur'anic studies. In addition, these were topics of which most medieval Islamic commentators on the Qur'an were unaware, and that modern scholars in the Islamic world were unlikely to explore for institutional and ideological reasons.

A continuing problem in the field is the knee-jerk rejection of works for ideological reasons. The problem is an old one. As previously noted, David Heinrich Müller wrote a daring work on the Ur-poetry of the Semites in which he argued that the composition of the Qur'an was yet another example of Semitic prophetic speech and followed strophic patterns of composition that were also found in biblical poetry, Babylonian myths, and even in the choruses of Greek tragedies. This book was rejected by contemporary scholars and was subsequently ignored by scholars except for Angelika Neuwirth, who made use of it in her work on the composition of the Meccan surahs. Another work that has been relatively ignored by subsequent scholarship is Neuwirth's work on the composition of the Meccan surahs. After several reviews by Alford Welch, Andrew Rippin, and Tilman Nagel, the work has not been investigated, addressed, or continued in other works. In both cases, the reasons for critiquing these works do not justify ignoring them, for each contains many valuable ideas about the structure of surahs and their interpretation. One could mention other works that have not been built on, such as Karl Voller's work on colloquial and written language in the Qur'an.

One weakness of Western scholarship has been the lack of expertise in Arabic and insufficient knowledge of Arabic grammar and rhetoric. A number of the greatest scholars in Western studies of the Qur'an were excellent

Arabists, but this has not been the case as a general rule. The level of expertise in Arabic texts has often been higher among scholars specializing in Arabic literature, history, theology, law, and other topics. Scholars writing on the Qurʾan have long been able to rely on translations to a large extent for certain types of investigations, more than scholars in other facets of Islamic studies. There are now concordances of the Qurʾan in English and other European languages. The recently published *Encyclopaedia of the Qurʾan* provides access to some of the more technical aspects of Qurʾanic grammar and lexicography without requiring a profound knowledge of Arabic.

Another weakness has been a lack of awareness of medieval Islamic scholarship on many aspects of the Qurʾan, whether commentary, grammatical analyses, lexicography, rhetoric, legal and theological hermeneutics, and so on. Nöldeke and Goldziher were exceptional in this regard, for they made full use of the material that had been published in their day. One could argue that Nöldeke's work would have been impossible without the publication of al-Suyūṭī's *al-Itqān fī ʿulūm al-Qurʾān*. Many later scholars were not as thorough in their use of medieval Islamic sources, particularly as the amount of material available grew exponentially. For a long time, it was assumed that the discovery of the commentary of al-Ṭabarī would solve the bulk of problems with the interpretation of the Qurʾan. When the work was discovered, and published, scholars realized that it did not, in fact, resolve many issues, despite its tremendous value for the preservation of earlier exegetical material.

The latter half of the twentieth century witnessed the publication of earlier exegetical works such as those of Muqātil b. Sulaymān and al-Mujāhid, but even those failed to explain some difficult aspects of the text. Because of the apparent gap between even the early commentaries and the *Sīrah* of the Prophet and the text of the Qurʾan itself, some Western scholars questioned the value of the *tafsīr* tradition as a whole. The result has been that many Western critics of the Qurʾan pay limited attention to the medieval discussions of the grammar, lexicon, rhetoric, and interpretation that may be relevant to the topics they are investigating.

Because scholars are coming to the Qurʾan from a variety of fields, disciplinary perspectives, and points of view, there is a continued problem regarding the continuity of research. Scholars in many cases are having one-sided conversations, in part because other scholars are simply unaware of their works and in part because of ideological divides. This is exacerbated by linguistic barriers, not just between those working in European languages and the languages of the Islamic world such as Arabic, Persian, Urdu, or Indonesian, but even between English, French, German, and Italian. Certain figures have been important in bridging the divide between German and English on the one hand—Richard Bell, especially—and German and French on the other—Régis Blachère and Claude Gilliot in particular. The recent institutional developments will help to streamline this process, and efforts are being made to translate particular works.

To some extent, research has been taking place in subdiscourses or research silos that are ideologically determined and remain somewhat isolated from each other. The radical revisionists have produced a number of studies that are cited and expanded upon by like-minded authors but which have not received sufficient critiques from other scholars. When critiques are made, the original authors have tended to ignore them and merely reiterate their claims rather than addressing the criticisms directly. In many cases, authors take pains to dismiss the methodology of their opponents as flawed without addressing their concrete results or claims about the text.

BIBLIOGRAPHY

Ahmed, Leila. *Women and Gender in Islam: Historical Roots of a Modern Debate.* New Haven: Yale University Press, 1992.

Ahrens, Karl. 'Christliches im Qoran'. *Zeitschrift der Deutschen Morgenländischen Gesellschaft* 84 (1930): 15–68, 148–90.

Aldeeb Abu Sahlieh, Sami. *Al-Qurʾān al-karīm bi-l-tasalsul al-tāʾrīkhī.* Ochettaz: Aldeeb, 2015.

Aldeeb Abu Sahlieh, Sami. *Le Coran: texte arabe et traduction française*, 2nd edn. Ochettaz: Aldeeb, 2016.

Ali, Kecia. *Sexual Ethics and Islam: Feminist Reflections on Qurʾan, Hadith, and Jurisprudence.* Oxford: Oneworld, 2006.

Ali, Kecia. *Marriage and Slavery in Early Islam.* Cambridge, MA: Harvard University Press, 2010.

Andrae, Tor. *Der Ursprung des Islams und das Christentum.* Uppsala: Almqvist & Wiksells, 1926.

Andrae, Tor. *Mohammed: sein Leben und sein Glaube.* Göttingen: Vandenhoeck & Ruprecht, 1932.

Azaiez, Mehdi. *Le contre-discours quranique.* Berlin: De Gruyter, 2015.

Azmeh, Aziz al-. *The Emergence of Islam in Late Antiquity: Allāh and His People.* Cambridge: Cambridge University Press, 2014.

Barlas, Asma. *'Believing Women' in Islam: Unreading Patriarchal Interpretations of the Qurʾan.* Austin: University of Texas Press, 2002.

Barth, Jakob. 'Studien zur Kritik und Exegese des Qorans', *Der Islam* 6 (1916): 113–48.

Bashear, Suleiman. *Studies in Early Islamic Tradition.* Jerusalem: The Max Schloessinger Memorial Foundation and the Hebrew University of Jerusalem, 2004.

Bauer, Karen. *Gender Hierarchy in the Qurʾān: Medieval Interpretations, Modern Responses.* Cambridge: Cambridge University Press, 2015.

Bauer, Thomas. 'The Relevance of Early Arabic Poetry for Qurʾanic Studies Including Observations on *Kull* and on Q 22:27, 26:225, and 52:21'. In Angelika Neuwirth, Nicolai Sinai, and Michael Marx, eds, *The Qurʾān in Context: Historical and Literary Investigations into the Qurʾānic Milieu.* Leiden: Brill, 2010, 699–732.

Baumstark, Anton. 'Jüdischer und christlicher Gebetstypus im Koran'. *Der Islam* 6 (1915): 113–48.
Beck, Edmund. 'Der ʿuthmanische Kodex in der Koranlesung des zweiten Jahrhunderts'. *Orientalia* 14 (1945): 355–73.
Beck, Edmund. 'Studien zur Geschichte der kufischen Koranlesungs'. I, II, II, IV. In *Orientalia* 17 (1948): 326–55; 19 (1950): 128–250; 20 (1951): 316–28; 22 (1953): 59–78.
Beck, Edmund. 'Die Zuverlässigkeit der Überlieferung von außer-ʿuṯmānischen Varianten bei al-Farrā'. *Orientalia* 23 (1954): 412–35.
Beck, Edmund. 'Die b. Mas'ūdvarienten bei al-Farrā'. I, II, III. *Orientalia* 25 (1956): 353–83; 28 (1959): 186–205, 230–56.
Bell, Richard. *The Origins of Islam in Its Christian Environment.* London: Macmillan, 1926.
Bell, Richard. *The Qurʾān. Translated, with a Critical Re-arrangement of the Surahs,* 2 vols. Edinburgh: Edinburgh University Press, 1937–1939.
Bell, Richard. *Introduction to the Qurʾān.* Edinburgh: Edinburgh University Press, 1953.
Bell, Richard. *A Commentary on the Qurʾān,* 2 vols, C. E. Bosworth and M. E. J. Richardson, eds. Manchester: University of Manchester, 1991.
Bellamy, James A. 'The Mysterious Letters of the Koran: Old Abbreviations of the *Basmalah'. Journal of the American Oriental Society* 93 (1973): 267–85.
Bellamy, James A. 'Some Proposed Emendations to the Text of the Koran'. *Journal of the American Oriental Society* 113.4 (1993): 562–73.
Bellamy, James A. 'More Proposed Emendations to the Text of the Koran'. *Journal of the American Oriental Society* 116.2 (1996): 196–204.
Bellamy, James A. 'Textual Criticism of the Koran'. *Journal of the American Oriental Society* 121.1 (2001): 1–6.
Ben-Shemesh, Aharon. 'Some Suggestions to Qurʾan Translators'. *Arabica* 16 (1969): 81–3; *Arabica* 17 (1970): 199–204.
Bergsträsser, Gotthelf. 'Die Koranlesung des Ḥasan von Baṣra'. *Islamica* 2 (1926): 11–57.
Bergsträsser, Gotthelf. 'Plan eines Apparatus Criticus zum Koran'. *Sitzungsberichte der philosophisch-philologischen Klasse der Bayerischen Akademie der Wissenschaften* 7 (1930): 3–11.
Birkeland, Harris. *'The Lord Guideth': Studies in Primitive Islam.* Oslo: Hos H. Aschehoug, 1956.
Blachère, Régis. *Introduction au Coran.* Paris: Maisonneuve, 1947.
Blachère, Régis. *Le Coran. Traduction selon un essai de reclassement des sourates.* Paris: G.-P. Maisonneuve, 1949.
Bobzin, Hartmut. *Koran im Zeitalter der Reformation.* Beirut: Orient-Institut, 1995.
Bobzin, Hartmut. 'Theodor Nöldekes *Biographische Blätter* aus dem Jahr 1917.' In Werner Arnold and Hartmut Bobzin, eds, *'Sprich doch mit deinen Knechten aramäisch, wir verstehen es!' 60 Beiträge zur Semitistik. Festschrift für Otto Jastrow zum 60. Geburtstag.* Wiesbaden: Harrassowitz, 2002, 90–104.
Bobzin, Hartmut. 'The Seal of the Prophets: Toward an Understanding of Muhammad's Prophethood'. In Angelika Neuwirth, Nicolai Sinai, and Michael Marx, eds, *The*

Qur'ān in Context: Historical and Literary Investigations into the Qur'ānic Milieu. Leiden: Brill, 2010, 565–84.

Bobzin, Hartmut. 'Pre-1800 Preoccupations of Qur'anic Studies'. *EQ* 4 (2004): 235–53.

Böwering, Gerhard. 'Chronology'. *EQ* 1:319–20. Leiden: Brill, 2001.

Bowersock, Glen. *Roman Arabia.* Cambridge, MA: Harvard University Press, 1983.

Bowersock, Glen. *Empires in Collision in Late Antiquity.* Waltham, MA: Brandeis University Press, 2012.

Bowersock, G. W. *The Throne of Adulis: Red Sea Wars on the Eve of Islam.* Oxford: Oxford University Press, 2013.

Bowman, John. 'The Debt of Islam to Monophysite Syrian Christianity'. *Nederlands Theologisch Tijdschrift* 19 (1964–65): 177–201.

Boyarin, Daniel. *Border Lines: The Partition of Judaeo-Christianity.* Philadelphia: University of Pennsylvania, 2004.

Boyarin, Daniel. 'Rethinking Jewish Christianity: An Argument for Dismantling a Dubious Category (to which is Appended a Correction of my *Border Lines*)', *Jewish Quarterly Review* 99 (2009): 7–36.

Brockett, Adrian Alan. 'The Value of the Ḥafṣ and Warsh Transmissions for the Textual History of the Qur'ān'. In Andrew Rippin, ed., *Approaches to the History of the Interpretation of the Qur'an.* Oxford: Clarendon Press, 1988, 31–45.

Brown, Peter. *The World of Late Antiquity, 150–750 A.D.* New York: Harcourt Brace Jovanovich, 1971.

Buhl, Frants. 'Über Vergleichungen und Gleichnisse im Qoran'. *Acta orientalia* 2 (1923–24): 97–108.

Burgmer, Christoph, ed. *Streit um den Koran. Die Luxenberg-Debatte. Standpunkte und Hintergründe.* Berlin: Hans Schiler, 2004.

Burton, John. *The Collection of the Qur'an.* Cambridge: Cambridge University Press, 1977.

Busse, Heribert. 'Herrschertypen im Koran'. In Ulrich Haarmann and Peter Bachmann, eds, *Die Islamische Welt zwischen Mittelalter und Neuzeit. Festschrift für Hans Robert Roemer zum 65. Geburtstag.* Beirut: Wiesbaden, 1979, 56–80.

Busse, Heribert. 'Jerusalem in the Story of Muhammad's Night Journey and Ascension'. *Jerusalem Studies in Arabic and Islam* 14 (1991): 1–40.

Cameron, Averil, ed. *The Byzantine and Early Islamic Near East III: States, Resources and Armies.* Papers of the Third Workshop on Late Antiquity and Early Islam. Studies in Late Antiquity and Early Islam 1, vol. 3. Princeton: The Darwin Press, 1995.

Cameron, Averil and G. R. D. King, eds. *The Byzantine and Early Islamic Near East* II: *Land Use and Settlement Patterns.* Papers of the Second Workshop on Late Antiquity and Early Islam. Princeton: The Darwin Press, 1994.

Casanova, Paul. *Mohammed et la fin du monde. Étude critique sur l'Islam primitive,* 2 vols. Paris: Geuthner, 1911–1924.

Chabbi, Jacqueline. *Le Seigneur des tribus: l'islam de Mahomet.* Paris: Noêsis, 1997.

Cook, Michael. 'The Stemma of the Regional Codices of the Koran'. *Graeco-Arabica* 9–10 (2004): 89–104.

Crone, Patricia. 'Islam, Judeo-Christianity and Byzantine Iconoclasm'. *Jerusalem Studies in Arabic and Islam* 2 (1980): 59–95.

Crone, Patricia. 'The First-Century Concept of *Hijra*'. *Arabica* 41 (1994): 352–87.

Crone, Patricia. 'Two Legal Problems Bearing on the Early History of the Qurʾān'. *Jerusalem Studies in Arabic and Islam* 18 (1994): 1–37.

Crone, Patricia. 'How Did the Quranic Pagans Make a Living?' *Bulletin of the School of Oriental and African Studies* 68 (2005): 387–99.

Crone, Patricia. 'Angels versus Humans as Messengers of God: the View of the Qurʾānic Pagans'. In P. Townsend and M. Vidas, eds, *Revelation, Literature, and Society in Late Antiquity*. Tübingen: Mohr Siebeck, 2010, 315–36.

Crone, Patricia. 'The Religion of the Qurʾanic Pagans: God and the Lesser Deities'. *Arabica* 57 (2010): 151–200.

Crone, Patricia. 'The Qurʾanic *Mushrikūn* and the Resurrection'. (Part I) *Bulletin of the School of Oriental and African Studies* 75.3 (2012): 445–72.

Crone, Patricia. *Collected Studies in Three Volumes*. Leiden: Brill, 2016.

Crone, Patricia. 'Jewish Christianity and the Qurʾān'. *Journal of Near Eastern Studies* 74 (2015): 225–53 and 75 (2016): 1–21.

Crone, Patricia and Michael Cook. *Hagarism: The Making of the Islamic World*. Cambridge: Cambridge University Press, 1977.

Cuypers, Michel. *Le Festin: une lecture de la sourate al-Mâʾida*. Paris: Lethielleux, 2007. English translation as *The Banquet: A Reading of the Fifth Sura of the Qurʾan*. Miami: Convivium Press, 2008.

Cuypers, Michel. *La Composition du Coran: Naẓm al-Qurʾân, rhétorique sémitique*. Paris: Gabalda, 2012.

Cuypers, Michel. *Une apocalypse coranique. Une lecture des trente-trois dernières sourates du Coran*. Pendé: Gabalda, 2014.

de Blois, François. 'Islam in Its Arabian Context'. In Angelika Neuwirth, Nicolai Sinai, and Michael Marx, eds, *The Qurʾān in Context: Historical and Literary Investigations into the Qurʾānic Milieu*. Leiden: Brill, 2010, 615–24.

Déroche, François. *Les Manuscrits du Coran*, 2 vols. Paris: Bibliothèque Nationale, 1983–1985.

Déroche, François. *La transmission écrite du Coran dans les débuts de l'islam. Le codex Parisino-pétropolitanus*. Leiden: Brill, 2009.

Déroche, François. *Qurʾans of the Umayyads: A Preliminary Overview*. Leiden: Brill, 2013.

Donner, Fred M. *Muhammad and the Believers: At the Origins of Islam*. Cambridge, MA: Harvard University Press, 2010.

Douglas, Mary. *Thinking in Circles: An Essay on Ring Composition*. New Haven: Yale University Press, 2007.

Dutton, Yasin. 'Red Dots, Green Dots, Yellow Dots & Blue: Some Reflections on the Vocalisation of Early Qurʾānic Manuscripts'—Part I: *Journal of Qurʾānic Studies* 1 (1999): 115–40; Part II: *Journal of Qurʾānic Studies* 2 (2000): 1–24.

Dutton, Yasin. 'An Early Muṣḥaf according to the Reading of Ibn ʿĀmir'. *Journal of Qurʾanic Studies* 3 (2001): 71–90.

Dutton, Yasin. 'Some Notes on the British Library's Oldest Qurʾān Manuscript (Or. 2165)'. *Journal of Qurʾanic Studies* 6 (2004): 43–71.

Dutton, Yasin. 'An Umayyad Fragment of the Qurʾan and Its Dating'. *Journal of Qurʾanic Studies* 10 (2008): 157–87.

Dye, Guillaume. 'Lieux saints communs, partagés ou confisqués: aux sources de quelques péricopes coraniques (Q 19: 16–33)'. In Isabelle Dépret and Guillaume Dye, eds. *Partage du sacré: transferts, dévotions mixtes, rivalités interconfessionnelles.* Brussels: E.M.E. & InterCommunications, 2012, 55–121.

Dye, Guillaume. 'Pourquoi et comment se fait un texte canonique? Quelques réflexions sur l'histoire du Coran'. In Christian Brouwer, Guillaume Dye, and Anja van Rompaey, eds, *Hérésies: une construction d'identités religieuses.* Brussels: Editions de l'Université de Bruxelle, 2015, 55–104.

El-Badawi, Emran. *The Qurʾān and the Aramaic Gospel Traditions.* London: Routledge, 2014.

Ess, Josef van. 'Rezension zu Wansbrough, *Qurʾanic Studies*', *Bibliotheca Orientalis* 35 (1978): 349–53.

Fahd, Toufic. *La divination arabe: études religieuses, sociologiques et folkloriques sur le milieu natif de l'islam.* Leiden: Brill, 1966.

Fahd, Toufic. *Le Panthéon de l'Arabie centrale à la veille de l'Hégire.* Paris: P. Geuthner, 1968.

Farrin, Raymond K. 'Surat al-Baqara: A Structural Analysis'. *Muslim World* 100:1 (2010): 17–32.

Farrin, Raymond K. *Structure and Qurʾanic Interpretation: A Study of Symmetry and Coherence in Islam's Holy Text.* Ashland, OR: White Cloud Press, 2014.

Fedeli, Alba. 'Early Evidences of Variant Readings and Qurʾānic Manuscripts'. In Karl-Heinz Ohlig and Gerard Puin, eds, *Die Dunkele Anfänge: Neue Forschungen zur Entstehung und frühen Geschichte des Islam.* Berlin: Hans Schiler, 2005, 293–316.

Fedeli, Alba. 'Early Qurʾānic Manuscripts, Their Text, and the Alphonse Mingana Papers Held in the Department of Special Collections of the University of Birmingham'. Dissertation, University of Birmingham, 2015.

Flügel, Gustav. *Corani Textus Arabicus.* Leipzig: Tauchnitz, 1834.

Fowden, Garth. *Empire to Commonwealth: Consequences of Monotheism in Late Antiquity.* Princeton: Princeton University Press, 1993.

Fowden, Garth. *Before and After Muhammad: The First Millennium Refocused.* Princeton: Princeton University Press, 2014.

Fück, Johann. 'Die Originalität des arabischen Propheten'. *Zeitschrift der Deutschen Morgenländischen Gesellschaft* 90 (1936): 509–25.

Fudge, Bruce. *al-Ṭabrisī and the Craft of Commentary.* London: Routledge, 2011.

Geiger, Abraham. *Was hat Mohammed aus dem Judenthume aufgenommen?* Bonn: Baaden, 1833.

Gilliot, Claude. *Exégèse, langue, et théologie en Islam. L'exégèse coranique de Ṭabarî.* Paris: Librairie Philosophique J. Vrin, 1990.

Gilliot, Claude. 'Les informateurs juifs et chrétiens de Muhammad: reprise d'un problem traité par Aloys Sprenger et Theodor Nöldeke'. *JSAI* 22 (1998): 84–126.

Gilliot, Claude. 'Reconsidering the Authorship of the Qurʾān: Is the Qurʾān Partly the Fruit of a Progressive and Collective Work?'. In Gabriel S. Reynolds, ed., *The Qurʾān in its Historical Context.* London: Routledge, 2008, 88–108.

Gimaret, Daniel. *Une Lecture muʿtazilite du Coran.* Louvain: Peeters, 1994.

Goitein, Fritz [Shlomo Dov]. 'Das Gebet im Koran'. Dissertation, Frankfurt am Main, 1923.

Goitein, Fritz, ed. *Studies in Islamic History and Institutions*. Leiden: Brill, 1966.

Goldziher, Ignaz. *Muhammedanische Studien*, 2 vols. Halle: Max Niemeyer, 1888–1889.

Goldziher, Ignaz. *Die Richtungen der islamischen Koranauslegung*. Leiden: Brill, 1920.

Graham, William A. *Divine Word and Prophetic Word in Early Islam*. Oxford: Oxford University Press, 1977.

Graham, William A. 'The Earliest Meaning of Qurʾān'. *Der Islam* 23–4 (1984): 361–77.

Graham, William A. *Beyond the Written Word: Oral Aspects of Scripture in the History of Religion*. Cambridge: Cambridge University Press, 1987.

Griffith, Sidney. 'Christian Lore and the Arabic Qurʾān: "The Companions of the Cave" in *Sūrat al-Kahf* and Syriac Christian Tradition'. In Gabriel S. Reynolds, ed., *The Qurʾān in its Historical Context*. London: Routledge, 2008, 109–37.

Griffith, Sidney. *The Bible in Arabic: The Scripture of the 'People of the Book' in the Language of Islam*. Princeton: Princeton University Press, 2013.

Grohmann, Adolf. 'The Problem of Dating Early Qurʾāns'. *Der Islam* 33 (1958): 213–31.

Grohmann, Adolf. 'Die Entstehung des Korans und die ältesten Koranhandschriften'. *Bustan* 1 (1961): 33–8.

Gross, Markus and Karl-Heinz Ohlig. *Schlaglichter: Die beiden ersten islamischen Jahrhunderte*. Berlin, 2008.

Guillaume Dye and Manfred Kropp. 'Le nom de Jésus ('Îsâ) dans le Coran, et quelques autres noms bibliques: remarques sur l'onomastique coranique'. In Guillaume Dye and Fabien Nobilio, eds, *Figures bibliques en islam*. Brussels: E.M.E. & InterCommunications, 2011, 171–98.

Gwynne, Rosalind Ward. *Logic, Rhetoric, and Legal Reasoning in the Qurʾān: God's Arguments*. New York: Routledge/Curzon, 2004.

Hamdan, Omar. *Studien zur Kanonisierung des Korantextes. Al-Ḥasan al-Baṣrī's Beiträge zur Geschichte des Korans*. Wiesbaden: Harrassowitz, 2006.

Hamdan, Omar. 'The Second *Maṣāḥif* Project: A Step towards the Canonisation of the Qurʾānic Text'. In Angelika Neuwirth, Michael Marx, and Nicolai Sinai, eds, *The Qurʾān in Context: Historical and Literary Investigations into the Qurʾānic Milieu*. Leiden: Brill, 2009, 795–835.

Hammer-Purgstall, Joseph von. 'Die letzten vierzig Suren des Korans als eine Probe einer gereimten Uebersetzung desselben'. In *Fundgruben des Orients*, vol. 2. Vienna: Anton Schmid, 1811–12, 25–46.

Hassan, Riffat. 'Made from Adam's Rib: The Woman's Creation Question'. *Al-Mushir Theological Journal of the Christian Study Centre* (Rawalpindi, Pakistan) 27 (3) (1985): 124–56.

Hawting, Gerald R. *The Idea of Idolatry and the Emergence of Islam. From Polemic to History*. Cambridge: Cambridge University, 1999.

Henninger, Joseph. 'Spuren christlicher Glaubenswahrheiten im Koran'. *Neue Zeitschrift für Missionswissenschaft* 1 (1945): 306–7.

Hibri, Aziza al-. 'A Study of Islamic Herstory: Or How Did We Ever Get Into This Mess?'. *Women and Islam: Women's Studies International Forum Magazines* 5 (1982): 207–19.

Hidayatullah, Ayesha. *Feminist Edges of the Qurʾan*. Oxford: Oxford University Press, 2014.

Hilali, Asma. 'Le Palimpseste de Ṣan'ā' et la canonisation du Coran: nouveaux éléments'. *Cahiers Glotz* 21 (2010): 443–8.
Hilali, Asma. 'Was the Ṣan'ā' Qur'ān Palimpsest a Work in Progress?'. In David Hollenberg, Christoph Rauch, and Sabine Schmidtke, eds, *The Yemeni Manuscript Tradition*. Leiden: Brill, 2014, 12–27.
Hirschberg, Joachim W. *Jüdische und chrisliche Lehren im vor- und frühislamischen Arabien. Ein Beitrag zur Entstehungsgeschichte des Islams*. Krakow: Nakł. Polskiej Akademii Umiejętności, 1939.
Hirschfeld, Hartwig. *Jüdische Elemente im Koran: ein Beitrag zur Koranforschung*. Berlin: Selbstverlag, 1878.
Hirschfeld, Hartwig. *Beiträge zur Erklärung des Koran*. Leipzig: Schulze, 1886.
Hirschfeld, Hartwig. *New Researches into the Composition and the Exegesis of the Qoran*. London: Royal Asiatic Society, 1902.
Horovitz, Josef. *Koranische Untersuchungen*. Berlin: De Gruyter, 1926.
Horovitz, Josef. 'Bemerkungen zur Geschichte und Terminologie des islamischen Kultus'. *Der Islam* 15–16 (1926–7): 249–63.
Horovitz, Josef. *Jewish Proper Names and Derivatives in the Koran*. Hildesheim: G. Olms, 1964.
Hoyland, Robert G. *Seeing Islam as Others Saw It: A Survey and Evaluation of Christian, Jewish and Zoroastrian Writings on Early Islam*. Princeton: Darwin Press, 1997.
Izutsu, Toshihiko. *God and Man in the Qur'an*. Tokyo: Keio University, 1964.
Izutsu, Toshihiko. *Ethico-Religious Concepts in the Qur'an*. Montreal: McGill University Press 1966.
Jeffery, Arthur. 'The Mystic Letters of the Qur'an', *The Moslem World* 14 (1924): 247–60.
Jeffery, Arthur. 'Progress in the Study of the Qur'ānic Text'. *Muslim World* 25 (1935): 4–16.
Jeffery, Arthur. *The Foreign Vocabulary of the Qur'ān*. Baroda, 1938.
Jeffery, Arthur. *Materials for the History of the Text of the Qur'ān: The Old Codices*. Leiden: Brill, 1937.
Jeffery, Arthur. 'Abū 'Ubayd on the Verses Missing from the Qur'ān'. *Muslim World* 28 (1938): 61–5.
Jeffery, Arthur. *The Qur'an as Scripture*. New York: R. F. Moore, 1952.
Kandil, Lamya. 'Die Schwüre in den mekkanischen Suren'. In Stefan Wild, ed., *The Qur'an as Text*. Leiden: Brill, 1996, 41–57.
Katsch, Abraham Isaac. *Judaism in Islam: Biblical and Talmudic Backgrounds of the Koran and Its Commentaries*. New York: New York University Press, 1954.
Kellermann, Andreas. 'Die Mündlichkeit des Koran. Ein forschungsgeschichtliches Problem der Arabistik'. *Beiträge zur Geschichte der Sprachwissenschaft* 5 (1995): 1–33.
Khaṭīb, 'Abd al-Laṭīf al-. *Mu'jam al-qirā'āt*. Damascus: Dār Sa'd al-Dīn, 2002.
Kister, M. J. '*Labbayka, Allāhumma, Labbayka*...On a monotheistic Aspect of a *Jāhiliyya* Practice'. *Jerusalem Studies in Arabic and Islam* 2 (1980): 33–57.
Klamroth, Martin. *Die fünfzig ältesten Suren des Korans. In gereimter deutscher Übersetzung*. Hamburg: Herold'sche Buchhandlung, 1890.
Krone, Susanne. *Die arabische Gottheit al-Lāt*. Bern: Peter Lang, 1992.

Kropp, Manfred. *Results of Contemporary Research on the Qur'an. The Question of a Historico-Critical Text.* Beirut: Institut Allemand des Études Orientales, 2007.

Kropp, Manfred. 'Beyond Single Words: Mā'ida, Shayṭān, jibt and ṭāghūt. Mechanisms of transmission into the Ethiopic (Gəʿəz) Bible and the Qur'ānic Text'. In Gabriel Said Reynolds, ed., *The Qur'ān in its Historical Context.* London: Routledge, 2008, 204–16.

Lammens, Henry. *Le culte des bétyles et les processions religieuses chez les Arabes préislamiques. Bulletin de l'Institut Français d'Archéologie Orientale* 17. Cairo: Institut français d'archéologie orientale, 1920.

Lane, Andrew. *A Traditional Muʿtazilite Commentary: The Kashshāf of Jār Allāh al-Zamakhsharī.* Leiden: Brill, 2006.

Lawrence, Bruce, B. 'Approximating *sajʿ* in English Renditions of the Qur'ān: A Close Reading of Sura 93 (*al-Ḍuḥā*) and the *basmala*', *Journal of Qur'ānic Studies* 7.1 (2005): 64–80.

Lohmann, Theodor. 'Die Gleichnisse im Koran'. *Mitteilungen des Instituts für Orientforschung* 12 (1966): 75–118, 241–87.

Loth, Otto. 'Ṭabarī's Korankommentar'. *Zeitschrift der Deutschen Morgenländischen Gesellschaft* 35 (1881): 588–628.

Lüling, Günter. *Über den Ur-Qur'ān: Ansätze zur Rekonstruktion vorislamischer christlicher Strophenlieder im Qur'ān.* Erlangen: Lüling, 1974. [reprinted 1990, 3rd, corr. ed., 2004].

Lüling, Günter. *A Challenge to Islam for Reformation. The Rediscovery and Reliable Reconstruction of a Comprehensive Pre-Islamic Christian Hymnal Hidden in the Koran under Earliest Islamic Reinterpretations.* New Delhi: Motilal Banarsidass Publishers, 2003.

Luxenberg, Christoph. *Die syro-aramäische Lesart des Koran. Ein Beitrag zur Entschlüsselung der Koransprache.* Berlin, 2000.

Luxenberg, Christoph. 'Noël dans le Coran'. In Anne-Marie Delcambre and Joseph Bosshard, eds, *Enquêtes sur l'Islam: en hommage à Antoine Moussali.* Paris: Éditions Desclée de Brouwer, 2004, 117–38.

Luxenberg, Christoph. 'Weihnachten im Koran'. In Christoph Burgmer, ed., *Streit um den Koran. Die Luxenberg-Debatte. Standpunkte und Hintergründe.* Berlin: Schiler, 2004, 35–41.

Luxenberg, Christoph. *The Syro-Aramaic Reading of the Koran: A Contribution to the Decoding of the Language of the Koran.* Berlin: Hans Schiler, 2007.

Madigan, Daniel. *The Qur'ān's Self-Image: Writing and Authority in Islam's Scripture.* Princeton: Princeton University Press, 2001.

Marshall, David. *God, Muhammad and the Unbelievers.* Richmond: Curzon, 1999.

Masri, Ghassan el-. 'Ma'sal: What the Ṭalal Would Tell Us'. In Michael Sells and Angelika Neuwirth, eds, *Quranic Studies Today.* London: Routledge, 2016, 249–61.

McAuliffe, Jane D. *Qur'ānic Christian: An Analysis of Classical and Modern Exegesis.* Cambridge: Cambridge University Press, 1991.

McElwain, Thomas. *The Beloved and I.* 5th edn. Adams and McElwain, 2014.

Melchert, Christopher. 'Ibn Mujāhid and the Establishment of the Seven Qur'ānic Readings'. *Studia Islamica* 91 (2000): 5–22.

Melchert, Christopher. 'The Relation of the Ten Readings to One Another'. *Journal of Qur'anic Studies* 10 (2008): 73–87.

Mingana, A. 'Syriac Influence on the Style of the Kur'ān'. *Bulletin of the John Rylands Library Manchester* 11 (1927): 77–98.

Mir, Mustansir. *Coherence in the Qur'ān: A Study of Iṣlāḥī's Concept of Naẓm in Tadabbur-i Qur'ān*. Indianapolis, IN: American Trust Publications, 1986.
Mir, Mustansir. *Verbal Idioms of the Qur'an*. Ann Arbor, MI: Center for Near Eastern and North African Studies, University of Michigan, 1989.
Mir, Mustansir. *Understanding the Islamic Scripture: A Study of Selected Passages from the Qur'an*. New York: Pearson Longman, 2007.
Mir, Mustansir. 'Continuity, Context, and Coherence in the Qur'an: A Brief History of the Idea of *Nazm* in the *Tafsir* Literature'. *Al-Bayan* 11 (2013): 2:15–29.
Mourad, Suleiman A. 'From Hellenism to Christianity and Islam: The Origin of the Palm Tree Story Concerning Mary and Jesus in the Gospel of Pseudo-Matthew and the Qur'an'. *Orientalia Christiana* 86 (2002): 206–16.
Muir, W. *The Coran: Its Composition and Teaching, and the Testimony It Bears to the Holy Scriptures,* 2nd edn. London: SPCK, 1878.
Müller, David Heinrich. *Die Propheten in ihrer ursprünglichen Form. Die Grundgesetze der ursemitischen Poesie, erschlossen und nachgewiesen in Bibel, Keilschriften und Koran, und in ihren Wirkungen erkannt in den Chören der griechischen Tragiker,* 2 vols. Vienna: A. Hölder, 1896.
Müller, Friedrun. *Untersuchungen zur Reimprosa im Koran.* Bonn: Selbstverlag des Orientalischen Seminars der Universität, 1969.
Nagel, Tilman. 'Vom Qur'an zur Schrift—Bells Hypothese aus religionsgechichtlicher Sicht'. *Der Islam* 60 (1983): 143–65.
Nagel, Tilman. *Medinensische Einschübe in mekkanischen Suren.* Göttingen: Vandenhoeck & Ruprecht, 1995.
Nasser, Shady Hekmat. *The Transmission of the Variant Readings of the Qur'ān: The Problem of Tawātur and the Emergence of Shawādhdh.* Leiden: Brill, 2012.
Neuwirth, Angelika. *Studien zur Komposition der mekkanischen Suren.* Berlin: De Gruyter, 1981.
Neuwirth, Angelika. 'Rezension zu Wansbrough, *Qur'anic Studies*'. *Die Welt des Islams* 23–24 (1984): 539–42.
Neuwirth, Angelika. *Der Koran als Text der Spätantike: Ein europäischer Zugang.* Berlin: Verlag der Weltreligionen, 2010.
Neuwirth, Angelika. *Scripture, Poetry and the Making of a Community.* Oxford: Oxford University Press, 2014.
Neuwirth, Angelika, Michael Marx, and Nicolai Sinai, eds. *The Qur'ān in Context: Historical and Literary Investigations into the Qur'ānic Milieu.* Leiden: Brill, 2009.
Nevo, Yehuda D. and Judith Koren. *Crossroads to Islam: The Origins of the Arab Religion and the Arab State.* Amherst, NY: Prometheus Books, 2000.
Newby, Gordon D. *A History of the Jews of Arabia: From Ancient Times to their Eclipse under Islam.* Columbia, SC: University of South Carolina Press, 1988.
Newby, Gordon D. and Vernon K. Robbins. 'A Prolegomenon to the Relation of the Qur'an and the Bible'. In John C. Reeves, ed., *Bible and Quran: Essays in Scriptural Intertextuality.* Leiden: Brill, 2003, 23–42.
Nöldeke, Theodor. 'Hatte Muhammad christliche Lehrer?'. *Zeitschrift der Deutschen Morgenländischen Gesellschaft 12* (1858): 699–708.
Nöldeke, Theodor. *Geschichte des Qorans.* 1st edn. Göttingen, 1860. 2nd, expanded edn with Friedrich Schwally. Leipzig: Dieterich, 1909. *Tārīkh al-Qur'ān,* Arabic

translation, Georges Tamer. Beirut: Konrad-Adenauer, 2004. English translation by Wolfgang Behn. Leiden: Brill, 2013.

Ohlig, Karl-Heinz and G. R. Puin, eds. *The Hidden Origins of Islam: New Research into its Early History*. Amherst, New York: Prometheus Books, 2010.

Paret, Rudi. *Mohammed und der Koran: Verkündigung und Geschichte des arabischen Propheten*. Stuttgart: Kohlhammer, 1957.

Paret, Rudi. *Der Koran*. Stuttgart: Kohlhammer, 1966.

Paret, Rudi. *Der Koran, Kommentar und Konkordanz*. Stuttgart: Kohlhammer, 1971.

Paret, Rudi. 'Textkritische verwertbare Koranlesarten'. In Richard Gramlich, ed., *Islamwissenschaftliche Abhandlungen. F. Meier zum 60. Geburtstag*. Wiesbaden: F. Steiner, 1974, 189–204.

Penn, Michael Philip. *Envisioning Islam: Syriac Christianity and the Early Muslim World*. Philadelphia: University of Pennsylvania Press, 2015.

Penn, Michael Philip. *When Christians First Met Muslims: A Sourcebook of the Earliest Syriac Writings on Islam*. Berkeley: University of California Press, 2015.

Peters, Frances E. 'The Quest of the Historical Muhammad'. *International Journal of Middle East Studies* 23 (1991): 291–315.

Pink, Johanna. *Sunnitischer Tafsir in der modernen islamischen Welt: akademische Traditionen, Popularisierung und nationalstaatliche Interessen*. Leiden: Brill, 2011.

Pohlmann, Karl-Friedrich. *Die Entstehung des Korans: Neue Erkenntinesse aus Sicht der historisch-kritischen Bibelwissenschaft*, 2nd edn. Darmstadt: Wissenschaftliche Buchgesellschaft, 2013.

Powers, David S. *Muḥammad Is Not the Father of Any of Your Men: The Making of the Latest Prophet*. Philadelphia: University of Pennsylvania Press, 2011.

Powers, David S. *Zayd*. Philadelphia: University of Pennsylvania Press, 2014.

Pretzl, Otto. 'Die Fortführug des Apparatus Criticus zum Koran'. In Otto Pretzl, ed., *Sitzungsberichte der bayerischen Akademie der Wissenschaften* 5. Munich: Verlag der Bayerischen Akademie der Wissenschaften, 1934.

Pretzl, Otto. 'Die Wissenschaft der Koranlesung'. *Islamica* 6 (1934): 1–47, 230–46, 290–331.

Pritchard, James B. *Ancient Near Eastern Texts Relating to the Old Testament*, 2nd edn. Princeton: Princeton University Press, 1955.

Puin, Elisabeth. 'Ein früher Koranpalimpsest aus Ṣanʿāʾ (DAM 01-27.1)'. In Markus Gross and Karl-Heinz Ohlig, eds, *Schlaglichter: Die beiden ersten islamischen Jahrhunderte*. Berlin: Hans Schiler, 2008, 462–93.

Puin, Gerd. 'Observations on Early Qurʾān Manuscripts in Sanaa'. In Stefan Wild, ed. *The Qurʾān as Text*. Leiden: Brill, 1996, 107–11.

Rabb, Intisar A. 'Non-Canonical Readings of the Qurʾān: Recognition and Authenticity (the Ḥimṣī Reading)'. *Journal of Qurʾanic Studies* 8 (2007): 84–127.

Rabin, Chaim. *Ancient West-Arabian*. London: Taylor's Foreign Press, 1951.

Reda [El-Tahry], Nevin. *Textual Integrity and Coherence in the Qurʾan: Repetition and Narrative Structure in Surat al-Baqara*. Dissertation, Toronto, 2010.

Reeves, John C., ed. *Bible and Qurʾan: Essays in Scriptural Intertextuality*. Leiden: Brill, 2003.

Reynolds, Gabriel S. *The Qurʾān in its Historical Context*. London: Routledge, 2008.

Reynolds, Gabriel S. *The Qurʾan and its Biblical Subtext*. London: Routledge, 2010.

Reynolds, Gabriel S. 'Le problème de la chronologie du Coran'. *Arabica* 58 (2011): 477–502.

Richter, Gustav. *Der Sprachstil des Koran, aus dem Nachlass von Dr. G. Richer herausgegeben*, edited by Otto Spies. Leipzig: Harrassowitz, 1940. [review by W. Björkman in *Die Welt des Islams* 23 (1941): 92–3.]

Rippin, Andrew. 'Ibn ʿAbbās's Al-lughāt fī'l-Qurʾān'. *Bulletin of the School of Oriental and African Studies* 44 (1981): 15–25.

Rippin, Andrew. 'Ibn ʿAbbās's Gharīb al-Qurʾān'. *Bulletin of the School of Oriental and African Studies* 46 (1983): 332–3.

Rippin, Andrew. 'The Qurʾān as Literature: Perils, Pitfalls and Prospects'. *British Society for Middle Eastern Studies Bulletin* 10 (1983): 38–47.

Rippin, Andrew. 'Al-Zarkashī and al-Suyūṭī on the "Occasion of Revelation" Material'. *Islamic Culture* 59 (1985): 243–58.

Rippin, Andrew. 'The Exegetical Genre *asbāb al-nuzūl*: A Bibliographical and Terminological Survey'. *Bulletin of the School of Oriental and African Studies* 48 (1985): 1–15.

Rippin, Andrew, ed. *Approaches to the History of the Interpretation of the Qurʾān*. Oxford: Oxford University Press, 1988.

Rippin, Andrew. 'The Function of *asbāb al-nuzūl* in Qurʾānic Exegesis'. *Bulletin of the School of Oriental and African Studies* 51 (1988): 1–20.

Rippin, Andrew. 'Epigraphical South Arabian and Qurʾānic Exegesis'. *Jerusalem Studies in Arabic and Islam* 13 (1990): 153–74.

Rippin, Andrew. 'The Poetics of Qurʾānic Punning'. *Bulletin of the School of Oriental and African Studies* 57 (1994): 193–207.

Robin, Christian Julien. 'Les Filles de dieu de Saba' à la Mecque: réflexions sur l'agencement des panthéons dans l'Arabie ancienne'. *Semitica* 50 (2001): 113–92.

Robin, Christian Julien. 'Arabia and Ethiopia'. In Scott Fitzgerald Johnson, ed., *The Oxford Handbook of Late Antiquity*. Oxford: Oxford University Press, 2012, 247–332.

Robin, Christian Julien. 'Les signes de la prophétie en Arabie à l'époque de Muhammad (fin du Vie et début du VIIe siècle de l'ère chrétienne)'. In Stella Georgoudi, Renée Koch Piettre, and Francis Schmidt, eds, *La raison des signes: presages, rites, destin dans les societies de la Méditerranée ancienne*. Leiden: Brill, 2012, 433–76.

Robinson, Neal. *Christ in Islam and Christianity: The Representation of Jesus in the Quran and Classical Muslim Commentaries*. London: Macmillan, 1991.

Robinson, Neal. *Discovering the Qurʾan: A Contemporary Approach to a Veiled Text*. London: SCM, 1996.

Robinson, Neal. 'Hands Outstretched: Towards a Re-reading of *Sūrat al-Māʾida*'. *Journal of Qurʾanic Studies* 3.1 (2001): 1–19.

Roggema, Barbara. *The Legend of Sergius Baḥīrā: Eastern Christian Apologetics and Apocalyptic in Response to Islam*. Leiden: Brill, 2009.

Rosenthal, Franz. 'The History of Heinrich Speyer's *Die biblischen Erzählungen im Qoran*'. In Dirk Hartwig, Walter Homolka, Michael J. Marx, and Angelika Neuwirth, eds,*'Im vollen Licht der Geschichte': Die Wissenschaft des Judentums und die Anfänge der kritischen Koranforschung*. Würzburg: Ergon, 2008, 113–16.

Rubin, Uri. *Between Bible and Qurʾan: The Children of Israel and the Qurʾanic Self-Image*. Princeton: Darwin Press, 1999.

Rückert, Friedrich. *Die Verwandlungen des Ebu Said von Serûg oder die Makâmen des Hariri, in freier Nachbildung, Teil 1.* Stuttgart und Tübingen: Johann Friedrich Cotta, 1826. (Complete edn in 2 vols. Stuttgart und Tübingen: Johann Friedrich Cotta, 1837.)

Rückert, Friedrich. *Der Koran*, August Müller, ed. Franfurt am Main: J.D. Sauerländer, 1888.

Rudolph, Wilhelm. *Die Abhängigkeit des Korans von Judentum und Christentum.* Stuttgart: Kohlhammer, 1922.

Sadeghi, Behnam. 'The Chronology of the Qurʾān: A Stylometric Research Program'. *Arabica* 58 (2011): 210–99.

Sadeghi, Behnam and Uwe Bergman. 'The Codex of a Companion of the Prophet and the Qurʾān of the Prophet'. *Arabica* 57.4 (2010): 343–436.

Sadeghi, Behnam and Mohsen Goudarzi. 'Ṣanʿāʾ 1 and the Origins of the Qurʾān'. *Der Islam* 87 (2012): 1–129.

Saleh, Walid A. *The Formation of the Classical Tafsīr Tradition: The Qurʾān Commentary of al-Thaʿlabī (d. 427/1035).* Leiden: Brill, 2004.

Saleh, Walid A. *In Defense of the Bible. A Critical Edition and an Introduction to al-Biqāʿī's Bible Treatise.* Leiden: Brill, 2008.

Schapiro, Israel. *Die aggadische Elemente im Erzählender Teil des Korans.* Leipzig: Fock, 1907.

Schoeler, Gregor. 'The Codification of the Qurʾān: A Comment on the Hypotheses of Burton and Wansbrough'. In Angelika Neuwirth, Nicolai Sinai, and Michael Marx, eds, *The Qurʾān in Context: Historical and Literary Investigations into the Qurʾānic Milieu.* Leiden: Brill, 2009, 779–94.

Segovia, Carlos A. *The Quranic Noah and the Making of the Islamic Prophet: Study of Intertextuality and Religious Identity Formation in Late Antiquity.* Berlin: De Gruyter, 2015.

Sells, Michael. 'Sound, Spirit and Gender in Surat al-Qadr'. *Journal of the American Oriental Society* 111 (1991): 239–59.

Sells, Michael. 'Sound and Meaning in Surat al-Qāriʿa'. *Arabica* 40 (1993): 403–30.

Sells, Michael. 'A Literary Approach to the Hymnic Surahs in the Qurʾan: Spirit, Gender and Aural Intertextuality'. In Issa Boullata, ed., *Literary Structures of Religious Meaning in the Qurʾan.* Richmond: Curzon, 2000, 3–25.

Shah, Mustafa. 'The Early Arabic Grammarians' Contribution to the Collection and Authentication of the Qur'anic Readings: The Prelude to Ibn Mujāhid's *Kitāb al-Sabʿa*'. *Journal of Qurʾanic Studies* 6.1 (2004): 72–102.

Shahid, Irfan. *Byzantium and the Arabs in the Fourth Century.* Washington, DC: Dumbarton Oaks, 1984a.

Shahid, Irfan. *Rome and the Arabs: A Prolegomenon to the Study of Byzantium and the Arabs.* Washington, DC: Dumbarton Oaks, 1984b.

Shahid, Irfan. *Byzantium and the Arabs in the Fifth Century.* Washington, DC: Dumbarton Oaks, 1989.

Shahid, Irfan. *Byzantium and the Arabs in the Sixth Century.* Washington, DC: Dumbarton Oaks, 1995.

Shoemaker, Stephen J. 'Christmas in the Qurʾān: The Qurʾānic Account of Jesus' Nativity and Palestinian Local Tradition'. *Jerusalem Studies in Arabic and Islam* 28 (2003): 11–39.

Shoemaker, Stephen J. *The Death of a Prophet: The End of Muhammad's Life and the Beginnings of Islam*. Philadelphia: University of Pennsylvania Press, 2012.
Silverstein, Adam. 'Hāmān's transition from the Jāhiliyya to Islam'. *Jerusalem Studies in Arabic and Islam* 34 (2008): 285–308.
Silverstein, Adam. 'The Quranic Pharaoh'. In Gabriel S. Reynolds, ed., *New Perspectives in the Qurʾān: The Qurʾan in Historical Context*. London: Routledge, 2011, 467–77.
Sinai, Nicolai. *Fortschreibung und Auslegung: Studien zur frühen Koraninterpretation*. Wiesbaden: Harrassowitz, 2009.
Sinai, Nicolai. 'The Qurʾān as Process'. In Angelika Neuwirth, Nicolai Sinai, and Michael Marx, eds, *The Qurʾān in Context: Historical and Literary Investigations into the Qurʾānic Milieu*. Leiden: Brill, 2010, 407–39.
Sinai, Nicolai. 'Religious Poetry from the Quranic Milieu: Umayya b. Abī l-Ṣalt on the Fate of the Thamūd', *Bulletin of the School of Oriental and African Studies* 74 (2011): 397–416.
Sinai, Nicolai. 'When Did the Consonantal Skeleton of the Quran Reach Closure? Part I'. *Bulletin of the School of Oriental and African Studies* 77.2 (2014): 273–92.
Sinai, Nicolai. 'When Did the Consonantal Skeleton of the Quran Reach Closure? Part II'. *Bulletin of the School of Oriental and African Studies* 77.3 (2014): 509–21.
Sirry, Mun'im. *Scriptural Polemics: The Qurʾan and Other Religions*. Oxford: Oxford University Press, 2014.
Sister, M. 'Metaphern und Vergleiche im Koran'. *Mitteilungen des Seminars für Orientalische Sprachen* 34 (1931): 194–254.
Small, Keith E. *Textual Criticism and Qurʾan Manuscripts*. Lanham, Maryland: Lexington Books, 2011.
Smith, David E. 'The Structure of *Surat al-Baqarah*'. *The Muslim World* 91 (2001): 121–36.
Sperl, Stefan. 'The Literary Form of Prayer: Qurʾān Sura One, the Lord's Prayer and a Babylonian Prayer to the Moon God'. *Bulletin of the School of Oriental and African Studies* 57 (1994): 213–27.
Speyer, Heinrich. *Die biblischen Erzählungen im Qoran*. Gräfenheinichen: Schulze, 1931.
Spitaler, Anton. *Die Verszählung des Koran im islamischer Überlieferung*. Munich: Bayerischen Akademie der Wissenschaften, 1935.
Sprenger, Aloys. *Das Leben und die Lehre des Mohammad, nach bisher größtenteils unbenutzten Quellen*. 3 vols. 1st edn, Berlin: Nicolai, 1861–1865; 2nd edn, Berlin: Nicolai, 1869.
Stefanidis, Emmanuelle. 'The Qurʾan Made Linear: A Study of the *Geschichte des Qorâns*' Chronological Reordering'. *Journal of Qurʾanic Studies* 10.2 (2008): 1–22.
Stetkevytch, Jaroslav. *Muhammad and the Golden Bough: Reconstructing Arabian Myth*. Bloomington: Indiana University Press, 1996.
Stewart, Devin J. '*Sajʿ* in the Qur'an: Prosody and Structure'. *Journal of Arabic Literature* 21 (1990): 101–39.
Stewart, Devin J. 'Understanding the Koran in English: Notes on Translation, Form, and Prophetic Typology'. In Zeinab Ibrahim, Nagwa Kasabgy, and Sabiha Aydelott, eds, *Diversity in Language: Contrastive Studies in English and Arabic Theoretical and Applied Linguistics*. Cairo: American University in Cairo Press, 2000, 31–48.

Stewart, Devin J. 'Notes on Medieval and Modern Emendations of the Qur'ān'. In Gabriel S. Reynolds, ed., *The Qur'ān in its Historical Context.* London: Routledge, 2008, 225–48.

Stewart, Devin J. 'Poetic License in the Qur'an: Ibn al-Ṣā'igh al-Ḥanafi's *Iḥkām al-Rāy fī Aḥkām al-Āy*'. *Journal of Qur'anic Studies* 11.1 (2009): 1–54.

Stewart, Devin J. 'The Mysterious Letters and Other Formal Features of the Qur'an in Light of Greek and Babylonian Oracular Texts'. In Gabriel S. Reynolds, ed., *New Perspectives on the Qur'ān: The Qur'an in Context 2.* London: Routledge, 2011, 321–46.

Stewart, Devin J. 'Divine Epithets and the *Dibacchius*: *Clausulae* and Qur'anic Rhythm'. *Journal of Qur'anic Studies* 15.2 (2013): 22–64.

Stewart, Devin J. 'Poetic License and the Qur'anic Names of Hell: The Treatment of Cognate Substitution in al-Rāghib al-Iṣfahānī's Qur'anic Lexicon'. In Stephen Burge, ed., *The Meaning of the Word.* London: I. B. Tauris, 2015, 195–253.

Stewart, Devin J. 'Wansbrough, Bultmann, and the Theory of Variant Traditions in the Qur'ān'. In Angelika Neuwirth and Michael A. Sells, eds, *Qur'ānic Studies Today.* London: Routledge, 2016, 17–51.

Stowasser, Barbara Freyer. *Women in the Qur'an, Traditions, and Interpretation.* Oxford: Oxford University Press, 1994.

Stroumsa, Guy G. 'Jewish Christianity and Islamic Origins'. In Behnam Sadeghi, Asad Q. Ahmed, Adam Silverstein, and Robert Hoyland, eds, *Islamic Cultures, Islamic Contexts: Essays in Honor of Professor Patricia Crone.* Leiden: Brill, 2015, 72–96.

Tesei, Tommaso. 'Deux légendes d'Alexandre le Grand dans le Coran. Une étude sur les origines du texte sacré arabe et sur ses liens avec les littératures chrétiennes et juives de l'Antiquité Tardive'. Doctoral dissertation, Sapienza University of Rome, 2013.

Tesei, Tommaso. 'The Prophecy of Ḏū-l-Qarnayn and the Origins of the Qur'ānic Corpus'. In A. Arioli, ed., *Miscellanea Arabica* (2013–14). Rome: Aracne Editrice, 2014, 273–90.

Tillschneider, Hans Thomas. *Typen historisch-exegetischer Überlieferung: Formen, Funktionen und Genese des asbāb an-nuzūl-Materials.* Würzburg: Ergon-Verlag, 2011.

Tisdall, W. St. Clair. *The Original Sources of the Qur'ān.* London: SPCK, 1905.

Toorawa, Shawkat M. '"The Inimitable Rose", Being Qur'ānic *saj'* from *Surat al-Ḍuhâ* to *Surat al-Nâs* (Q. 93–114) in English Rhyming Prose', *Journal of Qur'ānic Studies* 8.2 (2006): 143–53.

Toorawa, Shawkat M. 'Referencing the Qur'ān: A Proposal, with Illustrative Translations and Discussion', *Journal of Qur'ānic Studies* 9.1 (2007): 139–47.

Toorawa, Shawkat M. 'Hapless Hapaxes and Luckless Rhymes: The Qur'an as Literature'. *Religion and Literature* 41.2 (summer 2009): 221–7.

Toorawa, Shawkat M. 'Sūrat Maryam (Q. 19): Lexicon, Lexical Echoes, English Translation'. *Journal of Qur'anic Studies*, 13.1 (2011): 25–78.

Torrey, Charles Cutler. *The Jewish Foundation of Islam.* New York: Jewish Institute of Religion Press, 1933.

'Umar, Aḥmad Mukhtār and 'Abd al-'Āl Sālim Makram. *Mu'jam al-qirā'āt al-qur'āniyya*, 2nd edn, 8 vols. Kuwait: Maṭba'at Jāmi'at al-Kuwayt, 1988.

Van Bladel, Kevin. 'The Alexander Legend in the Qur'ān 18:83-102'. In Gabriel S. Reynolds, ed., *The Qur'ān in Its Historical Context*. London: Routledge, 2008, 175–213.
Vollers, Karl. *Volkssprache und Schriftsprache im Alten Arabien*. Strasbourg: Tübner, 1906.
Wadud, Amina. *Quran and Woman: Rereading the Sacred Text from a Woman's Perspective*. Oxford: Oxford University Press, 1999.
Wansbrough, John. *Quranic Studies: Sources and Methods of Scriptural Interpretation*. Oxford: Oxford University Press, 1977.
Wansbrough, John. *The Sectarian Milieu: Contents and Composition of Islamic Salvation History*. Oxford: Oxford University Press, 1978.
Watt, William Montgomery. *Bell's Introduction to the Qur'an*. Edinburgh: Edinburgh University Press, 1970.
Weil, Gustav. *Mohammed der Prophet: sein Leben und seine Lehre: aus handschriftlichen Quellen und dem Koran geschöpft und dargestellt*. Stuttgart: Metzler, 1843.
Weil, Gustav. *Historisch-kritische Einleitung in den Koran*. Bielefeld: Belhagen & Klasing, 1844. 2nd edn. Bielefeld: Belhagen & Klasing, 1878.
Weil, Gustav. *Biblische Legenden der Musulmänner*. Frankfurt am Main: Rütten, 1845.
Welch, Alford T. 'Formulaic Features of the Punishment Stories'. In Issa J. Boullata, ed., *Literary Structures of Religious Meaning in the Qur'an*. Richmond, UK: Curzon, 2000, 77–116.
Welch, Alford T. 'Kur'ān'. *EI*^{2}, 5 (1986): 400–32.
Wellhausen, Julius. *Reste arabischen Heidentums*. Berlin, 1887.
Wensinck, Arent J. *Muhammad and the Jews of Medina*. Leiden: Brill, 1928.
Wheeler, Brannon M. *Moses in the Quran and Islamic Exegesis*. London: Routledge, 2002.
Whelan, Estelle. 'Evidence for the early codification of the Qur'an'. *JAOS* 118 (1998): 1–14.
Wild, Stefan, ed. *The Qur'ān as Text*. Leiden: Brill, 1996.
Wild, Stefan. 'An Arabic Recitation: The Metalinguistics of Qur'anic Revelation'. In Stefan Wild, ed., *Self-Referentiality in the Qur'ān*. Wiesbaden: Harrassowitz, 2006, 135–58.
Wild, Stefan, ed. *Self-Referentiality in the Qur'ān*. Wiesbaden: Harrassowitz, 2006.
Winkler, Helmut. 'Fātiḥa und Vaterunser'. *Zeitschrift für Semitistik und verwandte Gebiete* 6 (1928): 238–46.
Witztum, Joseph. 'The Foundations of the House (Q 2:127)'. *Bulletin of the School of Oriental and African Studies* 72.1 (2009): 25–40.
Witztum, Joseph. 'Joseph among the Ishmaelites: Q 12 in Light of Syriac Sources'. In Gabriel S. Reynolds, ed., *New Perspectives on the Qur'ān: The Qur'ān in its Historical Context 2*. London: Routledge, 2011, 425–48.
Witztum, Joseph. 'The Syriac Milieu of the Qur'ān: The Recasting of Biblical Narratives'. Ph.D. dissertation, Princeton University, 2011.
Witztum, Joseph. 'Variant Traditions, Relative Chronology, and the Study of Intra-Quranic Parallels'. In Behnam Sadeghi et al., eds, *Islamic Cultures, Islamic Contexts*. Leiden: Brill, 2015, 1–50.

Zahniser, Mathias. 'Guidance and Exhortation: The Composition of Sūratu n-nisā''. In Asma Afsaruddin and A. H. Mathias Zahniser, eds, *Humanism, Culture, and Language in the Near East. Studies in Honour of Georg Krotkoff*. Winona Lake: Eisenbrauns, 1997, 71–85.

Zammit, Martin R. *A Comparative Lexical Study of Qurʾānic Arabic*. Leiden: Brill, 2001.

Zellentin, Holger Michael. *The Qurʾān's Legal Culture: The Didascalia Apostolorum as a Point of Departure*. Tübingen: Mohr Siebek, 2013.

Zwettler, Michael. 'A Mantic Manifesto: the Sura of the Poets and the Qurʾanic Foundations of Prophetic Authority'. In James Kugel, ed., *Poetry and Prophecy: The Beginnings of a Literary Tradition*. Ithaca: Cornell University Press, 1990, 75–119.

2

Processes of Literary Growth and Editorial Expansion in Two Medinan Surahs

Nicolai Sinai

INTRODUCTION

That various qurʾanic surahs contain secondary insertions and expansions is a thoroughly traditional notion: pre-modern Islamic scholars already maintained that many surahs revealed during Muhammad's 'Meccan' period (i.e., surahs promulgated before the emigration to Medina traditionally dated to 622) include later 'Medinan' passages and vice versa.[1] Such claims, of course, rest on the crucial assumption that we can defensibly make relative chronological judgements about different parts of the qurʾanic corpus, that is, claims of the kind that (most of) surah 37 predates (most of) surah 2. Assuming that one subscribes to this premise, as I do,[2] how are we to distinguish between earlier and later components of a given surah? Post-qur'anic Islamic literature frequently purports to have pertinent information to offer: on the one hand, reports about the so-called 'occasions of revelation' (*asbāb al-nuzūl*) of particular qurʾanic passages often place these latter in a recognizably Meccan or Medinan setting.[3] On the other hand, miscellaneous sources

Completion of this article was supported by the UK's Arts and Humanities Research Council (grant reference AH/M011305/1). English translations of qurʾanic passages are based on Alan Jones (trans.), *The Qurʾān* ([Cambridge:] Gibb Memorial Trust, 2007), which I have felt free to modify throughout. I am grateful to Prof. Jones and to the Gibb Memorial Trust for giving me permission to use this translation as I saw fit. Like Jones, I employ superscript 's' and 'p' in order to disambiguate verbs and pronouns for which singular and plural forms are undistinguishable in modern English.

[1] For instance, one scholar speaks of 'Medinan verses in Meccan surahs, and Meccan verses in Medinan surahs'. See Jalāl al-Dīn al-Suyūṭī, *al-Itqān fī ʿulūm al-Qurʾān*, 7 vols (Medina: Majmaʿ al-Malik Fahd li-ṭibāʿat al-muṣḥaf al-sharīf, AH 1426), vol. 1, 44, l. 3 (towards the beginning of *nawʿ* 1).

[2] See Nicolai Sinai, 'Inner-Qurʾanic Chronology', forthcoming in Muhammad Abdel Haleem and Mustafa Shah (eds), *The Oxford Handbook of Qurʾanic Studies* (Oxford: Oxford University Press).

[3] See Andrew Rippin, 'The Function of *Asbāb al-Nuzūl* in Qurʾānic Exegesis', *Bulletin of the School of Oriental and African Studies* 51 (1988): 1–20.

preserve statements (often traced back to early exegetical authorities or even to Companions of the Prophet) that summarily assign individual surahs to the Meccan or Medinan period and enumerate verses believed to constitute exceptions to this general attribution. For instance, we are informed that Ibn ʿAbbās considered surah 6 to be Meccan but held verses 151–3 to be Medinan.[4]

Although the distinction between an earlier 'Meccan' cluster of surahs and a later 'Medinan' one is another traditional premise that I am prepared to accept,[5] any attempt to base the identification of secondary additions to a given surah on post-qur'anic traditions of the sort just illustrated must appear irredeemably doubtful. With regard to the *asbāb al-nuzūl*, it is virtually never possible to rule out conclusively the possibility that a given report might only have emerged ex post facto in order to serve certain exegetical or ideological aims or simply by way of narrative amplification. With respect to the second class of material, too, it would be inappropriately credulous simply to accept the ascription of such traditions to contemporaries of Muhammad, given the very real possibility that the latter's names might merely be functioning as pegs that anonymous later exegetes draped with their own guesswork. Hence, we have no choice but to attempt to bypass the indigenous Islamic tradition on the matter at hand: as is the case with biblical literature, judgements about the presence of later insertions in a given unit of text will first and foremost need to be justified on the basis of a close reading of that text itself and in terms of features inherent in it. Of course, adopting such a procedure may subsequently turn out to corroborate, for example, that Q 6:151–3 are indeed likely to have been secondarily incorporated into surah 6; yet the existence of a report attributing this claim to Ibn ʿAbbās will not as such qualify as admissible evidence in support of the claim itself.

How, then, might one go about constructing an argument to the effect that a given verse or verse group A forms a secondary addition to surah S?[6] To begin with, one will need to show that it is possible to lift A from its literary context without generating an unsustainable gap in the text. In addition, one's case for an alleged insertion will be considerably strengthened if one is able to offer some kind of explanation for why A was placed at its present position within S. This might, for instance, take the form of showing that A clarifies, modifies, expands, or counterbalances a statement made elsewhere in S. Now, the

[4] For a conspectus of such traditions see Tilman Nagel, *Medinensische Einschübe in mekkanischen Suren* (Göttingen: Vandenhoeck & Ruprecht, 1995). My example is found on p. 20.

[5] For an attempt to isolate a Medinan stratum of the Qurʾan based on criteria inherent in the text see Nicolai Sinai, 'The Unknown Known: Some Groundwork for Interpreting the Medinan Qurʾan', *Mélanges de l'Université Saint-Joseph* 66 (2015–2016): 47–96.

[6] An earlier attempt to state criteria for identifying later additions to qurʾanic surahs is made in Nicolai Sinai, *Fortschreibung und Auslegung: Studien zur frühen Koraninterpretation* (Wiesbaden: Harrassowitz, 2009), 157, n. 8.

requirement that a verse or verse cluster be removable without leaving behind a gaping lacuna is clearly a necessary condition for considering it to be a later insertion. It will serve to keep our redactional speculations within limits if we treat the availability of some sort of explanation for a conjectured act of insertion as a near-necessary condition as well. I propose to subsume both considerations under the designation 'Class 0 arguments'. Without ruling out that in certain cases they might appear not only necessary but also sufficient, it would evidently be preferable for them to be topped up with further evidence.

Two classes of such additional arguments may be distinguished:

(i) We might appeal to A's stylistic and lexical peculiarities. For example, A's verse length might palpably diverge from that of its immediate context; or A might employ diction that is associated with a period of the Qurʾan assumed to be later than S, or diction associated with verses that have already been shown to be likely insertions. I shall refer to arguments based on such stylistic and terminological considerations as 'Class 1 arguments'.

(ii) We might also try to demonstrate that the content of A stands in tension with statements made elsewhere in S, such that removal of A would improve the surah's overall consistency. Or A might in some way appear to be structurally out of place or intrusive, or cause its literary context to deviate from compositional patterns that can be discerned elsewhere in the Qurʾan. I shall refer to such arguments from propositional incompatibility or from structural intrusiveness, awkwardness, and deviance as 'Class 2 arguments'.

Arguably, arguments falling into Class 2 will generally be much more open to challenge than those from Class 1. For instance, arguments from a perceived inconsistency of content are apt to trigger the question whether we are in fact entitled to expect the Qurʾan 'to conform to modern expectations about consistency'.[7] True, the basic principle underlying such reasoning appears sound: if a text articulates irreconcilable claims or norms, it is reasonable to explore the hypothesis that the clash might result from the text's having undergone secondary expansion or reworking. However, it is to be expected that it will frequently be possible to harmonize our putative insertion A with the rest of the surah in such a way as to eliminate any perceived inconsistencies. In such a case, the force of our argument from propositional incompatibility will stand or fall with the force of a particular construal of A—namely, the one construing A as standing in tension with other parts of S. As regards arguments from structural intrusiveness and compositional deviance, the

[7] The quotation is taken from John C. Collins' appraisal of classical nineteenth-century biblical source criticism, exemplified by the work of Wellhausen. See John C. Collins, *Introduction to the Hebrew Bible* (Minneapolis: Fortress Press, 2004), 16.

worry that they might be guilty of anachronistically imposing modern expectations on the Qurʾan is even more acute, given that contemporary notions of ideal literary structure or compositional consistency are likely to exhibit significant divergence from those current in seventh-century Arabia. In any case, none of the types of arguments just surveyed will be unassailably sufficient by itself. The case for a presumed addition will thus inevitably be a cumulative and probabilistic one.

The above taxonomy is not meant to be novel: at least in part, it merely codifies the different kinds of considerations informing earlier Western scholars' judgements about the presence of secondary insertions in the Qurʾan. Nöldeke and Schwally's *Geschichte des Qorāns* (1909), whose default position is to treat a given surah as a unity, already singles out specific verses and passages as later additions.[8] Much more far-reaching redactional conjectures are put forward in Richard Bell's 1937 translation of the Qurʾan, which dissects many surahs into brief paragraphs deemed to have been joined together only secondarily.[9] Famously, Bell posited that consecutive sections of qurʾanic text owe their adjacent position to the mere fact that they had been recorded on different sides of the same scrap of writing material, which caused the redactor or redactors of the Qurʾan to misread them as a continuous sequence.[10]

Although both works are still eminently valuable, they can hardly be considered a definitive treatment of the topic of secondary additions to qurʾanic surahs. Nöldeke and Schwally's assessments are partly based, as they should be, on observations about style, terminology, and content, yet their respective comments are often tantalizingly brief and hampered by significant reliance on post-qur'anic traditions. As for Bell, his analyses frequently rest on the dubious assumption that mere shifts in rhyme and/or in topic constitute sufficient ground for considering a surah to be redactionally composite. Equally problematic is Bell's persistent appeal to '[a]ll the possibilities of confusion in written documents',[11] which enables him to posit numerous instances of secondary expansion without having to account for why a given block of material ended up in one place rather than another.[12] I would submit that my insistence above that the identification of putative additions be

[8] See the diachronic survey of the qurʾanic surahs in Theodor Nöldeke and Friedrich Schwally, *Geschichte des Qorāns*, 2nd edn, vol. 1: *Über den Ursprung des Qorāns* (Leipzig: Dieterich'sche Verlagsbuchhandlung, 1909), 74–234.

[9] Richard Bell (trans.), *The Qurʾān*, 2 vols (Edinburgh, T. & T. Clark, 1937), vol. 1, and idem, *A Commentary on the Qurʾān*, 2 vols (Manchester: University of Manchester, 1991). See also Andrew Rippin, 'Reading the Qurʾān with Richard Bell', *Journal of the American Oriental Society* 112 (1992): 639–47.

[10] For a random example see Bell (trans.), *The Qurʾān*, vol. 1, 205–7 (on Q 11:1–7, according to the now standard Kufan system of verse division).

[11] Bell, *The Qurʾān*, vol. 1, vi.

[12] To put it differently, if we were to ask, 'Why did the hypothetically reconstructed *Urtext* of a given passage come to evolve into its canonical form?', then Bell's standard answer would

accompanied by the identification of intelligible motives offers a firm guarantee that our redactional hypotheses will not run amok, as Bell's frequently do.[13]

Despite such misgivings, previous scholarship on the Qurʾan is to be unequivocally credited with having successfully identified a number of fairly uncontroversial cases of later expansion. Many of these are found in the brief and largely eschatologically dominated surahs that Nöldeke and Schwally would assign to the early Meccan period, and Neuwirth has produced a useful conspectus of the verses in question.[14] Two especially conspicuous instances are Q 73:20 and Q 74:31. Having briefly discussed the former verse elsewhere, I shall limit myself to a few concise remarks on Q 74:31.[15] My aim in doing so is to present a benchmark case of secondary expansion to which all three classes of arguments surveyed above are pertinent.

Q 74:31 follows a brief description of the fire of hell, here referred to by the feminine noun *saqar*,[16] that runs from v. 26 to v. 30. After a terse introductory threat (v. 26: 'I shall roast him in *saqar*!'), a didactic question (v. 27: 'What can give you[s] knowledge of what *saqar* is?')[17] triggers a response consisting of three brief verses (vv. 28–30): 'It [literally, "she"] does not spare nor does it leave alone; / scorching the skin.[18] / Over it are nineteen.' This is followed by

consist in invoking 'confusion in written documents'. Such a generic, one-size-fits-all solution is scarcely satisfactory.

[13] But note that my own analysis of the opening section of surah 9 as put forward below partly overlaps with Bell's.

[14] Angelika Neuwirth, *Studien zur Komposition der mekkanischen Suren*, 2nd edn (Berlin: De Gruyter, 2007), 201–3. A more recent treatment of these verses can be found in Angelika Neuwirth, *Der Koran*, vol. 1: *Frühmekkanische Suren: Poetische Prophetie* (Berlin: Verlag der Weltreligionen, 2011). For a general discussion specifically of those additions to qurʾanic surahs that would appear to be motivated by interpretive concerns, see Nicolai Sinai, 'Two Types of Inner-Qurʾanic Interpretation', forthcoming in Georges Tamer, ed. *Exegetical Crossroads* (Berlin: De Gruyter).

[15] On Q 73:20, which mitigates the surah's opening injunction to lengthy vigils, see Sinai, 'Two Types of Inner-Qurʾanic Interpretation'.

[16] The word (which also appears at Q 74:42 and 54:48) is treated as feminine in Q 74:28 and is generally vocalized as a diptote, as required for proper names that are feminine in meaning according to classical Arabic grammar. Despite being used like a proper name, the word *saqar* does have significant semantic connotations due to its proximity to *saqrun*, 'scorching', the *maṣdar* of the verb *saqara, yasquru*, 'to scorch'. (The synonym *lāḥa* occurs in v. 29; see n. 18.) As a matter of fact, the Qurʾan's original audience may well have understood *saqarun* as an acceptable variant of *saqrun*, given that the *maṣdars* of other basic-stem verbs also show the morpheme pattern *faʿalun* (*ʿamalun, ṭalabun, naẓarun*, etc.).

[17] On such didactic questions see Neuwirth, *Studien*, 132, 190, and Neal Robinson, *Discovering the Qurʾan: A Contemporary Approach to a Veiled Text*, 2nd edn (London: SCM Press, 2003), 119–20.

[18] Arabic: *lawwāḥatun li-l-bashar*. Note that the verb *lāḥa* is to all intents and purposes synonymous with *saqara*, thus implying what is virtually an etymological explanation of the enigmatic name *saqar* (see n. 16). *Bashar*, of course, cannot only mean 'skin' but also 'mankind'. As a matter of fact, this second meaning of *bashar* occurs elsewhere in the same surah: v. 25 cites the Qurʾan's opponents as maintaining that 'this is only human speech' (*in hādhā illā qawlu l-bashar*); v. 31 concludes with a self-referential statement that 'it (*hiya*) is only an admonition for mankind' (*dhikrā li-l-bashar*); and v. 36 describes *saqar* itself as a 'warning to mankind'

v. 31, our putative addition, which supplies further information about the enigmatic 'nineteen' creatures alluded to in the previous verse by stating that the 'masters of the fire' (*aṣḥāb al-nār*) are in fact angels. V. 31 also explains why v. 30 advances such a puzzlingly precise quantification in the first place: the aim is to put the Unbelievers to the 'test' (*fitna*), to provide the inheritors of earlier scriptural revelations with certainty, and to ensure that 'those who believe may have even greater belief'.[19] This is followed by an oath (vv. 32–4) and a further characterization of *saqar* (vv. 35–7).

V. 31 stands out from its literary context on multiple counts. Most strikingly, the verse runs to the extraordinary length of 366 transcription letters, which is more than ten times the mean verse length displayed by the remainder of the surah (21.28 transcription letters, with a standard deviation of 7.16 letters).[20] Furthermore, v. 31 employs phraseology that is distinctively late Meccan and even Medinan (*yuḍillu llāhu man yashāʾu wa-yahdī man yashāʾu*, 'God sends astray those whom He wishes and guides those whom He wishes'; *alladhīna ūtū l-kitāb*, 'those who have been given the Scripture'; *alladhīna fī qulūbihim maraḍun*, 'those in whose hearts is sickness').[21] Such Class 1 arguments compellingly date the final version of v. 31 to a much later time, most likely to the Medinan period.[22] In addition, v. 31 also qualifies as an insertion in Class 0 terms, meaning that it fulfils the necessary conditions that any presumed addition must satisfy: it can easily be removed from its context without leaving behind any gap; and there is a reasonable explanation for why it came to be incorporated into the text—namely, in order to clarify and

(*nadhīran li-l-bashar*). Against this background, the occurrence of *bashar* in the alternative meaning of 'skin' in v. 29 would appear to be a deliberate rhetorical choice. Cf. Neuwirth, *Frühmekkanische Suren*, 369–71.

[19] Conceivably, it is the complex communicative function thus attributed to v. 30—its alleged ability to bring to light the borderline between Believers and Unbelievers—that underlies the fact that v. 31 implicitly describes the previous verse as a *mathal* or 'parable'. For a different view see Frants Buhl, 'Über Vergleichungen und Gleichnisse im Qur'ân', in Rudi Paret, ed. *Der Koran* (Darmstadt: Wissenschaftliche Buchgesellschaft, 1975), 75–85 [reprinted from *Acta Orientalia* 2 (1924): 1–11], at p. 84 (construing the expression *mathal* in Q 74:31 in the general meaning of 'account', 'description').

[20] For details on how these values were computed see Sinai, 'Inner-Qurʾanic Chronology'.

[21] For a similar observation see already Nöldeke and Schwally, *Geschichte des Qorāns*, vol. 1, 88–9. For *yuḍillu llāhu man yashāʾu wa-yahdī man yashāʾu* see e.g. Q 14:4 or 16:93. For *alladhīna ūtū l-kitāb* see, for instance, Q 2:101, 144, 145 and 3:19, 20, 23, 100, etc. There are some isolated occurrences of this phrase that would *prima facie* seem to be late Meccan, at 13:36 and 28:52 (cf. also 42:14), which may form the inner-qur'anic origin of the phrase; but the original version of surah 74 must be considerably earlier than surahs 13 and 28. On *alladhīna fī qulūbihim maraḍun* see Q 2:10, 5:52, 8:49, 9:125, 24:50, 33:12, 32, 60, and 47:20, 29 (all of which are plausibly considered to be Medinan). Q 22:53 appears in a part of surah 22 that might well be Meccan (at least according to Nöldeke and Schwally, *Geschichte des Qorāns*, vol. 1, 213).

[22] The notion of *fitna* deployed by v. 31 also appears in Q 37:63 and 17:60. At least the former verse is highly unlikely to constitute a Medinan insertion. It is not impossible that the present wording of Q 74:31 may have grown out of a shorter insertion that was incorporated into the surah already during the Meccan period.

comment on the immediately preceding statement that there are nineteen guardians set over the fire of hell. Finally, one may also adduce a Class 2 argument: the feminine pronoun appearing in v. 35 (*innahā la-iḥdā l-kubar*, 'it is one of the gravest matters') must refer back to the feminine noun *saqar* in vv. 26–30, yet this antecedent is to all intents and purposes obliterated due to the inordinate length of v. 31. Removing the putative insertion thus increases the passage's literary coherence. In sum, a discussion of Q 74:31 can rely on all three classes of evidence outlined above, making the verse a veritable textbook example for secondary additions.[23]

If a certain number of Meccan surahs underwent later expansion, as exemplified by surah 74, the same may be suspected to apply to the Medinan ones. Pursuing this conjecture, the present chapter will attempt to discern traces of secondary expansion in the opening sections of two Medinan surahs, Q 5 and 9.[24] We must recognize from the outset that in embarking on such an enquiry we are unlikely to encounter instances of secondary expansion that are as clear-cut as Q 74:31. For the latter verse confronts us with a much later (probably Medinan) addition embedded in an early Meccan environment, thus giving us a maximum time lag and, consequently, a stark contrast between the basic layer and the later insertion. Once we turn to qur'anic proclamations whose basic layer is itself Medinan, however, the terminological and stylistic disparity between a surah's original nucleus and any secondary additions will inevitably be much fainter. For instance, we will not be able to rely on marked discrepancies in verse length of the sort encountered in surahs 73 and 74 in order to identify additions. Thus, in setting out to detect instances of secondary expansion in the Medinan surahs we must brace ourselves for the possibility of having to make do with arguments falling into Classes 0 and 2. Inevitably, this expected lack of Class 1 evidence will make the redactional analysis of Medinan surahs considerably more speculative in nature than that of our paradigm case Q 74:31.

Still, I would submit that the unlikelihood of reaching certain, or even compellingly probable, results should not lead us to abandon the question. Rather, an enquiry into whether the Medinan surahs admit of internal diachronic distinctions—that is, of judgements to the effect that a given verse or

[23] Although Q 74:31 is highly likely to constitute a Medinan insertion, the verse is nevertheless not identified as one in any of the indigenous Islamic traditions about Medinan insertions that are compiled in Nagel, *Medinensische Einschübe* (see p. 89). This confirms the need for a high degree of cautionary scepticism regarding such traditions.

[24] The question of Medinan insertions in the later Meccan surahs also requires further attention. For a case study, see Angelika Neuwirth, 'Meccan Texts—Medinan Additions? Politics and the Re-reading of Liturgical Communications', in Rüdiger Arnzen and Jörn Thielmann, eds, *Words, Texts, and Concepts Cruising the Mediterranean Sea: Studies on the Sources, Contents, and Influences of Islamic Civilization and Arabic Philosophy and Science* (Leuven: Peeters, 2004), 71–93, arguing for the presence of Medinan insertions in surahs 20 and 7 (namely, Q 20:80–2 and Q 7:145–7, 7:152–3, and 7:155–7).

passage was incorporated into the respective surah later than other passages—is crucially important. This is so because the structural organization and thematic coherence especially of the Medinan long surahs (Q 2–5 and 8–9), or their lack thereof, continue to baffle scholars.[25] Despite recent attempts to construe these texts as well-organized ring-compositional wholes,[26] one wonders whether the task of understanding their present shape might not require us to invoke, at least on occasion, operations of editorial reworking and expansion. To offer an initial example, the brief treatment of fasting in Q 2:183–7 is plausibly viewed as consisting of two or three different and temporally successive pronouncements. Here, an original command demanding that the qurʾanic community fast 'on a number of days' in line with the practice of 'those before you^{p}' (vv. 183–4) was later supplemented by the institution of a month-long and specifically qurʾanic fast in Ramadan (vv. 185–7, with v. 187 possibly constituting yet a later pronouncement than vv. 185–6).[27] The present shape of the section thus lends itself to being explained as an outcome of incremental aggregation.

Taking our cue from this brief passage on fasting, it is tempting to speculate whether the manner in which surah 2 as a whole reached its canonical shape might not be similar to the way in which many biblical scholars would explain the canonical shape of many of the prophetic books of the Hebrew Bible—namely, as an outcome of gradual and complicated processes of literary growth.[28] The Islamic tradition, of course, is perfectly comfortable with this general notion yet confines such textual growth to the lifetime of the Prophet. For instance, a *ḥadīth* describes how Muhammad would instruct his scribes to

[25] See, e.g., Angelika Neuwirth, 'From Recitation through Liturgy to Canon: Sura Composition and Dissolution during the Development of Islamic Ritual', in Angelika Neuwirth, *Scripture, Poetry and the Making of a Community: Reading the Qurʾan as a Literary Text* (Oxford: Oxford University Press, 2014), 141–63 (originally published in German in 1996), at p. 154, describing some of the Medinan long surahs as 'repositories of dispersed groups of [...] verses'.

[26] See Michel Cuypers, *The Banquet: A Reading of the Fifth Sura of the Qurʾan*, trans. Patricia Kelly (Miami: Convivium Press, 2009); Carl Ernst, *How to Read the Qurʾan: A New Guide, With Select Translations* (Chapel Hill: University of North Carolina Press, 2011), 155–204; Raymond Farrin, *Structure and Qurʾanic Interpretation: A Study of Symmetry and Coherence in Islam's Holy Text* (Ashland: White Cloud Press, 2014), esp. 9–21 (on surah 2). Note that Farrin and Cuypers do not limit the applicability of their ring-compositional approach to the Medinan layer of the Qur'an.

[27] See provisionally Kees Wagtendonk, 'Fasting', in Jane Dammen McAuliffe, ed., *Encyclopaedia of the Qurʾān*, 6 vols, vol. 2 (Leiden: Brill, 2002), 180–5.

[28] For a stimulating exploration of this comparative perspective, see Karl-Friedrich Pohlmann, *Die Entstehung des Korans: Neue Erkenntnisse aus Sicht der historisch-kritischen Bibelwissenschaft* (Darmstadt: Wissenschaftliche Buchgesellschaft, 2012). Pohlmann argues that scribal circles consisting of Jewish and Christian converts continued to shape and expand the qurʾanic corpus after the death of Muhammad. While I harbour considerable reservations about his conclusions (on which see Sinai, 'Two Types of Inner-Qurʾanic Interpretation'), the contention that the Medinan long surahs might usefully be studied in the light of redactional models developed by scholars of the Hebrew Bible is extremely plausible.

insert newly revealed passages into existing surahs.[29] While we should naturally be wary of accepting this report as an authentic glimpse of Muhammad at work, it does present a model of textual development that would seem to fit the appearance of surah 2's fasting section as well as the two passages to be analysed below. In any event, Pohlmann's recent plea that such redactional activity must inevitably have constituted a post-prophetic phenomenon is far from conclusive: there would seem to be no a priori reason to rule out the possibility that the scribal revision of existing qurʾanic proclamations could have got under way already while further qurʾanic revelations were still being delivered.[30] At the same time, there is equally no a priori reason for ruling out that such editorial activity could have continued in the wake of Muhammad's death, although the time frame available for such hypothetical post-prophetic editing would appear to come to a close around 650.[31]

THE OPENING SECTION OF SURAH 5

Q 5:1–11 (the full text of which is given in Table 2.1 in the Appendix) forms a succession of paragraph-like subsections to do, inter alia, with food taboos and the performance of ablution before praying. The passage is followed by an extended portion of text centred on debates with, and exhortations about, the People of the Scripture, which runs from v. 11 or 12 until the end of v. 86.[32] In

[29] See al-Tirmidhī, *al-Jāmiʿ al-ṣaḥīḥ*, Aḥmad Muḥammad Shākir et al. (eds), 5 vols (Cairo: Maṭbaʿat Muṣṭafā al-Bābī al-Ḥalabī, 1978–1986), vol. 5, 272, no. 3086 (48:10: *Kitāb tafsīr al-Qurʾān*, on Q 9).

[30] See Pohlmann, *Die Entstehung des Korans*, and Sinai, 'Two Types of Inner-Qurʾanic Interpretation'.

[31] See Nicolai Sinai, 'When Did the Consonantal Skeleton of the Quran Reach Closure?', *Bulletin of the School of Oriental and African Studies* 77 (2014): 273–92 and 509–21.

[32] According to Neal Robinson, 'Hands Outstretched: Towards a Re-reading of *Sūrat al-Māʾida*', *Journal of Qurʾanic Studies* 3 (2001): 1–19, at 3–4, the first section of the surah ends at v. 9, which he takes to be followed by a free-standing verse. I am sceptical about this, mainly because vv. 9–10 constitute one of the Qurʾan's frequent antithetical juxtapositions of Believers and Unbelievers and would thus appear to be sufficiently closely linked in order to merit allocation to the same surah part. In any case, Robinson's proposal to consider the vocative 'O you who believe' at the beginning of v. 11 to open the surah's second section is plausible. Still, v. 11 also displays very close links to the preceding verses: as Figure 2.1 shows, its opening vocative as well as the injunctions to 'remember God's grace upon you' and to 'fear God' are all resonances of preceding verses. One might thus toy with the idea of having v. 11 conclude the first part rather than opening the second one, although this would have the disadvantage of making the second section begin with the somewhat less conspicuous *wa-la-qad* (v. 12) rather than a vocative (v. 11). Rather than attempting to settle this alternative either way, the matter is perhaps best seen as an expression of the more pervasive difficulty of deciding where exactly the boundary between two consecutive parts of a long qurʾanic surah is to be drawn. For some pertinent reflections, see A. H. Mathias Zahniser, 'Major Transitions and Thematic Borders in

terms of its internal thematic organization, vv. 1–11 may be subdivided as follows:

1–2 Prohibition of consuming hunting prey during the pilgrimage (including a warning not to clash with pagan participants in the pilgrimage ritual).

3–5 General dietary regulations, permission to consume hunting prey, permission of commensality and limited intermarriage with Jews and Christians.

6–7 Ablution before prayer, exhortation.

8–10 General paraenesis.

11 Conclusion.

While these subsections might at first appear to be self-contained, closer inspection reveals them to be woven together by an intricate web of recurrent words, roots, and phrases (e.g. the vocative 'O you who believe', the root *ḥ-l-l*, and injunctions to be fearful of God). Figure 2.1, again found in the Appendix, attempts to map out this network of terminological correspondences. In the interest of transparency, I do not include the complete text of the passage but only retain those expressions and phrases that are interlinked with others. Incidentally, while some of these correspondences also figure in Michel Cuypers' detailed study of surah 5, my presentation illustrates that it would be an oversimplification to follow Cuypers in describing these miscellaneous superimposed correspondence patterns as yielding an unequivocally concentric structure.[33]

The hypothesis I shall attempt to develop in what follows is that parts of verse 3 as well as verses 4 and 5 were inserted into the surah's opening sequence at a secondary stage. The basic idea is illustrated by Table 2.2, which puts forward a redactional model for the passage in which putative insertions are highlighted and indented. Note that for ease of reference, I have

Two Long Sūras: *al-Baqara* and *al-Nisāʾ*", in Issa J. Boullata, ed. *Literary Structures of Religious Meaning in the Qurʾān* (Richmond: Curzon, 2000), 26–55. Zahniser's concept of compositional 'hinges'—passages that exhibit discernible links both to the preceding and the following—is a helpful way of guarding against the (modern?) temptation to impose hard caesurae, that is, to require any verse to belong to one and only one surah part. Fortunately, the question where exactly the first part of surah 5 ends does not have any impact on my present argument.

33 See Cuypers, *The Banquet*, 61–115. Note that unlike Cuypers I have generally confined myself to terminological correspondences, that is, recurrences of the same word, phrase, or root. I am reluctant to take into account general thematic links not involving such verbal recurrence, given that they open up a much greater scope for the subjective imposition of preconceived structures. However, I have found it defensible to make two exceptions to this principle: firstly, I accept that there is a tenable parallel between the hardship clauses in vv. 3 and 6 despite the fact that they exhibit no literal overlap; and I am willing to consider the verb *khashiya* in 5:3 to correspond to the passage's multiple occurrences of *ittaqā*. (I translate the former verb as 'to be afraid' and the latter as 'to fear' in order to signal that the underlying Arabic words are not identical but merely synonyms.)

subdivided Q 5:3 into five smaller segments identified by the letters A, B, C, D, and E. I shall discuss the three verses in their canonical order.[34]

Q 5:3

The beginning of v. 3 enumerates four categories of prohibited meat ('carrion, blood, pork, and anything on which any other than God has been invoked'), while the end of the verse contains a hardship clause: if someone is 'compelled by hunger', it is forgivable to violate the dietary taboos set out before. This sequence of four dietary prohibitions followed by a hardship clause has three parallels elsewhere in the qur'anic corpus (Q 2:173, 6:145, 16:115), of which Table 2.3 offers a synopsis. In all three of these parallel verses the hardship clause follows immediately upon the four-part list of food taboos, whereas 5:3 intercalates a significant expanse of text between them. This is illustrated by Table 2.4, which juxtaposes Q 2:173 with 5:3. This table again subdivides 5:3 into five smaller segments identified by the superscript letters A, B, C, D, and E; the segments directly corresponding to Q 2:173 are 5:3A and 5:3E. It is the intervening segments B to D that are likely to have been grafted onto the text. Before I can make the case for this hypothesis, a brief exegetical treatment of each of these three intervening segments is indispensable.

Q 5:3B declares animals that have been strangled, or been beaten to death, or fallen to death, etc., to be forbidden unless they are 'purified', perhaps by draining them of their residual blood.[35] This part of the verse is best construed as an enumeration of various subcategories of carrion (*mayta*), the first kind of prohibited food listed in segment A. Segment B is therefore aptly described as a 'running gloss' on the term *mayta*.[36] This is so despite the fact that 5:3B is not of course positioned immediately after the word elucidated by it, which might make it appear as a continuation of the preceding food taboos rather than as a delayed clarification of the verse's opening taboo.

The following segment, 5:3C, adds two further prohibitions, namely, of meat that has been 'slaughtered on sacrifical stones' (*mā dhubiḥa ʿalā l-nuṣub*) and of 'practising *istiqsām* by means of arrows' (*an tastaqsimū bi-l-azlām*). The first of these interdictions, 'that which has been slaughtered on sacrifical

[34] It must be acknowledged that the literary evidence probably permits redactional scenarios that are even more complex than mine. For instance, one might deem Q 5:3D to be a second-order addition appended to the first-order addition Q 5:3B–C.

[35] In classical Islamic law, 'purification' denotes the emergency slaughter of an animal that still shows some signs of life. See *Encyclopaedia of Islam*, 2nd edn (Leiden: Brill, 1960–2006), s. v. 'Mayta' (Joseph Schacht).

[36] David M. Freidenreich, *Foreigners and Their Food: Constructing Otherness in Jewish, Christian, and Islamic Law* (Berkeley: University of California Press, 2011), 139.

stones'—a phrase that forms a qur'anic *hapax legomenon*—is to all intents and purposes a reformulation of 5:3A's ban of 'that on which any other than God has been invoked'. Thus, just as 5:3B elucidates the first item of the four-part list of general dietary taboos contained in segment A, so 5:3C paraphrases the last item of segment A. In this sense, the beginning of 5:3C, too, functions like a gloss on a part of 5:3A. Again, it is noteworthy that the explanation does not directly follow the phrase that forms its proper object.

The meaning of 5:3C's second prohibition (translated above as 'practising *istiqsām* by means of arrows') is not immediately evident. The root meaning of *q-s-m* and the dietary character of the preceding might invite the idea that reference is to a particular way of dividing up slaughtered meat. Such a reading would effectively consider the practice of *istiqsām* to be identical with or at least very similar to the *maysir* game, in which players gambled for portions of a she-camel by casting arrows.[37] Against such a conflation of *istiqsām* with *maysir*, Nadia Jamil inclines towards viewing *istiqsām* as an Arabian type of belomancy, or divination by means of arrows.[38] This position is borne out by Q 5:90, which condemns 'wine, *maysir*, sacrificial stones (*al-anṣāb*), and divining arrows (*al-azlām*)' as 'filth belonging to the work of Satan'. The list is clearly meant to be a catalogue of separate elements, entailing that the Qur'an views *maysir* and the use of *azlām* as distinct practices. This militates against identifying '*istiqsām* by arrows' in 5:3C with the *maysir* game and suggests that what is prohibited in segment C is not in fact a specific manner of dividing up meat. Belomancy fits the bill.[39] If this reasoning is accepted, then the second prohibition enunciated in 5:3C, unlike all preceding ones, does not constitute a dietary rule. The significance of this ancillary conclusion will become apparent further below.

The verse's penultimate segment, 5:3D, contains the first occurrence of the divine first person in the surah. Among other things, the divine voice maintains that 'today I have perfected your religion for you (*akmaltu lakum dīnakum*) and completed My grace upon you'. This could be understood as

[37] See in detail Nadia Jamil, 'Playing for Time: *Maysir*-Gambling in Early Arabic Poetry', in Robert G. Hoyland and Philip F. Kennedy, eds, *Islamic Reflections, Arabic Musings: Studies in Honour of Professor Alan Jones* ([Cambridge:] Gibb Memorial Trust, 2004), 48–90.

[38] Jamil, 'Playing for Time', 50–4.

[39] This conclusion tallies with al-Ṭabarī's paraphrase of '*istiqsām* by arrows' as consisting in 'searching the knowledge of that which has or has not been allotted to you (*mā qusima lakum aw lam yuqsam*) by means of arrows' (Abū Ja'far Muḥammad ibn Jarīr al-Ṭabarī, *Tafsīr al-Ṭabarī: Jāmiʿ al-bayān ʿan tafsīr āy al-Qurʾān*, Maḥmūd Muḥammad Shākir and Aḥmad Muḥammad Shākir, eds, 2nd edn [Cairo: Dār al-Maʿārif, n. d.], *ad* Q 5:30, vol. 9, 510). Whether al-Ṭabarī's explanation is etymologically correct or not, it shows that the root *q-s-m* does not necessitate construing Q 5:3C as referring to the division of meat. See also Erwin Gräf, *Jagdbeute und Schlachttier im islamischen Recht* (Bonn: Selbstverlag des Orientalischen Seminars der Universität Bonn, 1959), 51–3, as well as Holger Zellentin, *The Qurʾān's Legal Culture: The Didascalia Apostolorum as a Point of Departure* (Tübingen: Mohr Siebeck, 2013), 119, n. 56.

asserting the closure of revelation, implying that the verse styles itself as forming, or at least belonging to, Muhammad's last divine communication. This is how the statement of completion was understood by later Islamic readers, who believed it to have been proclaimed during Muhammad's Farewell Pilgrimage; as explained by al-Ṭabarī, a group of scholars 'maintained that after this verse, no further commandments were revealed to the Prophet (eulogy), neither the permission of anything nor the prohibition of anything, and that the Prophet (eulogy) only continued to live for another eighty-one nights after the revelation of this verse'.[40] If that is indeed the meaning of 5:3D, a secular historian may well wonder whether the segment, thus understood, might not postdate Muhammad's death and retrospectively inscribe into the qurʾanic corpus an unequivocal reassurance that the divine word had been communicated in its entirety. However, the purport of the assertion that the addressees' religion has now been 'perfected' may also have been much more limited—for example, the statement might simply mean that the dietary taboos of the qurʾanic community have now been fully and definitively elucidated, with the consequence that 'a defining characteristic of the nascent Islamic community in contrast to those who fall outside its bounds' has been articulated.[41]

Let us now take stock of the observations that might suggest that the present shape of 5:3 is not the original one. The hypothesis is not entirely original: Paret already tersely intimates that 5:3D could have been 'misplaced' from a different literary context.[42] Although he does not develop an explicit argument, he would appear to have been bothered by 5:3D's manifestly parenthetic status, that is, the fact that the segment shows virtually no obvious thematic or syntactic links with 5:3C nor with 5:3E (apart from the fact that all previous segments also contain occurrences of the second person plural). As a result of such minimal interlinking with its immediate context, segment D certainly satisfies the condition of being removable from its context without generating an unbridgeable lacuna. Going further than that, one may well consider 5:3D to be downright intrusive insofar as it interrupts the connection between the opening of the verse and the hardship clause in segment E. It is true that similarly parenthetic comments are a staple of qurʾanic discourse and that it

[40] al-Ṭabarī, *Tafsīr*, *ad* Q 5:3 (*al-yawma akmaltu lakum dīnakum*), vol. 9, 517f.; see also Nöldeke and Schwally, *Geschichte des Qorāns*, vol. 1, 227–8. Cuypers, *The Banquet*, 93, notes the absence of this verse from Ibn Isḥāq's version of Muhammad's Farewell Sermon.

[41] Freidenreich, *Foreigners*, 139. A similarly limited interpretation of the statement *al-yawma akmaltu lakum dīnakum* is also presented by al-Ṭabarī, who cites traditions to the effect that the completion of 'your religion' means merely the completion of the Islamic pilgrimage; cf. al-Ṭabarī, *Tafsīr*, *ad* Q 5:3, vol. 9, 519–20.

[42] Rudi Paret, *Der Koran: Kommentar und Konkordanz*, 2nd edn (Stuttgart: Kohlhammer, 1977), *ad* Q 5:3: 'Der Passus von *al-yauma yaʾisa lladīna kafarū* bis *wa-raḍītu lakumu l-islāma dīnan* [= 5:3D] ist vielleicht aus einem anderen Zusammenhang hierher versprengt.'

would be impossible to account for all such 'metatextual' asides or 'clausulae' in redactional terms.[43] Yet 5:3D is considerably longer than other metatextual interjections in the Qurʾan, encompassing as it does an initial statement introduced by *al-yawma* ('Today those who are Unbelievers have despaired of your religion') followed by a double imperative ('So do not be afraid of them, be afraid of Me!') and a tripartite concluding statement, likewise opened by *al-yawma* ('Today I have perfected your religion for you, completed My grace upon you, and approved submission / Islam as a religion for you'). Indeed, 5:3D by itself has a length (135 transcription letters) that is higher than or equal to that of many entire verses of surah 5.[44] At the same time, 5:3D exhibits none of the formulaic patterns characteristic of other metatextual parentheses in the Qurʾan.[45]

All of these observations support the suspicion that 5:3D entered the text at a secondary stage. Yet the insertion is likely to include a larger part of the verse than just segment D. One indication for this consists in the fact that 5:3E does not actually link up very well with 5:3C. As I have argued above, 5:3C proscribes not only meat that has been 'slaughtered on sacrificial stones' but also belomancy. However, the hardship clause contained in 5:3E is only intelligible as applying to dietary prohibitions: it makes good sense to except those 'compelled by hunger' from the prohibition of carrion or blood etc., but not to except them from the prohibition of belomancy. Thus, segment E would fit as a continuation of segments A or B but not of C. This suggests that the insertion is not confined to 5:3D, as conjectured by Paret, but includes at least segment C as well. Additional observations indicate that 5:3B is likewise part of the addition: first, it shares with 5:3C the function of clarifying one of the prohibitions appearing in 5:3A; and secondly, as we saw above, all three qurʾanic parallels to 5:3A and 5:3E—namely, Q 2:173, 6:145, 16:115—have the hardship clause (corresponding to 5:3E) follow immediately upon the four-part list of dietary prohibitions (corresponding to 5:3A). Our putative addition is therefore likely to encompass the entire stretch of text running from the beginning of 5:3B to the end of 5:3D—all of which can be lifted from the verse without generating an overt lacuna. The original version of the verse, consisting of segments A and E, would therefore have formed a near-identical parallel to Q 2:173, 6:145, and 16:115.

[43] For a detailed taxonomy and analysis of different types of qurʾanic clausulae see Neuwirth, *Studien*, 157–70; cf. also Robinson, *Discovering the Qurʾan*, 198–201. On my use of 'metatextual' here, see Nicolai Sinai, 'Qurʾānic Self-Referentiality as a Strategy of Self-Authorization', in Stefan Wild, ed., *Self-Referentiality in the Qurʾān* (Wiesbaden: Harrassowitz, 2006), 103–34, at 111 as well as 122–3, which discusses a similar aside occurring in Q 38:24.

[44] The mean verse length of surah 5 is 150.06 transcription letters, with a standard deviation of 83.67. Details on how these values were computed may be found in Sinai, 'Inner-Qurʾanic Chronology'.

[45] See the survey of the most common clausula patterns in Neuwirth, *Studien*, 160–3.

As emphasized above, it is preferable for any conjectures about secondary insertions to be accompanied by an explanation of why the insertion at hand would have been made. In the present case, 5:3B–D serve to clarify two of the components of segment A, providing us with an intelligible editorial motive for the suspected addition. As pointed out above, the first part of the addition, 5:3B, catalogues various cases of carrion and thus elucidates the prohibition of *mayta* at the beginning of 5:3A. Incidentally, this clarification appears to be informed by some acquaintance with Jewish (and perhaps also Christian) discussions about the kinds of dead animals falling under the biblical prohibition of consuming *nevelah* and *trefah*.[46] 5:3C, too, plays a clarificatory role with regard to 5:3A by paraphrasing its formulaic prohibition of that 'on which any other than God has been invoked' (see also 2:173, 6:145, and 16:115) as proscribing 'that which has been slaughtered on sacrificial stones'. This is then supplemented by the prohibition of belomancy discussed above.[47]

Regarding segment D, it functions in the first place as a 'wrap-up unit'[48] that closes out the entire insertion 5:3B–D. As observed above, 5:3D may either be read as asserting the general closure of the qurʾanic revelations or simply as underscoring the significance of the preceding elucidation of the qurʾanic dietary regulations. In addition, its use of the temporal qualifier *al-yawma* (twice in Q 5:3D, once more in 5:5) evokes the frequent use of 'today', *hayyom*, in the book of Deuteronomy and thus has the effect of implicitly styling surah 5 as a farewell speech analogous to that delivered by Moses.[49] Finally, segment D's use of the verbal noun *islām* (literally, 'submission'—namely, to

[46] Josef J. Rivlin, *Gesetz im Koran: Kultus und Ritus* (Jerusalem: Bamberger & Wahrmann, 1934), 71 (see also 78–9), remarks that this part of the verse has the effect of extending the qurʾanic prohibition of *mayta* to cases which rabbinic law classifies as *trefah* (animals that have been torn by a beast), as opposed to *nevelah* (animals that have died a natural death); Rivlin points to Talmud Chullin 43a. *Nevelah* is prohibited in Deuteronomy 14:21 (see also Leviticus 11:39–40) and *trefah* in Exodus 22:30; both are prohibited in Leviticus 17:15. See also Gräf, *Jagdbeute und Schlachttier*, 52. On the two terms see Aharon Shemesh, *Halakhah in the Making: The Development of Jewish Law from Qumran to the Rabbis* (Berkeley: University of California Press, 2009), 77–80. In addition to these Jewish parallels, one should also note that 'strangled' animals are already prohibited in Acts 15:19–20 and that the Pseudo-Clementine Homilies ban animals 'caught by wild beasts' (Zellentin, *The Qurʾān's Legal Culture*, 79–80).

[47] Note that v. 90 also condemns sacrificial stones and divining arrows, listed consecutively and in the same order as in v. 3C, in addition to wine and *maysir*. I would tentatively date v. 90 later than the final version of v. 3, just as vv. 94–96 would appear to be later clarifications pertaining to vv. 1–2.

[48] The term 'wrap-up unit' is taken from Zahniser, 'Major Transitions', 32. According to Zahniser, wrap-up units 'reinforce the content of the passages they cap off, act as motivational support for them, or reinforce the worldview of the Qurʾān in general'.

[49] Hartwig Hirschfeld, *New Researches into the Composition and Exegesis of the Qoran* (London: Royal Asiatic Society, 1902), 133. See e.g. Deuteronomy 5:1: 'Hear, O Israel, the statutes and judgements which I speak in your ears this day'. Parallels between the opening verses of surah 5 and Moses' 'testament-address' in Deuteronomy are also pointed out in Cuypers, *The Banquet*, 93–7. Inter alia, Cuypers notes the triple occurrence of *al-yawma* in Q 5:3.5, although without reference to Hirschfeld, and the fact that both texts contain injunctions to 'fear' God.

God)[50] to designate the qur'anic religion ('I have approved submission [to God] as a religion for you') is salient: the concatenation of the nouns *islām* and *dīn* in the sense of 'religion' has only a limited number of qurʾanic parallels,[51] suggesting that 5:3D might also serve as a prominently placed reinforcement of this nomenclature.

It is noteworthy that segment D picks up some of the diction punctuating the literary environment into which it was embedded: apart from its call to 'be afraid' (*khashiya*) of God, which echoes the passage's multiple uses of *ittaqā* and *taqwā*, the statement 'I have completed My grace upon you' anticipates the end of verse 6 ('He wishes... to complete His grace upon you') and the opening of verse 7 ('And remember God's grace upon you!'). We shall have occasion to make similar observations below. Complex patterns of terminological correspondences like those illustrated in Figure 2.1 may thus in part be an outcome of literary growth over time rather than necessarily indicating that the passage at hand forms a genetic unity.

Q 5:4

V. 4 is introduced by a responsa formula, 'They ask you ... Say: ... (*yasʾalūnaka ... qul ...*).' The *yasʾalūnaka* formula, which appears nowhere else in surah 5, enables the qurʾanic proclamations to engage with an audience query (or at least to style themselves as doing so).[52] V. 4 is best understood as latching onto the prohibition of consuming animals that have been 'devoured by beasts of prey' in v. 3B, its point being to explain that animals killed by hunting beasts do not count as having been 'devoured by beasts of prey', which according to v. 3B would make them illicit. Instead, hunting prey may be consumed if God's name is invoked over it—provided, of course, that hunting does not take place in the pilgrim state, which is prohibited in v. 1.[53] Note that

[50] See Q 2:131, 133, 136 and Q 3:20, which speak of 'submitting to (*li-*)' God or 'submitting one's face (*wajh*) to' God.

[51] Derivatives of *aslama* occur several times in Q 2:124–41 (vv. 128, 131, 132, 133, 136), where Abraham is presented as the prototype of 'submission' to God, and in various places in surah 3 (vv. 20, 64, 67, 68, 80, and 84). Both surahs contain verses concatenating forms of *aslama* with the noun *dīn*; see Q 2:132 (where Abraham and Jacob enjoin their sons, 'God has chosen the [true] religion for you, so die as *muslimūn*'), Q 3:19 ('[true] religion with God is submission [to God]', *inna l-dīna ʿinda llāhi l-islām*), and Q 3:85 (condemning 'those who seek some religion other than submission [to God]', *man yabtaghi ghayra l-islāmi dīnan*). For other occurrences of the verbal noun *islām*, see Q 6:125 ('Whomsoever God wishes to guide, He expands his breast to submission', *fa-man yuridi llāhu an yahdiyahū yashraḥ ṣadrahū li-l-islām*), Q 39:22 (similarly refers to 'him whose breast God has expanded to submission'), and Q 61:7 (condemns those who ascribe falsehoods to God 'while they are called to submission').

[52] For some occurrences of *yasʾalūnaka* outside surah 5 see Q 2:189, 215, 217, 219, 220, 222.

[53] Cf. Freidenreich, *Foreigners*, 139.

the clarification also serves to exclude a potential contradiction between v. 3B and v. 2, which explicitly permits hunting once the addressees have left the pilgrim state. It is thus readily possible to conjecture a motive for the insertion of v. 4.

Significantly, the prohibition of consuming animals that have been 'devoured by beasts of prey' in v. 3B does not appear in any of the other qurʾanic lists of food taboos. Thus, if we take the formulation 'they ask you' at face value, as introducing a question that had been really put to the qurʾanic Messenger, the query at hand can only have been prompted by the immediately preceding verse. This entails that v. 4 postdates v. 3 and that v. 4 was only secondarily embedded in the passage.[54] Of course, the self-contained character of v. 4 ensures that it fulfils the Class 0 requirement of being removable from its context without leaving behind an untenable lacuna. In sum, what appears to have happened is that the prohibition of consuming animals 'devoured by beasts of prey' in Q 5:3B triggered a query among the qurʾanic audience a response to which was then slotted in immediately after the verse that had given rise to it. The text thus exhibits an interpretive snowball effect: v. 3A was clarified by the inserted segment v. 3B, which became itself an object of clarification in yet another insertion, v. 4. Interestingly, v. 4, like v. 5:3D, echoes terminology from the literary context into which it was inserted, since it is closed out by the same injunction to 'fear God' that concludes v. 2, v. 7, and v. 8.

Q 5:5

V. 5 broaches the topic of relations with the 'People of the Scripture', which is otherwise absent from surah 5's opening sequence but figures later in the text. Again, the verse satisfies the Class 0 requirement of being removable from its current position without generating an unbridgeable gap. Of course, this is not by itself sufficient warrant that it constitutes a later addition. However, additional support for this consists in the fact that v. 5 does not easily cohere with other statements found in surah 5. The case for considering v. 5 to be a secondary insertion, as set out in what follows, is thus to a significant degree based on a Class 2 argument from propositional incompatibility. Admittedly, this is not a fail-safe basis on which to ground redactional hypotheses. However, in the present case the force of such Class 2 arguments is significantly augmented by my analysis of the preceding verses, which I take to have established that 5:3B–D and 5:4 are later additions, too.

[54] It would appear that self-contained *yasʾalūnaka* statements of the sort exemplified by v. 4 generally merit exploration of the possibility that they might be insertions.

The lynchpin of my case is the statement in v. 5 that 'the food of those who have been given the Scripture is permitted to you, and your food is permitted to them'. Placing this statement alongside the dietary prohibitions listed in v. 3 gives rise to a puzzle: how can v. 5 assert that Scripturalist food—which presumably includes the food of pork-eating Christians—is permitted while v. 3 explicitly prohibits the consumption of pork?[55] Various ways of addressing the difficulty have been proposed. Freidenreich suggests that v. 5 implicitly assumes that 'the food of those who have been given the Scripture' 'conforms to the standards of permissibility articulated in previous verses'.[56] He consequently takes v. 5 to decree that 'believers may eat *otherwise acceptable* [my italics] food prepared by Jews and Christians'.[57] The point of v. 5 would thus be that food does not become illicit simply by virtue of being Jewish or Christian food (whereas Christians did prohibit Jewish food merely on account of being prepared in accordance with rabbinic dietary rules).[58] Griffith would limit the reference of 'those who have been given the Scripture' in v. 5 to Jews alone.[59] By contrast, de Blois and Crone prefer to remove the tension by assuming that the Christians with whom the qurʾanic community was primarily confronted were Jewish Christians, who would have shunned pork.[60] A further attempt at harmonization is offered by Zellentin.[61]

[55] Late antique Christian authorities promoted the consumption of pork 'as a symbol of the distinction between Christian and Jewish dietary practices'; see Freidenreich, *Foreigners*, 133 (with further references given in n. 11). On the tension between v. 3 and v. 5 see, for instance, Zellentin, *The Qurʾān's Legal Culture*, 160, and Patricia Crone, 'Jewish Christianity and the Qurʾān (Part One)', *Journal of Near Eastern Studies* 74 (2015): 225–53, at 233.

[56] Freidenreich, *Foreigners*, 141. See also Freidenreich, 131–2, 139–40, construing the word *ṭaʿām* in v. 5 to be restricted in reference to 'all foodstuffs that God has not prohibited and especially to permissible meat, the subject of the passage as a whole'.

[57] Freidenreich, *Foreigners*, 140.

[58] Freidenreich, *Foreigners*, 110–28.

[59] Sidney Griffith, 'Al-Naṣārā in the Qurʾān: A Hermeneutical Reflection', in Gabriel S. Reynolds (ed.), *New Perspectives on the Qurʾān: The Qurʾān in its Historical Context 2* (Abingdon: Routledge, 2011), 301–22, at 315–16.

[60] François de Blois, '*Naṣrānī* (*Ναζωραος*) and *ḥanīf* (*ἐθνικός*): Studies on the Religious Vocabulary of Christianity and of Islam', *Bulletin of the School of Oriental and African Studies* 65 (2002): 1–30, at 15–16; Crone, 'Jewish Christianity and the Qurʾān', 233. For a critique of de Blois's theory that the qurʾanic *naṣārā* are Jewish Christians, see Griffith, 'Al-Naṣārā in the Qurʾān'.

[61] Zellentin, *The Qurʾān's Legal Culture*, 155–74. Zellentin notes that the Qurʾan considers the complex Jewish dietary laws to have been imposed as a punishment (see Q 4:160–1, 6:146) and to have been subsequently revoked by Jesus (Q 3:49–50), who thereby restituted the food laws of the original Torah. These, Zellentin maintains, are assumed to be identical with the four qurʾanic dietary prohibitions listed in Q 5:3 and its parallels (see Zellentin, *The Qurʾān's Legal Culture*, 169). Thus, Zellentin seems to take the statement that 'the food of those who have been given the Scripture is permitted to you' to permit the food of those Jewish and Christian Scripturalists *who abide by Jesus' restitution of the food laws of the original Torah*. This solution applies the same basic exegetical operation as Freidenreich, namely, to posit a contextual restriction of the reference of a key term. However, given the considerable amount of qurʾanic polemics against the 'People of the Scripture' or 'those who have been given the Scripture', such phrases are likely to function as descriptive terms

All of these proposals attempt to find some way of eliminating the ostensible tension between v. 3 and v. 5. However, it is by no means clear that we should not simply let the tension stand. At the very least, v. 5 makes no effort to exclude pork from the general lawfulness ascribed to the food of the Scripture people—despite the fact that the possibility of understanding v. 5 as overriding the preceding ban on pork in v. 3 would arguably have needed to be reckoned with, at least if the qurʾanic addressees had some awareness of pork-consuming mainstream Christians.[62] I would thus be inclined to construe v. 5 as substantially qualifying the dietary prohibitions set out in v. 3 and as maintaining that whatever is considered licit food by Christians and Jews is thereby also licit to the qurʾanic Believers, without any need for additional vetting. Thus understood, the verse permits unrestricted commensality.[63] That such a reading is not a bold imposition on the Qurʾan is borne out by v. 93, which discounts the importance of dietary rules by asserting that 'there is no sin for those who believe and do righteous deeds concerning what they have eaten'.

My suggestion that v. 5 might represent a partial abrogation of the food taboos in v. 3 rather than tacitly presupposing their continuing validity receives further support from the fact that v. 5 also stands in tension, if not with the letter, then at least with the general spirit of another passage in surah 5, beginning in v. 51: 'O you who believe, do not take the Jews and Christians as friends / patrons (*awliyāʾ*). They are friends / patrons of each other. Whoever of you makes them his friends / patrons is one of them. God does not guide the people who do wrong.'[64] Especially in light of the sustained polemic against Jewish and Christian unbelief that is found in later sections of the surah (e.g. vv. 17–18, 59–81), v. 51 might well be taken to imply a categorical prohibition of *all* kinds of intermarriage and commensality

designating all those who self-identified as Jews and Christians—and thus to include Jews who observed traditional dietary laws as well as Pauline (and pork-eating) Christians.

[62] It is really only the prohibition of pork that sets the qurʾanic dietary laws apart from those of late antique mainline Christianity. Contemporary Christians (and also Jews) could all reasonably have been expected to shun consumption of carrion, blood, and 'anything on which any other than God has been invoked'. See Freidenreich, *Foreigners*, 142, and Crone, 'Jewish Christianity and the Qurʾān', 233.

[63] Incidentally, the stance that v. 5 would advocate on this reading is similar to that expressed by Freidenreich himself in his personal preface (*Foreigners*, xi): 'Although I am an ordained rabbi and consider myself an observant Jew, I eat food prepared by non-Jews and I share meals with non-Jews [...].' The second part of the pronouncement ('your food is permitted to them') probably expresses the expectation that the Jews ought to drop their far-reaching dietary regulations, which the Qurʾan considers to have been imposed as divine punishment (cf. Zellentin, *The Qurʾān's Legal Culture*, 127–54). Thus, v. 5 would reiterate the abrogation of the full system of Jewish dietary laws which Zellentin argues the Qurʾan ascribes to Jesus (Q 3:49–50). This line of interpretation is also suggested in Rivlin, *Gesetz im Koran*, 65.

[64] On the meaning of *awliyāʾ* see Arne A. Ambros (with the collaboration of Stephan Procházka), *A Concise Dictionary of Koranic Arabic* (Wiesbaden: Reichert 2004), 296.

between Muhammad's followers, on the one hand, and all Jews and all Christians other than the 'believing' Christians described in vv. 82–6, on the other. Drawing such a rigid boundary around the qurʾanic community would actually have conformed to well-established Jewish and Christian precedents.[65] Yet against such precedents v. 5 displays what David Freidenreich describes as an 'unparalleled permissiveness regarding food prepared by and, presumably, eaten with Jews and Christians'.[66]

The significant tensions that are discernible between v. 5, on the one hand, and v. 3 and v. 51, on the other, back the hypothesis that v. 5, like v. 4, is a later addition to the passage. It is certainly possible to pinpoint a plausible motive for inserting the verse, insofar as it pre-empts the surah's recipients from concluding that v. 51 requires them to observe scrupulous segregation from the Scripturalists. Against such a potential inference, which would by no means be unreasonable within the context of the surah as a whole, v. 5 explicitly condones 'a partially porous boundary between believers and People of the Scripture by allowing food exchange across this border'[67] and also by allowing limited intermarriage.[68] This permission of intercommunal food exchange involved partially overriding—or, to put it in traditional Islamic terms, a partial 'abrogation'—of the dietary prohibitions laid down in verse 3.

We can only guess whether v. 5 was lodged in the passage before or after the insertion of v. 4. The fact that v. 5 repeats the 'Deuteronomistic' temporal qualifier *al-yawma* occurring twice before in 5:3D could be taken to indicate that v. 5 is contemporary with the latter. Yet it can hardly be ruled out that v. 5 might postdate v. 4. In any case, whatever the relative temporal order of v. 4 and v. 5, the later of the two verses evidently echoes the earlier one, since both begin by invoking the principle that consumption of 'the good things' is permitted to the qurʾanic community[69]—verse 4 doing so in order to justify the general licitness of hunting prey, while verse 5 uses it as a springboard for

[65] On the negative attitude of Judaism and Christianity to interfaith marriages, see Yohanan Friedmann, *Tolerance and Coercion in Islam: Interfaith Relations in the Muslim Tradition* (Cambridge: Cambridge University Press, 2003), 160–1. On Christian prohibitions against commensality with Jews, see Freidenreich, *Foreigners*, 113–18.

[66] Freidenreich, *Foreigners*, 140.

[67] Freidenreich, *Foreigners*, 140 (substituting 'Scripture' for 'Book').

[68] On interfaith marriage in Islamic law generally (based upon Q 2:221, 5:5, and 60:10), see Friedmann, *Tolerance and Coercion*, 160–93, emphasizing the contrast between the general disapproval of interfaith marriages in Judaism and Christianity and its limited permissibility in Islam (male Muslims may marry female Scripturalists, but male Scripturalists may not marry female Muslims).

[69] The principle has a wider presence in the Qurʾan, as demonstrated by Q 2:172, 7:157, and 23:51. Its polemical undertone is that the qurʾanic revelations do not impose onerous and arbitrary dietary restrictions of the sort associated with Jewish law and also with pagan taboos; see Joseph E. Lowry, 'When Less is More: Law and Commandment in *Sūrat al-Anʿām*', *Journal of Qurʾanic Studies* 9 (2007): 22–42.

approving unrestricted commensality with Jews and Christians. Once more, we find an insertion taking up the diction of the literary context into which it was implanted.

THE OPENING SECTION OF SURAH 9

The second passage examined in this article consists in the opening passage of surah 9. My focus will be on vv. 1–13, an English rendering of which is once again reproduced in the Appendix (Table 2.5). The Appendix also contains an attempt to illustrate the redactional scenario for which I shall argue (Table 2.6).[70] The entire passage would doubtless merit a terminological correspondence analysis similar to Figure 2.1, but I shall dispense from undertaking this exercise here.

It may be helpful to begin with a few remarks on how the opening section fits into the surah as a whole. Surah 9, traditionally known under the names *Barāʾa* or *al-Tawba*,[71] can be subdivided into two main parts. The first, which encompasses vv. 1–37, centres on a confrontation with the 'Associators' (*al-mushrikūn*)[72] and the unbelieving Scripturalists, while the second—and far longer—part mostly polemicizes against certain members of the qurʾanic community who are reviled as 'hypocrites' (*al-munāfiqūn*) and charged, among other things, with their unwillingness to fight (cf. 9:38–57, 81–96, 119–23). Somewhat schematically, we might summarize the surah's structure by saying that the first part engages external opponents while the second one engages internal ones—the link between the two parts being that the main accusation levelled against the internal opponents is their insufficiently confrontational stance towards the external ones. Within this macrostructural context, the opening section sets the surah's general mood by decreeing a state of military confrontation with the Associators. In order to assist the reader in navigating the following analysis, here is a thematic subdivision of the surah's first twenty-odd verses:

[70] An earlier attempt to unravel the redactional history of surah 9 is Richard Bell, 'Muhammad's Pilgrimage Proclamation', *Journal of the Royal Asiatic Society of Great Britain and Ireland* 2 (1937): 233–44. As noted below, I accept Bell's hypothesis that v. 1 and v. 3 belong to different textual layers but reject other aspects of his model, especially his decision to separate v. 2 from v. 1 and to place it after the first half of v. 36, to be followed by v. 5 (Bell, 236).

[71] The first name is based on the surah's opening word, the second one presumably on its frequent occurrences of the verb *tāba*, meaning 'to repent' when said of humans and 'to relent' when said of God (see vv. 3, 5, 11, 15, 27, 74, 102, 104, 106, 112, 117, 118, and 126).

[72] I prefer the literal rendering of *mushrik* as 'associator' to 'polytheist' (thus Jones) in order to avoid prejudging the question of the *mushrikūn*'s religious belief system by a mere act of translation. See Gerald R. Hawting, *The Idea of Idolatry and the Emergence of Islam: From Polemic to History* (Cambridge: Cambridge University Press, 1999, 48–9) as well as Patricia Crone, 'The Religion of the Qurʾānic Pagans: God and the Lesser Deities', *Arabica* 57 (2010): 151–200.

1–2 Revocation of treaties with the Associators (including stipulation of grace period).

3 General dissociation from the Associators.

4 Exception: agreements with covenant-abiding Associators remain valid.

5 The 'Sword Verse': injunction to fight the Associators until conversion.

6 Individual Associators may petition for refuge without being required to convert.

7–10 Justification for abolition of treaties with Associators (including exception for covenant-abiding Associators).

11 Possibility of the Associators' conversion reaffirmed.

12–16 Associators who violate covenants are to be fought; addressees urged to fight.

17–22 Associators barred from the sanctuary; promise of eschatological reward for those who have emigrated and fought 'in the path of God'.

Before moving on to examine the passage's literary growth, we shall need to address a number of exegetical queries and highlight various features of the text whose pertinence will become clear later on. The next section therefore provides a cursory exegetical treatment of vv. 1–16.

A CURSORY COMMENTARY ON Q 9:1–16

The surah begins with what appears like a heading: 'A *barāʾa* from God and His Messenger to those Associators with whom you^{P} have made a covenant.'[73] In the present verse, the word *barāʾa* is traditionally understood in the sense of a 'proclamation of dissociation'.[74] This construal is naturally suggested by the fact that v. 3 declares God and His Messenger to be 'quit (*barīʾ*) of the

[73] As al-Ṭabarī observes, a functionally similar surah opening is encountered, for example, in Q 24:1 ('A surah that We have sent down and imposed . . . '); see al-Ṭabarī, *Tafsīr*, *ad* Q 9:1, vol. 14, 95.

[74] This reading is represented, for instance, by Ibn Kathīr's gloss of the word as equivalent in meaning to *tabarruʾ*, the *maṣdar* of the fifth-form verb *tabarraʾa*, 'to declare oneself quit of (*min*) someone', 'to dissociate oneself from someone'; see Ibn Kathīr, *Tafsīr al-Qurʾān al-ʿaẓīm*, Sāmī ibn Muḥammad al-Salāma (ed.), 2nd edn, 8 vols (Riyadh: Dār Ṭayba, 1999/AH 1420), *ad* Q 9:1, vol. 4, 102. This is also the interpretation adopted by Bell, 'Muhammad's Pilgrimage Proclamation' and Uri Rubin, '*Barāʾa*: A Study of Some Quranic Passages', *Jerusalem Studies in Arabic and Islam* 5 (1984): 13–32. As emerges from al-Ṭabarī, *Tafsīr*, *ad* Q 9:1, vol. 14, 96, the verbal construction understood to underlie the concatenation *barāʾa ilā* is *bariʾa* <subject> *ilā* <object 1> *min* <object 2>. Here, the first object is a person, while the second one, which remains implicit in the wording of Q 9:1, would be the treaties that the Prophet had concluded with some of the Associators. See al-Suyūṭī, *al-Durr al-manṯūr*, *ad* Q 9:1, vol. 7, 234, citing Ibn ʿAbbās as stating: *bariʾa ilayhim rasūlu llāhi min ʿuhūdihim* [. . .].

Associators'. However, a strong case can also be made for *barāʾa* meaning something like a 'grant of immunity', which is the meaning that the word has in Q 54:43.[75] This interpretation of the word *barāʾa* would be reinforced if v. 1 and v. 3 were not originally part of the same literary continuum, which is in fact what I shall maintain below. Understood in this second sense, v. 1 would function as a sort of superscript to v. 2, which accords the Associators a grace period of four months during which they may 'travel in the land'—presumably, without fear of molestation.

The *barāʾa* declaration in vv. 1–2 is followed by another 'proclamation' (*adhān*), said to be made 'to the people on the day of the great pilgrimage'. It is syntactically coordinated with the term *barāʾa* by means of the conjunction *wa-*: '[1]A *barāʾa* . . . [3] and an *adhān* . . .'. Note that v. 3 targets a wider circle of addressees than v. 1, namely, 'the people' at large, whereas the *barāʾa* declaration concerns only a particular subgroup of Associators, those with whom a covenant has been concluded. V. 3's reference to the 'day of the great pilgrimage' might seem to coincide with the fact that the Islamic tradition associates the surah's opening passage with the pilgrimage of 631, during which it was allegedly proclaimed by ʿAlī in lieu of Muhammad.[76] But of course such convergence could simply indicate that the extra-scriptural reports in question are in part inspired by the wording of Q 9:3 rather than being based on independent historical memory. In any case, as Bell has pointed out, Q 9:3 does imply that 'Muhammad or his representative must have been free to attend the pilgrimage, and to make an important proclamation there, that is, he must already have had command of Mecca'.[77] Whether the phrase 'the day

[75] Paret, *Kommentar*, *ad* Q 9:1. In Q 54:43, the opponents of the qurʾanic Messenger are asked whether they are able to adduce 'a grant of immunity (*barāʾa*) in the [earlier] scriptures'. The word's meaning in Q 54:43 would also make sense in Q 9:1 and furthermore yield a good fit with the immediately following v. 2, where pagan treaty partners are conceded a grace period of four months.

[76] For a convenient compilation of traditions purporting to describe the circumstances under which the opening of surah 9 was first revealed and promulgated, see al-Suyūṭī, *al-Durr al-manthūr fī l-tafsīr bi-l-maʾthūr*, ʿAbd Allāh ibn ʿAbd al-Muḥsin al-Turkī (eds), 17 vols (Cairo: Markaz li-l-buḥūth wa-l-dirāsat al-ʿarabiyya wa-l-islāmiyya, 2003), *ad* Q 9:1, vol. 7, 227–33; for a brief overview of the material see Bell, 'Muhammad's Pilgrimage Proclamation', 233–5. The traditions compiled by al-Suyūṭī exhibit significant differences: for example, in some of them, it is only ʿAlī who is instructed to promulgate the surah—or, more specifically, the first ten verses of the surah—after the Prophet had initially entrusted Abū Bakr with this task, while other reports have ʿAlī join forces with Abū Bakr or Abū Hurayra. The exact relationship between Q 9:1ff. and these extra-qur'anic reports, as well as between the different versions of the latter, would clearly require a separate study. The dating of v. 3 to 631 is rejected in Uri Rubin, 'The Great Pilgrimage of Muḥammad: Some Notes on Sūra IX', *Journal of Semitic Studies* 27 (1982): 241–60, at 256–9; instead, Rubin argues (largely on the basis of extra-qur'anic reports pertaining to the phrase *yawm al-ḥajj al-akbar*) for dating the verse's proclamation to Muhammad's Farewell Pilgrimage in 632. Later sections of the surah are linked by the Islamic tradition to the summer of 630, when Muhammad allegedly ordered preparations for a raid against Byzantine forces (see Nöldeke and Schwally, *Geschichte des Qorāns*, vol. 1, 223–4).

[77] Bell, 'Muhammad's Pilgrimage Proclamation', 235. The point is directed specifically against Grimme, who proposed dating the opening of surah 9 before the conquest of Mecca in

of the great pilgrimage' (*yawm al-ḥajj al-akbar*) is simply an expansive equivalent of the *ḥajj tout court* or denotes the pilgrimage of a particular year may be left undecided in the present context.[78]

The content of the *adhān* made 'on the day of the great pilgrimage' is that 'God and His Messenger' are 'quit (*barīʾ*) of the Associators'.[79] Clearly, if we choose to interpret the word *barāʾa* in v. 1 as meaning a 'proclamation of dissociation', there will be significant overlap between vv. 1 and 3: v. 1 would merely anticipate a particular consequence (namely, the lapse of all treaties with the Associators) following from the more general declaration of disassociation in v. 3. If, on the other hand, we construe the word *barāʾa* in v. 1 as meaning 'a proclamation of immunity', then v. 3 would go significantly beyond v. 1. In early seventh-century Arabia, to declare oneself 'quit of' some individual or collective would presumably have meant the severance of all genealogical, social, and contractual ties.[80] Interestingly, v. 114 depicts Abraham as having dissociated himself from his unbelieving father (*tabarraʾa minhu*), an act that is surely meant to function as an antetype to the surah's opening pronouncements.

Arrestingly, the *barāʾa* and the *adhān* display far-reaching structural parallelism (see Table 2.7). Both begin with a superscript or heading (v. 1 and the first half of v. 3) that is followed by a second-person plural address of the Associators (v. 2 and the second half of v. 3). In both cases, this announcement contains an exhortatory warning that the addressees 'will not frustrate God' (*annakum ghayru muʿjizī llāh*). (In v. 3 alone, this is rounded off by an

630. Bell's observation does not of course imply that the entire surah must therefore postdate the takeover of Mecca. For example, Nöldeke and Schwally place vv. 13–22 before the conquest of Mecca (Nöldeke and Schwally, *Geschichte des Qorāns*, vol. 1, 223).

78 Paret understands the 'great pilgrimage' to contrast with the *ʿumra* (Paret, *Kommentar*, *ad* Q 9:3). By contrast, Rubin argues that the 'great pilgrimage' was 'Muḥammad's last pilgrimage, which was performed in 10/631, shortly before the Prophet's death' (Rubin, 'The Great Pilgrimage of Muḥammad', 243).

79 The structure of the phrase *anna llāha barīʾun mina l-mushrikīna wa-rasūluhu* ('God is quit of the Associators, and [likewise] His Messenger'), with the second subject *rasūluhu* being delayed until the end, deserves comment. An amusing anecdote reports how a Bedouin misread the phrase as *anna llāha barīʾun mina l-mushrikīna wa-rasūl<u>ihi</u>*, yielding the shocking meaning that God is 'quit of the Associators and of His Messenger' (al-Suyūṭī, *al-Durr al-manthūr*, *ad* Q 9:3, vol. 7, 240–1). The story underlines the point that the syntactical status of *rasūluhu* is exclusively conveyed by its desinential ending; due to its position at the end of the phrase, the verse would be seriously ambiguous if read without *iʿrāb*. I share the view that qurʾanic verses for which this is the case constitute a significant difficulty for Karl Vollers' hypothesis that the Qurʾan was originally recited in uninflected Arabic (Karl Vollers, *Volkssprache und Schriftsprache im alten Arabien* [Straßburg: K. J. Trübner], 1906), but see Clive Holes, *Modern Arabic: Structures, Functions, and Varieties*, revised edn (Washington, D.C.: Georgetown University Press, 2004), 17. For a similar delay of part of the subject, albeit without any serious danger of ambiguity, see Q 2:127: *wa-idh yarfaʿu ibrāhīmu l-qawāʿida mina l-bayti wa-ismāʿīlu*.

80 Cf. vv. 23–4, where the addressees are admonished to dissolve family ties with the Associators: 'O you who believe, do not take your fathers and your brothers as friends / patrons (*awliyāʾ*) if they prefer unbelief to belief!' (v. 23).

eschatological wrap-up unit addressing the qurʾanic Messenger.) Furthermore, v. 1 and the first half of v. 3 follow virtually the same internal order, consisting of an initial characterization of the subsequent message (as a *barāʾa* or an *adhān*) followed by the message's origin ('from God and His Messenger') and its intended addressees. One is reminded of the formulaic identification of sender and recipient in Pauline letter openings. Possibly, the wording of the text here adheres to established conventions.[81] Whatever the truth of the above-mentioned reports about the passage's promulgation during the pilgrimage of 631, both vv. 1–2 and v. 3 are plausibly imagined as public pronouncements.

V. 4 is explicitly marked as an exception by the verse-initial *illā*, 'except' or 'though that is not the case with respect to': if Associators with whom a treaty has been concluded have honoured their treaty, then the latter remains valid until its original date of expiry. This exception is followed by the passage's best-known component, the so-called Sword Verse (v. 5): 'when the sacred months have elapsed' the Believers are to 'kill the Associators wherever you^{P} find them', unless the Associators 'repent and perform prayer and give alms'. Since prayer and almsgiving are elsewhere associated with belief in the Day of Judgement and the worship of the one God,[82] v. 5 would minimally appear to require the Associators to convert to a generic form of monotheism; more probably, prayer and almsgiving here function as a metonymy for full conversion to the qurʾanic community, including acknowledgement of the prophetic authority of Muhammad.

At this point, a serious interpretive difficulty arises: what is the relationship between the 'sacred months' mentioned in v. 5 and the four-month grace period declared in v. 2? The matter is further complicated by v. 36, which like v. 2 speaks of four months while also characterizing them, similarly to v. 5, as 'sacred' (pl. *ḥurum*): 'The number of the months with God is twelve, [laid down] in God's decree on the day that He created the heavens and the earth. Four of them are sacred. That is the right religion. Do not wrong yourselves in them. But fight all the Associators [in them], just as they fight all of you

[81] This possibility is further supported by a certain isomorphism with the opening of the so-called 'Constitution of Medina', a treaty allegedly concluded by Muhammad whose authenticity is accepted by most scholars. To appreciate this, note that Table 2.7 distinguishes three components in v. 1 and the first half of v. 3: (i) a qualification of the message, (ii) an identification of the sender, and (iii) and identification of the recipient. The first and second of these components also appear at the beginning of the text of the 'Constitution' as transmitted by Ibn Isḥāq: 'This is a written compact (*kitāb*) [= (i)] from Muhammad the Prophet [= (ii)] between the Believers and Submitters of Quraysh and Yathrib and those who join them as clients, attach themselves to them, and strive in war (*jāhada*) together with them [cf. (iii)].' For the text, see Michael Lecker, *The 'Constitution of Medina': Muḥammad's First Legal Document* (Princeton: Darwin Press, 2004), 32 (translation modified).

[82] See, for instance, Q 9:18: 'The only ones to administer (*yaʿmuru*) God's places of prostration are those who believe in God and the Last Day and perform prayer and give alms and fear only God.' Cf. also Q 21:73, 24:37, and 70:22–7. On the meaning of *ʿamara* see Ambros, *Concise Dictionary*, 194.

[in them]! And know that God is with those who are fearful [of Him].'[83] Now, the four sacred months mentioned in v. 36 are best taken to be the four sacred months of the ancient Arabian calendar, namely, the three consecutive months of Dhū l-Qaʿda (the 11th month of the year), Dhū l-Ḥijja (no. 12), and Muḥarram (no. 1), as well as Rajab (no. 7).[84] So should we assume that these are also the months meant in v. 2 and in v. 5?

One possible answer, found in the Islamic tradition, is to equate the 'four months' referred to in v. 2 with the 'sacred months' from v. 5 and to consider both verses to refer to a one-off grace period of four consecutive months.[85] This requires the four months referred to in vv. 2 and 5 to be distinct from the four Arabian sacred months mentioned in v. 36, which are cyclically recurrent and not consecutive. We might summarize this view as follows:

'four months' (v. 2) = 'the sacred months' (v. 5) ≠ 'four of them are sacred' (v. 36)

The plausibility of this view rests primarily on the proximity of v. 2 and v. 5, which invites the assumption that both refer to the same time period. It does have a manifest weakness, though, which is the fact that both v. 5 and v. 36 employ the same adjective 'sacred'. It seems improbable that one and the same word would carry two different meanings in what are obviously very similar contexts,[86] making it preferable to equate the sacred months mentioned in v. 5

[83] Jones understands the accusative *kāffatan* (literally, 'entirely', 'altogether') in *wa-qātilū l-mushrikīna kāffatan ka-mā yuqātilūnakum kāffatan* to refer to all of *the sacred months*. This would appear to be inspired by Bell's translation of the expression as 'continuously'; see Paret, *Kommentar*, *ad* Q 9:36 (where this construal is questioned) as well as Reuven Firestone, *Jihād: The Origin of Holy War in Islam* (New York: Oxford University Press, 1999), 75. I accept the view that Q 9:36 mandates warfare against the Associators during the four sacred months just listed, a point that would appear to be made more explicitly in Q 2:194 and 2:217 (on which see Firestone, *Jihād*, 74–5 and 86–8). *Pace* Jones, however, I am not convinced that this aspect is expressed by *kāffatan*; more likely, the prepositional phrase *fīhinna* in *fa-lā taẓlimū fīhinna anfusakum* simply carries over into the following segment. However, it is not impossible to interpret Q 9:36 as making the opposite point, namely, that the Associators must *not* be fought during the sacred months, although during other periods of the year they are to be fought in their entirety. This would make Q 9:36 reiterate the command given in Q 9:5.

[84] On the ancient Arabian calendar and sacred months see Julius Wellhausen, *Reste arabischen Heidentums*, 2nd edn (Berlin: G. Reimer, 1897), 94–101, and Firestone, *Jihād*, 38–9.

[85] See, for instance, al-Suyūṭī, *ad-Durr al-manthūr*, *ad* Q 9:5, vol. 7, 244, according to which Mujāhid maintained with regard to 'And when the sacred months have elapsed' that these are 'the four [with regard to] which He [God] said 'Travel in the land for four months.' That the four months in question are considered to be consecutive emerges, inter alia, from the tradition about the proclamation of surah 9's opening section that is cited in al-Suyūṭī, *ad-Durr al-manthūr*, *ad* Q 9:1, vol. 7, 227–8, and according to which ʿAlī and Abū Bakr told pagans with whom Muhammad had previously concluded a treaty 'that they are safe for four months, and these are the consecutive sacred months that have elapsed (*wa-hiya l-ashhuru l-ḥurumu l-munsalikh-ātu l-mutawāliyāt*)', partially quoting Q 9:5.

[86] Proponents of the foregoing view—namely, that v. 2's 'four months' = v. 5's 'sacred months' ≠ the four sacred months of v. 36—must understand the attribute 'sacred' in v. 5 differently from v. 36 in order to resist identification of the time periods that feature in both

with those mentioned in v. 36. Assuming that v. 5, like v. 3, is meant to have been promulgated on the 'day of the great pilgrimage', v. 5 therefore instructs the audience that the Associators are to be killed when the present holy season has ended, that is, at the end of Muḥarram.[87] At the same time, this equation of the time periods referred to in v. 5 and v. 36 must not be allowed to carry over to v. 2, at least not if we retain the reasonable premise that v. 2 imposes a one-off grace period of four consecutive months.[88] This yields the following construal:

'four months' (v. 2) ≠ 'the sacred months' (v. 5) = 'four of them are sacred' (v. 36)

After this somewhat tortuous discussion, the remainder of the passage can be scanned in a much more perfunctory fashion. V. 6 demands that an individual Associator demanding refuge be protected 'until he can hear the words (*kalām*) of God' and then be conducted to a place of safety. This is followed by a cluster of verses justifying the preceding abolition of covenants with the Associators (vv. 7–10). What is noteworthy here is that the second part of v. 7 closely parallels v. 4: both constitute exceptive clauses introduced by *illā*, and both stipulate, albeit in different words, that treaties with Associators who have honoured their agreements with the qurʾanic community remain valid (see Table 2.8). V. 11 reiterates, in line with the second part of v. 5, that Associators have the option of becoming fully fledged members of the qurʾanic community through conversion. Finally, vv. 12–16 return to the possibility,

verses. For example, the four consecutive months that are referred to in v. 5 might be held to be 'sacred' in the sense that they must not be violated by fighting. See Ibn Kathīr, *Tafsīr*, *ad* Q 9:5, vol. 4, 111, paraphrasing 'the four sacred (*ḥurum*) months' as 'the four months in which We [= God] have prohibited you from fighting them [= the pagans] (*ḥarramnā ʿalaykum fīhā qitālahum*)'.

87 See, for instance, al-Ṭabarī, *Tafsīr*, *ad* Q 9:5, vol. 14, 134, stating that the expression the 'sacred months' denotes the months Dhū l-Qaʿda, Dhū l-Ḥijja, and Muḥarram. Cf. also Ibn Kathīr, *Tafsīr*, *ad* Q 9:1–2, vol. 4, citing Ibn ʿAbbās with the view that v. 5 refers to a time period of fifty nights, lasting from the 10th of Dhū l-Ḥijja (when the surah's opening section was purportedly first proclaimed) to the end of Muḥarram.

88 Why could the 'four months' mentioned in v. 2 not be the ancient Arabian sacred months Dhū l-Qaʿda, Dhū l-Ḥijja, Muḥarram, and Rajab—that is, why could v. 2 not refer to the same non-consecutive months as v. 5? According to such a non-consecutive understanding of v. 2, Associators with whom the qurʾanic community has concluded treaties would need to be spared in Dhū l-Qaʿda, Dhū l-Ḥijja, Muḥarram, and Rajab but would be legitimate targets of aggression during all other months (whether only in the present year or also in future years); by contrast, all other Associators could presumably be fought even during the four months in question. Thus construed, v. 2 would amount to an exceedingly odd half-way house that neither fully endorses the sacrality of the ancient Arabian sacred months (for in this case it ought to be prohibited to fight *any* of the Associators) nor fully abolishes it (for in this case it ought to be permissible to fight *all* Associators during any month). For an understanding of v. 2 as referring to the four Arabian sacred months (and as identical with both the 'sacred months' of v. 5 and the four sacred months of v. 36), see Rubin, '*Barāʾa*', 17. Rubin's position can be symbolically expressed as follows: 'four months' (v. 2) = 'the sacred months' (v. 5) = 'four of them are sacred' (v. 36).

envisaged in v. 4 and also in v. 7, that treaties with Associators might continue to be valid even after their general revocation in v. 1. Against this background, vv. 12ff. insist that if the pre-condition of such continuing validity lapses because the Associators 'break their oaths after having entered into a covenant and revile your religion', then they must be fought after all (v. 12).

THE LITERARY GROWTH OF SURAH 9'S OPENING SECTION

After this preparatory commentary, we are in a position to consider whether surah 9's opening passage exhibits any signs of literary growth over time. As with Q 5:1–11, there are no Class 1 arguments supporting a redactional analysis: stylistically and terminologically, the text does not appear to be any less homogenous than other Medinan surahs. Any evidence that the beginning of surah 9 has been secondarily expanded falls squarely into Class 2 territory. Most importantly, the passage displays significant internal tensions.

At the centre of these tensions stands the Sword Verse, v. 5, which demands that at the end of the current season of sacred months (presumably, at the end of Muḥarram) the Associators are to be fought unless they convert. This conflicts with vv. 1–2, which accord a grace period of four months to Associators with whom a treaty has been concluded. If we assume that the implied time of proclamation for vv. 1–2 is 'the day of the great pilgrimage' from v. 3, that is, the 10th of Dhū l-Ḥijja, then Associators with a treaty would be protected well into Rabīʿ al-Ākhir rather than, as per v. 5, until the end of Muḥarram.[89] Moreover, the Sword Verse clashes with v. 4, according to which the qurʾanic community remains bound by agreements with treaty-abiding Associators until their stipulated expiry date. V. 4 essentially recognizes the legal *status quo*—in contrast to v. 3's categorical dissociation from the Associators and in contrast to the Sword Verse's injunction to fight the Associators until conversion. In addition to being at variance with the Sword Verse, vv. 1–2 and v. 4 are also difficult to reconcile with each other, given that they

[89] For this calculation see, for instance, al-Ṭabarī, *Tafsīr*, *ad* Q 9:2, vol. 14, 100 (no. 16,363), where Qatāda explains the 'four months' from v. 2 as consisting of 'twenty [days] of Dhū l-Ḥijja, [the full month of] Muḥarram, [the full month of] Ṣafar, [the full month of] Rabīʿ al-Awwal, and ten [days] of Rabīʿ al-Ākhir'. The only way to eliminate this tension between vv. 1–2 and v. 5 would be to assume that vv. 1–2 were promulgated at an earlier point than v. 3, perhaps at the beginning of Shawwāl. The four-month grace period referred to in v. 2 would then consist of Shawwāl, Dhū l-Qaʿda, Dhū l-Ḥijja, and Muḥarram, and it would end at exactly the same time at which 'the sacred months have elapsed' (v. 5). However, we would then have removed the tension between vv. 1–2 and v. 5 precisely by assuming what I am ultimately aiming to demonstrate, namely, that the passage at hand is not genetically unitary.

would appear to formulate fundamentally different ways of dealing with Associators with whom the qurʾanic community has concluded treaties: vv. 1–2 merely delay the lapse of these treaties by a limited grace period, whereas v. 4 recognizes their continuing validity if they are not breached by the Associators themselves.[90] The Sword Verse furthermore conflicts with v. 6, which requires that individual Associators who petition the Prophet for asylum be granted safe conduct; although they should be given the opportunity to 'hear the words of God', their safety is not made conditional on conversion—in contrast to v. 5, according to which hostilities may only cease if the Associators 'repent and perform prayer and give alms'. Finally, vv. 8–10 categorically predict that the Associators will not respect any treaties with the Believers, yet vv. 4 and 7B presuppose that this is a credible eventuality for which guidance must be provided; and even v. 12 only countenances the *possibility* that the Associators might break their oaths, without presenting this as inevitable, as do vv. 8–10. In sum, the passage, if read literally, is riddled with inconsistencies.

Naturally, these difficulties have not escaped the attention of pre-modern Islamic exegetes. Some of them attempt to overcome them by implicit harmonization. For instance, the tension between vv. 1–2 and v. 4 could be eliminated by taking the former to apply to Associators with whom covenants stipulating no expiry date have been concluded (*dhawū l-ʿuhūdi l-muṭlaqati ghayri l-muʾaqqattah*) and considering the latter to refer to Associators with covenants that do stipulate an expiry date (*man kāna lahu ʿahdun muʾaqqat*). Similarly, v. 5 could be reconciled with the rest of the passage by taking it to apply only to Associators with whom no treaty has been concluded (*man laysa lahu ʿahdun*).[91] By imposing such distinctions on the text, the first five verses of the surah would come to express a consistent system of rules for dealing with different classes of Associators, a system that lends itself to being represented by a flow chart (see Figure 2.2). The approach does have its price, though: it is predicated on reading into the qurʾanic text a system of subtle distinctions that are nowhere explicitly intimated.[92] Quite simply, I find this price too high.

The second response adopted by pre-modern Islamic readers is to deploy the category of abrogation (*naskh*). For instance, according to one scholar the Sword Verse abrogated 124 other qurʾanic verses, including v. 7 of the same

[90] I take it that vv. 1–2 do *not* mean to say that Associators *who break their treaties* have the right to travel freely for four months.

[91] See Ibn Kathīr, *Tafsīr*, *ad* Q 9:1–2, vol. 4, 102. Alternatively, vv. 1–2 are held to apply to Associators who possess covenants whose period of validity is less than four months (*man lahu ʿahdun dūna arbaʿati ashhur*).

[92] V. 4 does speak of the 'term' (*mudda*) of treaties concluded with the Associators, but read literally the text would appear to assume that any treaty will have such a term; at least there is no explicit reference to treaties without an expiry date.

surah.[93] To adopt the *naskh* approach is to acknowledge, quite reasonably in my view, that the text as it stands contains irreconcilable contradictions and to explain these as a result of textual growth: different statements in the passage were promulgated at different historical moments and may therefore override and repeal one another rather than necessarily yielding an internally consistent system of rules. At least in principle, this second approach has palpable affinity with the present article's interest in processes of gradual textual growth. Hence, while I would concede that a redactional analysis of Q 9:1ff. rests first and foremost on Class 2 arguments from propositional incompatibility, which is a less secure foundation than one would like, the worry that the relevant observations are mere products of Orientalist fault-finding is misplaced.

So what might a plausible redactional scenario for the surah's opening section look like? A compelling point of departure is provided by the observation, made in the foregoing section, that vv. 1–2 (the *barāʾa*) and v. 3 (the *adhān*) constitute two parallel proclamations. As a matter of fact, the order of exposition in vv. 1–3 is puzzling: if they were genetically of a piece, one might have expected the general statement of dissociation from the Associators (v. 3) to have preceded discussion of the more specific case of Associators with whom treaties have been concluded; and one might have expected the information that vv. 1–3 were (or are to be) pronounced 'on the day of the great pilgrimage' to have been front-loaded. Of course, such bewilderment is merely another Class 2 argument, namely, one from perceived structural awkwardness; yet while it would hardly inspire much trust by itself, it is significantly strengthened by the tensions pointed out above. A promising key to unlocking the passage's literary growth is therefore to posit that the present link between the *barāʾa* and the *adhān*, created by the placement of the conjunction *wa*- at the beginning of v. 3, is secondary. The assumption that the passage conflates two different proclamations, whose beginnings are found in v. 1 and v. 3, is also crucial to the redactional model developed by Bell: 'There are, therefore, two things to be sought in what follows, first a *barāʾa*, and second an adhān, intended to be delivered to the people at some pilgrimage.'[94] For the moment, the question which one of the two proclamations is the earlier one may be conveniently postponed, although we should note that whichever one came later would appear to have been structurally patterned on the other and to deliberately pick up its warning that the addressees 'will not frustrate God', which occurs both in v. 2 and in v. 3 (see Table 2.7).

[93] Hibat Allāh b. Salāma, *al-Nāsikh wa-l-mansūkh*, Muḥammad Zuhayr al-Shāwīsh and Muḥammad Kanʿān, eds, (Beirut: al-Maktab al-Islāmī, 1986), 98–9.

[94] Bell, 'Muhammad's Pilgrimage Proclamation', 237. Bell's statement correctly underscores that this detachment of the *barāʾa* from the *adhān* means that we cannot presume the former to have been delivered in the context of the pilgrimage, as evoked in v. 3.

Proceeding from the two starting points supplied by v. 1 and v. 3, we can now gradually feel our way into the text and examine whether subsequent verses are plausibly linked with either the *barāʾa* or the *adhān*. Bell immediately wields the knife and considers v. 2 to be 'out of place' due to the 'abrupt change of address' between the first verse, which addresses the qurʾanic community, and the second one, which ostensibly addresses the Associators. Bell therefore surmises that v. 2 originally followed v. 36, and was itself followed by v. 5.[95] He similarly dismantles v. 3 into two originally unconnected parts, the latter beginning with 'If you^{p} turn in repentance' and said to have been 'written on the back' of the second one. This, too, is justified in terms of a change of addressees: '"The people" for whom the proclamation [in the first part of v. 3] was intended must have been, to some considerable extent at least, Muhammad's own followers, while those addressed in the second half of the verse are evidently unbelievers.'[96] Yet this dissection of vv. 1–2 and v. 3 is questionable. Sudden shifts of grammatical person are far too pervasive in the Qurʾan and occur with too high a frequency to be used as a sound basis for redactional reconstructions.[97] In the present case, neither the shift in addressee from Muhammad's followers in v. 1 to the Associators in v. 2 nor that from 'the people' at large to the Associators in v. 3 is sufficiently jarring to require v. 2 to be severed from the *barāʾa* and the second part of v. 3 to be extricated from the *adhān*. Furthermore, if v. 1 does indeed function as a superscript to v. 2, the two verses' difference in addressee would be entirely intelligible.

Moving on to v. 4, we find that Bell allocates it to the *barāʾa* layer.[98] This, too, must be rejected in view of the incompatibility of vv. 1–2, on the one hand, and vv. 4 and 7, on the other, pointed out above. Instead, v. 4 and also v. 7 are best viewed as later additions to the *barāʾa* layer that partially reverse the latter's revocation of treaties with Associators: as long as Associators keep their treaties, these remain valid.[99] Apart from the *barāʾa* layer and the *adhān*

[95] Bell, 235–6. [96] Bell, 236.

[97] This is well illustrated by the second half of v. 3 itself, which shifts from a second-person plural address of the Associators to a second-person singular address of the qurʾanic Messenger: 'If you^{p} turn in repentance, it will be better for you; but if you turn your backs, know that you will not frustrate God.—Give^{s} to those who do not believe the tidings of a painful punishment!' Tellingly, Bell does not take this shift in addressee to warrant a further redactional cut (Bell, *The Qurʾān*, vol. 1, 173), probably because the degree to which this would atomize the text is patently absurd. On the general phenomenon of sudden shifts in grammatical person in the Qurʾan see Hans Zirker, *Der Koran: Zugänge und Lesarten*, 2nd edn (Darmstadt: Wissenschaftliche Buchgesellschaft, 2012), 75–9. For a diametrically opposed view see Pohlmann, *Die Entstehung des Korans*, 78, contending that abrupt shifts from third-person statements about God to first-person divine speech betray editorial intervention.

[98] Bell, 'Muhammad's Pilgrimage Proclamation', 237.

[99] Note that already the early Meccan surahs contain cases where *illā* clauses would appear to have been secondarily inserted (e.g., Q 84:25, discussed in Sinai, 'Two Types of Inner-Qurʾanic Interpretation').

layer, the text thus turns out to contain a third stratum that is supplementary to the *barāʾa* layer. I shall designate it as the 'mitigating layer' (see Table 2.6).

Pace Bell, who regards v. 5 as originally belonging neither to the *barāʾa* nor to the *adhān*,[100] it is actually highly plausible to allocate the verse to the latter stratum and thus to link it up with v. 3. Both verses situate themselves in the context of the pilgrimage: v. 3 presents itself as having been (or meant to be) delivered 'on the day of the great pilgrimage', while v. 5 calls for warfare against the Associators 'when the sacred months have elapsed'. Both verses are furthermore united by the theme of calling for or envisaging the Associators' repentance. As a matter of fact, the two verses are neatly complementary: v. 3 proclaims a general dissociation from the Associators and enjoins the latter to 'repent', while v. 5 spells out the practical consequences of this dissociation (namely, the commencement of offensive warfare against the Associators at the end of the pilgrimage season) as well as the nature of the repentance demanded (namely, conversion to the qurʾanic religion). A final feature shared by v. 3 and v. 5 is their lack of any references to the question, so prominent in vv. 1–2 and v. 4, of how the qurʾanic community is to behave towards Associators with whom they have previously concluded covenants. Note, however, that to ascribe v. 3 and v. 5 to the same textual layer is not necessarily to posit that they ever formed a contiguous sequence; if the *adhān* layer is considered to be temporally posterior to the *barāʾa* one (a matter taken up below), then the two verses in question may never have existed separately from vv. 1–2 and v. 4.

Although v. 6 could perhaps be viewed as part of the mitigating layer added to the *barāʾa*, it is equally conceivable that it qualifies the Sword Verse, which would make it a secondary addition to the *adhān* layer: while the Sword Verse proclaims a general state of offensive warfare against the Associators with the ultimate aim of forced conversion, v. 6 ensures that individual Associators who petition for refuge are not after all compelled to convert in return for being granted protection. V. 6 thus approaches the objective of conversion as an act of individual conscience that should ideally take place without any coercion.

Vv. 7–10 are concerned to justify the abolition of covenants with Associators in terms of the latter's inherent unreliability. The verse cluster thus provides a vindication of the *barāʾa*, suggesting that vv. 7–10 should be joined up with vv. 1–2.[101] However, as remarked above and illustrated by Table 2.8, the second part of v. 7B displays significant overlap with v. 4. Thus, v. 7B is best extricated from the overarching cluster vv. 7–10 and allocated to the same mitigating layer as v. 4. This entails that v. 7A and v. 8 would originally have

[100] Bell, 'Muhammad's Pilgrimage Proclamation', 236.

[101] Bell likewise allocates v. 7A and v. 8 to the *barāʾa*, although he would exclude vv. 9–10, for reasons I do not find compelling. See Bell, 'Muhammad's Pilgrimage Proclamation', 237.

formed one overarching verse, since v. 7A's lack of an appropriate rhyme precludes it from functioning as an independent verse.

Interestingly, if we compare v. 7B to v. 4, the latter emerges as considerably more specific (see Table 2.8): whereas v. 7B merely issues a vague call to 'act straight' with Associators who 'act straight' with the addressees, v. 4 stipulates the required behaviour in much more concrete terms ('who have then not failed you in anything and have not supported anyone against you'). V. 4 is also more specific about the consequences of such conduct, namely, as entitling the Associators to fulfilment of their covenant 'until the end of their term'. Such a noticeable difference in specificity might be taken as grounds for considering v. 4 to be a posterior clarification of v. 7B. Nevertheless, it makes rhetorical sense to assign both v. 4 and v. 7B to the same redactional layer: v. 7B is satisfactorily accounted for as a summary recapitulation of v. 4, encapsulating the latter's precise stipulations in the catchy motto *fa-mā staqāmū lakum fa-staqīmū lahum*, the double occurrence of the verb *istaqāma* serving to underline the reciprocity of the two communities' interaction.

V. 11 once more takes up the theme of the Associators' repentance and their conversion to the qurʾanic religion that characterizes the *adhān* layer (i.e. vv. 3 and 5). Going further than v. 5, it does not just instruct the audience to cease hostilities against converted Associators but to accept them as 'your brothers in religion'. In the canonical shape of the text, v. 11 serves to counterbalance the preceding verses' emphasis on the duplicity and dishonesty of the Associators by affirming that they may nevertheless become full members of the qurʾanic community. This observation suggests that the *adhān* layer is temporally posterior to the *barāʾa*, a point to which we shall return in a moment. The following verse cluster, vv. 12–16, complements the provisions made in vv. 4 and 7B to the effect that any agreement with treaty-abiding Associators must be honoured 'until the end of their term' (v. 4). As v. 12 explains, any violation of such agreements on the part of the Associators will immediately result in punitive warfare against them. Hence, the entire cluster vv. 12–16 ought to be allocated to the mitigating layer.[102]

It is beyond the scope of this chapter to examine how and whether the foregoing analysis can be extended to later sections of the surah. Suffice it to say that *prima facie*, the ban on the Associators' maintenance of and presence at the sanctuary that is contained in vv. 17–22 and v. 28 may be well envisaged as forming part of the *adhān* stratum, given the references to the pilgrimage and the pilgrimage season in vv. 3 and 5. The concern to reserve the 'sacred place of prostration' (*al-masjid al-ḥarām*, v. 19 and v. 28) exclusively to the

[102] Note that Bell, too, views v. 12 as the 'continuation of *7b*', although he assigns both to the *adhān* (Bell, 'Muhammad's Pilgrimage Proclamation', 238).

qur'anic community certainly fits with the *adhān*'s emphasis that Associators must be fought until conversion.[103]

Rather than probing further into later sections of the text, let us conclude our discussion by examining the temporal sequence of the three textual strata for which I have argued. That the mitigating layer complements the *barā'a* and is therefore posterior to it may be taken for granted, but what about the chronological order of the *barā'a* and the *adhān*? It is not immediately obvious that we must follow Bell in viewing the *barā'a* as chronologically anterior to the *adhān*.[104] Thus, it is at least conceivable that the passage's nucleus consists in the categorical dissociation from all Associators in vv. 3 and 5. This may subsequently have given rise to the question of how one was to deal with Associators who were in possession of treaties with the qur'anic community. Should they simply be fought as soon as the pilgrimage season was over, as v. 5 would imply? Vv. 1–2 would have responded by according the particular subgroup of Associators in question a longer grace period than that laid down in v. 5. At yet a later stage, this initial restriction of the *adhān* in vv. 1–2 would itself have become the object of further restriction through the insertion of vv. 4 and 7B (together with vv. 12ff.).[105] The scenario just sketched would envisage the passage as documenting a linear process of increasing mitigation, a process plausibly considered to have culminated in v. 6. The fact that this scenario would require the *barā'a* to have been positioned *before* rather than *after* the *adhān*, despite forming a later qualification of it, should not raise eyebrows.

Yet despite the foregoing remarks I would tentatively side with Bell's view that the *barā'a* is anterior, rather than posterior, to the *adhān*. Firstly, such a sequence agrees better with what appears to have been the general direction of early Islamic history, namely, the fact that by the time the Arab conquests erupted into the Fertile Crescent and Islam entered the wider Middle Eastern stage, the Associators seem to have been decisively marginalized, and the Meccan sanctuary to have become exclusively Islamic. This early post-qur'anic situation agrees better with a trajectory leading from the *barā'a* layer to the much harsher *adhān* layer rather than vice versa. Secondly, as observed above, v. 11, which is best assigned to the *adhān* stratum, can reasonably be taken as counterbalancing, and thus presupposing, vv. 7A and 8–10, which

[103] Also, note that v. 18 echoes the references to the performance of prayer and almsgiving in vv. 5 and 11.

[104] See Bell, 'Muhammad's Pilgrimage Proclamation', 242–4.

[105] This model would entail that vv. 3 and 5 were originally contiguous, but this is not impossible. True, it would give us two sudden changes of addressee in a row: after the abrupt address of the Associators in the second part of v. 3, v. 5 would shift to a second-person address of the qur'anic community. However, this is precisely what happens in the canonical version of the text (v. 4 also addresses the qur'anic community). Furthermore, such shifts are extremely frequent in the Qur'an (see n. 97). Thus, the change of addressee between v. 3 and v. 5 could hardly be adduced as conclusive evidence against the scenario just outlined.

belong to the *barāʾa* layer. There is thus circumstantial, although perhaps not conclusive, evidence supporting Bell's relative dating of the passage's two main strata. It is not impossible that the core of the *adhān* layer, vv. 3 and 5, might originally have formed a self-standing proclamation, although I am rather more attracted to the view that the entire *adhān* stratum only ever existed as a complement to the *barāʾa* layer and its subsequent mitigation in vv. 4 and 7B.

The view that the *adhān* is posterior to the *barāʾa* is somewhat reminiscent of the traditional Islamic belief that the Sword Verse is the Qurʾan's ultimate statement on relations with the Associators. However, as observed above, v. 6 might be yet later than v. 5 and constitute a partial modification of it. In any case, it is potentially significant that the much less militant statements of the mitigating layer were retained as part of the text even when the *adhān* layer was woven into it. Either the passage's redactor or redactors were unable to drop existing parts of the text,[106] or they deliberately aimed at creating a text in which the unequivocal militancy of the Sword Verse was counterbalanced by other material. In other words, the fact that the canonical version of the surah retains verses such as v. 4 and v. 7B, which recognize that there could in principle be valid treaties even with Associators, may carry meaning even if this position was later superseded by the Sword Verse.

CONCLUSION

The preceding analysis of the opening sequences of surahs 5 and 9 has found the canonical version of both passages to have emerged from multiple-stage processes of literary growth. This does not of course entail that the same sort of analysis can necessarily be extended to the remainder of both surahs, or to other Medinan surahs. Such a generalization would require a similarly detailed examination of a significant amount of further material. Still, I would contend that the present study has established that a redactional approach to the Medinan Qurʾan is both promising and feasible. This chapter's results also provide preliminary clues regarding the driving forces behind the literary growth of qurʾanic passages. In many instances, the primary impetus may be characterized as a broadly interpretive engagement with existing portions of

[106] Q 2:106 and 16:101 imply that some qurʾanic passages were suppressed and replaced, rather than added to. However, at least if we assume that the qurʾanic proclamations were viewed as revelatory utterances from the moment of their first public recitation, it is not likely that such suppression and substitution could have been widespread.

text, which are, for instance, clarified (as in Q 5:3B–D and Q 5:4) or mitigated (as in Q 9:4, 7). In other cases, the insertion of later segments appears to have been due to obvious thematic or terminological affinity, which accounts for the general interweaving of the *adhān* with the *barāʾa* in surah 9.

A corollary of this study that deserves to be highlighted once more is that there is nothing to preclude the possibility that networks of terminological correspondences of the sort exemplified by Figure 2.1 may at least in part be an outcome of incremental literary growth, with secondary additions tending to pick up some of the terminology characterizing the literary environment into which they were integrated. This was found to be the case in Q 5:3D as well as in Q 5:4–5 and also in Q 9:3 (with respect to 9:1–2). It would therefore be fallacious to consider terminological coherence of the kind mapped out by Figure 2.1 to entail genetic unity, or composition 'in one go'. It deserves to be noted that this is also cursorily pointed out by Raymond Farrin, one of the chief proponents of a ring-compositional approach to the Qurʾan.[107]

A final remark concerns the fairly ample use that the present chapter has made of pre-modern Islamic commentaries. While this would have been standard procedure for Western scholars until at least the late 1970s, contemporary students of the Qurʾan have become notably more averse to substantial, or indeed any, recourse to the Islamic exegetical tradition in working out what specific qurʾanic passages may have signified to their first addressees. There are certainly valid reasons for such caution, implied by the much more sophisticated grasp of the nature of the *tafsīr* tradition that scholars like Norman Calder, Andrew Rippin, Walid Saleh, Bruce Fudge, and others have achieved during the past three decades. Exegetical statements by Muslim scholars must often be read in the light of later theological developments rather than as a mere reflection of the qurʾan's initial thrust or purpose, and many Islamic reports about the historical circumstances under which certain qurʾanic verses were allegedly first revealed are transparently not authentic glimpses of real events but (often ingenious) attempts at creating plausible narrative frames for scriptural passages.[108] It is appropriate to be highly sceptical about the claim that early Islamic exegesis preserves and transmits the ways in which the Qurʾan was understood by the original community of Muhammad's followers, for it appears that already the earliest layer of Islamic scriptural interpretation is separated from the Qurʾanic milieu by a significant cultural gap and engages in a considerable deal of exegetical guesswork (whose results, it must be said, are not therefore necessarily incorrect).[109] Some

[107] Farrin, *Structure and Qurʾanic Interpretation*, xv.

[108] Rippin, 'Function'.

[109] Patricia Crone, 'Two Legal Problems Bearing on the Early History of the Qurʾān', *Jerusalem Studies in Arabic and Islam* 18 (1994): 1–37. For a comprehensive case study examining how early Muslim scholars grappled with one particularly enigmatic term, see Pavel Pavlovitch, *The*

contemporary scholars have accordingly stressed that medieval Islamic exegesis is more likely to obscure rather than to illuminate what the qurʾanic proclamations meant to their original audience,[110] suggesting that it would be an important advance for historically minded readers of the Qurʾan if they resolutely emancipated their interpretive endeavours from the Islamic exegetical literature.

Nonetheless, many medieval Muslim scholars were expert readers of their scripture who possessed abundant philological acumen, interpretive creativity, literary sensitivity, and an intimate familiarity with the Qurʾanic corpus as a whole. It is true that these virtues were frequently exercised with the aim of harmonising the Qurʾan with later theological or legal developments in order to safeguard the text's ability to function as a scriptural canon. It is also undeniable that the medieval exegetical tradition has doctrinally motivated blind spots.[111] Yet even where interpretations proposed in Islamic sources prove to be unpersuasive from a historical-critical perspective, an understanding of the exegetical problems that sophisticated Muslim interpreters sought to resolve can help locate significant textual ambiguities or difficulties that also require addressing by historical-critical research. Whether implicitly or explicitly, the views of Muslim exegetes are frequently informed by textual observations and inferences that remain pertinent quite irrespective of the historical and doctrinal premises they might have brought to bear on the Qurʾan. For instance, the attempt to detect redactional seams in the Qurʾan via an identification of significant internal tensions and contradictions can undoubtedly benefit from an awareness of post-qurʾanic reports about the 'abrogation' (*naskh*) of certain scriptural verses by others: even if one were to adopt, as I would, a default view of all such reports as secondary interpretive constructs rather than as preserving authentic historical memory, they are often anchored in acts of close scriptural reading of which historical scholars are well advised to take note.

Formation of the Islamic Understanding of Kalālah *in the Second Century AH (718–816 CE): Between Scripture and Canon*, Leiden: Brill, 2016. For a hypothetical reconstruction of the development of early Muslim scriptural exegesis see Nicolai Sinai, 'The Qurʾanic Commentary of Muqātil b. Sulaymān and the Evolution of Early *Tafsīr* Literature', in Andreas Görke and Johanna Pink, eds Tafsīr *and Islamic Intellectual History: Exploring the Boundaries of a Genre* (Oxford: Oxford University Press), 2014, 113–43.

[110] For example, Gabriel S. Reynolds, *The Qurʾān and its Biblical Subtext* (Abingdon: Routledge, 2010), 200.

[111] An example is the Islamic tradition's tendency to overlook the importance of rhyme to the Qurʾan's literary fabric; see Devin Stewart, 'Poetic License in the Qurʾan: Ibn al-Ṣāʾigh al-Ḥanafī's *Iḥkām al-rāy fī aḥkām al-āy*', *Journal of Qurʾanic Studies* 11 (2009): 1–56.

APPENDIX: TABLES AND FIGURES

Table 2.1 An English translation of Q 5:1–11

Prohibition of consuming hunting prey during the pilgrimage
1 O you who believe,
fulfil the obligations!
Permitted to you^{P} is the beast of the herds,
except what is recited to you,
as long as you do not deem permissible [literally, 'not deeming permissible'] hunting prey
while you are in the pilgrim state.
God adjudicates as He wills.

2 O you who believe,
do not profane [literally, 'deem permissible'] God's rites
nor the sacred month nor the offerings nor the garlands
nor those repairing to the Sacred House,
seeking bounty and approval from their Lord.
When you leave the pilgrim state, you may hunt.
And let not hatred for a people
[that has arisen] because they barred you from the Sacred Mosque
incite you to commit a transgression.
Help one another to righteousness and fear of God;
but do not help one another to sin and transgression.
And fear God!
God is severe in punishment.

General dietary regulations, commensality and intermarriage with the People of the Scripture
3 Forbidden to you^{P} are carrion, blood, pork,
and that on which any other than God has been invoked.
And [forbidden are] the strangled, the beaten, the fallen, the gored,
and what has been devoured by beasts of prey –
except that which you purify.
And [also forbidden is] what has been slaughtered on sacrificial stones,
and to practise divination by means of arrows.
That is an abomination for you.
Today those who are Unbelievers have despaired of your religion.
So do not be afraid of them, be afraid of Me!
Today I have perfected your religion for you,
completed My grace upon you,
and approved submission [to God] (*al-islām*) as a religion for you.
As for those who are compelled by hunger, not deviating sinfully –
God is forgiving and merciful.

4 They ask you^{s} what is permitted to them.
Say: Permitted to you^{P} are the good things;
and [as regards] those hunting beasts that you teach,
training them, teaching them what God has taught you:
eat what they catch for you,
and mention God's name over it!
And fear God!
God is swift to reckon.

5 Today the good things have been permitted to you,
and the food of those who have been given the Scripture is permitted to you,

and your food is permitted to them.
And [permitted to you] are the chaste women of the Believers,
and the chaste women of those who have been given the Scripture before you,
if you give them their dowries [literally, 'wages'],
acting honourably, not committing fornication,
and not taking lovers.
If somebody denies the faith, his work is in vain,
and he will be among the losers in the next world.

Ablution before prayer, exhortation about covenant
[6] O you who believe,
when you rise to pray
wash your faces and your hands up to the elbows,
and wipe your heads, and [wash? wipe?] your feet up to the ankles.
If you are polluted, purify yourselves.
And if you are sick or on a journey
or one of you comes from the closet,
or if you have had contact with women
and you do not find water,
have recourse to clean soil
and wipe your faces and your hands with it.
God does not wish to place any difficulty on you,
but He wishes to purify you
and to complete His grace upon you,
so that you may be grateful.

[7] And remember[P] God's grace upon you
and the convenant that He took from you
when you said: we hear and obey!
And fear God!
God knows what is contained in men's breasts.

General paraenesis
[8] O you who believe,
be steadfast to God,
bearing witness to justice!
Let not hatred for a people incite you
to act unjustly.
Act justly!
This is closer to fear of God.
And fear God!
God is informed of what you do.

[9] God has made a promise to those who believe and do righteous deeds:
they will have forgiveness and a great reward;

[10] as for those who deny and deem our signs lies,
those are the companions of hell.

Conclusion
[11] O you who believe,
remember God's grace upon you
when a people tried to stretch out their hands towards you,
whereupon He restrained their hands from you!
And fear God!
It is in God that the Believers ought to put their trust.

Table 2.2 A redactional model for Q 5:1–11

Basic layer: food taboos during the pilgrimage

1 O you who believe, fulfil the obligations [...]
2 O you who believe, do not profane God's rites [...]

Basic layer continued: general dietary taboos

3A Forbidden to you[P] are carrion, blood, pork, and that on which any other than God has been invoked.

> **Insertion 1: further explanations, metatextual wrap-up**
> 3B And [forbidden are] the strangled, the beaten, the fallen, the gored, and what has been devoured by beasts of prey—except that which you purify.
> 3C And [also forbidden is] what has been slaughtered on sacrificial stones, and to practise divination by means of arrows. That is an abomination for you.
> 3D Today those who are Unbelievers have despaired of your religion. So do not be afraid of them, be afraid of Me! Today I have perfected your religion for you, completed My grace upon you, and approved submission [to God] (*al-islām*) as a religion for you.

Basic layer continued: hardship clause

3E As for someone who is compelled by hunger, not deviating sinfully—God is forgiving and merciful.

> **Insertion 2: responsum on hunting beasts**
> 4 They ask you[s] what is permitted to them. Say: Permitted to you[P] are the good things; and [as regards] those hunting beasts that you teach, training them, teaching them what God has taught you: eat what they catch for you, and mention God's name over it! And fear God! God is swift to reckon.
>
> > **Insertion 3: commensality and intermarriage with the people of the Scripture**
> > 5 Today the good things have been permitted to you, and the food of those who have been given the Scripture is permitted to you, and your food is permitted to them. And [permitted to you] are the chaste women of the Believers, and the chaste women of those who have been given the Scripture before you, if you give them their dowries, acting honourably, not committing fornication, and not taking lovers. If somebody denies the faith, his work is in vain, and he will be among the losers in the next world.

Basic layer continued: ablution before prayer

6 O you who believe, when you rise to pray [...]

Table 2.3 A synopsis of Q 2:172–3, 6:145, and 16:114–15

Q 2:172–3	Q 6:145	Q 16:114–15
172 O you who believe, eat of the good things that We have provided for you,		114 Eat[P] of the good and lawful food that God has provided for you,
and be grateful to God,		and be thankful for the grace of your Lord,
if it is Him whom you worship.		if it is Him you serve.

dietary prohibitions	173 He has forbidden to you carrion, blood, pork, and that on which any other than God has been invoked.	145 Say: I do not find in what is revealed to me anything forbidden to eat other than carrion or blood shed or pork – for that is an abomination – or filth on which any other than God has been invoked.	115 He has forbidden to you only carrion, blood, pork, and that on which any other than God has been invoked.
hardship clause	As for someone who is compelled, without being covetous and transgressing – it is no sin for him. God is forgiving and compassionate.	As for someone who is compelled, without being covetous and transgressing – your[s] Lord is forgiving and compassionate.	As for someone who is compelled, without being covetous and transgressing – God is forgiving and compassionate.

Table 2.4 A synopsis of Q 2:173 and 5:3

	Q 2:173	Q 5:3
dietary prohibitions	He has forbidden to you[P] carrion, blood, pork, and that on which any other than God has been invoked.	3A Forbidden to you[P] are carrion, blood, pork, and that on which any other than God has been invoked. 3B And [forbidden are] the strangled, the beaten, the fallen, the gored, and what has been devoured by beasts of prey—unless you purify it. 3C And [also forbidden is] what has been slaughtered on sacrificial stones, and to practise divination by means of arrows. That is an abomination for you. 3D Today those who are Unbelievers have despaired of your religion. So do not be afraid of them, be afraid of Me! Today I have perfected your religion for you, completed My grace upon you, and approved submission [to God] (*al-islām*) as a religion for you.
hardship clause	As for someone who is compelled, without being covetous and transgressing – it is no sin for him. God is forgiving and merciful.	3E As for someone who is compelled by hunger, not deviating sinfully – God is forgiving and merciful.

Table 2.5 An English translation of Q 9:1–13

Revocation of covenants with Associators, general dissociation
1 A grant of immunity from God and His Messenger
to those Associators with whom you[P] have made a covenant:

2 Travel[P] [freely] in the land for four months
and know that you will not frustrate God
and that God will shame the Unbelievers.

3 And a proclamation from God and His Messenger
to the people on the day of the great pilgrimage
that God is quit of the Associators, and [likewise] His Messenger.
If you[P] turn in repentance,
it is better for you;
and if you turn your backs,
know that you will not frustrate God.
- Give[s] to those who do not believe the tidings of a painful punishment!

Exception: agreements with covenant-abiding Associators remain valid
4 Though that is not the case with those Associators with whom you[P] have made a covenant
and who have then not failed you in anything
and have not supported anyone against you.
Fulfil their covenant to them to the end of their term.
- God loves those who are fearful [of Him].

Sword Verse
5 And when the sacred months have elapsed,
kill[P] the Associators wherever you find them
and take them and confine them
and lie in wait for them at every place of ambush.
If they repent and perform prayer and give alms,
then release them.
- God is forgiving and compassionate.

Refuge for individual Associators
6 If one of the Associators seeks your[s] protection,
grant him protection until he can hear the words of God
and then convey him to his place of safety.
That is because they are a people who do not know.

Justification for revocation of covenants with Associators, exception for covenant-abiding Associators
7 How can the Associators have a covenant with God and His Messenger?
Though that is not the case with those with whom you[P] have made a covenant at the sacred place of prostration.
As long as they act straight with you, act straight with them.
- God loves those who are fearful [of Him].

8 How? If they get the better of you[P],
they will not observe any pact or treaty concerning you.
They satisfy you with their mouths, but their hearts refuse.
Most of them are sinners.

9 They have acquired little gain for God's signs,
and they have barred [others] from His path.
How evil is that which they have been doing!

10 They do not observe any pact or treaty concerning a Believer.
These are the transgressors.

Possibility of conversion reaffirmed
11 If they repent and perform prayer and give alms,
then they are your^{P} brothers in religion.
- We expound the signs for a people who know.

Response to covenant violations, addressees urged to fight
12 And if they break their oaths after having entered into a covenant
and revile your^{P} religion,
fight the leaders of unbelief
- they have no [binding] oaths -
so that they desist.

13 Will you^{P} not fight a people who broke their oaths
and strove to drive out the Messenger,
taking the initiative against you first?
Do you fear them?
God is more deserving of your fear,
if you are Believers.

Table 2.6 A redactional model for Q 9:1–13

Barā'a layer	Mitigating layer	*Adhān* layer
Revocation of covenants with Associators 1 A grant of immunity from God and His Messenger to those Associators with whom you^{P} have made a covenant: 2 Travel^{P} [freely] in the land for four months and know that you will not frustrate God and that God will shame the Unbelievers!		
		General dissociation from Associators 3 And a proclamation from God and His Messenger to the people on the day of the great pilgrimage that God is quit of the Associators, and [likewise] His Messenger. If you^{P} turn in repentance, it is better for you; and if you turn your backs, know that you will not frustrate God.—Give^{S} to those who do not believe the tidings of a painful punishment!
	Exception for covenant-abiding Associators 4 Though that is not the case with those Associators with whom you^{P} have made a covenant and who have then not failed you in anything and have not supported anyone against you. Fulfil their covenant to them to the end of their term. —God loves those who are fearful [of Him].	
		Sword Verse 5 And when the sacred months have elapsed, kill^{P} the Associators wherever you find them and take them and confine them and lie in wait for them at every place of ambush. If they repent and perform prayer and give alms, then release them. —God is forgiving and compassionate.
		Refuge for individual Associators 6 If one of the Associators seeks your^{S} protection, grant him protection until he can hear the words of God and then convey him to his place of safety. That is because they are a people who do not know.

Table 2.6 Continued

Barāʾa layer	Mitigating layer	*Adhān* layer

Justification for revocation of covenants with Associators

7A How can the Associators have a covenant with God and His Messenger?

> **Exception for covenant-abiding Associators**
>
> 7B Though that is not the case with those with whom you[P] have made a covenant at the sacred place of prostration. As long as they act straight with you, act straight with them.—God loves those who are fearful [of Him].

{8} How? If they get the better of you[P], they will not observe any pact or treaty concerning you. They satisfy you with their mouths, but their hearts refuse. Most of them are sinners.

9 They have acquired little gain for God's signs, and they have barred [others] from His path. How evil is that which they have been doing!

10 They do not observe any pact or treaty concerning a Believer. These are the transgressors.

> > **Possibility of conversion**
> >
> > 11 If they repent and perform prayer and give alms, then they are your[P] brothers in religion.—We expound the signs for a people who know.

> **Response to covenant violations**
>
> 12 And if they break their oaths after having entered into a covenant and revile your[P] religion, fight the leaders of unbelief—they have no [binding] oaths—so that they desist.
>
> 13 Will you[P] not fight a people who broke their oaths and strove to drive out the Messenger, taking the initiative against you first? Do you fear them? God is more deserving of your fear, if you are Believers.

Table 2.7 The structure of Q 9:1–2 and 9:3 compared

		barāʾa (vv. 1–2)	*adhān* (v. 3)
(1) heading	*qualification of message*	1 A *barāʾa*	3 and a proclamation (*adhān*)
	sender of message	from God and His Messenger	from God and His Messenger
	recipient of message	to those Associators with whom you[P] have made a covenant:	to the people on the day of the great pilgrimage
		–	that God is quit of the Associators, and [likewise] His Messenger:
(2) address (second person plural)		2 Travel[P] [freely] in the land for four months,	If you[P] turn in repentance, it is better for you;
		and	and if you turn your backs,
	exhortation about divine power	know that you will not frustrate God	know that you will not frustrate God.
		and that God will shame the Unbelievers.	
(3) wrap-up unit		–	Give[s] to those who do not believe the tidings of a painful punishment!

Table 2.8 The structure of Q 9:4 and 9:7 compared

		Q 9:4	Q 9:7
(1) rhetorical question		–	^{A} How can the Associators have a covenant with God and His Messenger?
(2) **exception**	*condition 1: conclusion of covenant*	Though that is not the case with those Associators with whom you^{P} have made a covenant	^{B} Though that is not the case with those with whom you^{P} have made a covenant at the sacred place of prostration.
	condition 2: observance of covenant	and who have then not failed you in anything and have not supported anyone against you.	As long as they act straight with you,
	consequence: convenant remains valid	Fulfill their covenant to them to the end of their term.	act straight with them.
(3) concluding injunction to fear God		– God loves those who are fearful [of Him].	– God loves those who are fearful [of Him].

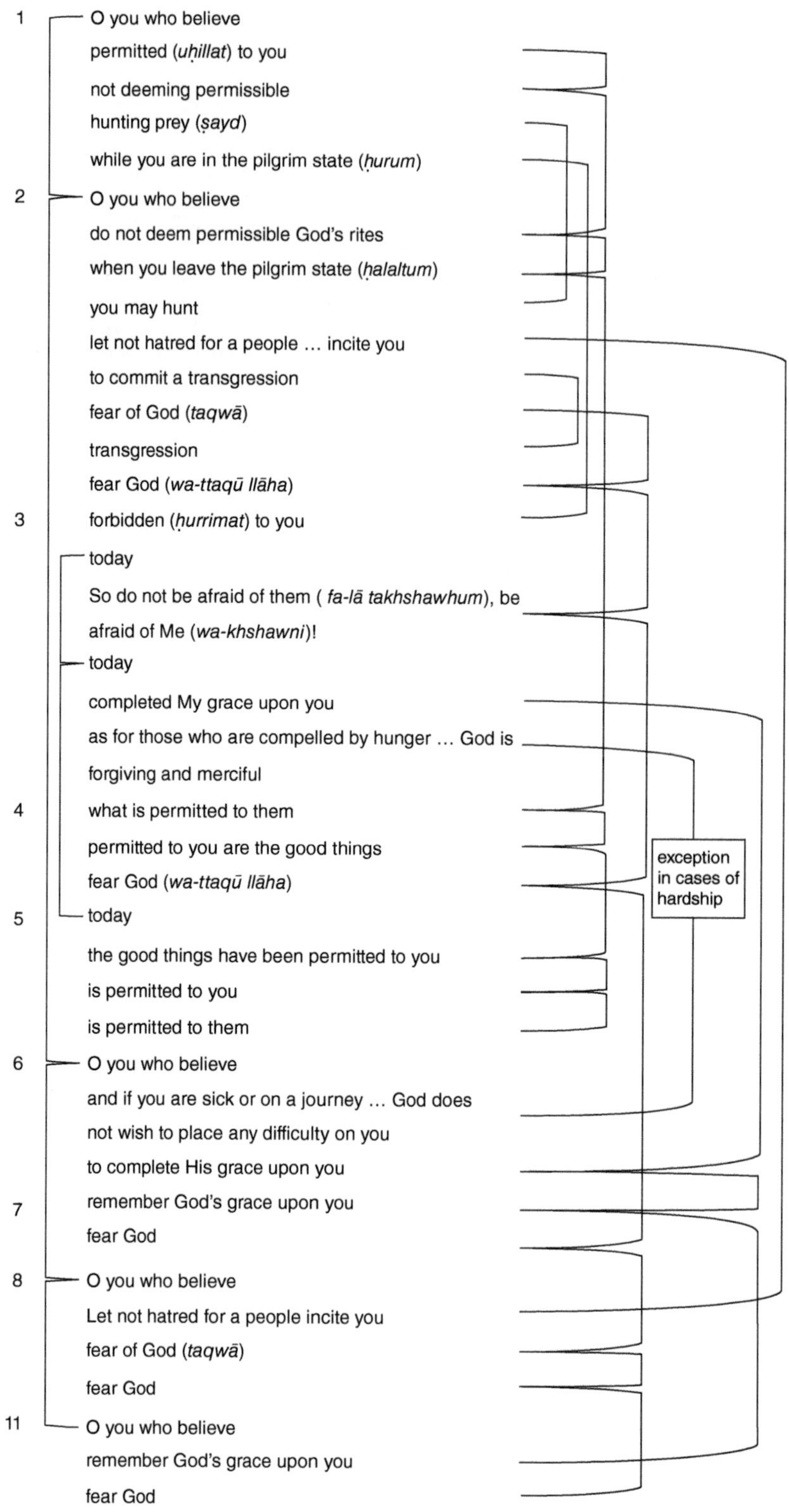

Figure 2.1 Terminological correspondences in Q 5:1–11

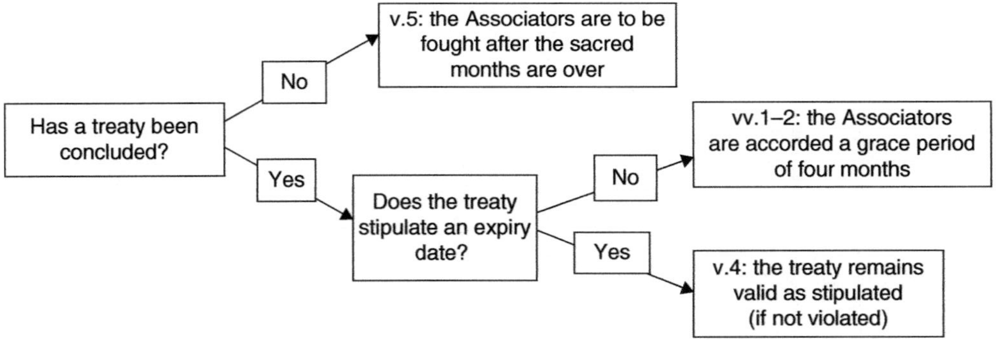

Figure 2.2 A harmonizing reading of Q 9:1–5 (based on Ibn Kathīr)

BIBLIOGRAPHY

Ambros, Arne A. (with the collaboration of Stephan Procházka). *A Concise Dictionary of Koranic Arabic*. Wiesbaden: Reichert, 2004.

Bell, Richard, trans. *The Qurʾān*, 2 vols. Edinburgh: T. & T. Clark, 1937.

Bell, Richard. 'Muhammad's Pilgrimage Proclamation'. *Journal of the Royal Asiatic Society of Great Britain and Ireland* 2 (1937): 233–44.

Bell, Richard. *A Commentary on the Qurʾān*, 2 vols. Manchester: University of Manchester, 1991.

Blois, François de. '*Naṣrānī* (*Ναζωραῖος*) and *ḥanīf* (*ἐθνικός*): Studies on the Religious Vocabulary of Christianity and of Islam'. *Bulletin of the School of Oriental and African Studies* 65 (2002): 1–30.

Buhl, Frants. 'Über Vergleichungen und Gleichnisse im Qurʾân'. In Rudi Paret, ed. *Der Koran*. Darmstadt: Wissenschaftliche Buchgesellschaft, 1975, 75–85. Reprinted from *Acta Orientalia* 2 (1924): 1–11.

Collins, John C. *Introduction to the Hebrew Bible*. Minneapolis: Fortress Press, 2004.

Crone, Patricia. 'Two Legal Problems Bearing on the Early History of the Qurʾān'. *Jerusalem Studies in Arabic and Islam* 18 (1994): 1–37.

Crone, Patricia. 'The Religion of the Qurʾānic Pagans: God and the Lesser Deities'. *Arabica* 57 (2010): 151–200.

Crone, Patricia. 'Jewish Christianity and the Qurʾān (Part One)'. *Journal of Near Eastern Studies* 74 (2015): 225–53.

Cuypers, Michel. *The Banquet: A Reading of the Fifth Sura of the Qurʾan*. Patricia Kelly, trans. Miami: Convivium Press, 2009.

Encyclopaedia of Islam. 2nd edn. Peri J. Bearman, C. E. Bosworth et al. (eds). Leiden: Brill, 1960–2006.

Ernst, Carl. *How to Read the Qurʾan: A New Guide, With Select Translations*. Chapel Hill: University of North Carolina Press, 2011.

Farrin, Raymond. *Structure and Qurʾanic Interpretation: A Study of Symmetry and Coherence in Islam's Holy Text*. Ashland: White Cloud Press, 2014.

Firestone, Reuven. *Jihād: The Origin of Holy War in Islam*. New York: Oxford University Press, 1999.

Freidenreich, David M. *Foreigners and Their Food: Constructing Otherness in Jewish, Christian, and Islamic Law*. Berkeley: University of California Press, 2011.

Friedmann, Yohanan. *Tolerance and Coercion in Islam: Interfaith Relations in the Muslim Tradition*. Cambridge: Cambridge University Press, 2003.

Gräf, Erwin. *Jagdbeute und Schlachttier im islamischen Recht*. Bonn: Selbstverlag des Orientalischen Seminars der Universität Bonn, 1959.

Griffith, Sidney. 'Al-Naṣārā in the Qurʾān: A Hermeneutical Reflection'. In Gabriel S. Reynolds, ed. *New Perspectives on the Qurʾān: The Qurʾān in its Historical Context 2*. Abingdon: Routledge, 2011, 301–22.

Hawting, Gerald R. *The Idea of Idolatry and the Emergence of Islam: From Polemic to History*. Cambridge: Cambridge University Press, 1999.

Hibat Allāh b. Salāma. *al-Nāsikh wa-l-mansūkh*. Muḥammad Zuhayr al-Shāwīsh and Muḥammad Kanʿān, eds. Beirut: al-Maktab al-Islāmī, 1986.

Hirschfeld, Hartwig. *New Researches into the Composition and Exegesis of the Qoran.* London: Royal Asiatic Society, 1902.

Holes, Clive. *Modern Arabic: Structures, Functions, and Varieties.* Revised edn. Washington, DC: Georgetown University Press, 2004.

Ibn Kathīr, Ismāʿīl ibn ʿUmar. *Tafsīr al-Qurʾān al-ʿaẓīm.* 2nd edn. Sāmī ibn Muḥammad al-Salāma, ed. Riyadh: Dār Ṭayba, 1999 (AH 1420).

Jamil, Nadia. 'Playing for Time: *Maysir*-Gambling in Early Arabic Poetry'. In Robert G. Hoyland and Philip F. Kennedy, eds. *Islamic Reflections, Arabic Musings: Studies in Honour of Professor Alan Jones.* [Cambridge:] Gibb Memorial Trust, 2004, 48–90.

Jones, Alan, trans. *The Qurʾān.* [Cambridge:] Gibb Memorial Trust, 2007.

Lecker, Michael. *The 'Constitution of Medina': Muḥammad's First Legal Document.* Princeton: Darwin Press, 2004.

Lowry, Joseph E. 'When Less is More: Law and Commandment in *Sūrat al-Anʿām*'. *Journal of Qurʾanic Studies* 9 (2007): 22–42.

Nagel, Tilman. *Medinensische Einschübe in mekkanischen Suren.* Göttingen: Vandenhoeck & Ruprecht, 1995.

Neuwirth, Angelika. 'Meccan Texts—Medinan Additions? Politics and the Re-reading of Liturgical Communications'. In Rüdiger Arnzen and Jörn Thielmann, eds. *Words, Texts, and Concepts Cruising the Mediterranean Sea: Studies on the Sources, Contents, and Influences of Islamic Civilization and Arabic Philosophy and Science.* Leuven: Peeters, 2004, 71–93.

Neuwirth, Angelika. *Studien zur Komposition der mekkanischen Suren.* 2nd edn. Berlin: De Gruyter, 2007.

Neuwirth, Angelika. *Der Koran*, vol. 1: *Frühmekkanische Suren: Poetische Prophetie.* Berlin: Verlag der Weltreligionen, 2011.

Neuwirth, Angelika. 'From Recitation through Liturgy to Canon: Sura Composition and Dissolution during the Development of Islamic Ritual'. In Angelika Neuwirth, *Scripture, Poetry and the Making of a Community: Reading the Qurʾan as a Literary Text.* Oxford: Oxford University Press, 2014, 141–63.

Nöldeke, Theodor and Friedrich Schwally. *Geschichte des Qorāns.* 2nd edn. Vol. 1: *Über den Ursprung des Qorāns.* Leipzig: Dieterich'sche Verlagsbuchhandlung, 1909.

Paret, Rudi. *Der Koran: Kommentar und Konkordanz.* 2nd edn. Stuttgart: Kohlhammer, 1977.

Pavlovitch, Pavel. *The Formation of the Islamic Understanding of* Kalālah *in the Second Century AH (718–816 CE): Between Scripture and Canon.* Leiden: Brill, 2016.

Pohlmann, Karl-Friedrich. *Die Entstehung des Korans: Neue Erkenntnisse aus Sicht der historisch-kritischen Bibelwissenschaft.* Darmstadt: Wissenschaftliche Buchgesellschaft, 2012.

Reynolds, Gabriel S. *The Qurʾān and its Biblical Subtext*, Abingdon: Routledge, 2010.

Rippin, Andrew. 'The Function of *Asbāb al-Nuzūl* in Qurʾānic Exegesis'. *Bulletin of the School of Oriental and African Studies* 51 (1988): 1–20.

Rippin, Andrew. 'Reading the Qurʾān with Richard Bell'. *Journal of the American Oriental Society* 112 (1992): 639–47.

Rivlin, Josef J. *Gesetz im Koran: Kultus und Ritus.* Jerusalem: Bamberger & Wahrmann, 1934.

Robinson, Neal. *Discovering the Qurʾan: A Contemporary Approach to a Veiled Text*, 2nd edn. London: SCM Press, 2004.

Robinson, Neal. 2011. 'Hands Outstretched: Towards a Re-reading of *Sūrat al-Māʾida*'. *Journal of Qurʾanic Studies* 3 (2001): 1–19.

Rubin, Uri. 'The Great Pilgrimage of Muḥammad: Some Notes on Sūra IX'. *Journal of Semitic Studies* 27 (1982): 241–60.

Rubin, Uri. '*Barāʾa*: A Study of Some Quranic Passages'. *Jerusalem Studies in Arabic and Islam* 5 (1984): 13–32.

Shemesh, Aharon. *Halakhah in the Making: The Development of Jewish Law from Qumran to the Rabbis*. Berkeley: University of California Press, 2009.

Sinai, Nicolai. 'Qurʾānic Self-Referentiality as a Strategy of Self-Authorization'. In Stefan Wild, ed. *Self-Referentiality in the Qurʾān*. Wiesbaden: Harrassowitz, 2006, 103–34.

Sinai, Nicolai. *Fortschreibung und Auslegung: Studien zur frühen Koraninterpretation*. Wiesbaden: Harrassowitz, 2009.

Sinai, Nicolai. 'When Did the Consonantal Skeleton of the Quran Reach Closure?' *Bulletin of the School of Oriental and African Studies* 77 (2014): 273–92 and 509–21.

Sinai, Nicolai, 'The Qurʾanic Commentary of Muqātil b. Sulaymān and the Evolution of Early *Tafsīr* Literature'. In Andreas Görke and Johanna Pink, eds. Tafsīr *and Islamic Intellectual History: Exploring the Boundaries of a Genre*. Oxford: Oxford University Press, 2014, 113–43.

Sinai, Nicolai. 'Inner-Qurʾanic Chronology'. In Muhammad Abdel Haleem and Mustafa Shah, eds, *The Oxford Handbook of Qurʾanic Studies*. Oxford: Oxford University Press, forthcoming.

Sinai, Nicolai. 'Two Types of Inner-Qurʾanic Interpretation'. In Georges Tamer, ed., *Exegetical Crossroads*. Berlin: De Gruyter, forthcoming.

Sinai, Nicolai. 'The Unknown Known: Some Groundwork for Interpreting the Medinan Qurʾan'. *Mélanges de l'Université Saint-Joseph* 66 (2015–2016): 47–96.

Stewart, Devin. 'Poetic License in the Qurʾan: Ibn al-Ṣāʾigh al-Ḥanafī's Iḥkām al-rāy fī aḥkām al-āy'. *Journal of Qurʾanic Studies* 11 (2009): 1–56.

Suyūṭī, Jalāl al-Dīn al-. *al-Durr al-manthūr fī l-tafsīr bi-l-maʾthūr*. ʿAbd Allāh ibn ʿAbd al-Muḥsin al-Turkī, ed. 17 vols. Cairo: Markaz li-l-buḥūth wa-l-dirāsat al-ʿarabiyya wa-l-islāmiyya, 2003.

Suyūṭī, Jalāl al-Dīn al-. *al-Itqān fī ʿulūm al-Qurʾān*. 7 vols. Medina: Majmaʿ al-Malik Fahd li-ṭibāʿat al-muṣḥaf al-sharīf, AH 1426.

Ṭabarī, Abū Jaʿfar Muḥammad ibn Jarīr al-. *Tafsīr al-Ṭabarī: Jāmiʿ al-bayān ʿan tafsīr āy al-Qurʾān*. Maḥmūd Muḥammad Shākir and Aḥmad Muḥammad Shākir, eds. 2nd edn. Cairo: Dār al-Maʿārif, n.d.

Tirmidhī, Muḥammad ibn ʿĪsā al-. *al-Jāmiʿ al-ṣaḥīḥ*. Aḥmad Muḥammad Shākir et al. (eds). 5 vols. Cairo: Maṭbaʿat Muṣṭafā al-Bābī al-Ḥalabī, 1978–1986.

Vollers, Karl. *Volkssprache und Schriftsprache im alten Arabien*. Straßburg: K. J. Trübner, 1906.

Wagtendonk, Kees. 'Fasting'. In Jane Dammen McAuliffe, ed. *Encyclopaedia of the Qurʾān*. 6 vols, vol. 2. Leiden: Brill, 2002, 180–5.

Wellhausen, Julius. *Reste arabischen Heidentums*. 2nd edn. Berlin: G. Reimer, 1897.

Zahniser, A. H. Mathias. 'Major Transitions and Thematic Borders in Two Long Sūras: *al-Baqara* and *al-Nisā*''. In Issa J. Boullata, ed. *Literary Structures of Religious Meaning in the Qur'ān*. Richmond: Curzon, 2000, 26–55.
Zellentin, Holger. *The Qur'ān's Legal Culture: The Didascalia Apostolorum as a Point of Departure*. Tübingen: Mohr Siebeck, 2013.
Zirker, Hans. *Der Koran: Zugänge und Lesarten*. 2nd edn. Darmstadt: Wissenschaftliche Buchgesellschaft, 2012.

3

'O Believers, Be Not as Those Who Hurt Moses'

Q 33:69 and Its Exegesis

Joseph Witztum

INTRODUCTION

The exegesis of Q 33:69 is a fine example of the degree to which early Islamic sources are steeped in biblical lore.[1] This chapter will first survey the various interpretations of this enigmatic verse in the classical exegetical sources and briefly trace the history of the traditions reflected in these interpretations.[2] Special attention will then be given to the Qur'an itself in an attempt to establish the verse's original meaning on the basis of textual and contextual considerations. Although the interpretation I will offer is itself not new, I will adduce new arguments in its favour.

[1] I first formulated the main argument presented here while preparing for Patricia Crone's Qur'an reading group. As an expression of my deep gratitude for all that she taught me, I dedicate this article to her memory. I thank Meir Bar-Asher, Etan Kohlberg, Michael Lecker, Judith Loebenstein Witztum, and the editors for their comments on earlier drafts. The research for this chapter was supported in part by the Mandel Scholion Center at the Hebrew University. Unless stated otherwise, the translations of biblical verses follow the New Revised Standard Version. The translations of qur'anic verses are usually my adaptations of Arthur J. Arberry, *The Koran Interpreted* (London: Allen & Unwin, 1955), often drawing on renditions of the many other translations of the Qur'an.

[2] In this part of the chapter I refer primarily to rabbinic parallels to the Islamic traditions; this is not to deny the possible existence of Christian parallels. Schwarzbaum's comment on the Islamic legend of 'those who affronted Moses' is noteworthy: 'A thorough folkloristic dissection of this interesting legend calls for a separate monograph'; Haim Schwarzbaum, *Biblical and Extra-Biblical Legends in Islamic Folk-Literature* (Walldorf-Hessen: Verlag für Orientkunde, 1982), 64.

THE RIDDLE

Q 33:69 reads as follows:

> *yā ayyuhā lladhīna āmanū lā takūnū ka-lladhīna ādhaw mūsā fa-barra'ahu llāhu mimmā qālū wa-kāna ʿinda llāhi wajīhan*
>
> O believers, be not as those who hurt Moses, but God declared him innocent of what they said, and he was well-esteemed in God's sight.[3]

What did the attack against Moses consist of? Though the verb *ādhā* may also refer to a physical attack, here it clearly refers to a verbal assault—'but God declared him innocent of what they said'.[4] While it is possible to argue that this refers generally to the Israelites' adversarial attitude towards Moses, the mention of God's vindication suggests that a specific incident of verbal affront is being alluded to here.[5] Indeed the classical exegetes offer a few interpretations that identify a singular event to which this verse refers.[6]

THE CLASSICAL INTERPRETATIONS

According to one group of traditions, the verse refers to an allegation that Moses suffered from a physical deformity, usually identified as a scrotal hernia or leprosy. Moses is said to have been extremely bashful and to have avoided undressing in public. This aroused the Israelites' suspicions that he had something to hide. God then proved them wrong by causing a rock to run away with Moses' clothes when he was bathing, thus forcing him to pursue it

[3] Compare Q 61:5 ('And when Moses said to his people: "O my people, why do you hurt me [*tu'dhūnanī*], though you know I am the Messenger of God to you?" When they deviated, God caused their hearts to deviate; and God never guides the disobedient people').

[4] For this verb in the Qur'an, see Arne A. Ambros with Stephan Procházka, *A Concise Dictionary of Koranic Arabic* (Wiesbaden: Reichert, 2004), 23.

[5] For verses in which the verb describes the sufferings of the messengers generally, see Q 6:34 and Q 14:12. Fakhr al-Dīn al-Rāzī wishes to interpret Q 33:69 without recourse to extra-qur'anic material and sees in it an allusion to the hurtful utterances of the Israelites addressed to Moses in verses such as Q 5:24 ('Go forth, you and your Lord, and fight'), Q 2:55 ('we will not believe you till we see God openly'), and Q 2:61 ('we will not endure one sort of food'). The problem with this is that these verses do not contain accusations concerning which God could declare Moses innocent. Therefore al-Rāzī explains *fa-barra'ahu llāhu mimmā qālū* as denoting God's freeing Moses from the responsibility of supplying their demands; Fakhr al-Dīn al-Rāzī, *al-Tafsīr al-kabīr aw Mafātīḥ al-ghayb* (Beirut: Dār al-Kutub al-ʿIlmiyya, 1990), 25:201.

[6] For an earlier discussion of these interpretations and their background, see Abraham Geiger, *Was hat Mohammed aus dem Judenthume aufgenommen?* (Leipzig: M. W. Kaufmann, 1902), 152 and 165–8 (English translation in Abraham Geiger, *Judaism and Islam* [New York: Ktav, 1970], 121 and 133–5). An agnostic approach to Q 33:69 is found in William Montgomery Watt, *Companion to the Qur'ān* (Oxford: Oneworld, 1994), 195.

and display his nakedness to the Israelites.[7] Though this story incorporates several biblical motifs, it is unknown in non-Islamic sources.[8]

In the collection of the stories of the prophets attributed to ʿUmāra Ibn Wathīma (d. 902) Q 33:69 is said to refer to a different verbal affront to Moses.[9] According to this interpretation, the Israelites would mock Moses and find fault with his reliance on his staff and the rock for their water supply.[10] They raised doubts about their fate should something happen to the staff and the rock and claimed that Moses wanted to bring about their ruination. In order to prove that the source of their sustenance is none other than God, He commanded Moses to speak to the rock rather than strike it with his staff. Initially Moses failed to fulfil the command and incurred God's wrath, but at last he did as he was told and water gushed out of the rock.[11] Elsewhere the Israelites' concerns are not linked to Q 33:69 but rather are mentioned in the context of the miracle of the rock and the water, so that the link to Q 33:69 may be secondary.[12] Be that as it may, this tradition clearly derives ultimately

[7] See e.g. Muḥammad b. Jarīr al-Ṭabarī, *Tafsīr al-Ṭabarī: Jāmiʿ al-bayān ʿan taʾwīl āy al-Qurʾān*, ʿAbd Allāh al-Turkī, ed. (Cairo: Hajar, 2001), 19:190–4, where such traditions are adduced in the names of the Prophet, Ibn ʿAbbās, Abū Hurayra, Saʿīd b. Jubayr, and Ibn Zayd. Some of these traditions also mention that after Moses retrieved his clothes he struck the rock with his staff.

[8] See Geiger, *Was hat Mohammed aus dem Judenthume aufgenommen?*, 167, where it is noted that the story is unknown in Jewish sources. For a discussion of this story, see David J. Halperin, 'The Hidden Made Manifest: Muslim Traditions and the "Latent Content" of Biblical and Rabbinic Stories', in D. P. Wright et al., eds, *Pomegranates and Golden Bells: Studies in Biblical, Jewish, and Near Eastern Ritual, Law, and Literature in Honor of Jacob Milgrom* (Winona Lake: Eisenbrauns, 1995), 581–94, at 587–94. Halperin notes that the travelling rock motif is known from both rabbinic and Christian sources (e.g. Tosefta Sukka 3:11 and 1 Corinthians 10:4) and that the striking of the rock is found in Exodus 17:1–7 and Numbers 20:2–13. See also Ze'ev Maghen, *After Hardship Cometh Ease: The Jews as Backdrop for Muslim Moderation* (Berlin: de Gruyter, 2006), 74–5. Might the notion of Moses hiding a deformity somehow stem from the veil with which he was said to have covered his shining face (Exodus 34:29–35)? Compare the comment of Ḥiwi al-Balkhi quoted in Ibn Ezra's exegesis of Exodus 34:29. As for Moses being afflicted with leprosy, see e.g. Exodus 4:6, and Gohei Hata, 'The Story of Moses Interpreted within the Context of Anti-Semitism', in Louis H. Feldman and Gohei Hata, eds, *Josephus, Judaism, and Christianity* (Detroit: Wayne State University Press, 1987), 180–97, and Louis H. Feldman, *Josephus's Interpretation of the Bible* (Berkeley: University of California Press, 1998), 384–6.

[9] On ʿUmāra Ibn Wathīma's work, see Roberto Tottoli, *Biblical Prophets in the Qurʾān and Muslim Literature* (London: Routledge, 2002), 144–6.

[10] In Q 2:60 and Q 7:160 Moses is commanded to strike the rock with his staff and twelve springs gush forth from it.

[11] Raif Georges Khoury, *Les légendes prophétiques dans l'Islam depuis le Ier jusqu'au IIIe siècle de l'Hégire* (Wiesbaden: Harrassowitz, 1978), 33–6 (Arabic text). The presentation of this tradition in ʿUmāra's text is complicated since it is intertwined with the tradition concerning Moses' alleged deformity in a manner which is not entirely clear to me.

[12] The following tradition is attributed to Wahb ibn Munabbih without any mention of Q 33:69: '[...] Moses would strike the nearest rock in a rocky terrain and springs would break forth from it, one for each of their tribes, they being twelve tribes [...] The (people) said: "If Moses lost his staff, we would die of thirst". So God inspired Moses: "Do not strike the rock with your staff, but speak to it, and it will obey you; perhaps they will reflect on it". So he did that, and

from Numbers 20:2–13. Following the Israelites' complaints regarding the lack of water, God commands Moses to take the staff, assemble the congregation, and speak together with Aaron to the rock (Numbers 20:8). Moses, however, proceeds to strike it twice (Numbers 20:11) and he and Aaron are informed that they will not enter the Holy Land (Numbers 20:12). Although it is unclear in the biblical text what exactly Moses did wrong, a common interpretation holds that he sinned in striking the rock—rather than speaking to it.[13] This notion is shared by ʿUmāra's narrative, which in addition explains why the command in this instance was to speak to the rock rather than strike it (compare Exodus 17).[14] The Israelites' assumption in ʿUmāra's narrative that only one specific rock could supply them with water is also reminiscent of Jewish texts, according to which the Israelites challenged Moses to bring out water from a rock of their choice.[15]

Another tradition finds in Q 33:69 a reference to an episode in which the Israelites accused Moses of murdering his brother Aaron after they had both ascended the mountain and Aaron had died. God then vindicated Moses by commanding the angels to display Aaron's body to the Israelites. From the angels' mention of his death the Israelites realized that no foul play was involved.[16] This tradition harks back to a legend that embellished the biblical

they said: "How will it be for us if we cross over to sands and to terrain where there are no rocks?" So He commanded Moses to take a rock with him, and whenever he encamped he cast it down'; slightly adapted from William M. Brinner, trans., *ʿArāʾis al-Majālis fī Qiṣaṣ al-Anbiyāʾ or 'Lives of The Prophets'* (Leiden: Brill, 2002), 405. See also Maḥmūd b. ʿUmar al-Zamakhsharī, *al-Kashshāf ʿan ḥaqāʾiq ghawāmiḍ al-tanzīl wa-ʿuyūn al-aqāwīl fī wujūh al-taʾwīl*, ʿĀdil Aḥmad ʿAbd al-Mawjūd and ʿAlī Muḥammad Muʿawwaḍ, eds (Riyadh: Maktabat al-ʿUbaykān, 1998), 1:274, and Abraham I. Katsh, *Judaism in Islām: Biblical and Talmudic Backgrounds of the Koran and Its Commentaries* (New York: New York University Press, 1954), 60–2. Note that whereas God's response in Wahb's version addresses the concerns regarding the rock and the staff, His response in ʿUmāra's text does not address the concern regarding the rock, at least not directly.

13 For surveys of ancient and modern approaches to the riddle posed by the condemnation of Moses in Numbers 20, see e.g. Steven D. Fraade, 'Moses at Meribah: Speech, Scepter and Sanctification', *Orim: A Jewish Journal at Yale* 2.1 (1986): 43–67, and Johnson Lim Teng Kok, *The Sin of Moses and the Staff of God: A Narrative Approach* (Assen: Van Gorcum, 1997) and the literature mentioned there. For the interpretation that the sin consisted of striking the rock, see e.g. Yelammedenu (in Yalkut Shimʿoni) to Numbers 20:8 and 12 (cf. Sifre Deuteronomy §340), as well as the sources cited and discussed in Lim, *The Sin of Moses*, 109, 111, and 126–31.

14 For a different explanation, see Yelammedenu (in Yalkut Shimʿoni) to Numbers 20:8.

15 See e.g. Numbers Rabba §19.9, Tanḥuma Ḥuqqat §9, Tanḥuma Buber Ḥuqqat §29, and parallels. The notion that there was an argument about the choice of the rock upon which the miracle would be performed is derived from Numbers 20:10 ('Listen, you rebels, shall we bring water for you out of this rock?'). See Fraade, 'Moses at Meribah', 52.

16 See al-Ṭabarī, *Jāmiʿ al-bayān*, 19:194, where the tradition is attributed to ʿAlī. See also Jalāl al-Dīn al-Suyūṭī, *al-Durr al-manthūr fī al-tafsīr bi-l-maʾthūr*, ʿAbd Allāh al-Turkī, ed. (Cairo: Markaz Hajar, 2003), 12:152, where Ibn ʿAbbās, Ibn Masʿūd, and other unnamed disciples of the Prophet are said to have transmitted a similar tradition. The reference to the angels talking about Aaron's death (*takallamat al-malāʾikatu bi-mawtihi*) is probably to be understood in the light of sources such as Sifre Deuteronomy §305 (quoted below) according to which God and the angels eulogized Aaron. In Muḥammad b. Aḥmad al-Qurṭubī, *al-Jāmiʿ li-aḥkām al-Qurʾān*, ʿAbd Allāh

description of Aaron's death.[17] In Numbers 20:22–29, Moses is ordered to ascend to Mount Hor together with Aaron and his son Eleazar in order for Aaron to die on the mountain top. After fulfilling God's command, Moses and Eleazar descend from the mountain and it is said that 'when all the congregation saw that Aaron had died, all the house of Israel mourned for Aaron for thirty days' (v. 29). Since the Bible does not mention that the Israelites were privy to God's plan regarding Aaron's death, a rabbinic legend posits that Moses and Eleazar's return without Aaron aroused the Israelites' misgivings. Their suspicion was then quelled by a miraculous display of Aaron's bier.[18] This legend finds a textual peg in a literal reading of Numbers 20:29 ('when all the congregation saw that Aaron had died'); since Aaron had died at the top of the mountain the Israelites could not have seen this unless God had somehow miraculously demonstrated it to them in order to reassure them.

According to another tradition, Q 33:69 alludes to an instance in which Korah (Qārūn in Arabic) paid a prostitute to accuse Moses of having had intimate relations with her. In the end, however, Moses was vindicated since the woman confessed and revealed the plot. An examination of the attestations of this tradition suggests that initially it addressed another qur'anic passage

al-Turkī, ed. (Beirut: Mu'assasat al-Risāla, 2006), 17:241–2, al-Qushayrī is cited as quoting a tradition of ʿAlī according to which God resurrected Aaron who informed the Israelites that Moses had not murdered him and then died.

[17] See Geiger, *Was hat Mohammed aus dem Judenthume aufgenommen?*, 166–7. A collection of rabbinic and Islamic versions of this legend is found in Max Grünbaum, *Neue Beiträge zur semitischen Sagenkunde* (Leiden: Brill, 1893), 173–6.

[18] See e.g. Sifre Deuteronomy §305: '[. . .] all Israel gathered before Moses and said to him: "Where is your brother Aaron"? He replied: "God has secreted him for life in the world to come". They did not believe him and said to him: "We know that you are cruel. It may be that he had said something improper before you, and you condemned him to death". What did the Holy One, blessed be He, do? He brought back Aaron's bier and suspended it in the upper heavens, and the Holy One, blessed be He, stood over him eulogizing him, while the ministering angels responded after Him. What did they say? *The Torah of truth was in his mouth, and unrighteousness was not found in his lips; he walked with Me in peace and uprightness, and did turn many away from iniquity* (Malachi 2:6)'; Reuven Hammer, trans., *Sifre: A Tannaitic Commentary on the Book of Deuteronomy* (New Haven: Yale University Press, 1986), 296. See also the sources listed in Louis Ginzberg, *The Legends of the Jews* (Philadelphia: Jewish Publication Society, 1909–38), 6:112–13, note 641, as well as Ephraim E. Urbach, ed., *Sefer Pitron Torah* (Jerusalem: Magnes, 1978), 189; Midrash Aggada to Numbers 20:28; Jacob Mann and Isaiah Sonne, *The Bible as Read and Preached in the Old Synagogue*, vol. 2 (Cincinnati: Mann-Sonne Publication Committee, 1966), 158 (Hebrew part); and Midrash Haggadol to Numbers 20:28. In some of these sources the displaying of Aaron's bier serves to assuage the Israelites' suspicion that he did not really die; see e.g. Pirqe de-Rabbi Eliezer §17. See also Haim Schwarzbaum, 'Jewish, Christian, Moslem and Falasha Legends of the Death of Aaron, The High Priest', *Fabula* 5 (1962): 185–227, and cf. Bernhard Heller, 'Muhammedanisches und Antimuhammedanisches in den Pirke Rabbi Eliezer', *Monatsschrift für Geschichte und Wissenschaft des Judentums* 69 (1925): 47–54, at 50–2. Unaware of Sifre Deuteronomy §305, Heller argues that Pirqe de-Rabbi Eliezer §17 is a polemical response to Islamic legends concerning Muhammad's coffin. See the responses in Louis Ginzberg, *On Jewish Law and Lore* (Philadelphia: Jewish Publication Society, 1955), 72, and Joseph Heinemann, *Aggadah and its Development* (Jerusalem: Keter, 1974), 243, note 22 (in Hebrew).

and only subsequently was it applied to Q 33:69.[19] This tradition too may be related to a rabbinic idea, which, on the basis of Psalms 106:16, 'They were jealous of Moses in the camp' (compare Numbers 5), introduced to the story of Korah's rebellion the notion that the rebels suspected Moses of committing adultery with their wives.[20]

A Shiʿite interpretation would seem to link Q 33:69 to the story of Korah differently. At the heart of the biblical Korah narrative stands the complaint against Aaron's high position (see Numbers 16–17) and the Shiʿite interpretation appears to understand the accusation against Moses in the Qur'an as referring to his preferential treatment of his brother Aaron.[21] In this tradition preserved in a ninth-century text and related in the name of the Imams, our verse is reformulated as follows: 'O believers, do not hurt the Messenger of God concerning ʿAlī as did those who hurt Moses concerning Aaron (*ka-lladhīna ādhaw mūsā fī hārūna*), but God declared him innocent of what they said.'[22] Though we are not given any further details, the comparison to Muhammad and ʿAlī suggests that the allegations had to do with Moses/Muḥammad appointing Aaron/ʿAlī to an official position.[23] Geiger too considered linking Q 33:69 to the Korah dispute independently of any acquaintance with this Shiʿite tradition.[24]

[19] For this tradition (in the name of Abū al-ʿĀliya) in the context of Q 33:69, see e.g. Abū Isḥāq Aḥmad al-Thaʿlabī, *al-Kashf wa-l-bayān ʿan tafsīr al-Qur'ān*, Ṣalāḥ Bāʿuthmān et al., eds (Jeddah: Dār al-Tafsīr, 2015), 21:580. In al-Ṭabarī, *Jāmiʿ al-bayān*, 18:331–6, this tradition is quoted in several versions in the name of Ibn ʿAbbās and his disciple ʿAbd Allāh b. al-Ḥārith in the context of Korah's story in Q 28:76–81. It is noteworthy that the version attributed to ʿAbd Allāh b. al-Ḥārith (without mention of Ibn ʿAbbās) may reflect influence of Q 33:69 in that it repeatedly uses the language of *īdhā'* and attributes the woman's change of heart to divine intervention.

[20] See Geiger, *Was hat Mohammed aus dem Judenthume aufgenommen?*, 166, BT Moʿed Qaṭan 18b and Sanhedrin 110a, Numbers Rabba §18.20, Tanḥuma Korah §10, Tanḥuma Buber Korah §25, Targum Pseudo-Jonathan to Numbers 16:4, and Midrash Tehillim §106.5. See also Grünbaum, *Neue Beiträge*, 170–2.

[21] For ancient interpreters of the Bible who understood that Korah accused Moses of nepotism, see James L. Kugel, *Traditions of the Bible: A Guide to the Bible as It Was at the Start of the Common Era* (Cambridge, MA: Harvard University Press, 1998), 783–4.

[22] See tradition §429 in Etan Kohlberg and Mohammad Ali Amir-Moezzi, eds, *Revelation and Falsification: The* Kitāb al-qirā'āt *of Aḥmad b. Muḥammad al-Sayyārī* (Leiden: Brill, 2009), 111 (Arabic text) and 202 (English notes). As the editors note in the name of al-Majlisī (d. 1699), it is unclear whether this tradition consists of a variant version of the verse or is simply an exegetical gloss. Al-Majlisī also explains that the attack against Moses might concern the appointment of Aaron as his legatee (*waṣiyyat hārūn*); Muḥammad Bāqir al-Majlisī, *Biḥār al-anwār* (Tehran: Dār al-Kutub al-Islāmiyya, 1956–74), 23:303.

[23] See e.g. al-Majlisī's comment mentioned in the previous footnote. For the parallel between ʿAlī and Aaron in Shiʿite sources, see §286 and §345 in Kohlberg and Amir-Moezzi, eds, *Revelation and Falsification*, 74 and 88 (Arabic text) and 157 and 176 (notes), as well as Meir M. Bar-Asher, 'La place du judaïsme et des Juifs dans le shīʿisme duodécimain', in Mohammad Ali Amir-Moezzi, ed., *Islam: identité et altérité: hommage à Guy Monnot, o.p.* (Tourhout: Brepols, 2013), 57–82, at 73, and G. Miskinzoda, 'The Significance of the *ḥadīth* of the Position of Aaron for the Formulation of the Shīʿī Doctrine of Authority', *Bulletin of the School of Oriental and African Studies* 78 (2015): 67–82.

[24] Geiger, *Was hat Mohammed aus dem Judenthume aufgenommen?*, 152 and 165.

A different interpretation makes do with qur'anic data and does not resort to extra-qur'anic lore. Taking its inspiration from the accusations against Muhammad and other qur'anic verses, this approach claims that Moses was accused of lying, engaging in magic, and being possessed.[25] These accusations are indeed levelled at Moses in the Qur'an (see especially Q 51:38–9), but by Pharaoh and his people, not by the Israelites. It would seem then that according to this interpretation the adversaries are to be identified as the Egyptians. This creates a problem, however, with Q 61:5 ('And when Moses said to his people: "O my people, why do you hurt me [*lima tu'dhūnanī*], though you know I am the Messenger of God to you?"'). Therefore it is preferable to understand this interpretation as arguing that the Israelites too made similar accusations.[26] Indeed al-Ṭabrisī and Ibn al-Jawzī explicitly state that these accusations were made by the Israelites.[27]

THE LINK TO NUMBERS 12

A different suggestion was put forward in 1828 by Samuel Friedrich Günther Wahl and was subsequently adopted by Abraham Geiger, Heinrich Speyer, and later scholars.[28] These scholars linked our verse to Numbers 12 where Moses is criticized by his siblings, Miriam and Aaron, but receives most elaborate praise from God in response:

> (1) Miriam and Aaron spoke against Moses because of the Cushite woman he had married: 'He married a Cushite woman!'[29] (2) They said, 'Has the Lord spoken only through Moses? Has He not spoken through us as well?' The Lord heard it.

[25] See the opinion of Abū Muslim al-Iṣfahānī in al-Faḍl b. al-Ḥasan al-Ṭabrisī, *Majmaʿ al-bayān fī tafsīr al-Qur'ān*, Ibrāhīm Shams al-Dīn, ed. (Beirut: Dār al-Kutub al-ʿIlmiyya, 1997), 8:141, and ʿAlī b. Muḥammad al-Māwardī, *al-Nukat wa-l-ʿuyūn: tafsīr al-Māwardī* (Beirut: Dār al-Kutub al-ʿIlmiyya, 1992), 4:426–7.

[26] Note that the verse which follows Q 61:5 mentions the Israelites' rejection of Jesus, which consisted of their saying 'this is manifest sorcery'. Note also that in Q 40:23–4 Moses is sent with miracles to Pharaoh, Haman, and Korah and they accuse him of being a sorcerer. Although in this verse Korah seems to be part of Pharaoh's court, he was an Israelite. See also Q 51:52.

[27] See al-Ṭabrisī, *Majmaʿ al-bayān*, 8:141, and Abū al-Faraj ʿAbd al-Raḥmān b. ʿAlī Ibn al-Jawzī, *Zād al-masīr fī ʿilm al-tafsīr* (Beirut: Dār al-Kutub al-ʿIlmiyya, 2002), 6:226.

[28] See e.g. Samuel Friedrich Günther Wahl, *Der Koran oder das Gesetz der Moslemen durch Muhammed den Sohn Abdallahs* (Halle: Gebauer, 1828), 407–8; Geiger, *Was hat Mohammed aus dem Judenthume aufgenommen?*, 152 and 167; Heinrich Speyer, *Die biblischen Erzählungen im Qoran* (Gräfenhainichen: Schulze, 1931), 344–5; Rudi Paret, *Der Koran: Kommentar und Konkordanz* (Stuttgart: Kohlhammer, 1980), 401; and Arthur J. Droge, *The Qur'ān: A New Annotated Translation* (Sheffield: Equinox, 2013), 280.

[29] Note the different understanding of the verse reflected in the New Revised Standard Version: 'Miriam and Aaron spoke against Moses because of the Cushite woman whom he had married (for he had indeed married a Cushite woman).'

(3) Now Moses was a very humble man, more so than any other man on earth. (4) Suddenly the Lord called to Moses, Aaron, and Miriam, 'Come out, you three, to the Tent of Meeting.' So the three of them went out. (5) The Lord came down in a pillar of cloud, stopped at the entrance of the Tent, and called out, 'Aaron and Miriam!' The two of them came forward; (6) and He said, 'Hear these My words: When a prophet of the Lord arises among you, I make Myself known to him in a vision, I speak with him in a dream. (7) Not so with My servant (*'avdi*) Moses; he is trusted throughout My household; (8) with him I speak mouth to mouth, plainly and not in riddles, and he beholds the likeness of the Lord. How then did you not shrink from speaking against My servant (*'avdi*) Moses?'[30]

The text is far from clear. We are told that Miriam and Aaron's criticism addressed the issue of Moses' Cushite wife and his authority as a prophet, but the precise relationship between these two elements is not spelled out.[31] Nor is the nature of the criticism concerning Moses' wife made explicit. Rabbinic sources explain that Moses was censured for separating from his wife after becoming a prophet.[32] A more straightforward interpretation sees this as a criticism of his marriage to a foreigner, but other interpretations exist.[33] Whatever the correct interpretation may be, it is clear that some element related to his wife was the focus of the attack and that in His response God stressed the high esteem in which He holds Moses.

Q 33:69 shares with the biblical account both the attack on Moses and the divine defence that stresses his high rank in God's eyes. As has been noted, the final part of Numbers 12:7, 'he is trusted throughout My household'

[30] In this passage I quote the new Jewish Publication Society translation.

[31] For some exegetical approaches, see Kugel, *Traditions of the Bible*, 778–9. See also Joseph T. Lienhard, ed., *Ancient Christian Commentary on Scripture: Old Testament III Exodus, Leviticus, Numbers, Deuteronomy* (Downers Grove: InterVarsity Press, 2001), 220.

[32] For these rabbinic traditions, see e.g. Daniel Boyarin, *Carnal Israel: Reading Sex in Talmudic Culture* (Berkeley: University of California Press, 1993), 159–65, and especially Menahem I. Kahana, *Sifre on Numbers: An Annotated Edition, Part III: A Commentary on Piska'ot 59–106* (Jerusalem: Magnes, 2011), 655–61 and 671–2 (in Hebrew). The tradition that Moses separated from his wife is used by Aphrahat in his polemics against the Jews. See the comparison between Aphrahat and the rabbis on this in Naomi Koltun-Fromm, *Hermeneutics of Holiness: Ancient Jewish and Christian Notions of Sexuality and Religious Community* (Oxford: Oxford University Press, 2010), 175–209.

[33] For an early attestation of the foreigner explanation, see John F. Petruccione and Robert C. Hill, eds and trans., *Theodoret of Cyrus: The Questions on the Octateuch* (Washington, DC: The Catholic University of America Press, 2007), 2:124–5. See also Ceslas van den Eynde, ed. and trans., *Commentaire d'Išoʿdad de Merv sur l'Ancien Testament: II. Exode-Deutéronome*, Corpus Scriptorum Christianorum Orientalium 176, 179, Scriptores Syri 80, 81 (Louvain: Secrétariat du CorpusSCO, 1958), 93–5 (Syriac) and 126–8 (French trans.). For a survey of the exegesis of this verse and a critique of those interpretations which focus on the wife's colour, see David M. Goldenberg, *The Curse of Ham: Race and Slavery in Early Judaism, Christianity, and Islam* (Princeton: Princeton University Press, 2003), 26–9 and 52–9. According to Joseph ibn Kaspi (d.1340), Moses was criticized for marrying a second wife; see Nehama Leibowitz, *Studies in Bamidbar (Numbers)*, translated and adapted by Aryeh Newman (Jerusalem: World Zionist Organization, 1980), 130–3.

finds a parallel at the end of the qur'anic verse, 'and he was well-esteemed in God's sight'.[34]

The suggestion to link Q 33:69 to Numbers 12 may be reinforced by an examination of the verb that describes God's vindication of Moses, *barra'ahu*. The only other instances of *b-r-'* in the second form in the Qur'an are in Q 12:53 ('I do not declare myself innocent') and Q 24:26 ('good women for good men, and good men for good women—these are declared innocent of what they say [about them]'). In both verses the context is sexual: the episode of Joseph and his master's wife, and slander concerning sexual misconduct. This suggests that Q 33:69 too should be understood in a sexual context, that is, in the light of Numbers 12. The link to Numbers 12 may be further supported by examining Q 33:69 in its literary context and by considering a variant version of this verse.

THE IMMEDIATE LITERARY CONTEXT

Support for the link to Numbers 12 was offered by Hartwig Hirschfeld in 1902. Hirschfeld analysed Q 33 after noting that it 'shows some traces of artistic arrangement for which, however, the compilers are alone responsible'.[35] With regard to verse 69 he had the following to say:

> The concluding speech (vv. 69–73) seems to stand in connection with that in which Muhammed reproved those Moslims who had caused annoyance at the wedding feast.[36] Moses also had to bear annoyance, 'but Allah cleared him of what they said'. The Commentators refer this remark to charges brought against Moses by Korah, or other people who suspected Moses of having murdered Aaron. It seems, however, that Muhammed had the incident of Numb. ch. xii. in his mind, because the accusation referred to in this chapter also bears on a woman.[37]

Hirschfeld's contextual argument is a precursor of the growing attention given in the twentieth century to the coherence and structure of the surahs, including the longer ones. Whereas the classical exegetes and modern scholars often treated verses in an atomistic manner, it is now becoming clear that in many

[34] Speyer, *Die biblischen Erzählungen*, 344–5.

[35] Hartwig Hirschfeld, *New Researches into the Composition and Exegesis of the Qoran* (London: Royal Asiatic Society, 1902), 120.

[36] Hirschfeld is referring here to Q 33:53, which is often understood as a reaction to the behaviour of some of the believers at the feast celebrating Muhammad's wedding to Zaynab bint Jaḥsh.

[37] Hirschfeld, *New Researches*, 122. Hirschfeld is alluding to the criticism concerning Muhammad's marriage to Zaynab bint Jaḥsh, the former wife of his adopted son Zayd. I will elaborate on this shortly.

instances surahs display a large measure of coherence, and context may therefore serve as an exegetical tool.[38] Q 33 too has been examined from this angle.[39] More recently, Uri Rubin has noted the link between Q 33:69 and other verses in the surah that exonerate Muhammad of criticism concerning one of his marriages by emphasizing that his behaviour follows the precedent set by his prophetic predecessors.[40] After God tells the Prophet in verse 37 that He gave him Zayd's former wife in marriage 'so that there should not be any fault in the believers, in (marrying) the wives of their adopted sons, when they have accomplished what they would of them', the Qur'an continues:[41]

> (38) There is no fault in the Prophet doing what God has ordained for him–God's practice (*sunnata llāhi*) concerning those who passed away before; and God's commandment is a fixed decree; (39) (those) who delivered the messages of God, and feared Him, and feared not anyone except Him; and God suffices as a reckoner.

In stating that there is no flaw in Muhammad's actions, the Qur'an seems to be reacting to a possible or actual criticism of the Prophet for marrying his daughter-in-law.[42] To exonerate Muhammad the Qur'an adduces the precedent of God's conduct with earlier prophets. The exegetes often understand this as an allusion to the story of David and Bathsheba.[43] But seeing that David

[38] Scholarship on the structure and coherence of the surahs is growing rapidly. For examples of recent maximalist studies, see Raymond Farrin, *Structure and Qur'anic Interpretation: A Study of Symmetry and Coherence in Islam's Holy Text* (Ashland, OR: White Cloud, 2014) and Michel Cuypers, *The Composition of the Qur'an: Rhetorical Analysis*, translated by Jerry Ryan (London: Bloomsbury, 2015). See also the survey and comments in Joseph Witztum, 'The Syriac Milieu of the Quran: The Recasting of Biblical Narratives' (Princeton University dissertation, 2011), 266–9.

[39] See Salwa M. S. El-Awa, *Textual Relations in the Qur'ān: Relevance, Coherence and Structure* (London: Routledge, 2006), 45–100.

[40] Uri Rubin, 'The Seal of the Prophets and the Finality of Prophecy: On the Interpretation of the Qur'ānic Sūrat al-Aḥzāb (33)', *Zeitschrift der Deutschen Morgenländischen Gesellschaft* 164.1 (2014): 65–96, at 72–3. Cf. El-Awa, *Textual Relations*, 98.

[41] For the episode with Zayd's wife, see David S. Powers, *Muhammad Is Not the Father of Any of Your Men: The Making of the Last Prophet* (Philadelphia: University of Pennsylvania Press, 2009), 35–50, and his more recent work, *Zayd* (Philadelphia: University of Pennsylvania Press, 2014), 32–40 and 97–102; and Rubin, 'The Seal of the Prophets', 70.

[42] See Muqātil b. Sulaymān, *Tafsīr*, 'Abd Allāh Maḥmūd Shiḥāta, ed. (Cairo: al-Hay'a al-Miṣriyya al-ʿĀmma li-l-Kitāb, 1979–89), 3:473 and 496, where the Jews and the Munāfiqūn are said to have accused him of hypocrisy: Muhammad married his daughter-in-law, while forbidding this practice to them. Somewhat differently, Bobzin suggests that Q 33:37–40 attempts to refute the Jews' argument that Muhammad committed adultery and could therefore not be a true prophet; Hartmut Bobzin, 'The "Seal of the Prophets": Towards an Understanding of Muhammad's Prophethood', in Angelika Neuwirth et al., eds, *The Qur'ān in Context: Historical and Literary Investigations into the Qur'ānic Milieu*, (Leiden: Brill, 2010), 565–83, at 575–8.

[43] See e.g. Muqātil b. Sulaymān, *Tafsīr*, 3:496–7, and Powers, *Zayd*, 113–14. Other exegetes understand this as a reference to God's allowing David and Solomon to enjoy a great number of wives and concubines; see e.g. al-Zamakhsharī, *al-Kashshāf*, 5:75.

is not mentioned in Q 33, it seems preferable to link this to the explicit reference to Moses in verse 69, as Rubin argues.[44]

The defence of Muhammad's marriage to Zayd's former wife is not the only reference to marital issues in the surah.[45] In fact, Q 33 repeatedly refers to the marital relationships of members of the community (Q 33:4, 49), to the marital relationships of the Prophet and his wives (Q 33:28–34, 50–2, 59), as well as to the proper conduct of the believers towards the Prophet's wives (Q 33:6 and 53–5).[46]

Further support for a contextual reading of verse 69 is found in the repeated use of the verb *ādhā* in other verses in the surah.[47] In verse 53 the believers are warned not to linger in the houses of the prophet since 'that is hurtful to the Prophet (*yu'dhī l-nabiyya*)'. The verse then adds that when asking the Prophet's wives for an object, the believers should do this from behind a curtain and concludes: 'it is not for you to hurt (*an tu'dhū*) God's Messenger, neither to marry his wives after him, ever; surely that would be in God's sight a monstrous thing'. In verse 57 we are told that 'those who hurt (*yu'dhūna*) God and His Messenger' are cursed in this world and in the world to come. In verse 58 we read: 'And those who hurt (*yu'dhūna*) believing men and believing women without that they have earned it have laid upon themselves calumny and manifest sin (*iḥtamalū buhtānan wa-ithman mubīnan*).'[48] Finally, in verse 59 the Prophet is ordered to tell his wives and daughters as well as the wives of the believers to draw their cloaks over themselves in order that they not be hurt (*fa-lā yu'dhayna*). Thus we see that the verb *ādhā* is used in this surah in sexual and marital contexts, especially with regard to harming the Prophet's wives or his relationship with them. The use of the same verb with regard to Moses, as well as the address to the Qur'an's audience not to be like

[44] See Rubin, 'The Seal of the Prophets', 72–3, where Q 33:7 (God's covenant with the prophets, Muhammad, Noah, Abraham, Moses, and Jesus) is noted as well.

[45] The surah also contains a lot of references to women. See especially Q 33:35, which, when describing the righteous, lists ten characteristics, mentioning both men and women for each. Thus it reads: 'Indeed, the surrendering men and the surrendering women, and the believing men and the believing women, the obedient men and the obedient women... God has prepared for them forgiveness and a great reward.' For traditions which claimed that this verse was revealed in response to a grievance expressed by women that only men are mentioned in the Qur'an, see e.g. al-Ṭabarī, *Jāmiʿ al-bayān*, 19:110–11.

[46] Note also that the stoning verse which set the punishment for prohibited sexual intercourse was allegedly part of the original version of Q 33; see e.g. John Burton, *The Collection of the Qur'ān* (Cambridge: Cambridge University Press, 1977), 72–86; Hossein Modarressi, 'Early Debates on the Integrity of the Qur'ān: A Brief Survey', *Studia Islamica* 77 (1993): 5–39, at 11–12; Kohlberg and Amir-Moezzi, eds, *Revelation and Falsification*, 200 (notes to tradition §421).

[47] See also verse 48 where a related noun occurs: 'And obey not the unbelievers and the hypocrites; heed not their hurt (*adhāhum*), but put your trust in God; God suffices as a guardian.'

[48] Might this refer to false accusations of sexual misconduct? This is suggested by the context, the reference to men and women, and the vocabulary. Compare with Q 24:11ff where we find both *ithm* (Q 24:11) and *buhtān* (Q 24:16). The latter word appears in the context of false accusations of sexual misconduct in Q 4:156 as well.

those who hurt Moses, clearly draws a parallel between the situation of Muhammad and that of Moses.[49]

All this suggests that the hurting of Moses mentioned in Q 33:69 concerned his marital life;[50] this is indeed the case in Numbers 12.

A VARIANT READING

A striking similarity between Numbers 12 and our verse is to be found if a variant reading attributed to Ibn Masʿūd (d. 652/3) and others is followed. Whereas the standard reading states that Moses 'was well-esteemed in God's sight (*wa-kāna ʿinda llāhi wajīhan*)', Ibn Masʿūd interprets the same consonantal skeleton differently and reads the sentence as follows: 'and he was a servant to God, well-esteemed (*wa-kāna ʿabdan li-llāhi wajīhan*)'.[51] This

[49] The classical exegetes, or at least some of them, did not fail to notice this parallel. See e.g. the Shiʿite tradition of al-Sayyārī cited above as well as the traditions attributed to Ibn ʿAbbās and Ibn Masʿūd in al-Suyūṭī, *al-Durr al-manthūr*, 12:152–3. These traditions did not note the marital connotation of the parallel. The marital and sexual context of the surah might have partially inspired the interpretation mentioned above according to which Moses was accused of having been intimate with a whore.

[50] It should be noted that a contextual examination of the closest parallel to our verse, Q 61:5, leads to a different conclusion. In that verse Moses says: 'O my people, why do you hurt me (*tu'dhūnanī*), though you know I am the Messenger of God to you?' In Q 61 there is no mention of women or marital problems whatsoever. Rather, in Q 61:6 there is mention of the Jews' rejection of Jesus as one who engages in sorcery. This implies that the harm Moses suffered was of a similar nature. Thus we see that Q 33 and Q 61 contain similarly worded, but not identical, verses in very different contexts. What to make of this? I am not sure, though it seems to have implications for the relationship between the two surahs.

[51] Both readings would be written the same way in early manuscripts of the Qur'an which usually lack diacritics and in which the space between characters does not depend on whether they belong to the same word. See e.g. the reconstruction of the lower layer of the palimpsest of Ṣanʿāʾ 1 in Behnam Sadeghi and Mohsen Goudarzi, 'Ṣanʿāʾ 1 and the Origins of the Qurʾān', *Der Islam* 87 (2012): 1–129, at 80, and cf. the manuscripts available online at http://corpuscoranicum.de/handschriften/index/sure/33/vers/69. For Ibn Masʿūd's reading, see e.g. ʿUthmān b. Jinnī, *al-Muḥtasab fī tabyīn wujūh shawādhdh al-qirāʾāt wa-l-īḍāḥ ʿanhā*, ʿAlī al-Najdī Nāṣif et al., eds (Cairo: al-Majlis al-Aʿlā li-l-Shuʾūn al-Islāmiyya, 1966–69), 2:185. Compare this reading to Q 4:172 where it is said that Jesus does not disdain 'to be a servant to God (*an yakūna ʿabdan li-llāhi*)'. This reading is transmitted in a slightly different manner in other sources: 'and the servant of God was well-esteemed (*wa-kāna ʿabdu llāhi wajīhan*)'; compare Q 19:30 and Q 72:19 and see Ibn Khālawayh, *Mukhtaṣar fī shawādhdh al-Qurʾān*, Gotthelf Bergsträsser, ed. (Leipzig: F. A. Brockhaus, 1934), 120, where this reading is cited in the name of al-Aʿmash (d. 765), who often follows the reading of Ibn Masʿūd, Abū Ḥaywa (d. 818), and less certainly Ibn Masʿūd. That these are not two actual readings but rather two interpretations of the written transmission of the same reading seems clear from the fact that no medieval source, as far as I have seen, transmits both versions. Of the two the first seems preferable. See the argument in ʿAbd al-Laṭīf al-Khaṭīb, *Muʿjam al-qirāʾāt* (Damascus: Dār Saʿd al-Dīn, 2002), 7:321–2. Note also that usually it is impossible to tell which version (ʿ*abdan li-llāhi* or ʿ*abdu llāhi*) was intended by the medieval

reading enjoyed some currency until the tenth century when its non-canonical status was definitively determined.[52]

Which reading is better? *ʿinda* or *ʿabdan*?[53] Several authorities consider the 'servant' reading to be inferior since according to it the verse does not clarify in whose eyes was Moses honoured, and thus he is denied the great praise of being honoured by God.[54] Inconclusive in itself, this argument is even weaker when our verse is compared to the other instance of *wajīh* in the Qur'an. In Q 3:45 the angels give Mary the good tidings of Jesus, describing him as 'well-esteemed (*wajīhan*) in this world and the next, and of those brought close'. It is possible then to describe someone as *wajīh* without explicitly noting that this is in God's sight, even though this could very well be the intention.[55]

A stronger argument for the *ʿinda* reading might be the parallel verse noted above, Q 33:53. After dissuading the believers from harming the Prophet and marrying his wives after him, the verse concludes by saying: 'surely that would be in God's sight a monstrous thing (*kāna ʿinda llāhi ʿaẓīman*)'.[56] Though the content is different, the syntactical similarity between the two verses is striking—as long as we follow the *ʿinda* reading. This argument is, however, inconclusive.

One could offer an argument in favour of the *ʿabd* reading in the light of our previous discussion. The reference to Moses as God's servant provides us with yet another link to Numbers 12 where God twice refers to him in this way, using the cognate word *ʿeved*. At the beginning of Numbers 12:7 we read: 'Not so My servant (*ʿavdi*) Moses; he is trusted throughout My household', and

authors. The manner in which the phrase appears in print may merely be a misinterpretation of a scribe or editor.

[52] Ibn Khālawayh (d. 980) testifies that during Ramadan he heard Ibn Shanabūdh (d. 939) read the verse in prayer, pronouncing the disputed word as *ʿabd*; Ibn Khālawayh, *Mukhtaṣar fī shawādhdh al-Qur'ān*, 120. To Ibn Khālawayh's testimony one should add Ibn al-Anbārī's (d. 940) argument against a contemporary who claimed that *ʿinda* in Q 33:69 was a corruption of *ʿabd*; see al-Qurṭubī, *al-Jāmiʿ li-aḥkām al-Qur'ān*, 1:128 and 17:243. Though Ibn al-Anbārī's *Kitāb al-radd ʿalā man khālafa muṣḥaf ʿUthmān* is no longer extant, many passages are preserved in al-Qurṭubī's commentary; see Ghānim Qaddūrī al-Ḥamad, '*Kitāb al-radd ʿalā man khālafa muṣḥaf ʿUthmān l-Ibn al-Anbārī*', *Majallat al-Ḥikma* 9 (1996): 223–40. According to al-Ḥamad, Ibn al-Anbārī's criticism in his book was aimed primarily at Ibn Shanabūdh. I hope to elaborate on this elsewhere.

[53] Similar variants are found in Q 43:19, the first part of which reads according to ʿĀṣim's version: 'And they have made the angels, who are themselves servants (*ʿibādu*) of the Merciful, females.' Other readers are said to have read in that verse *ʿabdu* which would not affect the meaning. Yet others read *ʿinda* instead of *ʿibādu* (compare Q 7:206 and Q 21:19). Accordingly, the verse should be rendered: 'And they have made the angels, who are themselves with (*ʿinda*) the Merciful, females.' For the distribution of these readings, see al-Khaṭīb, *Muʿjam*, 8:357–9. In manuscripts which lack diacritic points, and do not always mark the long *ā* vowels in writing, all three words would look identical.

[54] See e.g. Ibn al-Anbārī in al-Qurṭubī, *al-Jāmiʿ li-aḥkām al-Qur'ān*, 17:243, and Ibn Jinnī, *al-Muḥtasab*, 2:185.

[55] See e.g. al-Ṭabarī, *Jāmiʿ al-bayān*, 5:410.

[56] Compare Q 48:5.

again in the next verse: 'How then did you not shrink from speaking against My servant (*'avdi*), Moses?'[57] The reference to Moses as God's servant in both a variant reading of Q 33:69 and Numbers 12, on the one hand, suggests that this variant is to be preferred, and, on the other hand, fortifies the link between the two passages.

THE PROPHET'S FAMILY LIFE AS REFLECTED IN THE QUR'AN AND LATER TRADITIONS

That the Qur'an alludes to Numbers 12 is not altogether surprising. The story of close relatives criticizing Moses for his marital behaviour and being subsequently rebuked would be of great interest to the Qur'an's audience; after all, the Qur'an seems to be preoccupied with the familial troubles of the Prophet and with false accusations of sexual misconduct. In addition to Q 33 and especially the verses treating the Zayd incident, mention should be made of two other passages, which, though somewhat opaque, clearly reflect the disquiet that afflicted the Prophet's large and complicated household as well as the danger of false accusations. The first passage is Q 66:1–5, which reads as follows:

> (1) O Prophet, why do you forbid that which God has made permissible to you, seeking to please your wives? And God is forgiving, merciful. (2) God has ordained for you the absolution of your oaths. God is your patron and He is the Knowing, the Wise. (3) (Remember) when the Prophet confided to one of his wives a certain matter; and then when she told it (to others) and God disclosed that to him, he made known part of it, and turned aside from part. Then when he told her of it, she said: 'Who told you this?' He replied: 'The Knowing, the Well-informed, told it to me.' (4) If you two repent to God (you will be forgiven), for your hearts certainly strayed;[58] but if you support one another against him, God is his patron, and Gabriel, and the righteous among the believers, and furthermore the angels are his helpers. (5) It is possible that, if he divorces you, his Lord will give him in exchange wives who are better than you, women who have surrendered, believing, obedient, penitent, devout, given to fasting, who have been married and virgins too.

[57] Note that the Jewish Targums, the Samaritan translation, and the Peshitta all use the Aramaic cognate *'abdā* in these verses so that the Qur'an may be echoing an Aramaic version of Numbers 12 rather than the original Hebrew. It should be noted that Moses is referred to as God's servant in other biblical passages as well.

[58] The sentence is difficult. Richard Bell translates it differently: 'If ye two repent towards Allah, then your hearts are well inclined'; Richard Bell, *The Qur'ān: Translated, with a Critical Re-arrangement of the Surahs* (Edinburgh: T & T Clark, 1937–39), 2:590.

The other passage is Q 24:11ff, which I will refrain from citing on account of its length. Suffice it to say that it speaks of a group who spread 'the slander' (Q 24:11), which was not rejected by the believers (Q 24:12). The Qur'an engages in polemics against this slander, which remains vague, asking: 'Why did they not bring four witnesses concerning it?' (Q 24:13), and 'Why, when you heard it, did you not say: "It is not for us to speak about this; glory be to You! This is a mighty calumny"?' (Q 24:16). That the said slander concerns sexual misconduct is clear from the context; consider, for example, Q 24:23, which states that 'Surely those who slander women who are chaste, innocent, and believing, shall be cursed in the present world and the world to come; and there awaits them a mighty chastisement.'[59]

When we turn to non-qur'anic Islamic traditions we find elaborate stories about accusations of adultery levelled at the Prophet's women as well as other criticism aimed at them, often by their rivals, the other wives of the Prophet.[60] Thus Q 24:11ff is usually understood as referring to the adultery accusation against ʿĀ'isha.[61] Likewise there are those who think Q 33:58 refers to this incident.[62] An accusation of a similar nature was made against one of the Prophet's concubines, Māriya the Copt.[63] According to the tenth-century Shiʿite exegete ʿAlī b. Ibrāhīm al-Qummī, the Shiʿites believe that Q 24:11ff refers to this slander, which was spread by ʿĀ'isha.[64]

Māriya was also said to have been the object of Ḥafṣa's jealousy. This supposedly caused the Prophet to take an oath to abstain from sexual intimacy with Māriya and set in motion the events hinted at in Q 66:1–5.[65] Jealousy between the Prophet's wives is a motif we find elsewhere. Of special interest is the tradition adduced in the name of Ibn ʿAbbās in the context of Q 49:11 ('neither let women scoff at women who may be better than themselves... neither revile one another by nicknames'). According to this tradition, when Ṣafiyya bint Ḥuyayy b. Akhṭab complained to the Prophet that other wives addressed her as a Jewess, the daughter of two Jews, the Prophet said that her answer should be: 'Indeed my father is Aaron, my uncle is Moses, and my husband is Muhammad.'[66] It is in the light of this that one should understand

[59] See also Q 24:4 and 6.

[60] For a useful collection of traditions, see Muḥammad b. Sulaymān b. Ṣāliḥ al-Rubaysh, *Ummahāt al-mu'minīna fī al-sunna al-nabawiyya* (Beirut: Dār Ibn Ḥazm, 2010).

[61] See e.g. W. Montgomery Watt, "Ā'isha bint Abī Bakr', *EI*², 1:307–8, and D. A. Spellberg, *Politics, Gender, and the Islamic Past: The Legacy of ʿA'isha bint Abi Bakr* (New York: Columbia University Press, 1994), 61–74.

[62] See al-Thaʿlabī, *al-Kashf wa-l-bayān*, 21:560.

[63] See al-Rubaysh, *Ummahāt al-mu'minīna*, 134–6.

[64] See Spellberg, *Politics, Gender, and the Islamic Past*, 80–4, and Meir M. Bar-Asher, *Scripture and Exegesis in Early Imāmī Shiism* (Leiden: Brill, 1999), 42–3.

[65] See F. Buhl, 'Māriya', *EI*², 6:575.

[66] See e.g. al-Qurṭubī, *al-Jāmiʿ li-aḥkām al-Qur'ān*, 19:388. See also Muḥammad b. ʿĪsā al-Tirmidhī, *al-Jāmiʿ al-ṣaḥīḥ wa-huwa Sunan al-Tirmidhī*, Aḥmad Muḥammad Shākir et al.,

Ibn ʿAbbās' identification of those who hurt the Messenger in Q 33:57 with those who criticized him for marrying Ṣafiyya.[67] Though Ibn ʿAbbās does not elaborate it seems likely that the criticism was based on her Jewish descent.

Naturally, one cannot be sure that all these incidents are indeed alluded to in the Qur'an or that they indeed took place as reported. They do, however, present an atmosphere that seems to be reflected in the Qur'an. It is in the light of this atmosphere, and especially the event with Zayd's wife, which is mentioned explicitly in Q 33, that we should understand the comparison between Moses and Muhammad in Q 33:69.

CONCLUSION

In this chapter I have attempted to offer further support for the link between Q 33:69 and Numbers 12, while integrating different approaches to the study of the Qur'an. The larger context of Q 33, as well as a variant reading of verse 69, both support the interpretation of the verse as referring to the criticism directed at Moses' marriage in Numbers 12. This interpretation of this verse as drawing a parallel between the familial problems common to Moses and Muhammad fits well with what we know of the Prophet's family life from the Qur'an and later Islamic traditions. Though the evidence adduced from post-qur'anic reports concerning the Prophet's domestic life necessarily carries less weight, it too sheds light on the Prophet's familial disharmony, which seems to have troubled the Qur'an and its audience. If this study is in any way indicative, qur'anic scholarship stands to benefit from combining lower criticism, contextual readings, attention to pre-Islamic lore, and a consideration of what we know, or at least think we know, of the Prophet's life.

BIBLIOGRAPHY

Ambros, Arne A. with Stephan Procházka. *A Concise Dictionary of Koranic Arabic.* Wiesbaden: Reichert, 2004.

Arberry, Arthur J. *The Koran Interpreted.* London: Allen & Unwin, 1955.

Awa, Salwa M. S. El. *Textual Relations in the Qur'ān: Relevence, Coherence and Structure.* London: Routledge, 2006.

eds (Cairo: Muṣṭafā al-Bābī al-Ḥalabī, 1937–), 5:708; V. Vacca and Ruth Roded, 'Ṣafiyya', *EI*², 8:817; and the sources collected in al-Rubaysh, *Ummahāt al-mu'minīna*, 594–5 and 600–1.

[67] Al-Ṭabarī, *Jāmiʿ al-bayān*, 19:178–9.

Bar-Asher, Meir M. *Scripture and Exegesis in Early Imāmī Shiism*. Leiden: Brill, 1999.
Bar-Asher, Meir M. 'La place du judaïsme et des Juifs dans le shīʿisme duodécimain'. In Mohammad Ali Amir-Moezzi, ed., *Islam: identité et altérité: hommage à Guy Monnot, o.p.* Turnhout: Brepols, 2013, 57–82.
Bell, Richard. *The Qur'ān: Translated, with a Critical Re-arrangement of the Surahs*. Edinburgh: T & T Clark, 1937–39.
Bobzin, Hartmut. 'The "Seal of the Prophets": Towards an Understanding of Muhammad's Prophethood'. In Angelika Neuwirth et al., eds, *The Qur'ān in Context: Historical and Literary Investigations into the Qur'ānic Milieu*. Leiden: Brill, 2010, 565–83.
Boyarin, Daniel. *Carnal Israel: Reading Sex in Talmudic Culture*. Berkeley: University of California Press, 1993.
Brinner, William M., trans. *'Arā'is al-Majālis fī Qiṣaṣ al-Anbiyā' or 'Lives of The Prophets'*. Leiden: Brill, 2002.
Buhl, F. 'Māriya'. *EI²*, 6:575, 1991.
Burton, John. *The Collection of the Qur'ān*. Cambridge: Cambridge University Press, 1977.
Cuypers, Michel. *The Composition of the Qur'an: Rhetorical Analysis*, translated by Jerry Ryan. London: Bloomsbury, 2015.
Droge, Arthur J. *The Qur'ān: A New Annotated Translation*. Sheffield: Equinox, 2013.
EI². *The Encyclopaedia of Islam: New Edition*. P. J. Bearman et al. (eds). Leiden: Brill, 1960–2009.
Farrin, Raymond. *Structure and Qur'anic Interpretation: A Study of Symmetry and Coherence in Islam's Holy Text*. Ashland, OR: White Cloud, 2014.
Feldman, Louis H. *Josephus's Interpretation of the Bible*. Berkeley: University of California Press, 1998.
Fraade, Steven D. 'Moses at Meribah: Speech, Scepter and Sanctification'. *Orim: A Jewish Journal at Yale* 2.1 (1986): 43–67.
Geiger, Abraham. *Was hat Mohammed aus dem Judenthume aufgenommen?*. Leipzig: W. M. Kaufmann, 1902. English translation: *Judaism and Islam*, translated by F. M. Young. New York: Ktav, 1970.
Ginzberg, Louis. *The Legends of the Jews*. Philadelphia: Jewish Publication Society, 1909–38.
Ginzberg, Louis. *On Jewish Law and Lore*. Philadelphia: Jewish Publication Society, 1955.
Goldenberg, David M. *The Curse of Ham: Race and Slavery in Early Judaism, Christianity, and Islam*. Princeton: Princeton University Press, 2003.
Grünbaum, Max. *Neue Beiträge zur semitischen Sagenkunde*. Leiden: Brill, 1893.
Halperin, David J. 'The Hidden Made Manifest: Muslim Traditions and the "Latent Content" of Biblical and Rabbinic Stories'. In D. P. Wright et al., eds, *Pomegranates and Golden Bells: Studies in Biblical, Jewish, and Near Eastern Ritual, Law, and Literature in Honor of Jacob Milgrom*. Winona Lake: Eisenbrauns, 1995, 581–94.
Ḥamad, Ghānim Qaddūrī al-. *'Kitāb al-radd ʿalā man khālafa muṣḥaf ʿUthmān l-Ibn al-Anbārī'*. *Majallat al-Ḥikma* 9 (1996): 223–40.
Hammer, Reuven, trans. 1986. *Sifre: A Tannaitic Commentary on the Book of Deuteronomy*. New Haven: Yale University Press, 1986.
Hata, Gohei. 'The Story of Moses Interpreted within the Context of Anti-Semitism'. In Louis H. Feldman and Gohei Hata, eds, *Josephus, Judaism, and Christianity*, Detroit: Wayne State University Press, 1987, 180–97.

Heinemann, Joseph. *Aggadah and its Development*. Jerusalem: Keter, 1974 (in Hebrew).
Heller, Bernhard. 'Muhammedanisches und Antimuhammedanisches in den Pirke Rabbi Eliezer'. *Monatsschrift für Geschichte und Wissenschaft des Judentums* 69 (1925): 47–54.
Hirschfeld, Hartwig. *New Researches into the Composition and Exegesis of the Qoran*. London: Royal Asiatic Society, 1902.
Ibn al-Jawzī, Abū al-Faraj ʿAbd al-Raḥmān b. ʿAlī. *Zād al-masīr fī ʿilm al-tafsīr*. Beirut: Dār al-Kutub al-ʿIlmiyya, 2002.
Ibn Jinnī, ʿUthmān. *Al-Muḥtasab fī tabyīn wujūh shawādhdh al-qirāʾāt wa-l-īḍāḥ ʿanhā*. ʿAlī al-Najdī Nāṣif et al., eds. Cairo: al-Majlis al-Aʿlā li-l-Shuʾūn al-Islāmiyya, 1966–9.
Ibn Khālawayh. *Mukhtaṣar fī shawādhdh al-Qurʾān*, Gotthelf Bergsträsser, ed. Leipzig: F. A. Brockhaus, 1934.
Kahana, Menahem I. *Sifre on Numbers: An Annotated Edition, Part III: A Commentary on Piska'ot 59–106*. Jerusalem: Magnes, 2011 (in Hebrew).
Katsh, Abraham I. *Judaism in Islām: Biblical and Talmudic Backgrounds of the Koran and its Commentaries*. New York: New York University Press, 1954.
Khaṭīb, ʿAbd al-Laṭīf al-. *Muʿjam al-qirāʾāt*. Damascus: Dār Saʿd al-Dīn, 2002.
Khoury, Raif Georges. *Les légendes prophétiques dans l'Islam depuis le Ier jusqu'au IIIe siècle de l'Hégire*. Wiesbaden: Harrassowitz, 1978.
Kohlberg, Etan and Mohammad Ali Amir-Moezzi, eds. *Revelation and Falsification: The* Kitāb al-qirāʾāt *of Aḥmad b. Muḥammad al-Sayyārī*. Leiden: Brill, 2009.
Koltun-Fromm, Naomi. *Hermeneutics of Holiness: Ancient Jewish and Christian Notions of Sexuality and Religious Community*. Oxford: Oxford University Press, 2010.
Kugel, James L. *Traditions of the Bible: A Guide to the Bible as It Was at the Start of the Common Era*. Cambridge, MA: Harvard University Press, 1998.
Leibowitz, Nehama. *Studies in Bamidbar (Numbers)*, translated and adapted by Aryeh Newman. Jerusalem: World Zionist Organization, 1980.
Lienhard, Joseph T., ed. *Ancient Christian Commentary on Scripture: Old Testament III Exodus, Leviticus, Numbers, Deuteronomy*. Downers Grove: InterVarsity Press, 2001.
Lim, Johnson Teng Kok. *The Sin of Moses and the Staff of God: A Narrative Approach*. Assen: Van Gorcum, 1997.
Maghen, Ze'ev. *After Hardship Cometh Ease: The Jews as Backdrop for Muslim Moderation*. Berlin: de Gruyter, 2006.
Majlisī, Muḥammad Bāqir al-. *Biḥār al-anwār*. Tehran: Dār al-Kutub al-Islāmiyya, 1956–74.
Mann, Jacob and Isaiah Sonne. *The Bible as Read and Preached in the Old Synagogue*, Vol. 2. Cincinnati: Mann-Sonne Publication Committee, 1966.
Māwardī, ʿAlī b. Muḥammad al-. *Al-Nukat wa-l-ʿuyūn: Tafsīr al-Māwardī*. Beirut: Dār al-Kutub al-ʿIlmiyya, 1992.
Miskinzoda, G. 'The Significance of the *ḥadīth* of the Position of Aaron for the Formulation of the Shīʿī Doctrine of Authority'. *Bulletin of the School of Oriental and African Studies* 78 (2015): 67–82.
Modarressi, Hossein. 'Early Debates on the Integrity of the Qurʾān: A Brief Survey'. *Studia Islamica* 77 (1993): 5–39.

Muqātil b. Sulaymān. *Tafsīr*, ʿAbd Allāh Maḥmūd Shiḥāta, ed. Cairo: al-Hayʾa al-Miṣriyya al-ʿĀmma li-l-Kitāb, 1979–89.

Paret, Rudi. *Der Koran: Kommentar und Konkordanz*. Stuttgart: Kohlhammer, 1980.

Petruccione, John F. and Robert C. Hill, eds and trans. *Theodoret of Cyrus: The Questions on the Octateuch*. Washington, DC: The Catholic University of America Press, 2007.

Powers, David S. *Muhammad Is Not the Father of Any of Your Men: The Making of the Last Prophet*. Philadelphia: University of Pennsylvania Press, 2009.

Powers, David S. *Zayd*. Philadelphia: University of Pennsylvania Press, 2014.

Qurṭubī, Muḥammad b. Aḥmad al-. *Al-Jāmiʿ li-aḥkām al-Qurʾān*, ʿAbd Allāh al-Turkī, ed. Beirut: Muʾassasat al-Risāla, 2006.

Rāzī, Fakhr al-Dīn al-. *Al-Tafsīr al-kabīr aw Mafātīḥ al-ghayb*. Beirut: Dār al-Kutub al-ʿIlmiyya, 1990.

Rubaysh, Muḥammad b. Sulaymān b. Ṣāliḥ al-. *Ummahāt al-muʾminīna fī al-sunna al-nabawiyya*. Beirut: Dār Ibn Ḥazm, 2010.

Rubin, Uri. 'The Seal of the Prophets and the Finality of Prophecy: On the Interpretation of the Qurʾānic Sūrat al-Aḥzāb (33)'. *Zeitschrift der Deutschen Morgenländischen Gesellschaft* 164.1 (2014): 65–96.

Sadeghi, Behnam and Mohsen Goudarzi. 'Ṣanʿāʾ 1 and the Origins of the Qurʾān'. *Der Islam* 87 (2012): 1–129.

Schwarzbaum, Haim. 'Jewish, Christian, Moslem and Falasha Legends of the Death of Aaron, The High Priest'. *Fabula* 5 (1962): 185–227.

Schwarzbaum, Haim. *Biblical and Extra-Biblical Legends in Islamic Folk-Literature*. Walldorf-Hessen: Verlag für Orientkunde, 1982.

Spellberg, D. A. *Politics, Gender, and the Islamic Past: The Legacy of ʿAʾisha bint Abi Bakr*. New York: Columbia University Press, 1994.

Speyer, Heinrich. *Die biblischen Erzählungen im Qoran*. Gräfenhainichen: Schulze, 1931.

Suyūṭī, Jalāl al-Dīn al-. *Al-Durr al-manthūr fī al-tafsīr bi-l-maʾthūr*, ʿAbd Allāh al-Turkī, ed. Cairo: Markaz Hajar, 2003.

Ṭabarī, Muḥammad b. Jarīr al-. *Tafsīr al-Ṭabarī: Jāmiʿ al-bayān ʿan taʾwīl āy al-Qurʾān*, ʿAbd Allāh al-Turkī, ed. Cairo: Hajar, 2001.

Ṭabrisī, al-Faḍl b. al-Ḥasan al-. *Majmaʿ al-bayān fī tafsīr al-Qurʾān*, Ibrāhīm Shams al-Dīn, ed. Beirut: Dār al-Kutub al-ʿIlmiyya, 1997.

Thaʿlabī, Abū Isḥāq Aḥmad al-. *Al-Kashf wa-l-bayān ʿan tafsīr al-Qurʾān*, Ṣalāḥ Bāʿuthmān et al., eds. Jeddah: Dār al-Tafsīr, 2015.

Tirmidhī, Muḥammad b. ʿĪsā al-. *Al-Jāmiʿ al-ṣaḥīḥ wa-huwa Sunan al-Tirmidhī*, Aḥmad Muḥammad Shākir et al., eds. Cairo: Muṣṭafā al-Bābī al-Ḥalabī, 1937–.

Tottoli, Roberto. *Biblical Prophets in the Qurʾān and Muslim Literature*. London: Routledge, 2002.

Urbach, Ephraim E, ed. *Sefer Pitron Torah*. Jerusalem: Magnes, 1978.

Vacca, V. and Ruth Roded. 'Ṣafiyya'. *EI*^{2}, 8:817, 1995.

Van den Eynde, Ceslas, ed. and trans. *Commentaire d'Išoʿdad de Merv sur l'ancien testament*, Corpus Scriptorum Christianorum Orientalium 176, 179, Scriptores Syri 80, 81. Louvain: Secrétariat du Corpus SCO, 1958.

Wahl, Samuel Friedrich Günther. *Der Koran oder das Gesetz der Moslemen durch Muhammed den Sohn Abdallahs*. Halle: Gebauer, 1828.

Watt, William Montgomery. "Ā'isha bint Abī Bakr'. *EI²*, 1:307–8, 1960.
Watt, William Montgomery. *Companion to the Qur'ān*. Oxford: Oneworld, 1994.
Witztum, Joseph. 'The Syriac Milieu of the Quran: The Recasting of Biblical Narratives'. Princeton University dissertation, 2011.
Zamakhsharī, Maḥmūd b. ʿUmar al-. *Al-Kashshāf ʿan ḥaqāʾiq ghawāmiḍ al-tanzīl wa-ʿuyūn al-aqāwīl fī wujūh al-taʾwīl*, ʿĀdil Aḥmad ʿAbd al-Mawjūd and ʿAlī Muḥammad Muʿawwaḍ, eds. Riyadh: Maktabat al-ʿUbaykān, 1998.

4

Pagan Arabs as God-fearers

Patricia Crone

The pagan Arabs to whom this chapter is devoted are those of the Qurʾan, more specifically the unbelievers who the Qurʾan informs us were the Messenger's own people (Q 62:2, cf. 2:151; 3:164, and implicitly elsewhere).[1] They represent the community in which he must be presumed to have grown up and from which he had broken away by the time we meet them in the Qurʾan, so they give us a glimpse of the milieu in which he had been formed, or at least in which he operated. What kind of milieu was it, then?

That is a big question and I shall only deal with it in terms of religion. Before I try to do so, however, I should explain that we only know the beliefs and practices of the Messenger's opponents from his own polemical statements about them, and that this evidently poses the question how far we can infer what they actually said or did from his account of them. There are certainly times when he is exaggerating, running several positions together, or expressing himself so obscurely that one can only guess at what he meant (a recurrent problem throughout the Qurʾan). Unlike most polemicists, however, he was not working at a safe distance from his opponents, but rather preaching to them face to face, hoping to convert them. This obviously placed a limit on the amount of distortion he could engage in if he was to have hope of gaining a hearing. His statements are often aggressive, but they are also coherent and accord well with what we know about religious patterns in the pre-Islamic Near East. In short, the Messenger does seem to give us enough genuine information about his opponents for us to reconstruct their views and internal divisions, if only in broad outline.

To return to the question of the religious milieu in which the Messenger was active, the answer is that his people were pagans, if only in the minimal sense of being neither Jews nor Christians. They did have at least one genuinely

[1] I should like to thank Angelos Chaniotis and Michael Cook for reading and commenting on an earlier draft of this article.

pagan habit, namely infanticide, a practice abhorred by Jews, Christians, and the Messenger alike; and by the Messenger's standard, they were downright polytheists, or more precisely 'associationists' (*mushrikūn*), meaning that they assigned 'associates' or 'partners' to God.[2] Some of them venerated the sun and moon (Q 27:24; 41:37), a habit also attested for the Arabs of the Syrian desert;[3] and others venerated a number of lesser deities. But they accepted God as the supreme deity whatever else they venerated, and this is presumably why the Messenger called them 'associationists'.

The lesser deities that the Qur'an condemns are indiscriminately referred to as deities and angels; some of them were female, and some or all were of pagan origin if we trust the names assigned to them in the Qur'an (al-Lāt, Manāt, al-Uzzā, Q 53:19f; Wadd, Suwā', Yaghūth, Ya'ūq, and Nasr, placed in Noah's time, Q 71:23).

The Messenger is outraged by the idea of female angels, and even more by the fact that the pagans credited the angels with divine status and power of their own. In his view, the angels were created beings wholly subordinated to God, so that whatever power they had was His: they had no agency separate from His. But the unbelievers saw them as sons and daughters of God (e.g. Q 6:100; 16:57; 37:149, 153; 43:16), or in other words as partaking of His essence, and also as capable of influencing Him, much as the Christians saw Christ. He too was both part of God and a separate person capable of influencing God, by serving as an intermediary to whom one would, or indeed should, address all prayers and petitions to God according to Origen (d. 253 or 4).[4] In the centuries before and after the beginning of the Christian era the dividing line between God and angels was also indistinct in the thought of Jews, Christians and pagans of the Greco-Roman world alike. The 'sons of God' who figure in the Hebrew Bible had come to be understood as angels already in the Hellenistic period, as seen in the Septuagint; and by the second and third centuries philosophically inclined pagans also identified their pagan deities as angels and sons of God (i.e. the supreme pagan deity), claiming that these beings formed part of God.[5] Some

[2] What follows is based on Patricia Crone, 'The Religion of the Qur'ānic Pagans: God and the Lesser Deities', *Arabica* 57 (2010): 151–200.

[3] 'Doctrina Addai', in Ilaria Ramelli, *Bardaisan of Edessa: A Reassessment of the Evidence and a New Interpretation* (Piscataway, NJ: Gorgias, 2009), 72 (sun and moon); cf. also Cyril of Alexandria on pagans in Phoenicia and Palestine, below (astral bodies).

[4] 'We have to send up every petition, prayer, intercession, and thanksgiving to the supreme God through the high priest of all angels, the living and divine *logos*' (Origen, *Contra Celsum*, IV 4, trans. Henry Chadwick [Cambridge: Cambridge University Press, 1953], 266). But cf. John Anthony McGuckin, ed., *The Westminster Handbook to Origen* (Louisville and London: John Knox Press, 2004), 53, s.v. 'angels', citing his Homily on Leviticus 9:8, where all the angels act as intercessors.

[5] Thus Maximus of Tyre, Oration 11:5; cf. also 39:55; the Oinoanda inscription in S. Mitchell, 'The Cult of Theos Hypsistos between Pagans, Jews, and Christians', in Polymnia Athanassiadi

early Christians accepted the equation of gods and angels as long as it did not amount to a legitimation of angel worship,[6] but most resisted it, and angel worship seems quickly to have been perceived as too great a danger for the angels to retain their divine status.[7] The Jews too stressed that angels should not be worshipped, implying that they were in fact being worshipped, or at least venerated in what the religious authorities felt to be an excessive manner.[8] Both the Jews and the Christians regarded the angels as intercessors who carried prayers and petitions to God, a view well represented in the apocryphal and pseudepigraphic literature;[9] and it was precisely for their intercession that the qur'anic pagans invoked their lesser deities or angels, as they themselves explained.[10] So there was nothing particularly odd about them by the standards of the Near East outside Arabia, except perhaps that they were somewhat out of date; for by the seventh century most Jews and the Christians had come to distinguish sharply between God and the created world. Created beings, whether angels or saints (in the sense of deceased holy people), could still act as intercessors,[11] but they had no power of their own. This was also the Messenger's view, except that he did not operate with the concept of saints.[12]

To a modern scholar, the qur'anic pagans do not really come across as polytheists at all, but rather as monotheists of the inclusive type that casts

and Michael Frede, eds, *Pagan Monotheism in Late Antiquity* (New York: Oxford University Press, 1999), 81–148, at 86.

[6] Cf. Origen, *Contra Celsum*, V 4; Augustine, *City of God*, IX 21.

[7] Scripture forbids angel worship, as Didymus the Blind (d. 398) pointed out. See Erik M. Heen and Philip D.W. Krey, eds, *Ancient Christian Commentary on Scripture: New Testament*, X (*Hebrews*) (Downers Grove, IL: InterVarsity Press, 2005), *ad* Hebrews 1:6.

[8] Cf. Crone, 'Religion of the Qur'ānic Pagans', esp. 194, based on Loren T. Stuckenbruck, *Angel Veneration and Christology: A Study in Early Judaism and in the Christology of the Apocalypse of John* (Tübingen: J. C. B. Mohr, 1995).

[9] Angels bring the prayers of men before God, or simply intercede for them (of their own accord?) in Zechariah 1:12; Tobit 12:12, 15; 1 Enoch, trans. George W. E. Nickelsburg and J. C. VanderKam, *I Enoch: A New Translation Based on the Hermeneia Commentary* (Minneapolis, MN: Fortress, 2004), 9:1–3; 15:2; 39:5; 40:6, 9, and elsewhere. In the Life of Adam and Eve, 9:3 (trans. M. D. Johnson in J. C. Charlesworth, ed., *The Old Testament Pseudepigrapha* (New York: Doubleday, 1983–5, vol. 2, 249–95, at 260), Satan, disguised as an angel, falsely reassures Eve that her repentance has been accepted: 'all we angels have entreated for you and interceded with the Lord'. See also *Encyclopedia Judaica*, Jerusalem 19712, s.v. 'angels'; Theodor Klauser, ed., *Reallexicon für Antike und Christentum: Sachwörtherbuch zur Auseinandersetzung des Christentums mit der antiken Welt* (Stuttgart: Hiersemann Verlag, 1962), 163 (s.v. 'Engel IV'). For the pagans, see the South Arabian example in Crone, 'Religion of the Qur'ānic Pagans', 186f.

[10] For the references, see Crone, 'Religion of the Qur'ānic Pagans', 158f.

[11] See Cyril of Jerusalem, *Lectures on the Christian Sacraments: Procatechesis and five Mystagogical Catecheses*, ed. F. L. Cross, trans. R. W. Church (New York: St. Vladimirs Seminary 1986), Mystagogical Catechesis V (On the Eucharistic Rite), para. 9, on commemorating those who have died before us: the patriarchs, prophets, apostles, and martyrs, 'that at their prayers and interventions God would receive our petition'.

[12] Cf. Crone, 'Religion of the Qur'ānic Pagans', 158–9.

other deities as manifestations, hypostases or aspects of the One, a form of monotheism well known from the ancient world, both pagan and Jewish (and preserved in a limited form in the Christian Trinity), as well as India and elsewhere.[13] But the *mushrikūn* were not pagan monotheists in the normal sense of that word, for they worshipped the same God as the Messenger, Allāh, who was indeed a pagan deity by origin but had come to be identified with the God of the biblical tradition.[14] They also accepted that God sent messengers to mankind, but they expected all such messengers to be angels: one of their gripes against the Messenger was that he was not an angel.[15] Maybe the problem was simply that to their ears he *called* himself an angel, for to them *rasūl* seems to have meant 'messenger' in the sense of angel (*angelos*) rather than apostle (*apostolos*); and they accepted Moses as a prophet, indeed the paradigmatic prophet whose example the Messenger ought to have been able to imitate in their view,[16] though they did not cast Moses as an angel.[17] But there was probably more to this question, for there does seem to have been a tradition in the Syro-Arabian region for regarding religious leaders as angels on earth. Unfortunately, however, the tradition is too poorly attested to help us.[18]

However this may be, the *mushrikūn* were also familiar with the concepts of the resurrection and the day of judgement, and some of them believed in them too, without assigning much importance to them in their lives: they did not think that the end was near. Others doubted or denied the reality of these concepts, sometimes denying that there was any kind of afterlife at all; and a radical fringe denied not just the afterlife, but also God's role as creator, ruler, and judge of this world.[19] But their denial was not pagan. Here is how they spoke: 'There is nothing but our first death. We won't be resurrected' (*in hiya*

[13] For the pagans of the ancient world, including late antiquity (up to the early fifth century), see Athanassiadi and Frede, *Pagan Monotheism*; S. Mitchell and P. van Nuffelen, eds, *One God: Pagan Monotheism in the Roman Empire* (Cambridge: Cambridge University Press, 2010). For one of the many examples in the Pentateuch, see Genesis 18:13, where we are told that the Lord appeared to Abraham: Abraham looked up and saw three men, i.e. angels, whom he addressed as 'my Lord'.

[14] Cf. J. T. Milik, 'Inscriptions grecques et nabatéennes de Rawwafah', *Bulletin of the Institute of Archaeology* 10 (1971): 54–8, at 58.

[15] P. Crone, 'Angels versus Humans as Messengers of God', in Philippa Townsend and Moulie Vidas, eds, *Revelation, Literature, and Community in Late Antiquity* (Tübingen: Mohr Siebeck, 2011), 315–36, at 317f (where the problem is not completely solved).

[16] 'Why hasn't he [the Messenger] been given the like of what Moses was given?' (28:48); cf. also 'We will not believe until you cause a spring to gush forth from the ground' (17:90); and 'Why was the reading (*qurʾān*) not sent down in one go?', where the implicit contrast is probably also with Moses.

[17] Cf. the discussion of 6:91 in Crone, 'Angels versus Humans', 323–7.

[18] Cf. Eusebius, *Historia Ecclesiastica*, VII 30.11: the congregation of Paul of Samosata, the bishop of Antioch who enjoyed the support of the Palmyrene queen Zenobia, claimed that their teacher was 'an angel come down from heaven'.

[19] This and what follows is based on P. Crone, 'The Quranic *Mushrikūn* and the Resurrection, part I', *Bulletin of the School of Oriental and African Studies* 75/3, (2012): 445–72.

illā mawtatunā ʾl-ūlā wa-mā naḥnu bi-munsharīna) (Q 44:35). This is odd: one would expect them to say 'nothing but our first *life*'. The reason that they formulate themselves as they do is that they are denying the second death. This expression does not appear in the Qurʾan, with the result that the exegetes had trouble with it, but it appears in the targums and the Apocalypse of John, and from there it spread to Syriac, Greek, Manichaean, Mandaean, and Ethiopic literature. It always means eternal damnation. For example, Oikoumenios, who wrote around 600 AD, tells us that John speaks 'of the first and the second death. The first one is the physical death that separates the soul and the body; the second death is spiritual death, resulting from sin'. Or, as a Christian martyr tells the Zoroastrian authorities, 'We are dying for the name of Jesus our Saviour, so that we may be delivered from the second death, which lasts for ever.'[20] So what the radical *mushrikūn* are saying when they claim that there is only the first death is that there is no eternal damnation; there is no hell, because there is no afterlife at all. Their radical views notwithstanding, the pagans were speaking the same theological language as all the other Near Eastern communities based on, or heavily influenced by, the biblical tradition.

The same is true when the pagans are quoted as saying, 'There is nothing but our life down here. We die and we live, we will not be resurrected' (Q 23:37) or 'There is nothing but our life down here. We die and we live. Nothing but time (*al-dahr*) destroys us' (Q 45:24). Here it is the word order that is odd: why do they say that 'we die and we live' rather than the other way round? The answer is that they are paraphrasing a famous biblical passage: 'I, even I, am He; there is no god besides me. I kill/make dead (*ʾmyt*) and I make alive (*ʾḥyh*)...' (Deuteronomy 32:39). It is echoed in two other biblical passages: 'The Lord kills (*mmyt*) and brings to life (*mḥyh*)' (1 Samuel 2:6), and 'Am I God to kill and make alive (*lhmyt wlhḥywt*)?' (2 Kings 5:7). Speaking of God's life-giving and life-destroying powers in inverted order had apparently become standard. This proved useful when the rabbis began to look for proofs of the resurrection in the Pentateuch: it now seemed self-evident that God was talking about death and the resurrection. Jewish opponents of the idea of resurrection countered this interpretation by construing God as saying that He would kill one person and give life to another, but the rabbis responded that the continuation 'I wound and I heal' proved God to be talking about one and the same person. The Muslim exegetes claim that when the *mushrikūn* used the inverted word order, they also meant that God killed some and gave life to others, but it is not clear whether they actually remember this to be the case or had worked it out for themselves trying to figure out what the *mushrikūn* could have meant, perhaps assisted by familiarity with the Jewish debate. In any case, it is clear that the *mushrikūn* were using the

[20] Sebastian Brock, 'Jewish Traditions in Syriac Sources', *Journal of Jewish Studies* 30 (1979): 212–32, at 220f.

Deuteronomic word order in polemics against the same interpretation of the Deuteronomic passage as the Jewish deniers of the resurrection, in proof of an even more radical point: it was not just that God did not resurrect people; He did not even cause them to die in the first place, only time did.

The inverted word order appears in several other passages and was used by the Messenger himself too, but for the most part he preferred to correct it. He also spoke of the 'first death' himself, if only once (or twice), but for the rest he opted for other expressions.[21] In both cases one would assume him to have started by sharing the vocabulary of his opponents, to devise his own formulations thereafter, so that it is mostly when he cites his opponents that the biblical origin of the vocabulary is clear.

Finally, it is a striking fact that the Messenger expects his audience to recognize the biblical stories to which he refers or alludes and which he sometimes retells. This has often been noted, and the implication is that the audience knew this material before it was exposed to the Messenger's preaching. In short, pagans though the unbelievers were, they were saturated with thought of biblical origin. How is that to be explained? In the old days this problem was largely ignored, for the study of the Qurʾan was narrowly focused on the Messenger rather than his audience and the assumption was that he had acquired familiarity with the biblical or para-biblical material during his trading journeys in Syria and/or by picking up information from holy men, ascetics, and (or including) his *ʿajamī* informant (Q 16:103); and he then passed on his knowledge to his fellow-tribesmen. That the latter could have picked up such knowledge themselves during their trading journeys was not denied, but there does not seem to have been any interest in the question. However, it evidently was not from the Messenger that his opponents knew the biblical tradition, for not only does he take it for granted that they knew it, their own understanding of it also differed from his.

A more plausible answer is that the *mushrikūn* had absorbed their knowledge from the Israelites in their locality. This solution is rarely considered because it seems to be taken for granted that there were no Israelites in the Messenger's hometown, only in Yathrib, but this is not correct. 'This reading/recitation (*qurʾān*) tells the sons of Israel most of what they are disagreeing about', a Meccan surah says (27:76), leaving no doubt that the Messenger was preaching to Israelites no less than to Arabs well before he went to Yathrib.[22] Of course, one can strike out all the references to Israelites in the Meccan surahs on the premise that the Messenger simply cannot have encountered them before he came to Yathrib, but there is too much to remove for this to carry conviction. I proceed on the assumption that there were indeed Israelites

[21] Cf. Crone, 'The Qurʾanic *Mushrikūn* and the Resurrection', I, 460, 462.

[22] In addition, the Jews are addressed directly in surah 17:5–8, and believing scriptuaries, including Israelites, are mentioned in several Meccan surahs (discussed below).

in 'Mecca', wherever 'Mecca' was.[23] I should add that the Israelites seem to have included both Jews and Jewish Christians—both unbelieving and believing Jews, as the Christians of late antiquity would say; but though I shall have occasion to refer to them again, their inner divisions are not important here. What does matter here is that the Arabs seem to have related to the Israelites in the same way as did the gentiles known in antiquity as God-fearers.

THE GOD-FEARERS OF ANTIQUITY

'God-fearers' are best known from Greek sources, where they appear under the names of *phoboumenoi, seboumenoi, sebomenoi* [*ton theon*], and *theosebeis*, 'those who fear/respect God'. They are also attested in rabbinic writings under the name of *yirei shamayim*, 'those who fear heaven', and *yirei YHWH* and *yirei elohim*, 'those who fear God'. Of these terms *yirei shamayim* seems always to refer to non-Jews (God-fearers in the sense of interest here), but the same is not true of *yirei YHWH* or *yirei elohim*. They appear in the Hebrew Bible as terms for the Jews themselves to highlight their cultic veneration of God or more simply their piety (similarly *yirei el* in the Qumran texts), but they are sometimes used of gentiles too.[24] The Greek terms were also used of both Jews and gentiles attracted to their ways. The Christians eventually took to calling themselves 'the race of God-fearers' (*to tōn theosebōn genos*), or those who 'fear God' (*theon sebein*) in a new way,[25] but we may ignore them here. Of God-fearers in the sense of pagan gentiles, we learn that they would attend synagogue service and observe some parts of Jewish law, such as the Sabbath or abstention from pork, without becoming formal proselytes. They

[23] The Qur'an describes the town in which the Messenger was active (and which is never named) as an agricultural settlement devoted to the cultivation of grain, grapes, pomegranates, and other fruits, including olives; and surah 6:141 makes it clear that the olives were grown by the 'Meccans' themselves: it mentions all kinds of produce, including olives and pomegranates and adds, 'so eat of their fruits, but pay the dues on them when the harvest is gathered' (*wa-ātū ḥaqqahu yawma ḥasādihi*). One could not have harvested olives in either Mecca or Medina, however, because the winter temperatures there are too high, nor could one have done so in Ṭā'if, except perhaps in unusually cold years (for all this, see P. Crone, 'How Did the Quranic Pagans Make a Living?', *Bulletin of the School of Oriental and African Studies* 68 (2005): 387–99, esp. 391–5; add the Ṭā'if temperature chart now available at Wikipedia, s.v. 'Ṭā'if'). This is only one of several features mentioned in the Qur'an with reference to the Messenger's locality that do not fit Mecca. The settlement must have been located somewhere in northern Arabia, and it must have been a separate place from the Abrahamic sanctuary in the uncultivated valley. Mecca undoubtedly existed and presumably played a role in the rise of Islam as well, but its relationship with the olive-growing settlement is hard to make out.

[24] For all this, see F. Siegert, 'Gottesfürchtige und Sympathisanten', *Journal for the Study of Judaism* 4 (1973): 109–64, at 112.

[25] Cf. Judith M. Lieu, 'The Race of God-Fearers', *Journal of Theological Studies* 46 (1995): 483–501, esp. 488–90, 499.

were not circumcised. This was evidently not only because the operation was painful, but also because it changed a person's identity: a circumcised God-fearer was no longer a member of his native community, but a Jew.[26]

God-fearers in the sense of gentiles attracted to Jewish ways are seemingly first attested under their Greek name of *phoboumenoi*, 'those who fear (the lord/God)', in the Septuagint (*c.* 200 BC) in its translation of 2 Chronicles 5:6: the Hebrew passage speaks of Solomon and all the congregation of Israel; the Greek translation adds 'and the God-fearers (*kai hoi phoboumenoi*) and those of theirs who had gathered together (*kai hoi episynēgmenoi autōn*)'. But exactly how that should be understood is obscure,[27] and we hear nothing of gentile God-fearers thereafter down to the New Testament. The Acts of the Apostles (hereafter Acts) describe Paul as preaching in diaspora synagogues and addressing 'Israelites and God-fearers' (Acts 13:16, 26; 16:14; 17:1–4; 18:7; cf. 10:1ff on the famous God-fearer Cornelius). Paul himself never mentions a synagogue context for his mission, and the Acts are widely regarded as ahistorical; but Paul's reliance on arguments drawn from scripture in his writings to gentiles certainly supports the view that the latter had frequented synagogues and that this was where he found them: in the mid-first century CE the synagogue was the only place where gentiles could acquire the familiarity with scripture that Paul presupposes.[28] It is widely believed that God-fearers played a key role in the early spread of Christianity.[29]

It is not only the Acts that have much to say about God-fearers. Josephus (d. *c.* 100) does too, and they figure in other Greek sources as well.[30] Josephus claims that the Jews throughout the *oikoumenē* and the God-fearers (*sebomenōn ton theon*), even those in Asia and Europe, had long been sending money to the temple;[31] that there was not a single city, whether Greek or barbarian, where the custom of Sabbath rest, fasting, lighting lamps, and many of the

[26] Josephus, *Antiquities*, XX 2, 39: Izates' mother tried to dissuade Izates from having himself circumcised, among other things because 'he would thereby bring about great disaffection among his subjects when they would find out that he was so devoted to rites that were to them strange and foreign, and that they would never bear to be ruled over by a Jew'.

[27] Cf. Siegert, 'Gottesfürchtige und Sympathisanten', 162.

[28] Paula Fredriksen, 'What "Parting of the Ways"? Jews, Gentiles, and the Ancient Mediterranean City', in Adam H. Becker and Annette Yoshiko Reed, eds, *The Ways that Never Parted: Jews and Christians in Late Antiquity and the Early Middle Ages* (Tübingen: Mohr Siebeck, 2003), 35–63, at 51.

[29] Noted by Graham N. Stanton, '"God-Fearers": Neglected Evidence in Justin Martyr's *Dialogue with Trypho*', in his *Studies in Matthew and Early Christianity*, Marcus Bockmuehl and D. Linicum, eds (Tübingen: Mohr Siebeck, 2013), 351–75, at 351.

[30] See Louis H. Feldman, *Jew and Gentile in the Ancient World* (Princeton: Princeton University Press, 1993), ch. 10.

[31] Josephus, *Antiquities*, XIV 7, 2 (110). For the question whether the Jews and the God-fearers are identical or two different groups here, see Siegert, 'Gottesfürchtige und Sympathisanten', 127f.

Jewish food prohibitions had not spread;[32] that the Jews of Antioch were constantly attracting a multitude of Greeks to their religious worship and in some measure (or somehow) making them part of themselves;[33] that with a few exceptions all the wives of the pagans in Damascus had been attracted to the religious worship of the Jews;[34] that Queen Helena of Adiabene and her son Izates were both converted by Jewish merchants;[35] and that Poppaea, the wife of Nero, was a God-fearer (*theosebēs*).[36]

Latin sources also mention God-fearers (*metuentes*). Juvenal, for example, speaks of how a father who is *metuentem sabbata* will be a respecter of the Sabbath and abstain from pork, while his son will worship nothing but heaven and undergo circumcision (i.e. become a full proselyte).[37] Both Horace and Suetonius may also refer to God-fearers, without using any name for them,[38] and a funerary inscription from Pola in Istria describes the mother of the dedicators as fearing (i.e. respecting or observing) the Jewish religion.[39] But other references are uncertain, as *metuens* is also used to describe respect for a pagan god.

There does not seem to have been any procedure for becoming a God-fearer: apparently, one simply declared oneself to be one, or others did so, or no special word was used.[40] The Jews seem not to have anticipated the appearance of God-fearers. Maybe they had inadvertently attracted them by performing many of their religious activities out of doors, singing, dancing, engaging in communal eating, and building *sukkot* in the open, thereby arousing the curiosity of outsiders and drawing them to the synagogues, which were open to anyone interested.[41] Or maybe the appearance of God-fearers was the unforeseen outcome of Jewish attempts at proselytization.[42]

[32] Josephus, *Contra Apion*, II 40 (282).

[33] Josephus, *Jewish War*, VII 3, 3 (45); cf. Siegert, 'Gottesfürchtige und Sympathisanten', 139.

[34] Josephus, *Jewish War*, II 20, 2 (560); cf. Siegert, 'Gottesfürchtige und Sympathisanten', 139n.

[35] Josephus, *Antiquities*, XX 1–4 (17–48).

[36] Josephus, *Antiquities*, XX 11 (195).

[37] Juvenal, Satire XIV 96–106.

[38] Cf. J. Reynolds and R. Tannenbaum, *Jews and God-Fearers at Aphrodisias* (Cambridge: Cambridge University Press, 1987), with reference to Horace, Satire 1.9.68–72 (which is enigmatic), and Suetonius, *Lives*, 'Domitian', 12.2 (which is open to a different interpretation).

[39] Siegert, 'Gottesfürchtige und Sympathisanten', 153.

[40] Thus, for example, Luke 7:5; Philo, 'On the Life of Moses', II 7 (41); Josephus, *Antiquities*, III 9 (217), on the Greeks who 'revere our customs'; and the companions of Trypho, who seem to have been God-fearers (thus Stanton, 'God-Fearers', 354ff).

[41] Fredriksen, 'What "Parting of the Ways"?', 51ff, with G. F. Moore in n. 50 on the openness of synagogues. There were many interested outsiders, from the top of the social scale to its bottom, where magicians used garbled biblical stories and magic Hebrew recipe books.

[42] Cf. Feldman, *Jew and Gentile*, 358. It is often objected that there was no Jewish proselytization at the time, but this rests on the assumption that proselytization is always done by officially sponsored religious specialists. In Judaism, as in Islam (with the exception of Ismailism), however, missionaries in that sense did not normally exist. Rather, laymen would act as informal missionaries, in the sense that they would try to convert any non-believer they

Both mechanisms may well have been at work. Either way, the Jews seem simply to have accommodated the God-fearers when they appeared, presumably because they were a valuable source of income and social and political connections for the community. The result was that the relationship seems largely to have been determined by the God-fearers themselves, and to have varied considerably from place to place. One Julia Severa is mentioned in an inscription as the builder of an edifice, which she must have donated to the Jews of Akmoneia in Asia Minor, for they refurbished it for use as a synagogue and put up the inscription mentioning her.[43] If modern scholars are right, this Julia Severa also served as a priestess of the imperial cult in Nero's time, thus providing us (if the identification is correct) with one out of several examples of God-fearers who retained their ancestral customs even though they were attracted to Judaism too, or at least had an interest in cultivating its practitioners.[44] The inscription does not actually call Julia Severa a God-fearer, but she behaved as one, just as Poppaea did when she obtained a favour for the Jews from Nero, causing Josephus actually to call her pious (*theosebēs*).[45] In any case, there were many women, including many of high rank, among the God-fearers.[46] Their prominence in the material is striking, but entirely in keeping with the part they played in the rise of Christianity[47] and with the role of women in spreading Islam in Europe today. A woman also figures in a story in Deuteronomy Rabba, in which the husband is called a God-fearer and the wife's sympathies are likewise with the Jews;[48] and it is a (Roman) *matrona*

happened to come across after the fashion of the two merchants who converted Helena and Izates to Judaism according to Josephus, *Antiquities*, XX 20.3 (34f), 20.4 (71).

[43] Judith M. Lieu, *Neither Jew nor Greek?: Constructing Early Christianity* (London: T & T Clark, 2002), 39; cf. Ekkehard W. Stegemann and Wolfgang Stegemann, *The Jesus Movement: A Social History of Its First Century* (Minneapolis: Fortress Press, 1999), 257, where Julia Severa is wrongly said to have furnished the synagogue too.

[44] The role of social and political networking is stressed by Lieu, *Neither Jew nor Greek*, 39ff.

[45] Josephus, *Antiquities*, XX 11 (195). She did the Jews a favour on a second occasion too (Josephus, *Vita*, 3 (16)), but this time Josephus does not call her *theosebēs*, perhaps because he was now too aware of her misdeeds. On the question of her Jewish leanings, see most recently T. Grüll and L. Benke, 'A Hebrew/Aramaic Graffito and Poppaea's Alleged Jewish Sympathy', *Journal of Jewish Studies* 62 (2011): 37–55.

[46] Noted by Reynolds and Tannenbaum, *Jews and God-Fearers*, 53; Stegemann and Stegemann, *Jesus Movement*, 257; Siegert, 'Gottesfürchtige und Sympathisanten', 128, 135f; and discussed by Lieu, *Neither Jew nor Greek*, 83ff.

[47] Rodney Stark, *One True God: The Historical Consequences of Monotheism* (Princeton: Princeton University Press, 2001), 71, by a sociologist who has done his historical homework, with further details on the overrepresentation of women in new religious movements in R. Stark and R. Finke, *Acts of Faith: Explaining the Human Side of Religion* (Berkeley and Los Angeles: University of California Press, 2000). Some of Stark's later books on the consequences of monotheism in the West are too crude to work, but his *One True God* is an absorbing read of great interest to historians of new religious movements.

[48] Deuteronomy Rabba 2:24, cited in Stegemann and Stegemann, *Jesus Movement*, 258; discussed in Siegert, 'Gottesfürchtige und Sympathisanten', 110f.

who asks difficult Bible questions of a second-century rabbi, who is by no means unfriendly to her.[49]

There is a related development in the appearance of worshippers of *theos hypsistos*, God the highest. Such worshippers were not always, or even usually, God-fearers, for the highest God was often a pagan deity, usually, but not always, Zeus; even a female deity appears as *thea hypsistē* in two inscriptions.[50] In some cases, however, the highest God was the God of the Jews and His devotees were God-fearers, with or without that term being used.[51] The father of Gregory of Nazianzus (d. 328 or 9), for example, belonged to a sect called Hypsistarians in Cappadocia who worshipped the highest God, the ruler of the cosmos, rejected idols and sacrifices, and observed the Sabbath along with other Jewish customs, but were not circumcised.[52]

The literary evidence for gentile God-fearers (of which there is more than mentioned here) is so ample and consistent that one is surprised to find that there was a time when many regarded them as a literary fiction,[53] or at least denied that the term 'God-fearer' referred to gentiles attracted to Jewish ways. It meant no more than 'pious' or 'devout', it was argued, so that when, for example, the gentile Cornelius is described in Acts 10:2, 22, as devout/righteous and God-fearing (*eusebēs/dikaios kai phoboumenos ton theon*), the reference is to his personal quality of devotion rather than to his status as a synagogue adherent.[54] This is probably true: Luke, the presumed author of the Acts, is not using the expression as a technical term for gentiles attracted to Jewish ways. But the reason he characterizes Cornelius as God-fearing is precisely that he envisages him as revering the Jewish God, praying and giving alms, and being well spoken of by the whole Jewish nation, who presumably knew him from the

[49] R. Gershenzon and E. Slomovic, 'A Second Century Jewish-Gnostic Debate: Rabbi Jose Ben Halafta and the Matrona', *Journal for the Study of Judaism*, 16 (1985): 1–41.

[50] See Mitchell, 'The Cult of Theos Hypsistos'; Mitchell, 'Further Thoughts on the Cult of Theos Hypsistos', in Mitchell and P. van Nuffelen, eds, *One God: Pagan Monotheism in the Roman Empire* (Cambridge: Cambridge University Press, 2010), 167–208, which is probably his clearest statement; for the *thea hypsistē*, see 182; for the God-fearer inscriptions, see p. 91. For an earlier statement see S. Mitchell, 'Wer waren die Gottesfürchtigen?', *Chiron* 28 (1998): 55–64 (drawn to my attention by A. Chaniotis).

[51] S. Mitchell, who assembled the *hypsistos* inscriptions, mostly from Anatolia, regards all varieties of *theos hypsistos* worship as part of a single phenomenon overlapping with that of God-fearers. It is easy to agree if one takes him to mean that there was a general trend towards centralization of the divine realm in late antiquity, mirroring that of the political world, but he means more than that.

[52] Cf. Mitchell, 'The Cult of Theos Hypsistos', 94–6.

[53] A. T. Kraabel, 'The Disappearance of the "God-Fearers"', *Numen* 28 (1981): 113–26, at 117: 'If we only had the synagogue inscriptions as evidence, there would be nothing to suggest that such a thing as a God-fearer had ever existed.' Kraabel is right that some of the literary evidence is exaggerated (Josephus) or shaped by the point the author wishes to make (Juvenal), but one needs a real phenomenon in order to exaggerate or reshape it.

[54] Max Wilcox, 'The "God-Fearers" in Acts—a Reconsideration', *Journal for the Study of the New Testament* 13 (1981): 102–22, at 105.

synagogue (Acts 10:2, 22). It was also objected that the terms *phoboumenoi* or *sebo[u]menoi (ton theon)* do not appear in the synagogue inscriptions (or indeed any inscription), which only speak of *theosebeis*. This was held to undermine the credibility of the literary tradition. When synagogue inscriptions describe *theosebeis* as making donations to synagogues, it was held that they were simply Jews.[55] In 1987, however, Reynolds and Tannenbaum published a long inscription from Aphrodisias in Asia Minor with an admirable survey of the whole God-fearer phenomenon.[56] This inscription has since been shown to consist of two separate parts, of which the longer has been tentatively placed between 311 and 381.[57] This part lists 52 God-fearers (*theosebeis*) and 55 Jews (originally more), clearly as donors, but both the cause to which they contributed and the names of some of the Jews are missing thanks to the loss of the top of the inscription. The second inscription is variously dated to the late fourth or fifth century (or even the sixth, which is hard to believe). It, too, is a donor inscription, and it also mentions God-fearers, though only two, along with sixteen Jews, including three proselytes. Some of the God-fearers were men of high status in gentile society: nine of the 52 mentioned in the long inscription were members of the local city council (*boulē*).[58] (The rest were craftsmen, traders, and workmen.) Most have ordinary gentile names, and those who have Jewish names have fathers with gentile names. By contrast, those who were not God-fearers or proselytes mostly have biblical names. Though the question whether the God-fearers in this or that passage are Jews or gentiles is often disputed, the Aphrodisias inscription leaves no doubt that gentiles attracted to Jewish ways were known as *theosebeis*, at least in some places. The expressions used in the Acts come across as experimental,[59] whereas *theosebēs* (first attested of gentiles in Josephus) seems gradually to have become a technical term for gentile God-fearers in inscriptions and literary texts alike.[60]

The God-fearer phenomenon survived the victory of Christianity, if only on the fringes of the empire.[61] In one of his sermons Cyril of Alexandria (d. 444)

[55] Thus Kraabel, 'Disappearance', 116. This is hard to square with Capitolina, who made a donation to a synagogue in Caria and called herself a God-fearer (*theosebēs*): she was surely a gentile (on her, see for example Stegemann and Stegemann, *Jesus Movement*, 257). But maybe she was still unknown in Kraabel's time.

[56] Reynolds and Tannenbaum, *Jews and God-Fearers*. The Greek text is reproduced with an English translation in Stephen R. Llewelyn et al., eds, *New Documents Illustrating Early Christianity*, IX: *A Review of the Greek Inscriptions and Papyri Published in 1986–87* (Grand Rapids, MI: W.B. Eerdmans, 2002), 73–80.

[57] Thus A. Chaniotis, 'The Jews of Aphrodisias: New Evidence and Old Problems', *Scripta Classica Israelica* 21 (2002): 209–42, at 218, 228f.

[58] Face b, II, lines 34–8.

[59] Cf. Wilcox's characterization of them as Lukanisms ('The "God-Fearers" in Acts', 103f, 118f).

[60] Cf. Cyril of Alexandria and the Venosa inscription (n. 61).

[61] In addition to the examples from the eastern empire which follow, see the inscription from Pola mentioned above, n. 39, which probably dates from the late empire, since that was when the

discusses Jethro, the Midianite priest and father-in-law of Moses who realized that the Lord was greater than all gods (Exod. 18:11). Cyril comments that Jethro worshipped the highest God (*hypsistō theō*), but that he also recognized other gods, such as the earth, sky, and astral bodies (the pattern attested for the pagans in the Qurʾan), and then adds that this has continued to the present day, for there were men in Phoenicia and Palestine who called themselves *theosebeis* and whose worship was not purely according to Jewish custom, nor yet wholly Greek (i.e. pagan); rather it was as if they were darting about and distributing themselves on both sides.[62] Earlier authors had said much the same: the God-fearers do not practise what they learn by studying, but behave in an undecided manner, Epictetus observes;[63] they are 'two-faced' and rush from synagogue to pagan shrine, Commodian, a convert to Christianity (f. *c.* 250), says;[64] and as we have seen, Julia Severa served as priestess to the emperor while at the same time donating a building to the Jews.[65] Maybe genuine indecision did play a role at times, but from a pagan point of view it was perfectly natural to add new cults to one's religious repertoire, and there were many reasons why one might wish to do so. Only Jews and Christians insisted that one had to renounce all of them in favour of just one.

A contemporary of Cyril, Sozomen (d. *c.* 450), also knew of pagan God-fearers, though he did not use that term. He locates them in Arabia, probably somewhere in the Gaza region, and probably on the basis of hearsay. Sozomen, whose Semitic name was Salamanes and who may have known Arabic,[66] tells us that the Saracens descend from Ishmael and that owing to their shared origin with the Hebrews,[67] they practise [in the present tense] circumcision like the Hebrews, abstain from pork, and observe many other customs of the people (*ethnōn*, i.e. the Jews). In so far as they deviate from them, it is because Moses legislated only for those that he led out of Egypt; the Ishmaelites were left to fall under the influence of their neighbours, who corrupted the unwritten

Jews first came to northern Italy (Reynolds and Tannenbaum, *Jews and God-Fearers*, 52); and even more strikingly, the inscription from Venosa in northern Italy in Baruch Lifshitz, 'Les Juifs à Venosa', *Rivista di Filologia e di Istruzione Classica* 90 (1962): 367–71, at 368, where a Latin funerary inscription from the sixth or seventh century describes the deceased youth as *teuseues* (*theosebēs*).

[62] Reynolds and Tannenbaum, *Jews and God-Fearers*, 63, with reference to Cyril, 'De Adoratione et Cultu in Spiritu et Veritate', 3.92.3 (in Migne, *Patrilogia Graeca*, vol. 68, 281).

[63] Epictetus, *Dissertations*, 2.9.19ff, as interpreted by Reynolds and Tannenbaum, *Jews and God-Fearers*, 62.

[64] See Commodian, *Instructions*, I, 24.11–14; I, 37.1, 8, 10; cf. Reynolds and Tannenbaum, *Jews and God-Fearers*, 62f.

[65] Cf. n. 43.

[66] At least he knows that the Saracens are still singing songs about Queen Mavia's round defeat of the Romans. See Sozomen, *Ecclesiastical History*, VI.38.4; ed. and trans. (French) A.-J. Festugière and B. Grillet, *Histoire ecclésiastique* (Paris: Cerf, 2005), 459; Edward Walford, trans., *Ecclesiastical History of Sozomen* (London: Henry G. Bohn, 1855), 308.

[67] Not 'Jews', as Walford has it.

laws given to them by Ishmael, with the result that his descendants came to worship the same false deities (*daimonia*) as their neighbours and eventually forgot what they once knew. Thereafter, however, some of them had dealings with the Jews (*Ioudaiois*) and learned about their true origin from them and so reverted to following Hebrew laws.[68] After this Sozomen goes on to discuss the conversion to Christianity of a chief called Sokomos.

The account does not make perfect sense. It is of the Arabs in general, apparently those of Sozomen's own time, that we are told that they practise circumcision like the Jews, abstain from pork, and observe many other customs of the people (*ethnōn*), that is, the Jews; but it evidently was not the case that all Arabs followed Hebrew or Jewish customs, and besides, Sozomen also tells us that they had forgotten their ancient law and become idolaters. As for the Arabs who learned about their origin from the Jews and reverted to Hebrew law, we are not told anything concrete about the customs they adopted. Sozomen presumably means that they renounced their idolatry (*daimonia*) in favour of monotheism and adopted all the customs that the others had forgotten, meaning circumcision and pork avoidance. But circumcision was an ancient custom once widespread in the western part of the Near East which the Jews and the Arabs simply happened both to have preserved: to outsiders it looked as if the Arabs owed the institution to the Jews, but this was not actually the case. Pork avoidance would be a better example if it were real, but though it may well be that the pre-Islamic Arabs did not eat pork, it will not have been for religious reasons, but simply because pigs did not thrive in desert areas. In short, most of Sozomen's information seems to be no more than inferences of the type made by outsiders.[69] But he does have one piece of information that cannot be explained in those terms: there were Arabs who had learned about their origin from the Jews and responded by adopting Hebrew customs.

Disappointing though the dearth of information is, this is what matters here: there were God-fearers in northern Arabia. Unlike their counterparts in the Greco-Roman world, they were drawn to Israelite religion on the basis of their kinship with the Jews,[70] and one cannot tell whether they frequented synagogues (though it was probably there that their kinship with the Jews had

[68] I am indebted to Emmanuel Papoutsakis for speedy and most helpful answers to questions about the Greek text of this passage.

[69] Another example is his claim that the Ishmaelites stopped calling themselves by that name because of its unflattering nature (Ishmael being the son of a slave girl) and called themselves Saracens instead. In fact, the Arabs never called themselves Saracens, and contrary to what the Greeks often said, the name has nothing to do with Sarah.

[70] Compare the Africans and Amerindians who came to see themselves as Jews, sometimes going so far as to adopt some Jewish law, thanks to Christians casting them as black Jews and/or lost tribes. Cf. Tudor Parfitt, *Black Jews in Africa and the Americas* (Cambridge, MA: Harvard University Press, 2013).

become known to them): what we can tell is that they adopted Israelite customs without going so far as to become proselytes. More precisely, if Sozomen is right, they adopted *Hebrew*, that is, pre-Mosaic, customs, having picked them out as more relevant to descendants of Ishmael than their Jewish equivalents. But the chances are that Sozomen is simply being a good student of Eusebius. It was the latter who introduced the distinction between Hebrews (pre-Mosaic Israelites, of whom he approved) and Jews (the Israelites from Moses onwards, whom he disliked);[71] and the fact that Sozomen was aware of the difference does not imply that the same was true of the Arabs he was writing about.

It has recently been suggested that the monotheist inscriptions of South Arabia also reflect a God-fearer relationship,[72] and I shall argue that it existed in the Messenger's town as well. In fact, one wonders if the God-fearer relationship did not develop wherever Jews and Arabs lived together for extended periods without being disturbed by gentile Christians. We need not postulate any direct carry-over from the Greco-Roman world to Arabia. In so far as there was continuity, it lay in the presence of the same two ingredients, Jews and pagans, in the same place. The word *muttaqūn*, 'fearers' (of God and His law), is common in the Qur'an, here as in antiquity in the sense of pious, but there is nothing to suggest that it is a translation of *theosebeis* or *phoboumenoi/sebo[u]menoi (ton theon)*. Besides, the Christians had aggressively marketed themselves as the real God-fearers by way of competition with the Jews and probably also in the hope of persuading gentile God-fearers that it was with Christianity that they belonged.[73] So even if we should find a term unquestionably meaning God-fearer in pre-Islamic Arabia, it would not necessarily mean that it was being used in the sense of gentiles attracted to Jewish ways who stopped short of conversion. Nor is that of importance here. The key point is that the relationship existed in Arabia.

THE QUR'AN

This then is the explanation proposed here for the fact that the Messenger's pagans were so well informed about the biblical and para-biblical literature:

[71] See his *Praeparatio evangelica* and, for example, Jean Sirinelli, *Les vues historiques d'Eusèbe de Césarée durant la période prénicéenne* (Dakar: Université de Dakar, 1961), 147–63.

[72] I. Gajda, *Le royaume de Ḥimyar à l'époque monothéiste: l'histoire de l'Arabie du sud ancienne de la fin du IVe siècle de l'ère chrétienne jusqu'à l'avènement de l'Islam*, Paris 2009, 244f; also in I. Gajda, 'Quel monothéisme en Arabie du sud ancienne?', in J. Beaucamp, F. Briguel-Chatonnet and C. J. Robin, eds, *Juifs et Chrétiens en Arabie aux Ve et VIe siècles: regards croisés sur les sources* (Paris: Association des amis du Centre d'histoire et civilisation de Byzance, 2010), 107–17, at 116; and Gajda, 'Remarks on Monotheism in Ancient South Arabia', in this volume.

[73] Cf. Lieu, 'The Race of the God-Fearers', 488. Lieu only mentions competition with the Jews.

Like Sozomen's Arabs, they knew that they were related to the Jews, presumably because the Jews had told them;[74] and like the God-fearers addressed by Paul (and perhaps those of Sozomen too), they must have acquired their learning by attending synagogue services. This presupposes that there were synagogues in the Messenger's locality, wherever it was;[75] and so indeed there must have been if Israelites lived there, but we have no textual (let alone archaeological) proof. Synagogues are only mentioned once in the Qurʾan (22:40: *ṣalawāt*, a translation of Greek *proseuchai*), and the reference is general, without any indication of where they might be found.

What then can be said to clinch the God-fearer hypothesis? As mentioned already, there is good evidence that the pagans had acquired Jewish (including Jewish Christian) beliefs, above all belief in the God of the biblical tradition, in prophets such as Abraham and Moses, and, in the case of some of them, the resurrection, day of judgement, and eternal afterlife in paradise or hell. But there does not seem to be any evidence that they had adopted Jewish (or Hebrew) customs. The Messenger does not castigate them for Sabbath observance, for example, though he inveighs against it in his anti-Jewish polemics.[76] And it is he himself who prescribes food laws indebted to the Apostolic Decree, which settled the minimum requirements for gentile converts to Christianity,[77] just as it is he who attaches great importance to prayer and charity, as did many God-fearers in antiquity.[78] 'Observing the prayer and paying *zakāt*' (*aqāma 'l-ṣalāta wa-āta 'l-zakāta*) is a fixed expression in the Qurʾan, where it recurs time and again, and next to monotheism, it is what singles out a believer.[79] Are we to see residues of the Messenger's days

[74] Sebeos (attrib.) (writing *c.* 660?), *Histoire d'Héraclius*, trans. F. Macler (Paris: Imprimerie Nationale, 1904), 95; trans. Robert W. Thomson with historical commentary by James H. Howard-Johnston and assistance from Tim Greenwood, *The Armenian History Attributed to Sebeos* (Liverpool: Liverpool University Press, 1999), I, 95, explicitly says that when the Jews came to Arabia, they informed the Ishmaelites of their kinship with them, which the latter accepted, though their different cults were a problem until Muḥammad united them. But the Arabs to whom the Messenger preached must have learned their Biblical genealogy well before this.

[75] Cf. n. 23.

[76] Thus the Medinese surahs 2:65; 4:47, 154, all alluding to the story told in the Meccan 7:163, where the Sabbath-violating fishermen are not identified as Israelites, however.

[77] See esp. 5:3; cf. also 2:173; 6:118–21, 145; compare Acts 15.

[78] The best known example is Cornelius (Acts 10:2).

[79] It is part of the definition of a believer in surah 8:2: 'The believers are those whose hearts are filled with fear when they hear Him mentioned . . . and who observe the prayer, and spend out of that which God has provided them with' (8:2–3). There is also a striking example in surah 9, where God and the Messenger are declared to be quit of the *mushrikūn* (verse 1), so that when the holy months are over, the believers should fight them, seize them, besiege them and lie in wait for them; but if the *mushrikūn* repent, observe the prayer and give *zakāt*, then they should be set free (verse 5) or, as we are told a couple of verses later, then they are 'your brothers in religion' (verse 11). Here repenting presumably means abandoning *shirk*, but even so, there does not seem to be much to separate the two sides, apart from political rivalry.

as a God-fearer here? Maybe, but with so little evidence one guess is as good as another.

What we can show is that the Messenger regarded the recipients of the earlier book (presumably meaning that of Moses) as a source of authoritative knowledge second only to God Himself, and that he assumed the same to be true of his audience, including his opponents. For example, in one of those passages in which he is so dispirited by his lack of success that he is beginning to doubt the veracity of his own revelations, God assures him that 'If you are in doubt about what We have sent down to you, ask those who recited/read the book before you' (Q 10:94). Defending his view that God's messengers did not consist of angels alone, the Messenger says that his predecessors were also human beings who had been granted revelation: 'Ask the people of *dhikr* if you do not know this' (16:43). 'Those to whom We have given the book know this [i.e. that there is only one God] as they know their sons. Those who have lost their own souls don't believe' (6:20; cf. the Medinese 2:146). Or again, 'Is it not a sign for them that the learned men of Israel know this to be true?' (26:197): this is where it is clear that he assumes his opponents to have the same respect for the religious knowledge of the scriptuaries, here identified as Israelites, as he has himself. There is no sense of rivalry between the religious communities here, merely of an extension of knowledge: the truth that God revealed to earlier communities He had now given to the Arabs too. Not everyone was ready to accept them in that role, however. In 46:10 the Messenger asks his unbelieving opponents whether they have considered what their situation would be 'if it (his revelation) was from God and you rejected it, whereas a witness from Banū Isrāʾīl testified to something similar and believed, while you were too arrogant to do so?' Once again it is the Israelites who are invoked as authoritative. The response of the unbelievers is that if it had been any good, 'they' would not have got it first. 'They' would appear to be the Messenger and his followers, and what the opponents are claiming seems to be that if his revelation had been genuine, it would have gone to an Israelite rather than an Arab.[80] Again it is clear that they had the same respect for Israelite knowledge as the Messenger; they just did not believe that the Messenger's own knowledge was of divine origin.

Further, in the Meccan surahs the Messenger repeatedly claims that the recipients of the earlier book believe in his message. Thus God says that He has sent down the book to the Messenger and that 'those who were given the book believe in it, as do some of these ones' (*wa-min hāʾulāʾi man yuʾminu bihi*) (29:47). This is a remarkable statement in that the recipients of the earlier

[80] These unbelievers could come from an Israelite or Arab background alike, and they may not have believed in scriptural authority at all, cf. their dismissal of the Messenger's preaching as an *ifkun qadīmun*, an old lie. For such unbelievers, see Crone, 'The Qurʾanic *Mushrikūn* and the Resurrection', I, 454–7, 470–2.

book are described as believers in the Messenger's revelation without qualification, whereas only some of 'these ones', presumably the Messenger's own people, accept it.[81] It cannot be the case that all the recipients of the earlier book believed in his message.[82] He must be speaking of a particular group among them and turning them into all of them in order to impress his opponents. Some exegetes claim that the reference is to ʿAbdallāh b. Salām and his companions, that is to say Jewish converts to Islam.[83] But for one thing, it is not obvious that the passage is speaking about conversion at all: the recipients of the earlier book still constitute a group of their own. For another thing, ʿAbdallāh b. Salām and his companions are envisaged as converting in Medina, whereas 29:47 must be earlier, since it reflects a stage at which the Messenger did not have many Arab followers (this we have to accept, for exaggerating the degree to which the scriptuaries believed in him did not require him to present them as outnumbering his Arab followers). Finally, ʿAbdallāh b. Salām and his companions were too few to be contrasted with *some* of 'these ones'. A better bet would be that the passage refers to a group of sympathizers, whom it is tempting to identify as Israelite Christians of the type that regarded Jesus as a purely human prophet, if only because Israelite Christians of this type ought to have been present somewhere in the Messenger's town.[84] But however this may be, the Messenger here seems to be presenting himself as emerging from an Israelite milieu to preach to his own people. This supports the view that he had started as a God-fearer.

There are several other Meccan passages in which the recipients of the earlier book are characterized as believers without qualification. 'Those to whom We have previously sent the book believe in this; when it is recited to them, they say, We believe in this, it is the truth from our Lord, we were Muslims before this' (28:52f). The exegetes take the recipients of the earlier book to have been Muslims in the sense of having worked out on the basis of their Scripture that a prophet called Muhammad would come,[85] but surely what they are saying here is that 'this is what we have always believed', or 'now we realize that we have always been Muslims'. The passage highlights the close similarity between their beliefs and those set out in the Qurʾan, perhaps with reference to a particular doctrine: it would be an apt comment for Jewish

[81] Reynolds and Tannenbaum, *Jews and God-Fearers*, 63, with reference to Cyril, 'De Adoratione et Cultu in Spiritu et Veritate', 3.92.3 (281).

[82] In fact, the preceding verse enjoins the believers to dispute nicely with the People of the Book, but surah 29 is regarded as composite, and verse 46 is likely to be Medinese.

[83] Thus for example Muqātil Ibn Sulaymān, *Tafsīr*, ʿAbdallāh Maḥmūd Shiḥata, ed. (Beirut: Mu'assasat al-Ta'rīkh al-ʿArabī, 2002), vol. 3, 385. But al-Ṭabarī only comments on *min hāʾulāʾi*, saying like others that they were the people of Mecca.

[84] Cf. Crone, 'Jewish Christianity and the Qurʾān (Part Two)', *Journal of Near Eastern Studies* 75 (2016), section 8.

[85] Cf. Jane Dammen McAuliffe, *Qurʾānic Christians: an Analysis of Classical and Modern Exegesis* (Cambridge: Cambridge University Press, 1991), 244–6.

Christians of the low Christological type to make in response to the qur'anic assertion of Jesus' status as a purely human prophet, which the Messenger was the first gentile ever to endorse as an article of faith. But again, we can only guess.

Or again, 'those to whom We have given the book rejoice in what has been revealed to you (sg.), but of the *aḥzāb* there are some who deny some of it' (13:36). The *aḥzāb* are elsewhere identified as people who reject the prophets sent to them and who are implicitly accused of polytheism too.[86] But here only some *aḥzāb* deny the Messenger's revelation, and then only some of it: one would have liked some more details. 'Whether you believe in it or not, those who were given knowledge before it [i.e. before the Messenger's revelation] fall down on their faces in prostration and say, Glory be to God, truly the promise of our Lord has been fulfilled. They fall on their faces weeping, and it increases their humility' (17:107–9). In this passage we can be reasonably sure that although the believing scriptuaries may have been Israelites, they were not Jews, for the Jews are coldly treated in this surah: their sins, twice punished by God with terrible destruction, are recounted and they are told they may put things right the third time if they will stop sinning; one way in which they might do so was apparently by believing in the Qur'an and the hereafter (17:4–10). The Messenger cannot have had them in mind. Again, however, he could be referring to Jewish Christians of the low Christological type.

The Messenger's tone changes drastically in the Medinese surahs. Here the best he can find to say about the recipients of the earlier book (now called 'People of the Book') is that *some* of them are believers. If the People of the Book had believed, it would have been better for them, he tells us, adding that in fact some of them do believe, but that *most of them* are wrongdoers (*fāsiqūn*) (3:110). The People of the Book are not all the same, he observes, taking it for granted that most of them are bad: *some* form a righteous nation (*umma qā'ima*) and recite God's verses all night while prostrating. They believe in God and the last day (a standard expression in the Medinese surahs for obeying the Messenger);[87] they also command right and prohibit wrong and hasten to do good works, and they will be rewarded, whereas those who reject the faith will go to hell (3:113–16). 'There are among the People of the Book those who believe in God and what He has sent down to you and to them, men humble to God, not selling His verses for a miserable gain' (3:199): no further identification of them is offered.[88] The Jews are guilty of many sins

[86] See 38:12, where the people of Noah, ʿĀd, Pharaoh Dhū 'l-Awtād, Thamūd, Lot, and the *aṣḥāb al-ayka* are enumerated as examples with the comment, 'those are the *aḥzāb*'.

[87] Cf. Crone, '*Mushrikūn* and the Resurrection', I, 472.

[88] The exegetical suggestions include the Jews in general and ʿAbdallāh b. Salām in particular (cf. McAuliffe, *Qur'ānic Christians*, 160ff).

and will suffer grievous punishment; but even so there are among them, or perhaps among the People of the Book, some who are firmly grounded in knowledge and who are believers: they accept what was revealed to the Messenger and to those before him, and they observe the prayer, give charity and believe in God and the last day; they will be rewarded (4:162). Elsewhere it is among the Israelites that there are a few who are rightly guided: 'We made a covenant with the children of Israel and sent Messengers; some they denied, others they slew... *many of them* are blind and deaf' (5:70–1). God took a covenant from the sons of Israel, but *except for a few* they violated it (2:83). If only the People of the Book had believed and feared God, their sins would have been blotted out and they would have been admitted to paradise. If only they had stuck by the Torah, Gospel, and everything sent down to them by God, they would have been fine; actually, as we are suddenly told, there is an *umma mutaqaṣida*, a moderate community or one that gets things right, among them, but *many* of them are evildoers (5:65). The believing scriptuaries in whom the Messenger sought support in the Meccan surahs seem to have been reduced to a minority. Or more probably, they had always been a minority and what had changed was only that the Messenger no longer needed to magnify them in order to impress his own people.

In the Medinese surah 5 the Christians (*naṣārā*), too, are presented as believers in the Messenger's revelation: here we are told that whereas the Jews and the *mushrikūn* were the most hostile to the believers, the Christians were the most filled with love towards them, for they had presbyters/priests (*qissīsūn*) and monks (*ruhbān*) who were not arrogant and who would weep when they heard the Messenger's revelations, declaring them to be the truth and asking why they shouldn't believe, given that they were longing to be with their Lord (5:82–4). The passage is odd, for in general the Messenger is as hostile to the *naṣārā* as he is to the Jews: he goes so far as to curse both of them for elevating 'Uzayr and Jesus along with their own sages (*aḥbār)* and monks to divine status (9:30f), and he also accuses the *aḥbār* and monks of devouring people's wealth, in some cases by burying it, and thus barring people from the path of God (9:34).[89] Why then are they here being praised in glowing terms, and at considerable length? It is all the more surprising in that the Christians here seem to be of the gentile rather than the Jewish Christian variety, for *qissīs* is derived from Syriac or Aramaic *qaīā*, meaning priest in Syriac, presbyter in Aramaic; and since they are concatenated with monks, one takes them to be priests.

This inference may be overhasty, however. Though Jewish Christians did not have priests, they shared with their ancestors the feature of having elders, known as *zeqenim* in the Hebrew Bible, and sometimes translated as

[89] In post-qur'anic Arabic *aḥbār* could stand for both Jewish and Christian leaders, but it seems only to stand for Jewish ones in the Qur'an.

presbyteroi in the Septuagint.[90] The Jerusalem church was run by elders (*presbyteroi*) according to Acts (11:30; 15:22f), and in that passage the *presbyteroi* are presumably rendering Aramaic *qaīē* rather than Hebrew *zekenim*.

It is possible, then, that the *qissīsūn* could be understood as presbyters.[91] Alternatively, we could follow Ubayy b. Kaʿb whose codex had *ṣiddīqūn*, pious or truthful people, rather than *qissīsūn*.[92] But did Jewish Christians have monks? They do in the tradition, in an exegetical story of how those followers of Jesus who refused to deify Christ (sometimes called 'the Muslims') fled into the desert when they were persecuted and lived there as monks until the coming of Muhammad.[93] But that aside, 57:27 tells us that God placed mildness (*raʾfatan*), mercy (*raḥmatan*), and *rahbāniyyatan* in the hearts of Jesus' followers, oddly continuing the statement by denouncing *rahbāniyya* as a Christian invention. Here as in 5:82, the Christians are a mild and humble lot endowed with something that came to be identified as monasticism/monks, described first as an admirable, God-given quality and next as a bad, human innovation. This suggests that *rahbāniyya* in Q 57:27 was originally meant in its literal sense of 'fear' (of God) and that a later person, perhaps the Messenger himself, took it to mean monasticism and so revised the oral or literary source in question to fit his own understanding;[94] but whether he understood the *ruhbān* of Q 5:82 as 'fearers' or as monks one cannot tell. De Blois, who argues that all the qurʾanic *naṣārā* were Jewish Christians (Nazoreans), does not seem to notice the problem.[95]

Whatever the solution may turn out to be, the facts remain that the qurʾanic pagans were semi-believers who did not apparently have any trouble understanding the qurʾanic references to the biblical tradition; that the Messenger himself regarded the earlier recipients of the scripture as authoritative to the point of regarding them as able to sit in judgement on the validity of his own revelations; that he assumed his audience to share this view; and that he was eager to have them, or a particular group (or groups) of them, on his side, even

[90] E.g. Numbers 11:25; Jeremiah 19:1; Joel 1:2.

[91] My thanks to Kevin van Bladel, Jack Tannous and others for illumination regarding the diverse meanings of *qaīē*.

[92] See Arthur Jeffery, *Materials for the History of the Text of the Qurʾān* (Leiden: Brill, 1937), 129, *ad* 5:82.

[93] See for example al-Ṭabarī, *ad* 57:27.

[94] That there are sometimes several chronological layers in one and the same qur'anic passage seems to have become widely accepted. But some hold all the layers to date from Muhammad's time, meaning that he revised earlier statements of his own; others believe the redactors to have added a layer after his death, and still others hold that there are layers which predate him. My own sympathies are with the third position (despite youthful statements going in the opposite direction), but the three possibilities are not mutually exclusive, of course.

[95] F. de Blois, '*Naṣrānī* (*nazōraios*) and *ḥanīf* (*ethnikos*): Studies on the Religious Vocabulary of Christianity and Islam', *Bulletin of the School of Oriental and African Studies* 65 (2002): 1–30, at 12–15.

depicting himself as emerging from an Israelite milieu. On this basis it seems reasonable to conclude that both he and the pagans who opposed him had grown up as God-fearers.

It is notable that the recipients of the earlier book/People of the Book who declare themselves to be believers or Muslims have not abandoned their Jewish or Christian identity. The tradition does know of individuals, both Jewish and Christian, who converted in Medina,[96] but the qurʾanic scriptuaries who declare themselves to be believers, or to have been Muslims even before they heard the Messenger's revelations (28:52f), are still addressed or referred to as People of the Book or the like. Even the fervently believing Christians of surah 5 are still known as Christians; they still have their own religious authorities, too; and when the Messenger describes them as closer to the believers than are the Jews, he acknowledges that they form a separate group. The reason that the communities stayed separate even when their beliefs were shared is presumably that they were based on different ethnicities. Jews and Jewish Christians could form communities *alongside* the Messenger's, but they were not Arabs and so could not merge with his community, nor for that matter could gentile Christians unless they were Arabs. There was no notion that one could *become* an Arab, which is why the Arabs resorted to clientage after the conquests to cope with the influx of non-Arab freedmen and converts; and the idea that the Muslim community was based entirely on faith rather than a combination of ethnicity and faith was still in the future. The believing *naṣārā* are problematic there again, for if they were gentile Christians living in Arabia, they were presumably Arabs and so could have merged with the Believers.[97] But the believing Israelites (Jewish or Christian) ended up in a sort of inverse God-fearer relationship: they accepted the message of the gentile prophet without abandoning their own ethnic and religious community.

By Muhammad's time there had been God-fearers for at least six hundred years, but no God-fearer that we know of had taken it upon himself to preach to other gentiles, let alone to the Israelites themselves. That is what Muhammad started doing. Eventually, he won enough political control to overrule everybody else in Arabia, and there were many more Arabs there than there were Israelites. So as in the case of the rise of Christianity, the upshot was that the gentiles took over and ousted the Israelites.

[96] For the Jewish converts (Ibn Salām and his companions), see Muqātil, *Tafsīr*, vol. 2, 555, *ad* 17:107–9; vol. 3, 85 (*ad* 29:47, cited above, note 82). For the Christians, see id., *Tafsīr*, vol. 3, 348f, where he takes 28:52f to refer to eight Syrian converts from Christianity, all whom he names; and id., *Tafsīr*, vol. 4, 246, where he takes 57:27 to refer to twelve Ethiopians and eight Christians from Syria. For other exegetes, see McAuliffe, *Qurʾānic Christians*, ch. 7.

[97] It is notable that while the Jews form an *umma* along with the believers in the Constitution of Medina, there is no mention of Christians.

BIBLIOGRAPHY

Beaucamp, J., F. Briguel-Chatonnet, and C. J. Robin, eds. *Juifs et Chrétiens en Arabie aux Ve et VIe siècles: regards croisés sur les sources*. Paris: Association des amis du Centre d'histoire et civilisation de Byzance, 2010.

Blois, F. de. '*Naṣrānī* (*nazōraios*) and *ḥanīf* (*ethnikos*): Studies on the Religious Vocabulary of Christianity and Islam'. *Bulletin of the School of Oriental and African Studies* 65 (2002): 1–30.

Brock, Sebastian. 'Jewish Traditions in Syriac Sources'. *Journal of Jewish Studies* 30 (1979): 212–32.

Chadwick, Henry, trans. *Origen: Contra Celsum*. Cambridge: Cambridge University Press, 1953.

Chaniotis, A. 'The Jews of Aphrodisias: New Evidence and Old Problems'. *Scripta Classica Israelica* 21 (2002): 209–42.

Charlesworth, James. *Old Testament Pseudepigrapha. Volume 2*. New York: Doubleday, 1985.

Crone, Patricia. 'How Did the Quranic Pagans Make a Living?' *Bulletin of the School of Oriental and African Studies* 68 (2005): 387–99.

Crone, Patricia. 'The Religion of the Qur'ānic Pagans: God and the Lesser Deities'. *Arabica* 57 (2010): 151–200.

Crone, Patricia. 'Angels versus Humans as Messengers of God'. In Philippa Townsend and Moulie Vidas, eds, *Revelation, Literature, and Community in Late Antiquity*. Tübingen: Mohr Siebeck, 2011.

Crone, Patricia. 'The Quranic *Mushrikūn* and the Resurrection, part I'. *Bulletin of the School of Oriental and African Studies* 75.3 (2012): 445–72.

Cross, Frank L. *Cyril of Jerusalem: Lectures on the Christian Sacraments: Procatechesis and five Mystagogical Catecheses*. Translated by R. W. Church. New York: St Vladimir's Seminary, 1986.

Feldman, Louis H. *Jew and Gentile in the Ancient World*. Princeton: Princeton University Press, 1993.

Festugière, A-J. and B. Grillet, eds and trans. *Sozemène: Histoire ecclésiastique*. Paris: Cerf, 2005.

Fredriksen, Paula. 2003. 'What "Parting of the Ways"? Jews, Gentiles, and the Ancient Mediterranean City'. In Adam H. Becker and Annette Yoshiko Reed, eds, *The Ways That Never Parted: Jews and Christians in Late Antiquity and the Early Middle Ages*. Tübingen: Mohr Siebeck, 35–63.

Gershenzon, R. and E. Slomovic. 'A Second Century Jewish-Gnostic Debate: Rabbi Jose Ben Halafta and the Matrona'. *Journal for the Study of Judaism* 16 (1985): 1–41.

Grüll, T. and L. Benke. 'A Hebrew/Aramaic Graffito and Poppaea's Alleged Jewish Sympathy'. *Journal of Jewish Studies* 62 (2001): 37–55.

Heen, Erik M. and Philip D. W. Krey, eds. *Ancient Christian Commentary on Scripture: New Testament*. Volume X: *Hebrews*. Downers Grove, IL: InterVarsity Press, 2005.

Jeffery, Arthur. *Materials for the History of the Text of the Qur'ān*. Leiden: Brill, 1937.

Klauser, Theodor, ed. *Reallexicon für Antike und Christentum: Sachwörtherbuch zur Auseinandersetzung des Christentums mit der antiken Welt*. Stuttgart: Hiersemann Verlag, 1962.

Kraabel, A. T. 'The Disappearance of the "God-Fearers"'. *Numen* 28 (1981): 113–26.
Lieu, Judith M. 'The Race of God-Fearers'. *Journal of Theological Studies* 46 (1995): 483–501.
Lieu, Judith M. *Neither Jew nor Greek?: Constructing Early Christianity*. London: T & T Clark, 2002.
Lifshitz, Baruch. 'Les Juifs à Venosa', *Rivista di Filologia e di Istruzione Classica* 90 (1962): 367–71.
Llewelyn, Stephen R., et al., ed. *New Documents Illustrating Early Christianity*, IX: *A Review of the Greek Inscriptions and Papyri Published in 1986–87*. Grand Rapids, MI: W.B. Eerdmans, 2002.
McAuliffe, Jane Dammen. *Qurʾānic Christians: an Analysis of Classical and Modern Exegesis*. Cambridge: Cambridge University Press, 1991.
McGuckin, John Anthony, ed. *The Westminster Handbook to Origen*. Louisville; London: John Knox Press, 2004.
Migne, Jacques-Paul. *Patrologia Graeca*. Vol. 68. Paris: Imprimerie Catholique, 1857–66.
Mitchell, Stephen. 'Wer waren die Gottesfürchtigen?' *Chiron* 28 (1998): 55–64.
Mitchell, Stephen. 'The Cult of Theos Hypsistos between Pagans, Jews, and Christians'. In Polymnia Athanassiadi and Michael Frede, eds, *Pagan Monotheism in Late Antiquity*. New York: Oxford University Press, 1999.
Mitchell, Stephen and P. van Nuffelen, eds. *One God: Pagan Monotheism in the Roman Empire*. Cambridge: Cambridge University Press, 2010.
Muqātil Ibn Sulaymān, *Tafsīr*, ʿAbdallāh Maḥmūd Shiḥata, ed. Beirut: Mu'assasat al-Ta'rīkh al-ʿArabī, 2002.
Nickelsburg, G. W. E and J. C. VandkerKam. *I Enoch: A New Translation Based on the Hermeneia Commentary*. Minneapolis: Fortress, 2004.
Parfitt, Tudor. *Black Jews in Africa and the Americas*. Cambridge: Harvard University Press, 2013.
Ramelli, Maria I.E. *Bardaisan of Edessa: A Reassessment of the Evidence and a New Interpretation*. Piscataway, NJ: Gorgias, 2009.
Reynolds, J. and R. Tannenbaum. *Jews and God-Fearers at Aphrodisias*. Cambridge: Cambridge University Press, 1987.
Siegert, F. 'Gottesfürchtige und Sympathisanten'. *Journal for the Study of Judaism* 4 (1973): 109–64.
Sirinelli, Jean. *Les vues historiques d'Eusèbe de Césarée durant la période prénicéenne*. Dakar: Université de Dakar, 1961.
Stanton, Graham N. '"God-Fearers": Neglected Evidence in Justin Martyr's *Dialogue with Trypho*'. In Graham Stanton, Marcus Bockmuehl, and D. Linicum, eds, *Studies in Matthew and Early Christianity*. Tübingen: Mohr Siebeck, 2013.
Stark, Rodney. *One True God: Historical Consequences of Monotheism*. Princeton: Princeton University Press, 2001.
Stark, Rodney and Roger Finke. *Acts of Faith: Explaining the Human Side of Religion*. Berkeley and Los Angeles: University of California Press, 2000.
Stegemann, Ekkehard W. and Wolfgang Stegemann. *The Jesus Movement: a Social History of its First Century*. Minneapolis: Fortress Press, 1999.
Stuckenbruck, Loren T. *Angel Veneration and Christology: A Study in Early Judaism and in the Christology of the Apocalypse of John*. Tübingen: Mohr Siebeck, 1995.

Thomson, Robert W., James H. Howard-Johnston, and Tim Greenwood. *The Armenian History Attributed to Sebeos*. Liverpool: Liverpool University Press, 1999.

Walford, Edward, trans. *Ecclesiastical History of Sozomen*. London: Henry G. Bohn, 1855.

Wilcox, Max. 'The "God-Fearers" in Acts—a Reconsideration'. *Journal for the Study of the New Testament* 13 (1981): 102–22.

5

Locating the Qur'an and Early Islam in the 'Epistemic Space' of Late Antiquity

Angelika Neuwirth

QUESTIONING PERIODIZATIONS

Global history studies have lately effected a change in evaluating the past: scholars have voiced the conviction that the Eurocentric view claiming Enlightenment—a momentous epistemic turning point in modernity—to be a specifically European achievement is no longer tenable.[1] Should the other prerogative of European historical superiority, the understanding of Late Antiquity—the formative period of European cultural history—as an essentially Christian epoch be more time-resistant? Though new discourses have arisen that venture on a closer synopsis of the cultures of Late Antiquity on both sides of the Mediterranean these historical works have not yet carved out the role of earliest Islam as an active player in the late antique culture of debate.[2] Questioning and undoing inherited periodizations appears a task not limited to modernity alone. Where does the Qur'an and early Islam belong? The answer will determine the way of reading the Qur'an as either a hermeneutically familiar text of monotheist theology or as the founding document of a foreign religious culture that arose out of the rich heritage of its particular historical moment, but was then to differentiate itself gradually over succeeding centuries—a document that pre-figures the 'other' culture of Islam. Both readings, though dedicated to one and the same text, follow different hermeneutic principles. It is here, in the hermeneutic realm, that the parting of the ways occurred, where the Western enemy image of Islam that was to prevail during the Middle Ages originally emerged. One cannot fairly dissociate the

[1] Sebastian Conrad, 'Enlightenment in Global History: A Historiographical Critique', *American Historical Review* (2012): 999–1012.

[2] Thomas Sizgorich, *Violence and Belief in Late Antiquity: Militant Devotion in Christianity and Islam* (Philadelphia: University of Pennsylvania Press, 2009).

currently incumbent task of accommodating the Qurʾan into world history from the peculiar history of the Western engagement with the Qurʾan.[3] Western qur'anic studies are burdened with an extremely problematic record: they carry with them a heavy load of prejudices accumulated since the age of the Qurʾan's first fierce critic, John of Damascus.[4] Polemics since then have made use of shockingly primitive misreadings of the qur'anic text, based on the Qurʾan's alleged character of a 'flat text' to be understood by the letter, completely lacking figurative speech. It was this hermeneutic mistake that proved to be the most momentous obstacle in the way of understanding the Qurʾan. Although qur'anic studies today are booming, scholars are still far from recognizing the status of the Qurʾan as a new, indeed revolutionary manifestation of the literary genre that was considered of paramount authority in Late Antiquity: a mantic text, that is, a text claiming supernatural origin.

To restart and explore the status of the Qurʾan in an age in which the ideological foundations of what was to become Western culture were laid is of course a highly political endeavour. The proton pseudos that has generated the Qurʾan's present status as an epigonal text, the practice of exclusion—which had earlier on been exercised against Jewish tradition—the uprooting of the Qurʾan from the intellectual scene it originated from, has still not been seriously rethought.[5] Qurʾanic studies will not become 'modern' through simply introducing new historical, archaeological, and codicological evidence into the discussion. What is needed today is to re-embed the Qurʾan into the discourses current in its epoch and most importantly, to consider the hermeneutics that was prevalent at the time. To take the text seriously requires that scholars before selecting particular textual details work towards a consensus about the basics, such as the genre of the Qurʾan, its oral or written character, its 'author' and recipients, and its spatial and temporal coordinates.[6] Such a consensus is still missing, investigations usually start—I would say arbitrarily—with the *textus receptus*, the *muṣḥaf* as a given, leaving the criteria mentioned undetermined. This 'impressionist approach' in a way reproduces the pre-modern image of the Qurʾan as a momentous but 'foreign' Book, an 'other', whose emergence—known in its perverted form from the polemic narrative—was not considered

[3] Hartmut Bobzin, 'Pre-1800 Preoccupations of Qurʾanic Studies' in Jane Dammen McAuliffe, ed., *Encyclopedia of the Qurʾan* (Leiden: Brill, 2004), 4: 235–53.

[4] Daniel Sahas, *John of Damascus: The 'Heresy of the Ishmaelites'* (Leiden: Brill 1972), Angelika Neuwirth, '*Jesus und Muhammad*—Zwei spätantike Lehrer? Ein Versuch, den Koran im Licht der Lehre Jesu "neu zu lesen"', in Thomas Fornet-Ponse, *Jesus Christus: von alttestamentlichen Messiasvorstellungen bis zur literarischen Figur* (Münster: Aschendorff, 2015), 133–48.

[5] Angelika Neuwirth, *Koranforschung—eine politische Philologie?: Bibel, Koran und Islamentstehung im Spiegel spätantiker Textpolitik und moderner Philologie* (Berlin: Walter de Gruyter, 2014).

[6] See the introduction to Angelika Neuwirth, *Scripture, Poetry and the Making of a Community: Reading the Qurʾan as a Literary Text* (Oxford: Oxford University Press, 2014).

worth further investigation. Studies in qur'anic history have never made serious efforts to reach the methodological level of biblical studies. The emergence of the alleged 'Book' still for many is a sort of taboo; it is at least scholarship-deterrent. The fact that this is a—secular and thus inverted—reproduction of the Muslim concept of the 'Book' as the ultimate Other should not be used as an excuse. Muslim critics themselves have identified this particular status of earliest Islamic history as the 'Unthought of Islamic Thought'.[7]

LATE ANTIQUITY AS THE EPISTEMIC SPACE OF THE QUR'AN'S GENESIS

The designation 'Late Antiquity' is usually taken to point to an epoch—whose beginning and end are controversial among historians. Peter Brown whose work has given rise to the currently lively discipline of Late Antiquity studies defined Late Antiquity as ranging until 750 CE, a period that would include the Qur'an.[8] Brown, however, left the Qur'an almost unmentioned considering it as a foreign import imposed on a society that was otherwise confined to the—allegedly limited—cultural horizons of the Peninsula. The Qur'an has also not been considered an active player by the scholars of Brown's school. The task of positioning the Qur'an in Late Antiquity thus still waits to be accomplished. In the following, Late Antiquity will not be taken as an epoch but as an 'epistemic space', a 'Denkraum',[9] where battles are fought between neither political foes nor the contesting empires, but where textual controversies are staged between confederates and opponents from diverse theological realms. Textual, not military, strategies are at play here, strategies which easily pass from one religious culture to another. The transfer of knowledge in Late Antiquity—once we proceed from a 'Denkraum'—is not confined to the transmission of semantically relevant traditions but is first of all a hermeneutic venture. 'Typology' will be highlighted as one of the most efficient textual strategies employed here.

To do justice to the literary character of the Qur'an,[10] we need to pursue its development as both a monotheist proclamation, an oral message, a *Verkündigung*, voiced by a messenger, and at the same time as a successively

[7] Mohammad Arkoun, *The Unthought in Contemporary Islamic Thought* (London: Saqi Books, 2002).

[8] Peter Brown, *Late Antiquity* (Cambridge: Harvard University Press, 1998).

[9] See Nora Schmidt et al., *Denkraum Spätantike: Reflexionen von Antiken im Umfeld des Koran* (Wiesbaden: Harrassowitz, 2016).

[10] Angelika Neuwirth, *Studien zur Komposition der Mekkanischen Suren* (Berlin: de Gruyter, 2007).

growing text reflecting a community's construction of identity. The first aspect highlights the Qurʾan as the document of a transfer of biblical knowledge to Arab recipients, whereas the second targets the reverse process, the community's response from within Arabian Late Antiquity. Both processes—each reflected in one of the two principal subgenres of the Qurʾan, narrative and debate—are easily recognizable as charged with political tension. The Qurʾan does not simply reflect a massive conversion process from paganism to monotheist faith but equally offers a rewriting of Arabian antiquity, of the rich literary and social heritage that is accessible to us in ancient Arabic poetry, as well as recent epigraphic and archaeological findings.[11] How do these two rival canons, the biblical and the Arabian, interact? Or more precisely, how does the audience, or later the community, reach a consensus about their respective validity? The fact that the Qurʾan in its final stage displays a successful osmosis between these two cultural heritages invites the question of the strategies applied to achieve this particular merger, which—in my view—equals a revolutionary expansion of monotheist religious thought in Late Antiquity.

To assume a development leading towards such an osmosis means to set a principal methodological course. It requires us to read the Qurʾan diachronically, following not the order of the surahs within the *muṣḥaf* but the sequence of their first dissemination, the recitation of the Prophet Muhammad.[12] The establishment of this sequence occupied the minds of not a few generations of traditional Muslim scholars whose insights into the so-called *ʿilm al-makkī wa-l-madanī* and *asbāb al-nuzūl* were to lay the basis for Theodor Nöldeke's 'Geschichte des Korans',[13] History of the Qurʾan, a still indispensable nineteenth-century attempt to establish a qur'anic chronology. Whereas the traditional Muslim scholars—roughly speaking—had tried to provide a *Sitz im Leben*, an embedding of individual proclamations into their social circumstances, critical scholarship focused textual criteria, particularly stylistic and terminological, thus downgrading or even eliminating the role of the community. This preference proved no academic trifle: until now Western scholarship tends to sever the Qurʾan from its Meccan and Medinan milieu, allegedly out of scepticism vis-à-vis the authenticity of the Islamic traditions about the Qurʾan's emergence. The shortsightedness of this approach has lately been exposed by Aziz al-Azmeh,[14] who justly laments some scholars' obsession with finding

[11] See Ute Franke, Ali al-Ghabban, Joachim Gierlichs, and Stefan Weber, eds. *Roads of Arabia: Archaeological Treasures of Saudi Arabia* (Berlin: Wasmuth, 2011).

[12] Nicolai Sinai, 'The Qurʾan as Process', in Angelika Neuwirth, Nicolai Sinai, and Michael Marx, eds, *The Qurʾān in Context, Historical and Literary Investigations into the Qurʾānic Milieu* (Leiden: Brill, 2009), 407–40.

[13] Theodor Nöldeke, Friedrich Schwally, Gotthelf Bergsträsser and Otto Pretzl, *Die Geschichte des Korantextes* (Leipzig: Dieterich, 1938, reprint Hildesheim: Olms, 1961).

[14] Aziz al-Azmeh, *The Emergence of Islam in Late Antiquity: Allah and His People* (Cambridge: Cambridge University Press, 2004).

precursors and antecedents to anything that can prove the derivative status of Islamic phenomena. To avoid the onerous step of exploring the cultural milieu of the Qur'an—which is still widely understudied—renders qur'anic scholarship an easy task, since it allows for the invention of a new context, identified today by many as Jewish aggadah and Christian postbiblical tradition.[15] The Qur'an is presently viewed by many scholars as the authorial work of one man or even more often as the outcome of a redaction carried out by a collective, resembling a Christian apocryphon more closely than a genuine Arabic scripture.

This assumption of the text's genesis from a premeditated authorial process, its emergence in one piece, so to say, is however belied by its literary composition. The Qur'an is a polyphonic text, the transcript of debates between various and often changing agents. In terms of genre it is not a continuous report or a chain of narratives but a drama with numerous protagonists involved. Present scholarship tends to focus the narrative parts exclusively, thus limiting its work to a kind of midrashic exegesis in the vein of rabbinic studies. Such a simple perception of the text as a given, however tempting it may be, cannot persist vis-à-vis the demands of modern philology which Sheldon Pollock in his famous manifesto has lately outlined.[16] In Pollock's view philology demands not only the analysis of the text under scrutiny, but equally the exploration of its context, the 'recipients' response', and last but not least, the carving out of 'the philologist's meaning', the text's implications relevant for today's intellectual discourse. Studying texts should bring to light and make meaningful the ways in which human communities interpret their environments.

To sever the text from its local societal context then is no viable solution. We have to read the Qur'an—in tune with relevant segments of Muslim traditional scholarship—as the document of a communication process which accompanied and gradually shaped social and intellectual developments within the community, a document whose chronology is therefore crucial. The Qur'an is from the very beginning connected to addressees who successively acquire new insights and who increase in number and diversity. It should be read as a drama staging the itinerary of the Prophet's listeners from a pious conventicle to a community with a distinctive religious identity.[17] The Qur'an is—one might claim—the 'property' of a community. (I will later try to argue that the Qur'an is at the same

[15] Gabriel Reynolds, *The Qur'ān and its Biblical Subtext* (New York: Routledge, 2010).

[16] Sheldon Pollock, 'Future Philology? The Fate of a Soft Science in a Hard World', in *Critical Inquiry* 33 (2009): 931–61.

[17] Such a dynamic perception is not a mere outsider's view. It comes close to the perception of one of the most prominent Muslims scholars of the Qur'an of our time, the late Nasr Hamid Abu Zayd. Nasr, who had dedicated his life's work to pondering the textuality of the Qur'an, in a later phase distanced himself from the notion of the 'Qur'an as text', preferring to discuss it as a discourse. See Nasr Hamid Abu Zayd, *Rethinking the Qur'an: Towards a Humanistic*

time universal 'property', a significant legacy to what we so often unhesitatingly call Western—Jewish and Christian—culture.)

LATE ANTIQUE HERMENEUTICS: TYPOLOGY VERSUS LITERALITY

It is striking to observe that both processes, the biblicization of Arabian knowledge and the Arabicization of biblical lore, involve the same hermeneutic strategy: typology. In view of the multiple manifestations of typology, the term in the following will be used in a very broad sense, as a collective concept to cover diverse textual strategies. Typology, which played an important role in the Christian reading of the Bible, is usually taken to denote the relationship between historical, that is, biblical events and their re-enactments in the present, thus structurally implying repetition which evokes a cyclical structure of history. In the Qurʾan, the mission of the Prophet is presented as the re-enactment of the dispatching of earlier prophets, an observation which has generated the stereotypical notion of the Qurʾan's prophetology as a whole following a cyclical pattern. Although there are in the early surahs purely additive enumerations of earlier prophetical missions, the notion of the sameness of these missions is overcome in later Meccan times to give way to a 'succession of prophets'. The insistence of scholars on the one mode of 're-enactment typology', leaving other modes of typology that involve historical progress unconsidered, has generated the erroneous image of the Qurʾan as a text devoid of significant development.[18]

Although examples of typology are ubiquitous, as will be shown, until now the perception that there is typology in the Qurʾan has not been met with much interest. Western qur'anic studies started with the literal reading of the text. Since Abraham Geiger's seminal work of 1833, the Qurʾan has been investigated primarily as a document interesting for the ways in which it reflects and receives earlier biblical and postbiblical conceptions and ideas.[19]

Hermeneutics (Utrecht: Humanistics University Press, 2004). See also Massimo Campanini, *Modern Muslim Interpretations* (London; New York: Routledge, 2011).

[18] A telling example is the still influential article by Rudi Paret, 'Das Geschichtsbild Mohammeds', *Welt als Geschichte 11* (1951): 214–24. Paret's thesis is approved not only by Heribert Busse, 'Herrschertypen im Koran', in Ulrich Haarmann and Peter Bachmann, eds, *Die Islamische Welt zwischen Mittelalter und Neuzeit. Festschrift für Hans Robert Roemer zum 65. Geburtstag* (Beirut; Weisbaden: In Kommission bei F. Steiner, 1979), 57, but still by many recent scholars.

[19] Geiger, *Was hat Mohammed aus dem Judenthume aufgenommen?* (Bonn: Baaden, 1833). For the school of historical critical scholarship established by Geiger, see Dirk Hartwig et al., eds, *'Im vollen Licht der Geschichte': Die Wissenschaft des Judentums und die Anfänge der kritischen Koranforschung* (Würzburg: Ergon, 2008).

The status of the Qur'an as a coherent scriptural text was outside the scope of the earliest historical critical scholarship. Although immense credit goes to Geiger and his successors for contextualizing the Qur'an within late antique traditions,[20] it is undeniable that they stopped short of considering the theological aspects of the Qur'an, thus leaving the hermeneutic aspects completely disregarded. This way of reading the Qur'an has continued into our days.

Among modern researchers few have paid attention to typology in the Qur'an. Some scholars tend to deny the presence of typology in the Qur'an altogether. Heribert Busse, one of the first scholars dedicated to an extensive study of particular manifestations of qur'anic typology, confined himself to one single qur'anic technique: the pairing of particular narrative figures, bearers of power and authority that match each other in virtue or—more often—in wickedness. Although recruited from historically and geographically unrelated contexts, they form ensembles in one and the same qur'anic narrative. Busse and after him Adam Silverstein have singled out a number of such narrative figures that in the Qur'an reappear 'typologically' coupled such as Firʿawn and Hāmān, Pharaoh and Haman, two wicked persecutors of believers who appear together.[21] Busse's classification of types of just and unjust rulers who are associated with each other in the Qur'an and thus throw light on each other is most relevant to explaining the narrative function of more marginal qur'anic figures, but it does not highlight their function in the gradual development of a biblically oriented world view.[22] Since the examples adduced by Busse concern rulers often in conflict with prophets, they cannot be denied a typological relationship to the present of the messenger. What comes far closer to a functional understanding of qur'anic typology is what Sidney Griffith in a recent publication has highlighted as 'prophetology based on typology'.[23] He holds that the Qur'an's most momentous doctrine, the concept of prophecy as the exclusively legitimate mediator between the transcendent and the real world, is based on a 'typological' portrayal of the prophets. Moses in this perception is typologically closest to the Prophet Muhammad.

All these manifestations of typology, however, do not match the model that patristic readings of Old Testament texts based on Paul's theology have established. Here biblical figures and events are regarded as foreshadowing what will reveal their significance in the fullness of time with the coming of the

[20] Heinrich Speyer, *Die biblischen Erzählungen im Qoran* (Gräfenhainichen: Schulze, 1931); Josef Horovitz, *Koranische Untersuchungen* (Berlin: De Gruyter, 1926).

[21] Busse, 'Herrschertypen im Koran', and Adam Silverstein, 'Hāmān's Transition from Jāhiliyya to Islām', *Jerusalem Studies in Arabic and Islam 34* (2008): 285–308.

[22] Thus, Busse, 'Herrschertypen im Koran', 57, realizes the typological relationship between Solomon's consecration of the Jerusalem Temple and Abraham's consecration of Kaʿba, without however noticing the developmental function of the similarity which serves to establish Mecca as the new Jerusalem.

[23] Griffith, *The Bible in Arabic*, 65.

Messiah. The earlier facts entail a promise to be fulfilled at a later stage which in the case of a re-enactment is not involved. Muhammad's ministry among the Meccans may appear in many respects as a re-enactment of that of Moses among the Israelites, but it is devoid of the figure of 'promise and fulfilment', which is so current in Jewish messianic and particularly in Christian typological thought. Thus Moses, who in Christian typology is reduced to a mere foreshadowing of Christ, in the Qur'an—though exhibiting strong similarities to Muhammad—preserves his status as the most eminent biblical prophet. He is in no way degraded to the rank of a typus.

Does this verdict of the non-existence of a promise—fulfilment pattern in qur'anic typology, however, hold true for the entire Qurʾan? On closer look from its very beginnings, the Qurʾan conveys a theology of covenant that heavily relies on the promise-fulfilment pattern.[24] Already some very early surahs reflect a field of tension between the two poles of the double event of primordial creation and divine instruction and its double denouement on the Last Day when the cosmos will dissolve and humans will render the token of divine instruction by accounting for their deeds. Divine teaching, according to this figure of thought, virtually entails a promise whose fulfilment makes it retrospectively meaningful. This very powerful creation-instruction theology which presupposes a divine-human covenant, based on the principle of a balance between act and retribution, though this concept is not yet made explicit in the early Qurʾan, could be identified with a mode of typology. Human acts are measured in terms of covenantal criteria. Although this does not bridge the gap between the Bible as an earlier scripture and the qur'anic message as a later one, it does connect the qur'anic message to a scriptural reference, undetermined as it may be. Instead of a biblical-qur'anic promise fulfilment figure, a theological field of tension familiar from biblical tradition is reactivated and highlighted in the Qurʾan.

Until the late Meccan period, typology appears predominantly in the shape of simple parallelization, the analogous depiction of biblical and contemporary figures, like Moses and the Prophet Muhammad. Biblical history is thus absorbed by the present which in turn acquires a new theological dimension as part of a biblical salvific project. It is true that typology may also work in the opposite direction, so, for example, biblical poetry is reshaped in the earliest poetically phrased surahs, thus inducing an Arabization of the biblical psalm tradition. Yet all these instances of typology aim at an inclusive effect: the qur'anic message appropriates biblical tradition and in some cases imprints it with Arabic patterns of thought. This leads to a shift in the collective self-perception: A kind of counter-history emerges, which rewrites local history in biblical terms. This, however, turns out to be a liability. Thus, at a later stage the community is challenged by its opponents to reconcile imagined biblical

[24] Neuwirth, *Der Koran als Text der Spätantike*, 436–50.

history with real Arabian history and social life. The counter-history that had been established by the hermeneutic tool of typology in turn needs to be rectified by the same tool. To connect the two views of history a more complex form of typology is required, involving the epistemic figure of 'promise and fulfilment'. The existence and the social role of the community needs to be embedded in Arabian memory. Here Abraham, rooted in both the biblical and the Arabian world, emerges as a figure of compromise.

The notion of promise in the Bible is most closely connected to Abraham. Being graced with the promise that his Israelite progeny will be settled in the Holy Land and acquire a momentous historical role, he is a figure of highly political significance. In the early Meccan surahs this political significance of his is completely muted. Abraham appears as a morally exemplary figure devoid, however, of collective significance. It is only in a late Meccan prayer that he slips into a political role. In surah 14, he seeks to secure for his Arab progeny a promise analogous to that received for his Israelite progeny: their destined home, Mecca, is to become the birthplace of Arabian monotheism.[25] Mecca is thus promoted to the rank of an Arabian Promised Land. At the time of the proclamation of the message the promise has already been fulfilled. The community is thus founded on an Abrahamic foundation.

Yet, this epistemic figure of promise and fulfilment at a still later phase will be eclipsed by an even more sophisticated approach. The ultimate breakthrough—the community's construction of an identity of its own—will be propelled by what we might call mythopoietic typology, that is, the discovery of archetypal events, mythemes, shaped in biblical narrative which the community identifies as underlying their own local cultic practices. Such an archetypal event, an 'original scene', is the sacrifice of Abraham, which the qur'anic community identifies as the subtext of the cultic practice of sacrifice at the Meccan pilgrimage.

Let us follow the community's itinerary from a pious conventicle following late antique cultic patterns with the intent to assimilate itself to the earlier pious communities, to its re-figuration as a new religious community engaging in a polemic exchange with its neighbours, again applying modes of typology that had been well established in Late Antiquity.

STAGING BIBLICAL TRADITION AND ADDRESSING AN ARAB PREDICAMENT

The earliest perusal of biblical tradition in the Qur'an can best be described as a 'staging' of biblical tradition, the re-enactment of psalmodic chant in

[25] See Nicolai Sinai, *Fortschreibung und Auslegung: Studien zur frühen Koraninterpretation* (Weisbaden: Harrassowitz, 2009).

qur'anic recitation. The audience of the Prophet thereby establishes itself as a liturgical community, re-embodying just the ideal of the Psalms and at the same time emulating the pious of the neighbouring traditions who all share the practice of praising God through the medium of short poetic compositions, 'psalms'. The early surahs closely resemble biblical Psalms. One of the earliest uses of the word *qur'ān* (Q 73:1–10) points to an already existing practice of nightly recitals, of vigils:

> O you enwrapped in the cloak,
> Keep vigil all the night, except a little
> A half of it, or diminish a little,
> Or add a little, and chant the Koran distinctly.
> We shall cast upon you weighty speech,
> Surely the first part of the night is heavier in tread, more upright in speech,
> Surely during the day you have long business.
> Remember the Name of your Lord, and devote yourself unto Him devoutly
> Lord of the East and West—there is no god but He, so take Him for a Guardian.

The liturgical frame of a vigil which is presented here would elsewhere be filled with Psalm readings. What is being read here is only vaguely determined as *al-qur'ān*—obviously a new genre of liturgical texts not known before in the Arabic language. The early surahs' close relationship to the biblical Psalms in terms of composition and topics has been acknowledged in scholarship—but what about their relationship to Arabic poetry? Josef Horovitz thought of shared topics: he assumed that the early qur'anic paradise scenarios reflected banquet scenes from ancient Arabic poetry.[26] The relationship, however, is not one of similarity but of rewriting, of supersession: the qur'anic paradise tableaus portraying groups of men and women in a lush natural environment furnished with aesthetically refined artefacts should not simply be taken as idyllic depictions. They respond rather to an intellectual crisis of ancient Arab society that is mirrored in poetry. We should read them as a reverse image of the 'landscape in ruins' depicted in the elegiac-philosophical introductory section of the Arabic *qaṣīda,* the *nasīb* which dwell on 'deserted encampments', which leave the poet in despair, overwhelmed by the feeling of futility of being abandoned to fate. His aporia finds expression in the compelling image of an inscription, a writing on a rock, curiously designated *waḥy*, a nonverbal message which forces itself on the beholder without, however, disclosing its meaning.

It is this perception of the world that the early Qur'an addresses: God Himself takes over the role of fate and reshapes the time of man, which now

[26] Josef Horovitz, Das Koranische Paradies', *Scripta Universitatis atque Bibliothecae Hierosolymitanarum* 6 (1923): 1–16. Reprinted in Rudi Paret, ed., *Der Koran* (Darmstadt: Wissenschaftliche Buchgesellschaft, 1975), 53–73.

is no longer cyclical as the pre-Islamic concept of time had it, but expands from primordial creation to its end on Judgement Day. The qur'anic description of paradise thus not only reverses the erstwhile image of nature as bleak and threatening, but equally reinstalls reflections on history by rewriting ancient Arabic poetry. The unreadable signs of the emblematic inscription, the *waḥy,* are thwarted by the intelligibility of the signs, *āyāt* of scripture. The enigma, *waḥy*, reappears in the Qur'an in the inverted function of a revelation thus offering the very key to understanding the world.[27]

PENETRATING BIBLICAL TRADITION

During the Middle Meccan phase of the Prophet's mission a shift in communal awareness occurred: the nascent community's adopting a new identity as the successors of the Israelites. The awareness of participating in a shared liturgical practice with earlier communities or pious individuals is not yet tantamount to sharing their historically rooted covenantal status. This new awareness comes about with the necessity of self-legitimation of the nascent community which arose in its situation of siege. The surahs of the Middle Meccan period in particular attest the community's attempt to dissociate itself from the Meccan cult centre and to relocate itself in an imagined space, the Holy Land, the landscape of biblical history which is dominated by the towering figure of Moses. This is achieved through diverse textual strategies. Most strikingly, there is a frequent re-narrating of biblical stories in the later surahs, which usually occupy the central part of the composition. Whereas the introductions and conclusions of the longer surahs offer treatments of topical issues, consoling addresses to the Prophet, polemics, and admonitions, the biblical story at the centre is outstanding. That is, it takes the listeners away from their real life into a remote time and to remote places pertaining to the world of the *Banū Isrā'īl*, which they in their situation of inner exile come to adopt as their textual homeland. It is not irrelevant to notice that this particular position of the biblical narration within the surah matches the position of the *lectio* or the *qeri'at Torah* in Christian and Jewish services respectively.[28] Thus, the surah at this stage may have served as a kind of libretto for a complete divine service. It is therefore hardly surprising to find Scripture as such, *al-kitāb*, as the ultimate reference to attest the truth of the proclaimer's message, explicitly called upon in the beginnings and the ends of

[27] Angelika Neuwirth, 'The "Discovery of Writing" in the Qur'an: Tracing an Epistemic Revolution in Late Antiquity', in Nuha al-Shaar, ed., *Qur'an and Adab* (Oxford: Oxford University Press in association with the Institute of Ismaili Studies), forthcoming.

[28] Neuwirth, *Der Koran als Text der Spätantike*, 360–78.

the middle Meccan surahs. This is in tune with Guy Stroumsa's thesis that the rise of Scripture to the rank of the highest authority is one of the chief 'religious mutations' of Late Antiquity.[29] Since this Text represents, on a certain level, the collective memory, it is necessary to make sense of it, to bridge the ontological differences that exist between contemporary situations and the sacred past. This occurs either through the expansion of scripture or—and this applies to the Qur'an—through exploring the manner in which Scripture can read itself intratextually and intertextually.

The celebration of Scripture in the Qur'an is no mere literary device, but the idea of scriptural remembrance induced a massive expansion of collective consciousness in the later Meccan period. Firstly, the topography of relevant history was extended beyond Arabia to include the homeland of earlier messengers; thus, the Holy Land emerges as a particularly blessed region. At some point during this period, the orientation towards the 'furthest sanctuary', the Jerusalem Temple, *al-masjid al-aqṣā*, was implemented on the ritual level as well, with the community adopting the Jerusalem *qibla* and sealing the expansion of the symbolic horizon into the world of the *Banū Isrāʾīl*, the people of Moses.[30] This cultic reform is closely connected to a personal experience of the Prophet Muhammad, his travel to the sanctuary in Jerusalem. In Q 17:1, Jerusalem functions as the destination of a nocturnal journey, *isrāʾ*, of the Prophet:

> Glory be to Him, who carried His servant by night (*asrā*)
> from the Holy Place of Worship to the Further Place of Worship
> the precincts of which We have blessed,
> that We might show Him some of Our signs. He is the All-hearing, the All-seeing.

Though the location is mentioned only obliquely, it is made unambiguous through its reference to the Holy Land, 'the precincts of which We have blessed', which was familiar to the community from various biblical narratives. The Jerusalem Temple as the destination of the Prophet's nocturnal journey is, however, not identical with the historical site, but has been adapted to the late antique image of sanctuaries. The Jewish *bayit*, the Temple as the 'House of God', is perceived as a *masjid*, a place where humans perform the ritual prayer. It is constructed as an analogue to the Kaʿba, and thus integrated into Arabian space. On the other hand, the Prophet's journey into the Land of the Israelites can be understood in biblical terms, as a mimesis of Moses. Moses was raised to a high mountain to receive the Tablets. Likewise the Prophet is transferred to a sacred place—though no longer for a mythical encounter with God but

[29] Guy A. Stroumsa, *Das Ende des Opferkults: Die religiösen Mutationen der Spätantike* (Berlin: Suhrkamp, 2011), 53–85.

[30] Neuwirth, 'The Spiritual Meaning of Jerusalem in Islam'.

rather for a personal experience of the sacred at the point of the *qibla*, the place towards which he oriented his prayers. The Moses typology is even more evident from the phrasing of the *isrā'*, which resonates with the divine order given to Moses in Q 20 and 26: *asri bi-'ibādī*, ('Go out with My servants' = Perform the Exodus). Though no real collective, but only a spiritual individual exodus is at stake, the *isrā'* still resounds with the triumphal feeling of liberation which permeates the exodus report—a Mosaic prerogative has been appropriated.

Many listeners of the Prophet did not understand the Moses typology, and refused to believe his experience. In the same surah, Q 17:93, they challenge him:

> They say: We will not believe you . . . till you go up to heaven and we will not believe your going up till you bring down on us a book that we may read. Say: Glory be to my Lord, am I not only a mortal, a messenger?

The opponents interpret the words of the Prophet in the literal sense. In view of his frequent claim to owe his speech to a heavenly writ—comparable to Moses who had received the heavenly writ in the shape of the tablets—they press him to present the transcendent Scripture in material form. In a milieu where revelations had long been familiar in the shape of codices or scrolls, mere oral proclamations like that of the Prophet appeared to lack authority. But the decisive handicap of the opponents is their inability to apply the new hermeneutics of typology that underlies the qur'anic speech where exterior meaning is elusive, truth being accessible only through references to a textual universe. The claim of the Qur'an to the rank of Scripture is firmly tied to the implementation of the hermeneutics of typology.

Is there a promise-fulfilment pattern involved here? It is striking to note that Moses' exodus which is narrated in Mecca a few times (Q 20, Q 26) is always presented as a punitive narrative—dramatic in view of the amount of violence involved—but completely devoid of its biblical political dimension. There are no Egyptian plagues needed, no catastrophes to endanger the entire state of Egypt, to move Pharaoh to let the people go. The Exodus is depicted as the Prophet Moses' salvation from vicious foes, an individual salvation which he shares only with his adherents. No nation building is at stake. Q 17:1 equally tells about a personal experience of a prophet, but also has a political tint, since it induces a promotion of the local Meccan Ka'ba to the rank of the great sanctuary as such, the Temple. The map of the *topographia sacra* is expanded with Mecca remaining the point of departure.

Mecca's rise in status thus achieved is mirrored in a prayer uttered by Abraham in a slightly later surah which puts the blessed Land—as the destination of the Israelites, promised to Abraham in Gen 15—on equal footing with the Meccan sanctuary, the home of the new people of the monotheist creed. In Q 14 Abraham intercedes for his Arab progeny asking for their subsistence and success not in a land flowing with milk and honey but in the barren region of Mecca whose dignity is however warranted by a sanctuary and which is to be the point of departure for a monotheist cult:[31]

> When Abraham said, My Lord, Make this land secure
> and turn me and my sons away from serving idols. . . .
> Our lord, I have made some of my seed to dwell in a valley where is no sown land by your Holy House. Our Lord, let them perform the prayer and make the hearts of men yearn towards them, and provide them with fruits, haply they will be thankful . . .
> Praise be to God who has given me, though I am old, Ishmael and Isaac; surely my Lord hears the petition.

The project of an ideologically determined 'nation' clearly looms behind this text. In view of the real presence of the monotheist community in situ, this promise has already come true. Yet, it is at this stage not more than a new self-perception of the community that regards itself as the implementer of an Abrahamic project which binds it to its Arabian setting. As is evident from the real history of the community, the re-reading of biblical history to include local Arabian memory, even the staging of Abraham as the progenitor of the Arabs in particular, did not dissolve the conflict with the pagans. That conflict continued and finally induced a parting of the ways, the community's emigration to Medina.

ECLIPSING BIBLICAL TRADITION: A NEW MYTHOPOIESIS

Once we turn to the last stage in the development, the community's encounter with the Bible in Medina, momentous changes emerge. With the community's establishment of close contacts with the *ahl al-kitāb,* or scriptural people (primarily educated Jews), another manifestation of the Bible, different from Griffith's concept of the universally accessible 'interpreted Bible', which was widely Christian-imprinted, enters the scene. It is the Bible in its Jewish use in liturgy and in debate where it is read through the lens of rabbinic exegesis. The encounter with the exegetically professional Jewish interlocutors enables the community to rediscover biblical evidence for their own theological positions.

The Jews of Medina—far from being opponents of the Prophet from the outset—need to be imagined as significant interlocutors of the community who introduced not only a more precise biblical knowledge but equally new hermeneutical approaches to biblical texts. The impact of their exegetical skills on the debates that took place between them and the new community—of

[31] Sinai, *Fortschreibung und Auslegung.*

which we only can trace remnants—must have been paramount. There is a sudden and unexpectedly keen interest attested in *Sūrat Āl ʿImrān*, Q 3, with respect to the issue of the 'openness', ambiguity, of scriptural texts which needs to be contextualized with the Jewish exegetical principle of the multiple faces of the Torah.[32] Verse 8 states:

> It is He who sent down upon you the Scripture, wherein are verses clear that are the Mother of the Scripture, and others ambiguous.
>
> As for those in whose hearts is swerving, they follow the ambiguous part, desiring dissension (or temptation, seduction) and desiring its interpretation; but none knows its interpretation, save only God.
>
> And those firmly rooted in knowledge say, 'We believe in it; all is from our Lord', yet none remembers, but men possessed of minds.

This verse, for the first time, raises the issue of hermeneutic ambiguity in scripture, which comes as a surprise in view of the numerous previous passages in which the Qurʾan describes itself as a particularly manifest (*mubīn*) text, such as Q 26:2: 'Those are the signs of the Manifest Book [Scripture]', tilka āyātu l-kitābi l-mubīn. Accordingly, why should there be verses that are ambiguous? The problem remains unresolved as long as the community's ongoing debate with adherents of the older religions is ignored.

We need, however, to remember that not only Christian but also much of Jewish exegesis builds on allegory and mythopoiesis. It is the hermeneutic experience exemplified by both Jews and Christians that we find negotiated in the later surahs of the Qurʾan. A particularly telling example is the Medinan re-interpretation of the concept of the remote sanctuary, *al-masjid al-aqṣā*. One of the earliest reforms carried out in Medina was the change of the direction of prayer from Jerusalem to Mecca, a step which involved the promotion of the Kaʿba to the rank of Jerusalem as the most dignified sanctuary, indeed the sacred centre of the world where prayers converge to rise to heaven. This momentous step, which had to be realized against vehement opposition, throws light on a newly induced hermeneutical turn.

Religious concepts that had until then been taken for granted now turn out to be bearing highly symbolic weight. The Jerusalem sanctuary looked upon through the eyes of Jewish and Christian neighbours in Medina presented itself to the emerging community in a new light. In rabbinic tradition it was the very foundation of the altar which Abraham together with Isaac had raised

[32] See Angelika Neuwirth, 'Mary and Jesus Counterbalancing the Biblical Patriarchs. A Re-reading of *Sūrat Maryam* in *Sūrat Āl ʿImrān* (Q 3.1–62)', *Parole de l'Orient* 30 (2005): 231–60, and Angelika Neuwirth, 'The House of Abraham and the House of Amram: Genealogy, Patriarchal Authority, and Exegetical Professionalism', in *The Qurʾān in Context*, edited by Neuwirth et al. (Leiden: Brill, 2009), 499–532.

for the sacrifice on Mount Moriah.[33] Christians as against that had completely unhinged the Temple from its topographical embedding. The Church Fathers transformed it into a spiritual edifice associated with Golgatha which had equally 'been erected' by means of a father–son synergy, this time by God and Christ, the antitypes of Abraham and Isaac, the 'two wise architects of belief', as Ephrem of Nisibis calls them.[34] This image of Jerusalem was no longer in tune with the long cherished *al-masjid al-aqṣā*, the universal centre of monotheism. Yet, both traditions are built on a shared typological basis: monotheist sanctuaries obviously need to be of Abrahamic origin and they are owed to a sacrifice offered synergetically by a father and a son. It is on this axiom that the qur'anic foundation story of the Kaʿba as the new Temple builds.

The Abrahamic sacrifice had already been a topic of a Meccan surah, in a story told to exemplify Abraham's utmost loyalty. Both the victim's name and the local setting of the act had remained undetermined. The edificatory story unrelated to the discourse of sacrifice had to be rewritten in Medina where among learned Jews the idea of the Akedah and of sacrifice in general possessed paramount significance. To adjust the story to the new theological requirements, the nation-building dimension of the Akedah needed to be addressed. To balance his rank as the progenitor of the Israelites, Abraham also needed to be regarded as the progenitor of the Arab tribes—a rank that is biblically warranted but had been little cherished in Jewish or Christian theology. Let us look briefly at the Meccan text of the Akedah (Q 37) and its Medinan extension which is easily recognizable from its greater verse-length (102).

> Then We gave him the good tidings of a prudent boy
> And when he had reached the age to perform the rite of *al-saʿy* with him Abraham said, my son, I see in a dream that I shall sacrifice you, consider what do you think?
> He said, My father do as you are bidden. You will find me—God willing—one of the steadfast.
> When both had surrendered and he flung him upon his brow, We called upon him: Abraham.
> You have confirmed the vision. Even so We recompense the good-doers.
> This is indeed the manifest trial.
> And We ransomed him with a mighty sacrifice
> And left for him among the later folk: 'Peace be upon Abraham.'

The story without v. 102 matches Gen 22, the appended long verse 102, however, unmistakably locates it in Mecca, thus relating it to the myth of

[33] For the late traditions attached to the Akedah story, see Lukas Kundert, *Die Opferung, Bindung Isaaks: Gen 22:1–19 in frühen rabbinischen Texten* (Neukirchen-Vluyn: Neukirchner, 1998).

[34] The typological relationship between the Akedah story in Jewish and Christian exegesis and the Qur'an have been discovered by Joseph Witztum, 'The Foundations of the House (Q 2: 127)', *Bulletin of the School of Oriental and African Studies* 72.1 (2009): 25–40.

origin of the Ka'ba. According to verse 102, Abraham and his son were on their pilgrimage in Mecca preparing themselves for the ritual of the running between al-Ṣafā and al-Marwa,[35] when the *ru'yā*, the dream vision with the call to the son's sacrifice occurred. Both, father and son, together are willing to offer the sacrifice—in tune with rabbinic tradition where, however, the identity of the son as the patriarch Isaac is of central importance. In the Qur'an the son is named neither in the core text nor in the 'appendix', verse 102. But his identity is known from the foundation myth of the Ka'ba which had meanwhile emerged. This foundation story builds on the scenario of the father–son synergy as presented in the rabbinic sacrifice story. According to surah 2:126–8, Abraham together with his son lays the foundation of the sanctuary. But it is no longer the altar on Mount Moriah but the Ka'ba in Mecca that is established and the son involved in the act is not Isaac, the ancestor of the Jewish people, but Ishmael, the ancestor of the Arabs.

> When Abraham said, my Lord. Make this land secure and provide its people with fruits, such of them as believe in God and the Last Day...
> When Abraham, and Ishmael with him raised up the foundation of the House:
> Our lord receive this (sacrifice) from us. You are the all-hearing, the all-knowing.

The foundations of the Meccan sanctuary, the Ka'ba, are laid in a manner which is strikingly analogous to those that Abraham—according to rabbinic tradition—had laid for the Solomonic Temple. Mecca has thus emerged as a New Jerusalem.

The typological reconstruction of Mecca as a new Jerusalem does not, however, stop with the 'biblical' legitimation of the sanctuary through the construction of a parallel genealogy leading back to Abraham. Mecca is also to catch up with, indeed to outrun Jerusalem in its spiritual significance, namely as the point of departure for the promulgation of monotheist divine service, and verbal service in particular. The prayer uttered by Abraham and his son continues:

> Our lord, send among them a messenger, one of them who shall recite to them your signs,
> and teach them the Scripture and the Wisdom and purify them;
> you are the all-mighty, the all-wise.

This prayer comes very close to the prophecy uttered by Isaiah regarding Jerusalem, where it says (Isaiah 2:3): 'For out of Zion shall go forth Torah and the word of the Lord from Jerusalem.'

The prayer, like the previous one dating to back to the late Meccan period, is a *vaticinatio ex eventu*, an already fulfilled prophecy: the messenger craved for,

[35] For the rituals of the Islamic Ḥadjdj see Gerald Hawting, 'Pilgrimage', *Encyclopedia of the Qur'an* (Leiden: Brill, 2003), 3: 91–100.

who will teach Scripture and Wisdom, has already arrived in the person of the Prophet Muhammad. The Scripture which he is meant to teach—though not yet brought to an end at this time—is in the process of being completed.

REFLECTING TYPOLOGY

The Qurʾan, however, does not confine itself to the narrative genre to convey the conviction that reading the Bible is not reserved for Jews and Christians and that not a few of their readings are deficient. It is in debates and direct addresses that controversial issues are negotiated. One point of attack is the mode of thinking in genealogical categories which is manifest in the Jewish view of being privileged thanks to the 'merits of the fathers'. In the Qurʾan this article of faith is identified as a mistaken conclusion from the biblical promise of blessing that Abraham had received after agreeing to sacrifice his son. He is graced with the promise of a blessing which in qur'anic understanding is falsely focused by Jewish exegetes on Abraham's Israelite progeny alone. Abraham himself is evoked to correct this conclusion in Q 2:124:

> And *remember* when his Lord tried Abraham with certain commands which he fulfilled. He said, 'I will make thee a Leader of men.' *Abraham* asked, 'And from among my offspring?' He said, 'My covenant does not embrace the transgressors.'

The appropriation of Abraham by both Jews and Christians is undermined by an argument that Paul had already used: Abraham antedates the legislation of Moses and the coming of Christ. It is his exemplary piety that matters. His veneration of God is closely related to the concept of submission that underlies Islam—the word Islam can even be regarded as a verbal translation of submission, the Abrahamic virtue. In Q 3:66, 68 we read:

> O People of the Book! Why do you dispute concerning Abraham, when the Torah and the Gospel were not revealed till after him? Will you not then understand?
>
> Abraham was neither a Jew nor a Christian, but he was ever inclined *to God and* obedient *to Him*, and he was not of those who associate gods *with God*. Surely, the nearest of men to Abraham are those who followed him, and this Prophet and those who believe; and God is the friend of believers.

As the last step in the community's itinerary towards a new identity as an Abrahamic faith, the close relationship between the messenger and Abraham is vindicated. Muhammad is a prophet from the biblical tradition but he is at the same time a prophet from a counter-tradition, in the vein of the pre-Jewish and pre-Christian Abraham who was already identified by Paul as a servant of God before the emergence of the Israelite covenant and thus still belonged to 'the nations', the non-Jews. Accordingly the Prophet Muhammad is a prophet from among the nations (Q 7:159):

> Say, 'O mankind! Truly I am a Messenger to you all from God to Whom belongs the kingdom of the heavens and the earth. There is no God but He. He gives life, and He causes death. So believe in God and His Messenger, the Prophet from among the nations who believes in God and His words; and follow him that you may be rightly guided.'

CONCLUSION

The emergence of the Qurʾan as such is not only laden with biblical symbolism, it is no less imprinted with Late Antique textual politics. The hermeneutical strategies applied in the Qurʾan are the common property of the monotheist and even pagan groups in the milieu. Many of them can be classified as modes of typology. And yet, until now scholars have not succeeded in putting qur'anic and biblical traditions on the same footing. They still tend to differentiate between 'genuine biblical lore' in the Qurʾan and qur'anic typological readings of biblical narratives which appear as 'deviations' from the biblical models and thus are to be labelled 'legends'.[36] This way of grading betrays a still subsisting theological bias. Qurʾanic reshapings of biblical stories such as the Akedah story staged in Mecca, however, are not to be considered as fabrications but rather represent Late Antique elaborations, 'updatings' so to speak, of particular biblical texts. They reflect a creative perusal of antique exegetical models known from rabbinic, New Testament, and ecclesiastical practices. Looked upon from this perspective, the Qurʾan proves an active and innovative player in the Late Antique field of debate. Its effects are momentous: biblical topography is extended into Arabia, and Mecca is established as a new Jerusalem. Last but not least a new teacher of rectitude has established himself in the person of the Prophet Muhammad who in many respects follows in the footsteps of Jesus. His coming is announced by Abraham, who has charged him with the transformation of the ancient Arabian ritual religion into a scriptural religion: His mission is therefore inseparable from that of the figure of Abraham.

To properly understand these innovations of the Qurʾan we need to admit the Qurʾan into the textual and hermeneutical universe of Late Antiquity. It is not the Bible in the hands of the Jews and Christians that provides the ultimate criterion about what is a genuine monotheist lore in tune with the Bible, since this Christian or Jewish understanding is often the result of readings that

[36] Reuven Firestone, 'Abraham', *Encyclopedia of the Qurʾan* (Leiden: Brill, 2001), 1: 5–11.

privilege particular ideas over others. It may equally be the qur'anic reading of the Bible which can open the eye of the reader to the intent of a biblical text unit. In such cases the qur'anic reading can help to recheck established biblical readings so as to exclude marginalizations of particular texts in favour of more conventionally accepted ones, as was the case with the biblical traditions about Ishmael. In the light of our analysis of the qur'anic Abraham stories we probably will have to read the biblical Abraham-and Ishmael-texts anew, finally taking the measure of their intrinsic political dimension which Jewish and Christian traditions have seriously marginalized.

BIBLIOGRAPHY

Abu Zayd, Nasr Hamid. *Rethinking the Qurʾan: Towards a Humanistic Hermeneutics.* Utrecht: Humanistics University Press, 2004.

Arkoun, Mohammed. *The Unthought in Contemporary Islamic Thought.* London: Saqi Books, 2002.

Azmeh, Aziz al-. *The Emergence of Islam in Late Antiquity: Allah and His People.* Cambridge: Cambridge University Press, 2004.

Bobzin, Hartmut. 'Pre-1800 Preoccupations of Qurʾanic Studies'. In Jane Dammen McAuliffe, ed., *Encyclopedia of the Qurʾan.* Leiden: Brill, 2004, 4: 235–53.

Brown, Peter. *Late Antiquity.* Cambridge: Harvard University Press, 1998.

Busse, Heribert. 'Herrschertypen im Koran'. In Ulrich Haarmann and Peter Bachmann, eds, *Die Islamische Welt zwischen Mittelalter und Neuzeit. Festschrift für Hans Robert Roemer zum 65 Geburtstag.* Beirut; Weisbaden: In Kommission be F. Steiner, 1979, 56–80.

Campanini, Massimo. *Modern Muslim Interpretations.* London; New York: Routledge, 2011.

Conrad, Sebastian. 'Enlightenment in Global History: A Historiographical Critique'. *American Historical Review* 117 (4) (2012): 999–1027.

Firestone, Reuven. 'Abraham'. *Encyclopedia of the Qurʾan.* Leiden: Brill, 2001, 5–11.

Franke, Ute, Ali al-Ghabban, Joachim Gierlichs, and Stefan Weber, eds. *Roads of Arabia: Archaeological Treasures of Saudi Arabia.* Berlin: Wasmuth, 2012.

Geiger, Abraham. *Was hat Mohammed aus dem Judenthume aufgenommen?* Bonn: Baaden, 1833.

Griffith, Sidney. *The Bible in Arabic: The Scriptures of the 'People of the Book' in the Language of Islam.* Princeton: Princeton University Press, 2013.

Hartwig, Dirk, Walter Homolka, Michael J. Marx, and Angelika Neuwirth, eds. *'Im vollen Licht der Geschichte': Die Wissenschaft des Judentums und die Anfänge der kritischen Koranforschung.* Würzburg: Ergon, 2008.

Hawting, Gerald. 2003. 'Pilgrimage'. *Encyclopedia of the Qurʾan.* Leiden: Brill, 2003, 3: 91–100.

Horovitz, Josef. 'Das Koranische Paradies'. *Scripta Universitatis atque Bibliothecae Hierosolymitanarum* 6 (1923): 1–16. Reprinted in Rudi Paret, ed., *Der Koran.* Darmstadt: Wissenschaftliche Buchgesellschaft, 1975.

Horovitz, Josef. *Koranische Untersuchungen*. Berlin: De Gruyter, 1926.

Kundert, Lukas. *Die Opferung, Bindung Isaaks: Gen 22:1–19 in frühen rabbinischen Texten*. Neukirchen-Vluyn: Neukirchner, 1998.

Neuwirth, Angelika. 'The Spiritual Meaning of Jerusalem in Islam'. In Nitza Rosovsky, ed., *City of the Great King: Jerusalem from David to the Present*. Cambridge: Harvard University Press, 1996.

Neuwirth, Angelika. *Studien zur Komposition der Mekkanischen Suren*. Studien zur Sprache. Geschichte und Kultur des islamischen Orients. 2nd edn. Berlin: Walter De Gruyter, 2007.

Neuwirth, Angelika. *Der Koran als Text der Spätantike: Ein europäischer Zugang*. Berlin: Verlag der Weltreligionen im Insel Verlag, 2010.

Neuwirth, Angelika. *Koranforschung—eine politische Philologie?: Bibel, Koran und Islamentstehung im Spiegel spätantiker Textpolitik und moderner Philologie*. Litterae et Thologia. Berlin: de Gruyter, 2014.

Neuwirth, Angelika. *Scripture, Poetry and the Making of a Community: Reading the Qurʾan as a Literary Text*. Oxford: Oxford University Press, 2014.

Neuwirth, Angelika. '*Jesus und Muhammad*—Zwei spätantike Lehrer? Ein Versuch, den Koran im Licht der Lehre Jesu "neu zu lesen"'. In Thomas Fornet-Ponse, ed., *Jesus Christus: von alttestamentlichen Messiasvorstellungen bis zur literarischen Figur*. Münster: Aschendorff, 2015.

Neuwirth, Angelika. 'The "Discovery of Writing" in the Qurʾan: Tracing an Epistemic Revolution in Late Antiquity'. In Nuha al-Shaar, ed., *Qurʾan and Adab*. Oxford: Oxford University Press in association with the Institute of Ismaili Studies, 2017.

Nöldeke, Theodor, Friedrich Schwally, Gotthelf Bergsträsser, and Otto Pretzl. *Die Geschichte des Korantextes*. Leipzig, Dieterich, 1938. Reprint: Hildesheim: Olms, 1961.

Paret, Rudi. 'Das Geschichtsbild Mohammeds'. *Welt als Geschichte 2* (1951): 214–24.

Paret, Rudi, ed. *Der Koran*. Darmstadt: Wissenschaftliche Buchgesellschaft, 1975.

Reynolds, Gabriel. *The Qur'ān and its Biblical Subtext*. New York: Routledge, 2010.

Sahas, Daniel. *John of Damascus: The 'Heresy of the Ishmaelites'*. Leiden: Brill, 1972.

Schmidt, Nora, et al. *Denkraum Spätantike: Reflexionen von Antiken im Umfeld des Koran*. Episteme in Bewegung. Weisbaden: Harrassowitz, 2016.

Silverstein, Adam. 'Hāmān's Transition from Jāhiliyya to Islām'. *Jerusalem Studies in Arabic and Islam* 34 (2008): 285–308.

Sinai, Nicolai. *Fortschreibung und Auslegung: Studien zur frühen Koraninterpretation*. Weisbaden: Harrassowitz, 2009.

Sinai, Nicolai. 'The Qurʾan as Process'. In Angelika Neuwirth, Nicolai Sinai, and Michael Marx, eds, *The Qurʾān in Context: Historical and Literary Investigations into the Qurʾānic Milieu*. Leiden: Brill, 2010.

Sizgorich, Thomas. *Violence and Belief in Late Antiquity: Militant Devotion in Christianity and Islam*. Divinations: Rereading Late Ancient Religion (series). Philadelphia: University of Pennsylvania Press, 2009.

Speyer, Heinrich. *Die biblischen Erzählungen im Qoran*. Gräfenhainichen: Schulze, 1931.

Stroumsa, Guy G. *Das Ende des Opferkults: Die religiösen Mutationen der Spätantike*. Berlin: Verlag der Weltreligionen im Insel Verlag, 2011.

Witztum, Joseph. 'The Foundations of the House (Q 2: 127)'. *Bulletin of the School of Oriental and African Studies* 72 (2009): 25–40.

6

Were there Prophets in the Jahiliyya?

Gerald Hawting

THE PROBLEM

The tradition of prophecy associated with Muhammad is a specific one: he is portrayed as one of a series, in which his forerunners were mainly figures known in the Jewish and Christian scriptures. When he is referred to as a prophet, it is not meant merely that he had powers or gifts that were 'prophet-like', but that he was the heir of a tradition of prophecy that was centuries old and was shared, mutatis mutandis, by Jews and Christians. Accordingly, terms used in connection with prophets in that tradition are attached to him, notably *nabī* (= Greek *prophetes*), the Arabic form of the common Semitic word for 'prophet', and *rasūl* (= Greek *apostolos*, Hebrew *mal'akh*, *shalīaḥ*), 'messenger'.[1]

We would expect a prophet of this sort to appear in a society already to some extent familiar with that tradition, where there was some awareness and knowledge of it. For a new prophet to be accepted, some at least would need to be willing to envisage that another prophet might come. Perhaps there had been individuals claiming prophecy of this sort in the recent past. God could in theory send a prophet at any time or place of His choosing, but so far as we know He has not sent one of this type to any society completely untouched by Judaism, Christianity, or Islam.

From the Qur'an it is evident that awareness of prophecy must have been strong in the society from which the text came. The opponents of the qur'anic prophet do not need to be told what a prophet is, and the Qur'an presupposes, on the part of its audience, considerable knowledge and understanding of figures such as Noah, Abraham, Moses, and Jesus, presented in it as prophets.

Muslim tradition regarding Muhammad and his environment, however, is ambivalent about the extent to which there was an awareness of prophets and

[1] I am not here concerned with the issue of the possibly different significations of *nabī* and *rasūl*; in this chapter both terms are rendered by 'prophet'. For an example of the collocation of 'messengers' and 'prophets', see 2 Chronicles 36:16.

prophecy. Its portrayal of Mecca as an almost completely pagan town, and of the opponents of Muhammad there as idolaters and polytheists, does not suggest that we should expect to encounter much knowledge or understanding of the biblical idea of prophets. On the other hand, it reports that there were several individual monotheists, often called *ḥanīf*s and sometimes said to have been attached to Christianity, in the environment, and even that some of them were familiar with the Jewish or Christian scriptures.

Furthermore, there are reports about individuals living in the region associated with the life of Muhammad who claimed to be prophets, or were regarded by others as prophets, just before or contemporary with him. Those reports, which are the focus of this chapter, are not widespread or well known, but they have led some scholars to argue that Muhammad did not appear as a claimant to prophecy in what might be called a prophetic vacuum. Rather, the concept of prophecy was reasonably familiar and available to him and his contemporaries in the Ḥijāz, and there should be no surprise that he claimed to be, and was accepted by his followers as, a prophet in the biblical tradition.[2]

The ambivalence of Muslim tradition as a whole is especially evident if one considers its material about pre-Islamic Arabian prophets living shortly before the time of Muhammad in the light of its idea of the *fatra*. According to that idea, before the coming of Muhammad there was a significant length of time during which God had not sent any prophet, the Arabic word *fatra* here designating the interval between Muhammad and the prophet who preceded him.

This idea of an interval or gap in the succession of prophets before the coming of Muhammad is usually connected with Q 5:19. There, God tells the People of the Book that He has sent His messenger to them after a *fatra* (literally, 'relaxation' or 'abatement' and hence 'pause' or even 'conclusion')[3] in the succession of messengers. He had now sent them a messenger in case they should complain that no one had been sent to warn them of the end they would meet if they did not believe, or to inform them of the rewards of belief. God tells them that they have indeed been sent a messenger to warn and inform them.

Commentators on the passage most frequently identify the *fatra* as the period between Jesus and Muhammad, a length of time variously estimated in different reports,[4] although some saw the qur'anic verse as directed against Jews who claimed that prophecy had ceased with Moses.[5]

[2] For some of those who argue that way, see pp. 189–91.

[3] In his commentary on this verse al-Ṭabarī (d. 310/923) glosses *fatra* as *inqiṭāʿ*.

[4] The identification of the *fatra* as the time between Jesus and Muhammad is attested in the commentaries attributed to Muqātil b. Sulaymān (d. 150/767) and ʿAbd al-Razzāq (d. 211/826). Muṭahhar al-Maqdisī (mid 4th/10th century), *Kitāb al-Badʾ wa-l-taʾrīkh*, C. Huart, ed. (Paris: Ernest Leroux, 1899–1907), 3: 126, attributes views on the length of the *fatra* to both Ibn Isḥāq (d. 148/765) and Ibn Jurayj (d. 150/767), although in Ibn Hishām's redaction of Ibn Isḥāq's *Sīra* the word only seems to be used with reference to a gap in the succession of revelations to Muhammad.

[5] For the understanding that Q 5:19 was directed at Jews in Medina who insisted that prophecy had ceased with Moses, see Ṭabarī, *Tafsīr*, on that passage.

The qur'anic reference to the *fatra* must indicate that among the social and religious groups to which the passage was addressed (explicitly monotheists, People of the Book) there was no idea that they had had a prophet in the recent past, and probably they held that prophecy had ceased at some relatively remote time in the past, a view accepted by the rabbis and by the Church. On the other hand, the verse also illustrates their general familiarity with the concept of prophecy, which is what we would expect. It seems that the verse was addressed to people familiar with the concept but with no recent history of prophets.

The notion of the *fatra* is in tension with the reports about individuals claiming to be prophets living in Arabia in the period between Jesus and Muhammad, some of them just prior to him and some contemporary with him. Because some of those claimants to prophethood are accepted as genuine prophets in the tradition, the tension cannot be resolved, as might be thought initially, by arguing that they are all regarded as false prophets. Some Muslim scholars envisaged that there were indeed prophets in Arabia during the *fatra*.[6]

It might be thought that the tension is illusory because, while the idea of the *fatra* is obviously a religious doctrine (for whatever reasons it emerged), the reports about the prophets perhaps relate more to actual historical conditions in pre-Islamic Arabia. That would not be a unique example of a conflict between doctrine and reality. It will be suggested here, however, that much of the material on the prophets of the Jahiliyya, rather than recording historical facts, likely developed to meet the needs of Muslim tradition, and if that argument is persuasive, there are tensions within the tradition between ideas that perhaps originated independently for different reasons.

Another ambivalent group of reports are those that tell us that Muhammad did not understand the nature of his initial prophetic experience, did not comprehend that he had been called to be a prophet. Only when a relative who was familiar with the Jewish and Christian scriptures enlightened him did he come to understand it.[7]

If those reports show Muhammad as unaware of prophecy at the time of his first call, they also illustrate that some individuals—those who followed one or other tradition of monotheism—were familiar with the institution. In Ibn Hishām's report, Muhammad's uncle Waraqa was able, because of his knowledge of, presumably, the Bible, to explain that the experience his nephew had undergone was a call to be a prophet.

The reports about Waraqa are part of a relatively prominent body of material about the presence of monotheists in the environment. If taken at face value, they indicate that the biblical tradition of prophecy was known to at least some of the

[6] See especially pp. 200–4 for those regarded as genuine prophets.

[7] E.g., Ibn Hishām, *Al-Sīra al-nabawiyya*, Muṣṭafā al-Saqqā et al., eds (Cairo: Muṣṭafā al-Bābī al-Ḥalabī, 1955), 1: 233–41 = English translation, A. Guillaume, *The Life of Muhammad* (Oxford: Clarendon Press, 1955), 104–11.

population, but again it will be necessary to consider how far the reports about the pre-Islamic Arab monotheists exist in the tradition because it is concerned to relate historical facts, and how far those reports too reflect the ideas of those who narrate them. Of course, it cannot be denied that there were monotheists in pre-Islamic Arabia, and knowledge of the biblical tradition of prophecy, but the issue is whether the Islamic image of the Jahiliyya tells us about historical pre-Islamic Arabia or about the needs and impulses of the early Islamic scholars.

JĀHILĪ PROPHETS?

This chapter is concerned, then, with the traditional material that appears to show that there was not merely an awareness of the concept of prophecy in the Jahiliyya, but that there were a number of individuals just before or contemporary with Muhammad who claimed to be prophets.

This material tends to be found, not in the best-known traditional biographies of Muhammad or historical works, but in genres such as *adab* and collections of *ḥadīth*s. Some, but not all, of the individuals concerned are presented as false prophets, although for us the truth or falsity of their prophethood is not an issue. If it could be established that there were claimants to prophecy in the biblical tradition in Arabia just prior to the appearance of Muhammad, that would help us to understand his emergence as a prophet of that type in what generally seems to be an unlikely setting for it.

Some scholars, indeed, have used this material about prophets in the Jahiliyya to contest the idea that Muhammad appeared, as it were, out of the blue. According to Yohanan Friedmann, who has referred to a number of the figures to be discussed here, 'Prophethood was, of course, not a phenomenon unknown to the ancient Arabs . . . This material indicates that the emergence of Muhammad . . . was not a unique event in the history of Arabia.'[8]

As predecessors or contemporaries of Muhammad, Friedmann refers to several prophets in pre-Islamic Arabia. Best known are the 'Arabian prophets' (Hūd, Ṣāliḥ and Shuʿayb) of the remote past who figure largely in the Qurʾan but are unknown to the biblical tradition; and also those who appeared among the tribes that fought against Medina during the wars of the Ridda following Muhammad's death. In addition he mentions three whose names are provided in exegesis of Q 36:13–14, names which the scripture itself does not provide; and, as well as them, Ḥanẓala b. Ṣafwān; Riʾāb b. Zayd; and Khālid b. Sinān.

Since the three whose names are supplied in commentaries on Q 36:13–14, are purely the result of exegesis and are associated with an unknown time

[8] Yohanan Friedmann, *Prophecy Continuous. Aspects of Aḥmadī Religious Thought and Its Medieval Background* (2nd printing, New Delhi: Oxford University Press 2003), 64–5.

and place,[9] they are not really relevant for a discussion of claimants to prophecy in the Jahiliyya. The same might also be said of the 'Arabian prophets' of the Qur'an. While their prominence in the scripture may attest to the circulation, in the milieu from which the Qur'an came, of stories about ancient prophets who lived in Arabia,[10] they cannot really be viewed as historical individuals who would have influenced Muhammad and his contemporaries in Mecca and Medina to see the biblical tradition of prophecy as still alive. These ancient prophets of the Qur'an and Muslim tradition will not, therefore, figure in our discussion. Only the Ridda prophets and others, including the last three names in Friedmann's list, seem to require discussion here.

In a similar way, Al Makin has questioned 'the domination of the prophethood of Muhammad in the narrative of the seventh century of the Arabian Peninsula presented by both Muslim and Western scholars'. 'There were', he states, 'many other claimants to prophethood, who are ignored in Muslim and Western sources.' His article discusses the case of the poet Umayya b. Abī-l-Salṭ, whose life and career are said to have overlapped those of Muhammad, and who is sometimes said to have claimed to be a prophet.[11]

In an article that refers to reports in the *Iklīl* of al-Hamdānī (d. 334/945), first drawn attention to by G. Widengren, about pre-Islamic tombs that contained inscriptions referring to various individuals as messengers of God, Jarl Fossum wrote, 'The term "Apostle" apparently was a popular title in the religious vocabulary of the Arabs at the time of Muhammad.... Tombstone inscriptions in South Arabia, recorded by al-Hamdānī, tell us that there were several people who regarded themselves as a, or *the*, Apostle of God.'

Of the four cases referred to in the *Iklīl*, three relate to Arabian prophets of the Qur'an (two mention Shuʿayb and one ʿĀd b. Iram, the target of Hūd's preaching), and one refers to Ḥanẓala b. Ṣafwān (on whom see pp. 200–1). In fact, the reports do not say that the prophet in each case used the title *rasūl Allāh*, but rather *nabī Allāh*. That would not make the evidence less significant, but it seems obvious that the reports are inspired by knowledge of the Qur'an and are unlikely to be accurate records of authentic pre-Islamic tombstones. In each case the alleged inscription referring to one of the Arabian prophets of the Qur'an ends with a reference to the fact that he was rejected, and one of them mentions the sending of the wind, which, according to Q 46:24, destroyed the people of ʿĀd. The report relating to Ḥanẓala also

[9] Some commentators, indeed, identify the place as Antioch.

[10] It is also possible that the Qur'an has transformed into prophets figures who were not originally seen as prophets.

[11] Al Makin, 'Re-thinking Other Claimants to Prophethood: the case of Umayya b. Abī Ṣalt', *Al-Jāmiʿah: Journal of Islamic Studies*, Yogyakarta Indonesia: 48 (2010): 165–90.

mentions his rejection by those to whom he was sent, and it ends by identifying him as the 'martyr' of al-Rass (see further on pp. 200–1).[12]

A positivist attitude to the traditional material about prophets in Arabia prior to and contemporary with Muhammad is displayed too by Aziz al-Azmeh, who refers to some of them in his argument that what was to develop into Islam emerged against the background of an indigenous Arab pre-Islamic monolatry. As well as the Khālid b. Sinān mentioned by Friedmann, he discusses Ibn Ṣayyād (on whom see pp. 204–7), and has frequent references to Umayya b. Abī-l-Salṭ and the *Ridda* prophets.[13]

Before it can be used to reconstruct the religious situation in the Jahiliyya, however, the evidence for these and other claimants to prophecy needs more consideration, and that is the purpose here.

Some of the reports are so isolated and unforthcoming that it may be we can do little with them. A certain Niyār b. Rabīʿa of the tribe of ʿAbs, for example, is said to have been cursed by Muhammad as a false prophet, but is mentioned only in passing.[14] Where there is more material, though, it is necessary to discuss its nature and whether it is possible to account for its presence in the tradition, before trying to use it for the purposes of historical reconstruction. Rather than examining each case separately, it is possible to put some of these possible prophets in a number of different categories.

THE RIDDA PROPHETS

The reports about the individuals who claimed to be prophets among the tribes in Arabia in the years following Muhammad's death are certainly the

[12] Jarl E. Fossum, 'The Apostle Concept in the Qurʾān and pre-Islamic Near Eastern Literature', in Mustansir Mir, ed., *Literary Heritage of Classical Islam: Arabic and Islamic Studies in Honor of James A. Bellamy* (Princeton: Darwin Press, 1993), 149. See *The Antiquities of South Arabia: Being a Translation from the Arabic... of the Eighth Book of al-Hamdānī's al-Iklīl*, trans. Nabih Amin Faris (Princeton: Princeton University Press, 1938), 80, 82, 84, 87.

[13] Aziz al-Azmeh, *The Emergence of Islam in Late Antiquity. Allāh and His People* (Cambridge: Cambridge University Press, 2014), 253–4 (Khālid b. Sinān), 348–9 (Ibn Ṣayyād); for Umayya b. Abī-l-Salṭ, and the Ridda prophets see the index.

[14] See Ibn Shabba, *Taʾrīkh al-Madīna al-Munawwara*, Fahīm Muḥammad Shaltūt, ed. (Beirut: Dār al-Turāth, 1410/1990), 2: 429–30. The reference occurs in the course of Ibn Shabba's chapter devoted to the prophet Khālid b. Sinān, in a report with a quite precise provenance ('Zurayq b. Ḥusayn b. Mūkhāriq, the chief of the tribe of ʿAbs in the year 210 [825–6] told me'). According to the story, a group of the ʿAbs had lost a spring of theirs, and Niyār b. Rabīʿa b. Makhzūm, 'who proclaimed that he was a prophet (*adhāʿa anhu tanabbaʾa*)', said that he would cause it to come forth for them. His utterance of a soothsayer-like verse failed to do the trick, however. When Muhammmad was told of this, he said (after approving the prophethood of Khālid) that Niyār was a false prophet (*kādhib*), 'may God curse him'. The report concludes with a line of verse by an ʿAbsī poet in Islamic times, referring to God's having cursed Niyār. Possibly the material on Niyār reflects a wish to distinguish between the true prophet and the traditional soothsayer.

most widespread and best known of those we are concerned with. Unlike many of the other reports, those on the Ridda prophets appear in Muslim historical literature. The most prominent of these prophets is referred to, perhaps pejoratively, as Musaylima; he claimed prophethood among his tribe of Ḥanīfa.[15]

For some scholars these Ridda prophets offer the prospect of situating Muhammad as just one, although the most successful, of several claimants to prophecy in Arabia in the first half of the seventh century. Dale Eickelmann, who put forward that view, suggested that the various claims to prophethood originated as nativist responses to external pressures on the Arabs. What made Muḥammad more successful than the others was the pan-tribal nature of his message compared with the others who were able only to motivate particular tribes or tribal groups.[16]

In spite of the relative profusion of material about the Ridda prophets, however, it has to be said that we are only allowed to view them from a later Muslim perspective. Generally they are portrayed as pale and often risible imitators of Muhammad. Musaylima is reported to have been willing to accept Muhammad as a prophet if he would recognize his prophethood in return. Like Muhammad they are reported to use titles like *nabī* and *rasūl Allāh*, and to have claimed that God sent them revelations, but the examples transmitted of such revelations are often ridiculous and childish, and said to have been modelled upon the Qurʾan (*muḍāhāh li-l-Qurʾān*).[17]

It is the fact that most of the activity of these prophets comes later than that of Muhammad that makes the material on them of questionable value so far as this chapter is concerned. If their activity was sparked off by the earlier successes of Muhammad, they cannot really be used to help explain why it was that he appeared claiming to be a prophet some twenty years or so before them. For any theory like Eickelmann's it seems important to establish that at least some of the Ridda prophets were active considerably before the death of Muhammad and independently of his influence. If the traditional image of

[15] On the wars of the Ridda in general, see E. Shoufani, *Al-Riddah and the Muslim Conquest of Arabia* (Toronto: University of Toronto Press, 1972); *Encyclopaedia of Islam* (hereafter *EI2*) s.v. Ridda (by Michael Lecker).

[16] D. Eickelmann, 'Musaylima: An Approach to the Social Anthropology of Seventh Century Arabia', *Journal of the Economic and Social History of the Orient* 10 (1967): 17–52. Eickelmann does not ask why it was as an outbreak of prophecy that the Arab reaction expressed itself rather than in any other way. M.J. Kister, 'The Struggle against Musaylima and the Conquest of Yamama', *Jerusalem Studies in Arabic and Islam* 27 (2002): 1–56 also emphasizes the purely local ambitions of Musaylima compared with the universal reach of Islam. See too Claude Gilliot, 'Muhammad, le Coran et les "contraintes del'histoire"', in *The Qurʾān as Text*, S. Wild, ed. (Leiden: Brill, 1996), 3–26, esp. 24–5.

[17] Ibn Hishām, *Sīra*, 2: 576–7, 599, 600; al-Ṭabarī, *Taʾrikh al-rusul waʾl-mulūk*, ed. M.J. de Goeje et al. (Leiden: Brill, 1879–1901), Part 1, 1737–1738 and 1748; Kister, s.v. Musaylima in *Encyclopaedia of the Qurʾān*.

them as mere imitators persists, they are not relevant for understanding why Muhammad identified himself as a prophet. Al-Azmeh seems to recognize that when he says that it is not possible to tell whether Muhammad was merely the most effective of such claimants to prophethood, or whether the Ridda prophets were following his example.[18]

Evidence that some at least of the Ridda prophets were already active early in Muhammad's lifetime is needed. Ibn Isḥāq does indeed tell us that Musaylima in the Yamāmah and al-Aswad b. Kaʿb al-ʿAnsī in the Yemen had 'spoken' in the time of Muhammad (*qad kāna takallama fī ʿahd rasūl Allāh*), but the statement lacks substance. It is made together with a report about Muhammad having said, in a public address, that he had known the true date of the 'Night of Power' (*laylat al-qadr*) but had been caused to forget it,[19] and that he had seen two golden bracelets on his arms which he had disliked and blown into fragments: 'I interpreted them to be these two impostors—the fellow in the Yemen and he in the Yamāmah.' There then follows a well-known tradition in which Muhammad prophesies that the end of time will not come before 30 antichrists have appeared, each one claiming to be a prophet.[20]

Chronologically, the activity of al-Aswad has been dated to a couple of months or so in the spring and early summer of 632 (AH 10–11)—in the lifetime of Muhammad but quite late—and it is not really possible to say how far his claim to be a prophet was influenced by Muhammad. Some see him as more of a traditional Arabian soothsayer (*kāhin*)[21] rather than as someone who claimed to be a *nabī*, even though he claimed to speak on behalf of the God of monotheism (Allāh or al-Raḥmān), and Montgomery Watt thought it likely that his monotheism was influenced by local Yemeni Judaism or Christianity rather than by Islam. Nevertheless, Watt considered that his movement was directed against the spread of Muhammad's influence in the Yemen. The evidence regarding the nature of his prophethood, however, is limited.[22]

There are more reports about Musaylima than about al-Aswad, and it has sometimes been suggested that he was active at an early stage in Muhammad's career, perhaps even that he appeared as a prophet before Muhammad did. Kister supports the idea that Musaylima was already active before the Hijra in the article on this prophet he wrote late in his career, and more recently

[18] Al-Azmeh, *Emergence of Islam in Late Antiquity*, 394.

[19] It is accepted that this significant night falls late in Ramaḍān, but its precise date is not known.

[20] Ibn Hishām, *Sīra* 2: 599. Ṭabarī, *Taʾrīkh*, Part 1, 1796–1797 has the report about the bracelets in an account from Sayf b. ʿUmar that dates it to a time after Muhammad's final illness had begun.

[21] Sayf b. ʿUmar's account at Ṭabarī, *Taʾrīkh* Part 1: 1795 ff. says that al-Aswad was a *kāhin shiʿbādh*.

[22] W. M. Watt, *Muḥammad at Medina* (Oxford: Clarendon Press, 1956), 128–30 and s.v. al-Aswad in *EI2*. See too s.v. Ridda in *EI2* (by M. Lecker).

al-Azmeh has expressed the opinion that it is 'not improbable that Musaylima's prophecy antedated Muhammad's, and that the two may have met before the Hijra'.[23] Montgomery Watt, on the other hand, thought it 'virtually impossible' that Musaylima had claimed to be a prophet at least until towards the end of Muhammad's life.[24]

It is very likely that the idea that Musaylima was active as a prophet in the Yamāma even before the Hijra, results from a piece of qur'anic exegesis. According to Ibn Isḥāq, Q 13:30 with its reference to 'those who disbelieve in al-Raḥmān' was revealed to Muhammad in order to refute the charge of his Meccan opponents that he had been taught by a man of the Yamāma called al-Raḥmān (cf. Q 16:103 for the opponents' claim that the qur'anic prophet had been taught by a human being). The Meccans were 'those who disbelieve in al-Raḥmān' because they rejected Muhammad, whom they accused of having been taught by someone called al-Raḥmān in the Yamāma. The 'man of the Yamāma' must be Musaylima, and other accounts, indeed, identify this al-Raḥmān of the Yamāma as Musaylima. We are told that Musaylima claimed to have received revelations from al-Raḥmān, and that he was called by his companions *raḥmān al-Yamāma*.[25]

Unconvincing as the exegesis seems (and it is not widely attested in *tafsīr* on Q 13:30), it probably lies behind the idea that Musaylima had contacts with Muhammad early in the latter's prophetic career. Other reports first introduce Musaylima in connection with the delegation from the Banū Ḥanīfa that came to submit to Muhammad towards the end of his life around the year 10/632. Although the reports about that differ as to whether Muhammad met Musaylima at the time (some say Musaylima was left to guard the baggage while the others conferred with Muhammad), it is said that he began to claim to be a prophet after the delegation had returned to the Yamāma, taking advantage of something that Muhammad had said when he was told that one member of the delegation had not been able to come to meet him. I do not suggest that these accounts of the delegation are necessarily any more historical than other reports relating to Musaylima, but simply wish to illustrate that the material that we have may contain reports that originated independently

[23] Kister, 'The Struggle against Musaylima', 4–5; al-Azmeh, *Emergence of Islam*, 238. Kister based his statement on a report in the *Thimār al-qulūb* of ʿAbd al-Malik al-Thaʿālibī (d. 429/1038) that 'Musaylima falsely claimed prophethood while the Prophet was in Mecca before the *hijra*' (Kister cites p. 146, no. 207). Al-Azmeh relies on a work by Jamāl ʿAlī al-Ḥallāq, *Maslama al-Ḥanafī* (Cologne: Manshūrāt al-Jamal, 2008)—he refers to pp. 33 f. and 91 ff.

[24] Watt, s.v. Musaylima in *EI2*, and his *Muḥammad at Medina*, 135.

[25] According to al-Wāqidī, *Kitāb al-Maghāzī*, J. Marsden Jones, ed. (London: Oxford University Press, 1966), 1: 82–3, in the Jāhiliyya, ʿAbd al-Raḥmān b. ʿAwf had been called ʿAbd ʿAmr but had changed his name to ʿAbd al-Raḥmān when he became a Muslim. At the time of Badr (2/624), a former friend still refused to call him ʿAbd al-Raḥmān 'because Musaylima in the Yamāma calls himself al-Raḥmān and I will not call you after him'. This report was cited by Kister, 'The Struggle against Musaylima', 6; see too his article s.v. Musaylima in *EQ*.

of others and reflect different impulses in the tradition. At any rate, the evidence that Musaylima might have prepared the way for the appearance of Muhammad as a prophet seems very questionable.

In spite of its relative abundance, therefore, the material about the Ridda prophets does not help much in trying to establish some sort of context in the Jahiliyya for Muhammad's appearance as a prophet in the Jewish and Christian tradition of prophecy. It is certainly possible that the various prophets, including Muhammad, indicate a proliferation of prophetic activity in Arabia in the first half of the seventh century, but our evidence generally portrays the Ridda prophets as emerging under the influence of the success of Muhammad. For that reason they have to remain somewhat peripheral to our concerns here, and we turn to material about other alleged claimants to prophecy where there is no doubt about their suggested chronology in relation to Muhammad.

MONOTHEISTS IN THE JAHILIYYA SOMETIMES IDENTIFIED AS PROPHETS

The case of a certain Riʾāb or Ribāb, referred to by Friedmann, has features similar to those of better known individuals who are sometimes associated with claims to prophethood in the sources. Riʾāb is reported by Ibn al-Kalbī (d. 206/821) to have been claimed as a prophet by the tribe of ʿAbd al-Qays.[26] Ibn al-Kalbī seems to be the only early source that has such a report, for elsewhere this Riʾāb (Ibn al-Kalbī calls him Riʾāb b. Zayd) appears only as someone who had intimations of monotheism in the Jahiliyya.

Ibn al-Kalbī claims that he composed a verse that uses Qurʾan-like phraseology praising God for raising the firmament without any light and splitting the earth without any spade,[27] while Ibn ʿAbd Rabbihi has him as one of those who proclaimed the oneness of God in the Jahiliyya.[28] According to the *Kitāb al-Aghānī*, Ribāb (sic) al-Shannī came from a family of soothsayers and wished to break with the people of the Jahiliyya, so he followed the religion of the Messiah.[29]

[26] *Tazaʿʿama ʿAbd al-Qays annahu nabiyyan*; Friedmann, *Prophecy Continuous*, 64–5, citing the British Library ms. of Ibn al-Kalbī's *Jamharat al-nasab* [= Ibn al-Kalbī, *Jamharat al-nasab*, in the *riwāya* of al-Sukkarī from Ibn Ḥabīb, ed. Bājī Ḥasan (Beirut: ʿĀlam al-kutub, 1407/1986), 593–4].

[27] *Al-ḥamdu lillāhi ʾlladhī rafaʿa ʾl-samāʾa bi-ghayri manār wa-shaqqa ʾl-arḍa bi-ghayri miḥfār*: Cf. Q13:2 and 80: 26.

[28] Ibn ʿAbd Rabbihi, *Al-ʿIqd al-Farīd*, ed. ʿAbd al-Majīd al-Ruhaynī, ed. (Beirut: Dār al-Kutub al-ʿIlmīyah, 1404/1983), 3: 308.

[29] Abu-l-Faraj al-Iṣfahānī, *Kitāb al-Aghānī*, Iḥsān ʿAbbās et al., eds (Beirut: Dār al-Kutub al-ʿIlmīyah, 1423/2002), 16: 229.

The report about Riʾāb/Ribāb in the *Aghānī* also contains a story that appears in several other sources that refer to him. During the *fatra* (or before the sending of the Prophet, or in the Jahiliyya) a voice would be heard at night calling, 'The best of the people of the earth are three: Riʾāb al-Shannī, Baḥīrā the Monk, and one who has not yet come.' Whenever a descendant of Riʾāb's died a gentle shower (*ṭashsh*) would water his grave. Baḥīrā is, of course, a well-known Christian witness in Muslim tradition to the truth of Muhammad's prophethood,[30] and the one still to come is Muhammad himself.[31]

The impression that emerges, then, is that Riʾāb serves in the tradition predominantly, like Waraqa b. Nawfal, as a pre-Islamic monotheist witness to the authenticity of the Prophet Muhammad. As with Waraqa, the material on him associates him both with the *ḥanīf*s (that is implied in the *Aghānī*'s account of him, although it does not use the word *ḥanīf*) and with Christianity, and in addition he is connected to the Arabian soothsaying tradition, which he rejected. Ibn al-Kalbī does not tell us that he claimed to be a prophet but that his tribe claimed him as one. From the evidence used here, then, the association of Riʾāb with prophecy seems to be a minor, even isolated, feature of the material on him, which reflects more the desire to document the fact that Muhammad had been foretold by monotheists who lived in the Jahiliyya.

Much more widely known than Riʾāb is the poet Umayya b. Abī-l-Salṭ, associated with Ṭāʾif and an older contemporary of Muhammad. He has been prominent in discussions of Muhammad's milieu because some of the verses attributed to him reflect monotheistic concepts and treat narratives also found in the Bible and the Qurʾan.[32] It is sometimes said that he also claimed to be a prophet.[33]

[30] See, e.g., Ibn Hishām, *Sīra*, 180–3 (= Eng. tr., 79–81).

[31] *Aghānī*, 16: 229; al-Masʿūdī, *Murūj al-dhahab*, Barbier de Meynard and Pavet de Courteille, eds; revised by Ch. Pellat (Beirut: Manshūrāt al-Jāmiʿa al-lubnāniyya, 1966), 1: 76 (§§133–4); Ibn Qutayba, *Kitāb al-Maʿārif*, Tharwat ʿUkāsha, ed. (Cairo: Dār al-maʿārif, 1969), 58; Ibn Durayd, *Kitāb al-Ishtiqāq*, ʿAbd al-Salām Hārūn, ed. (Baghdad: Maktabat al-Muthannā, 1979), 325. According to Ibn ʿAbd Rabbihi, *ʿIqd* 3: 308, when the delegation of ʿAbd al-Qays came to visit Muhammad, he asked them about Riʾāb, the graves of whose descendants were moistened (by rain).

[32] J. Frank-Kamenetzky, *Untersuchungen über das Verhältnis der dem Umajja b. Abī s Salt zugeschriebenen Gedichte zum Qorân* (Kirchhain, 1911). For the argument that Umayya influenced the Qurʾan, see Clement Huart, 'Une nouvelle source du Qoran', *Journal Asiatique* ser. 10, 4 (1904): 125–67. For more recent discussion of the authenticity of Umayya's poetry, see pp. 198–9.

[33] Al Makin, 'Re-thinking Other Claimants to Prophethood', especially 174–5, refers to Umayya's claims to be a prophet, but is vague in documenting them (n. 25). Uri Rubin, '*Ḥanīfiyya* and Kaʿba. An enquiry into the Arabian pre-Islamic background of *dīn Ibrāhīm*', *Jerusalem Studies in Arabic and Islam* 13 (1990), 96, reflects the evidence more precisely: 'Umayya tended to consider himself a prophet.'

As with Riʾāb, however, the evidence that Umayya claimed to be a prophet is quite tenuous. According to the *Kitāb al-Aghānī*, which seems to be the sole source of the idea, Umayya 'aspired to prophethood (*ṭamiʿa fi-l-nubuwwa*) because he had read in the scriptures (*kutub*) that a prophet would be sent from among the Arabs, and he hoped that it would be him'.[34] Other early accounts of Umayya known to me do not explicitly mention his ambition to be a prophet.[35]

Most of the biographical information about Umayya produces a picture rather like that for the above-mentioned Riʾāb and other monotheist precursors of Muhammad. In al-Masʿūdī's account, he visited 'clergy' (*ahl al-kanāʾis*) among the Jews and Christians of Syria and read the scriptures, so that he knew that a prophet would be sent among the Arabs. But when Muhammad appeared, although initially he intended to accept Islam, eventually he rejected him out of jealousy. That last detail could have generated the claim that he aspired to be a prophet himself.[36]

Traditions about him collected in the *Aghānī* repeat the claim that he knew the scriptures, provide examples of names he used to refer to God (*al-Salṭīṭ, al-Taghrūr*), tell us that he wore hair-shirts (*al-musūḥ*) as an act of devotion, and include him among those who mentioned Abraham, Ishmael and the religion of the *ḥanīfs* (*al-ḥanīfiyya*). A verse attributed to him says that on the day of the resurrection the only religion acceptable to God will be that of the *ḥanīfs*. Further, he was sceptical about idols and sought the truth (he was a *muḥaqqiq*). Nevertheless, it is implied, he failed ultimately to find it because he did not recognize Muhammad. In exegesis he appears as one possible candidate for the person about whom Q 7: 175 was revealed: 'Recite to them the news of him to whom We gave Our signs, but he cast them off.'[37]

All of this is broadly similar to the material about Waraqa and Riʾāb discussed above, with the difference that whereas Waraqa recognized Muhammad's prophethood, and Riʾāb died before he had the opportunity, Umayya rejected it, as did some of the other *ḥanīfs* discussed by Rubin.[38] All the material illustrates that the coming of the Prophet was known to those

[34] *Aghānī*, 4: 97. T. Fahd, *La divination arabe: études religieuses, sociologiques at folkloriques sur le milieu natif de l'Islam* (Paris: Sinbad, 1987), 77, accurately translates the sentence from the *Aghānī*, but then says that tradition made Umayya a dangerous rival of Muhammad regarding prophecy.

[35] Of the sources other than the *Aghānī* referred to by Rubin, '*Ḥanīfiyya* and Kaʿba', 96, n. 62, neither Ibn Qutayba's *Maʿārif* nor Masʿūdī's *Murūj* mention a claim to prophecy. Al-Suyūṭī, *Al-Khaṣāʾiṣ al-kubrā*, Muḥammad Khalīl Harrās, ed. (Cairo: Dār al-Kutub al-Ḥadītha, 1967), 1:60 (from Ibn ʿAsākir) refers to Umayya's knowledge of a prophet to come, but does not mention his own claims or hopes.

[36] Masʿūdī, *Murūj*, 1: 78–9 (§§139–40). Masʿūdī further says that Umayya introduced the formula *biʾsmika Allāhumma* to the Quraysh of Mecca before Muhammad (*Murūj*, 1: 79, §142).

[37] *Aghānī*, 4: 97.

[38] Rubin, '*Ḥanīfiyya* and Kaʿba', 85–112.

with learning or to whom it had been revealed in some way, but that knowledge does not always determine behaviour.

Another possible ingredient in the report that Umayya aspired to be a prophet is the lack of clear distinction in the Qur'an and some *ḥadīths*, with regard to terminology and concepts, between poetic inspiration and prophetic revelation. It is well known that Umayya is reported to have had his breast opened and filled (with poetic inspiration) in a way similar to that in which Muhammad's was opened and purified. Possibly the mention of Umayya's ambition is intended to underline that, in spite of the apparent overlap between poets and prophets, the distinction is significant.[39]

Although slightly tangential to our main theme here, something should be said about the issue of the authenticity of the verses attributed to him. If those that relate to the Qur'an and to biblical tradition are genuinely compositions of the Umayya who lived in the Hijaz at the time of Muhammad, that would indicate that he, and presumably his audience, were likely to have been aware of the biblical tradition of prophecy.[40]

The summaries of his verses provided in the biographical material probably reflect what circulated in his name or was collected in the *dīwān* by Ibn Ḥabīb (d. 245/860). According to al-Masʿūdī and Ibn Qutayba, Umayya's verses included descriptions of the heavens and the earth, the sun and the moon, angels and prophets, the resurrection of the body (*al-baʿth wa-l-nushūr*), paradise and hell, and glorification of the one God.[41]

The authenticity of the verses, like that of much else of the so-called *jāhilī* poetry, has been much discussed.[42] In Ibn Hishām's redaction of Ibn Isḥāq's *Sīra*, the attribution of a verse or verses to Umayya is often done by Ibn Hishām while Ibn Isḥāq cites them as the work of someone else. James Montgomery is fundamentally non-committal on the issue of authenticity in his article on Umayya in *EI2*, while Tilman Seidensticker has argued that there may be some genuine material.[43] Aziz al-Azmeh, while finally admitting that

[39] See J. Wansbrough, *Quranic Studies* (Oxford: Oxford University Press, 1977), 59–63 and the sources referred to there.

[40] Authenticity is a slightly ambiguous concept here: it could be envisaged, for example, that a particular verse is genuinely pre-Islamic but its attribution to Umayya (with all that that implies about the culture from which the verse came) is secondary.

[41] Ibn Qutayba, *Al-ṣhiʿr wa-l-shuʿarāʾ*, cited by Montgomery s.v. Umayya b. Abī ʾl-Ṣalt in *EI2*; al-Masʿūdī, *Murūj*, 1: 78 (§ 139).

[42] Thomas Bauer, 'The relevance of early Arabic poetry for Qurʾanic Studies', in Angelika Neuwirth et al., eds, *The Qurʾān in Context* (Leiden and Boston: Brill, 2010), 699–732, especially 701–3, takes issue with what he sees as some of the more extreme denials of authenticity, yet recognizes the difficulties in establishing it. He refers to Umayya as one especially controversial case (702).

[43] T. Seidentsticker, 'The authenticity of the poems ascribed to Umayya b. Abīʾl-Ṣalt', in J. R. Smart, ed., *Tradition and Modernity in Arabic Language and Literature* (Richmond, Surrey: Curzon 1996), 87–101 (cited by Montgomery).

the problem cannot be solved definitively, would clearly like to find grounds in favour of some authenticity.[44]

Nicolai Sinai has argued for the genuineness of verses attributed to Umayya that tell of the fate of the people of Thamūd, to whom, according to the Qurʾan, God sent the prophet Ṣāliḥ. His argument is based on the fact that there is little in common, in vocabulary or thematic treatment, between the verses and what he takes to be the earliest of the Qurʾan's allusions to the story of Thamūd and Ṣāliḥ. The main difference between the two is the absence of any prophet from the story in the version attributed to Umayya, whereas in the Qurʾan the central point is that Thamūd were destroyed because they rejected their prophet. In Umayya's poem the destruction of Thamūd is entirely the result of their mistreatment of the camel. Sinai's conclusion is that the story of Thamūd circulated in the Hijaz around the beginning of the seventh century, found its way into both Umayya's poetry and the Qurʾan, but in the latter was reshaped and reworked to make it fit the recurrent qur'anic theme of God's punishment of people who reject the prophet sent to them.[45]

That argument suggests that the qur'anic and poetic versions of the Thamūd story are independent and different versions of ones already circulating, but to conclude that they establish the authenticity of the attribution of the verses to Umayya depends heavily on acceptance of the traditional data about him. There are still various possibilities about where and when the verses were composed, how they came to be attributed to Umayya, and how the biographical material about Umayya developed. Whether (some of) the poetry ascribed to Umayya is really evidence for awareness of stories about prophets and prophecy in and around Mecca in the first decades of the seventh century still seems debatable.

What the material on Riʾāb and Umayya seems to illustrate is that there was occasionally a tendency in the tradition to associate some of the monotheists of pre-Islamic Arabia with prophecy, but in these two cases, at least, that tendency is confined to isolated reports. More generally the material on the two has the effect of substantiating the idea that there were people in Arabia before Muhammad who knew that his coming was to be expected, in a manner reminiscent of Christian interpretations of the prophets of the Hebrew Bible and of the story of the prophets Simeon and Anna in Luke's Gospel.[46]

[44] Al-Azmeh, *Emergence of Islam in Late Antiquity*, especially 258, n. 647.

[45] Nicolai Sinai, 'Religious Poetry from the Quranic Milieu: Umayya b. Abī l-Salṭ on the Fate of the Thamūd', *Bulletin of the School of Oriental and African Studies* 74 (2011): 397–416.

[46] Luke 2: 22–38.

Prophets of the *Fatra*

There are some other cases, though, when an individual is accepted more widely and assertively as a prophet in Arabia before Muhammad, to the extent that the traditional idea of the *fatra* is called into question. As al-Masʿūdī says at the beginning of his section on the *fatra*:

> Between the Messiah [Jesus] and Muhammad in the *fatra* there was a group of people who attested the oneness of God and affirmed the resurrection of the dead. But there are differences of opinion regarding them. According to some, there were prophets among them, but others held a different opinion.[47]

Some of the claimants to prophethood treated by al-Masʿūdī in this section are situated outside Arabia, and so are not really relevant here, but he begins with the Ḥanẓala b. Ṣafwān, whom we have already met as the occupant of one of the tombs reported by al-Hamdānī (see p. 200) and in the list of Yohanan Friedmann. Like al-Hamdānī, al-Masʿūdī tells us that Ḥanẓala was a prophet sent to the people of al-Rass in the Yemen, but they rejected him and killed him. In a subsequent cross-reference to the story of Ḥanẓala, Masʿūdī calls him Ṣafwān al-ʿAbsī.

The material on Ḥanẓala is relatively sparse. He is not mentioned by Ibn Qutayba in his section on those who followed the true religion before Muhammad, which includes some of the same material given by al-Masʿūdī. In his *EI2* article on this prophet, Pellat indicates the *Tarbīʿ* of Jāḥiẓ (d. 255/ 868–9) as the earliest reference to him. Al-Muṭahhar al-Maqdisī has similar reports about a Ḥanẓala b. Afyūn (probably an orthographical variant of Ṣafwān) al-Ṣādiq in his section on the *fatra*.[48]

His identification as the prophet sent by God to the people of al-Rass, who rejected and killed him, makes it likely that he exists, at least in part, as the result of speculative exegesis of the Qurʾan. The people of al-Rass are mentioned twice in the Qurʾan (25:38 and 50:12), both times as an example of a community which was sent a prophet whom they rejected and was thereupon destroyed by God. No details are given and the prophet sent to them is anonymous. It is well known that Muslim tradition generally hates anonymity and constantly supplies (variant) names to identify individuals, places, and such things not specified in early versions of reports and stories. That happens here in connection with both the location of the community and the name of its prophet. It will be remembered that Friedmann's list of prophets also contains names for the three anonymous messengers sent to the anonymous town of Qurʾān 36:13–14. Whether that accounts entirely for the existence of Ḥanẓala—or whether there

47 Al-Masʿūdī, *Murūj*, 1:72 (§ 122).

48 See *EI2* s.v. Ḥanẓala b. Ṣafwān; al-Muṭahhar al-Maqdisī *Badʾ*, 3: 6, 126, 133.

was already some material on him which was developed to make him a prophet and to connect him with the people of al-Rass—is debatable.

Another candidate for identification as the prophet sent to the people of al-Rass, although it seems only in later texts, is Khālid b. Sinān al-ʿAbsī, who is a much more developed presence in the tradition than the somewhat shadowy Ḥanẓala.[49] Especially notable in the case of Khālid is the existence of reports that Muhammad himself recognized him as a prophet who had appeared in Arabia only two generations earlier.

Khālid has been treated summarily by Pellat in *EI2* and more fully by Ella Landau-Tasseron in an article that discusses material about his tomb, situated at various locations in North Africa.[50] The reports about this prophet of the tribe of ʿAbs[51] repeat in variant forms certain recurring themes and details.[52] Not all the accounts of him contain all of these, and it may be possible to analyse the material to show that certain elements came in later than others. On the whole, though, one has the impression that the basic material on Khālid is relatively early: he is known to a number of third/ninth-century scholars, who claim to cite reports through earlier authorities back to Companions of the Prophet and members of Khālid's tribe who had their information from his contemporaries.[53]

Repeated in these early accounts are what seem to be the most important details regarding his identification as a prophet: the Prophet Muhammad said of him that he was a prophet whose people had 'lost', 'neglected', or 'failed' him (*nabī ḍayyaʿahu/aḍāʿahu qawmuhu*), the possible explanation of which

[49] The association with the people of al-Rass is not found in the 13 reports occupying 13 pages devoted to Khālid in Ibn Shabba's *Taʾrīkh al-Madīna* or in the short notice devoted to him in Ibn Qutayba's *Maʿārif*.

[50] See Ch. Pellat, s.v. Khālid b. Sinān in *EI2*; Ella Landau-Tasseron, 'Unearthing a Pre-Islamic Arabian Prophet', *Jerusalem Studies in Arabic and Islam* 21 (1997): 42–61. As the latter notes, Goldziher referred to Khālid and his tombs in the Maghrib in his study of the cult of saints in Islam in the second volume of his *Muhammedanische Studien* (1890) [= I. Goldziher, *Muslim Studies*, S. M. Stern and C. R. Barber, eds and trans., vol. 2, London 1971, 321]. Al-Azmeh, *Emergence of Islam in Late Antiquity*, 253–4 and 349, does not refer to Landau-Tasseron but cites Muḥammad Saʿīd's *Anbiyāʾ al-badw*, said to be forthcoming and cited from a typescript.

[51] ʿAbs b. Baghīḍ of the Ghaṭafān tribal confederation (part of Qays ʿAylān according to the traditional genealogies).

[52] See Landau-Tasseron, 'Unearthing', n. 13 for an extensive list of sources.

[53] Ibn al-Kalbī (cited by, e.g., Ibn Shabba); al-Jāḥiẓ, *Kitāb al-Ḥayawān*, ʿAbd al-Salām Muḥammad Hārūn, ed. (Cairo: Muṣṭafā al-Bābī al-Ḥalabī, 1938–45), 4: 476 ff.; Ibn Qutayba, *Kitāb al-Maʿārif*, 62 (includes him, together with Umayya b. Abī-l-Ṣalt, Waraqa b. Nawfal and others, in a section headed 'Those who held true religion before the sending of the Prophet'); Ibn Shabba, *Madīna*, 2: 420–33; Ibn ʿAbd al-Ḥakam, *Futūḥ Miṣr wa-akhbāruhā*, C. Torrey, ed. (New Haven: Yale University Press, 1922), 111, 229 and n. 18: an ʿAbsī settler in Fusṭāṭ called Kaʿb b. Ḍinna, or Kaʿb b. Yasār b. Ḍinna, who turned down the offer of being appointed *qāḍī*, is identified as the son of Khālid's daughter or sister. Ms D [Leiden] of the *Futūḥ* then gives some of the reports about Khālid—quoted in n. 18 to p. 229.

will be referred to shortly.[54] Sometimes it is reported that the occasion on which Muhammad said it was a meeting with Khālid's daughter (variant, son). When she heard Muhammad reciting sura 112 (*al-Ikhlāṣ*)—*qul: huwa llāhu aḥad Allāhu l-ṣamad*—she told him that she had heard her father saying the same, whereupon Muhammad greeted her as the daughter of his brother, a prophet whose people had 'lost' him.[55]

A story prominent in the chapters devoted to Khālid tells how, when death approached, he asked his people to bury him in a certain place for three days and then disinter him—they would find him alive and he would tell them of everything that was to happen until the Day of Resurrection. However, they failed to fulfil his instructions, a fact sometimes attributed to the shame they would have experienced if the other Arabs knew that they had exhumed one of their dead.[56] This story is sometimes adduced as the explanation of the *ḍayyaʿahu qawmuhu* dictum: his people failed or lost him because by not following his instructions they did not receive the insights he would have communicated to them.[57]

Sometimes the burial story appears together with, and seems to be a consequence of, Khālid's miraculously extinguishing a huge fire that issued from the ground in the Ḥijāz. The fire is variously called Nār al-Ḥadathān, Nār al-Ḥarra (or al-Ḥarratayn), Badā', etc.[58]

Another element found in the material about Khālid is his role in killing the *ʿanqāʾ*, apparently a birdlike creature that terrified the pre-Islamic Arabs. Here again it seems that the material on Khālid overlaps with that on Ḥanẓala.[59]

In spite of the relatively wide circulation of these stories about Khālid b. Sinān, his prophethood seems to have been occasionally contested. Jāḥiẓ, who is happy to accept that Khālid was a prophet—he says that there was no prophet (*nabī*) among the descendants of Ishmael prior to him—reports that the *mutakallimūn* did not accept him as one, because he was a Bedouin Arab (of the tribe of ʿAbs), and God never sent any prophet from among the

[54] Ibn Shabba, *Madīna*, 421 (twice), 423 (twice), 426, 430, 433; Ibn Qutayba, *Maʿārif*, 62; Jāḥiẓ, *Ḥayawān*, 4: 477; Ibn ʿAbd al-Ḥakam, *Futūḥ*, 229, n. 18 (passage that appears in the Leiden ms. only); Muṭahhar al-Maqdisī, *Bad'*, 3: 135.

[55] See references in previous note. Al-Azmeh, *Emergence of Islam in Late Antiquity*, 254, rejects the implication that Khālid was a monotheist and suggests he may have been 'an advocate of some kind of supra-celestialist monolatry'.

[56] Muṭahhar al-Maqdisī, *Bad'*, 135, top. According to Jāḥiẓ, *Ḥayawān*, 4: 477, it was Khālid's son who forbade that his father be disinterred, since he (the son) would then have been called Ibn al-Manbūsh.

[57] Maqdisī cites the prophet Muḥammad: 'If they had exhumed him, he would have told them all about me and this community' (*Bad'*, 135).

[58] Jāḥiẓ, *Ḥayawān*, 4: 476–7; Ibn ʿAbd al-Ḥakam, *Futūḥ*, 220, n. 18 (text in ms. D only); Muṭahhar al-Maqdisī, *Bad'*, 3: 134–5.

[59] See Pellat in *EI2*, s.vv. al-Anḳā' and Khālid b. Sinān.

Bedouins or those who live in hair tents: He only sent prophets from among those who live in settlements and towns.[60]

Ella Landau-Tasseron, in her article on Khālid b. Sinān, clearly regards much of the material about him as legendary and formulaic, and treats him as an historical figure transformed in the tradition 'from an Arabian miracle worker to a prophet'.[61] That implies that she doubts that the presentation of him as a prophet was an original part of the material about him, and sees his prophethood as an accretion to accounts of someone who actually existed.

That is certainly possible—to envisage him as a legendary hero of ʿAbs, whom Muslim tradition has made into a prophet. It seems clear though that even in our earliest Muslim sources about him, it is his identity as a prophet that is at centre stage: Muhammad's identification of him as a brother prophet and as 'a prophet whom his people lost'. If we cannot conclude that in this case we do have a genuine Arabian prophet one generation before Muhammad, at least we have to consider why Muslim tradition would want to create (if it has) a monotheist prophet among the ʿAbs just one generation before Muhammad.

In some ways Khālid's case is comparable to that of other monotheists of the Jahiliyya such as Waraqa, Riʾāb, and Umayya. In those cases there was an emphasis on monotheist beliefs, and knowledge of the scriptures or other sources of revelation (such as soothsaying) leading to prognosis or attestation of Muhammad's prophethood. Khālid is not credited with prediction of the appearance of Muhammad,[62] but he is presented as a forerunner of Islamic monotheism who was able to recite the key qur'anic formula about God's oneness before Islam.

The story of the meeting between his daughter and Muhammad is a sort of attestation story. Although Muhammad attests to Khālid's prophetic status rather than the other way round, the story does accord with others in which Muhammad's prophethood is foretold or verified by one of the *ḥanīfs* or People of the Book: a link is made between the prophet Muhammad and previous adherents of true religion. While Waraqa is never, apparently, referred to as a prophet, and Riʾāb and Umayya are connected with prophethood only tentatively and in a limited number of reports, Khālid b. Sinān's

[60] Jāḥiẓ, *Ḥayawān*, 4: 478, noted by Pellat, s.v. Khālid b. Sinān in *EI2*, and Landau-Tasseron, 'Unearthing', 45 n. 2, who adds references to Ṭabrisī, Majlisī, and Rāwandī. The argument cites Qurʾan 12: 109 (*wa-mā arsalnā min qablika illā rijālan nūḥī ilayhim min ahli l-qurā*). The rejection of the prophetic status of Khālid by the *mutakallimūn* (i.e. the Muʿtazila?) does not seem to have been based on any fundamental objection to the idea that there were prophets in the *fatra*: some argued that the story of the people of al-Kahf, which most—but not all—dated to the *fatra*, implied that there must have been a prophet amongst them, since the miracle involving them was so great that it could only have been performed in association with a prophet (see, e.g., Maqdisī, *Badʾ*, 3: 129).

[61] Ella Landau-Tasseron, 'Unearthing', 44.

[62] Although Maqdisī (n. 57) points out that it was his people's failure to recover him from his grave that prevented his prophesying the advent of Muhammad.

identification is primarily as a prophet. It seems that the impulse to associate Muhammad with an Arabian tradition of monotheism had become so strong that it had overcome the early idea of the *fatra.*

IBN ṢAYYĀD (OR IBN ṢĀ'ID)

Our last candidate for prophethood in the traditional Muslim image of pre-Islamic Arabia (the Jahiliyya) is substantially different from those so far considered.

Presented as a younger contemporary of Muhammad, he is treated in Muslim tradition in a generally hostile manner, and most often appears as the personification of the Antichrist (al-Dajjāl).[63] The idea that he claimed to be a prophet rests largely on one particular story, although some reports ascribe characteristically prophetic behaviour to him. The stories about him occur in variant forms, and display many puzzling features. He has attracted the attention of several scholars.[64]

He is described as a Jewish boy, living in Medina at the time when Muhammad and his followers had moved there from Mecca. There are stories about confrontations between him and Muhammad, and between him and important Companions. The reports about these confrontations have surprised a number of scholars. One would perhaps expect them to show Muhammad decisively having the upper hand and overcoming a rival claimant to prophethood, but the outcome seems indeterminate. Morabia comments that we learn from several reports that Ibn Ṣayyād's 'behaviour and pretensions perplexed Muhammad in a way that is surprising for a prophet'.[65]

The idea that Ibn Ṣayyād claimed to be a prophet rests mainly on a report that occurs in variant forms. In one version, in response to Muhammad's asking him whether he recognized him as the Messenger of God, he replied, 'I witness that you are the Messenger of the Gentiles (*rasūl al-ummiyyīn*) . . . Do you witness that I am the Messenger of God?' Muhammad responds to that by

[63] On the Dajjāl as a figure in Muslim apocalyptic ideas, see s.v. Antichrist, in *EQ* (N. Robinson) and s.v. Dadjdjāl in *EI2* (A. Abel).

[64] D. Halperin, 'The Ibn Ṣayyād traditions', *Journal of the American Oriental Society* 96 (1976): 213–25; A. Morabia, 'L'antéchrist: s'est-il manifesté du vivant de l'envoyé d'Allah?', *Journal Asiatique* 267 (1979): 81–94; S. Wasserstrom, 'The Moving Finger Writes: Mughīra b. Saʿīd's Islamic Gnosis and the Myth of Its Rejection', *History of Religions* 25 (1985–86): 1–29 (esp. 23–7); D. Cook, *Studies in Muslim Apocalyptic* (Princeton: Princeton University Press, 2002), 110–17; Wim Raven, 'Ibn Ṣayyād as an Islamic "Antichrist"', in W. Brandes and F. Schmieder, eds, *Endzeiten. Eschatologie in den monotheistischen Weltreligionen*, (Berlin: Walter de Gruyter, 2008), 261–91. For earlier academic references to Ibn Ṣayyād, see Halperin, 'Ibn Ṣayyād Traditions', 214, n. 7.

[65] Morabia, 83.

saying, 'I believe in God and His messengers.'[66] In another version, Muhammad and he simply exchange assertions about their respective identity as the Messenger of God.[67]

In addition Ibn Ṣayyād's words and behaviour are sometimes described in ways reminiscent of those of a prophet. For example, he is credited with being able to sleep and yet know what people had said while he was sleeping. 'My eyes sleep, but my heart does not', he said, using a phrase that Muslim tradition attributes also to Muhammad who was sleeping at the time when he was taken on his Night Journey (*isrā*ʾ), and which Muhammad himself used when describing the Dajjāl.[68]

A prophet-like ability to attain knowledge hidden from others is also evident in the report that Muhammad came to Ibn Ṣayyād and told him that he had hidden something from him (*khabaʾtu laka khabīʾan*), to which he responded, *dukhkh*, and Muhammad then told him to 'push off' (*ikhsa*ʾ).[69] This report too occurs in numerous diverse forms that contain additional material, perhaps supplied by transmitters as an attempt to give meaning to this skeletal version. For example, some explain that what Muhammad had hidden was the apocalyptic verse 10 of *sūra* 44 (Sūrat al-Dukhān): *yawma taʾtī al-samāʾu bi-dukhānin mubīnin* (a day when the heavens produce evident smoke), and that Ibn Ṣayyād's response, '*dukhkh*', was his attempt to say *dukhān*.[70]

[66] ʿUmar b. Shabba, *Madīna*, 402. Here the Antichrist/pseudo-prophet is called Ibn Ṣāʾid. In another version (Ibn Shabba, *Madīna*, 403–4) the exchange between Muhammad and Ibn Ṣayyād/Ṣāʾid is preceded by the latter's mother introducing Muhammad to him as *rasūl al-ummiyyīn.*

[67] Bukhārī, *Ṣaḥīḥ, Kitāb al-Adab, bāb qawl al-rajul li-l-rajul: ikhsa*ʾ [= *Ṣaḥīḥ*, Muḥammad ʿAlī al-Quṭb, ed. Beirut: al-Maktaba al-ʿaṣriyya, 1991, 4: 1943, *bāb* 97], 2nd *ḥadīth*; Ibn Shabba, *Madīna*, 404; al-Muṭahhar al-Maqdisī, *Badʾ*, 2: 186–7. Halperin, 'Ibn Ṣayyād Traditions', 216 and 225, nos. 4, 6, and 7. Al-Azmeh, *Emergence of Islam in Late Antiquity*, 349, follows Halperin in interpreting this story as evidence that Muhammad did not deny Ibn Ṣayyād's claims to be a prophet (and assumes that that increases the authenticity of the reports and the reality of Ibn Ṣayyād as a claimant to prophethood in the time of Muhammad).

[68] For the story about Ibn Ṣayyād, see al-Tirmidhī, *Ṣaḥīḥ*, *Abwāb al-Fitan*, *Bāb mā jāʾa fī dhikr Ibn Ṣāʾid*, no. 3 [=*Ṣaḥīḥ*, with commentary of Ibn al-ʿArabī, 13 vols (Cairo: al-Maṭbaʿah al-Miṣrīyah bi-al-Azhar, 1931–4), 9: 102]. D. Cook points out that Ibn Ṣayyād is not mentioned by name in the tradition—but the context makes it clear that he is the subject. For the idea in connection with Muhammad, see, e.g., Ibn Hishām, *Sīra*, 1: 400 [= Eng.tr., Guillaume, 183]. On revelation received while asleep, see Fahd, *Divination*, 77, referring to the phrase, 'I sleep but my heart is awake', in the Song of Songs, 5: 2.

[69] For this skeletal form of the exchange (sometimes with additional dialogue or further incidents added) see, e.g., Bukhārī, *Ṣaḥīḥ*, *Kitāb al- Adab, Bāb qawl al-rajul li-l-rajul: ikhsa*ʾ [= *Ṣaḥīḥ*, ed. Muḥammad ʿAlī al-Quṭb, 4: 1943, *bāb* 97], 1st *ḥadīth*; Muslim, *Ṣaḥīḥ*, *K. al-Fitan wa-ashrāṭ al-sāʿa*, *Bāb dhikr Ibn Ṣayyād* [=*Ṣaḥīḥ*, M. Fuʾād ʿAbd al-Baqī, ed. (Beirut: Dār al-Fikr, 1398/1978), 4: 2240 ff., *bāb* 19] *ḥadiths* 86 and 95; Ibn Shabba, *Madīna*, 2: 403.

[70] E.g., Ibn Shabba, *Madīna*, 2: 404. Both Halperin, 219, and Morabia, 85–6, interpret the story, persuasively, as typical of material about the testing of soothsayers (*kahana*).

Halperin attempts to reconstruct, as far as possible, the development over time of the material on Ibn Ṣayyād. He expresses mistrust of what he regards as a significant number of later elaborations, but argues that there is a basic historical core that is authentic, averring that there was no reason why those who created the Muslim tradition would have invented material that seems to be unflattering to the prophet Muhammad. He concludes that Ibn Ṣayyād did in fact claim to be a prophet and that Muhammad was unable to refute him. After the death of their own prophet, the early Muslims began to portray the Jewish impostor as the Antichrist when the doctrine of the *Dajjāl* began to enter Islam.[71]

Halperin is clearly influenced by the fact that, while some of the material portraying Ibn Ṣayyād as the Dajjāl says that God removed him from Medina to a place whence he will appear at the appropriate apocalyptic moment, there are also reports that treat him as someone who accepted Islam and was involved in significant events in early Islamic history. Ṭabarī, from Sayf b. ʿUmar, reports that at the siege of Sūs in 17/638–9, the monks and priests of the town taunted the Muslims by calling out to them that they would be unable to conquer the town unless they had the Dajjāl with them. Thereupon Ṣafī b. Ṣayyād angrily strode up to the town gate and kicked it, calling on it to open, and it did, together with the other gates. The Muslims entered the town and took it.[72] Elsewhere, he is said to have disappeared around the time of the battle of the Ḥarra, when an Umayyad army fought against the Medinans, in 63/683.[73]

The story of his attempt to get Muhammad to accept that he was the Messenger of God, however, is only one element in a body of material that is much more concerned with his identity as the Antichrist, and traditionally the figure of the Antichrist is associated with pseudo-prophets.[74] It is not surprising that the purported Antichrist should be given prophet-like abilities, such as working miracles.[75] Whether there was a real person lying behind the

[71] Halperin, 'Ibn Ṣayyād Traditions', especially 214–16. Halperin's argument, 217–18, that one can see references to Markaba mysticism in the reports about Ibn Ṣayyād has been convincingly rejected by Morabia (86, n. 22) and Cook (110, n. 91). The fact that the Qurʾan has no mention of the Antichrist does not necessarily mean that the figure was unknown in the circles from which the text emerged.

[72] Ṭabarī, *Taʾrīkh*, part 1: 2565 (= tr. [G.H.A. Juynboll], 13: 145–6). This seems to be Ṭabarī's only allusion to Ibn Ṣayyād. Other reports say that when the Muslims conquered Iṣfahān, the Jews there took Ibn Ṣayyād as their king (Cook, *Muslim Apocalyptic*, 115 with sources). That seems connected with a *ḥadīth* that the Dajjāl will appear with 70,000 Jews of Iṣfahān in his train (A. J. Wensinck et al., *Concordance*, s.v. Dajjāl, Dajjālūn).

[73] Ibn Abī Shayba, *Muṣannaf*, 15: no. 19, 377 (in the *Kitāb al-Fitan*); Abū Dāʾūd, *Sunan*, *K. al-Malāḥim*, *Bāb khabar Ibn Ṣāʾid*, 4th *ḥadīth* [= *Sunan*, ʿIzzat ʿUbayd Al-Daʿʿās, ed. (Ḥimṣ: Muḥammad ʿAlī al-Sayyid 1393/1973), 4: 506, no. 4332]: *faqadnā ʾbna Ṣayyād yawma l-Ḥarra*.

[74] For the tradition in which Muhammad predicts the appearance of 30 Antichrists, each claiming to be a prophet, see Ibn Hishām, *Sīra*, 2: 599; and cf. Matthew 24: 11.

[75] Al-Qurṭubī, *Al-Tadhkira fī aḥwāl al-mawtā wa-umūr al-ākhira* (Cairo; Maktabat al-Kulliyyāt al-Azhariyya, 1400/1980), disputes the view, which he attributes to the Jahmiyya,

difficult material pertaining to Ibn Ṣayyād is impossible to say—the references to him in connection with events like the conquest of Sūs and the battle on the Ḥarra could suggest that the name was already associated with the idea of the Dajjāl and became attached to historical events because they were considered to have apocalyptic significance. The material on the battle of the Ḥarra and the associated struggle between the Umayyads and Ibn al-Zubayr sometimes gives an apocalyptic colouring to various episodes,[76] and it is not difficult to envisage how the Arab conquest of towns like Sūs, a town with a large Christian population and accepted by them and by Jews as the site of the tomb of the prophet Daniel, could come to be described by allusion to apocalyptic ideas.[77] It may, too, be that all the reports now associated with Ibn Ṣayyād did not originate with reference to the same (real or imaginary) person.

David Cook's conclusion that it is impossible to derive historical information about Ibn Ṣayyād from the Muslim reports (which are our only evidence for him) is persuasive. For Cook, Ibn Ṣayyād's role in the reports is primarily that of the Dajjāl, and the stress on his Jewish origins and inhuman characteristics is in accordance with that.[78] The material does not seem solid enough to conclude that there was indeed a rival to Muhammad as a prophet in Medina.

CONCLUSIONS

Leaving aside the Ridda prophets, for whom the evidence is difficult to interpret, most of the claimants to prophecy in the Jahiliyya considered here are connected with the theme of a pre-Islamic Arabian monotheism whether

that the miracles of the Dajjāl are merely tricks and sleight of hand (*makhāriq wa-ḥiyal*). If they were genuine miracles, they claimed, we would be unable to tell the difference between a true prophet (who is known through his evidentiary miracles) and a false one. Qurṭubī's response is that that would only be true if the Dajjāl claimed to be [merely] a prophet, but in fact he claims divinity. Furthermore, that he is the Dajjāl is evident from certain physical characteristics, such as the letters *k-f-r* on his forehead and being blind in one eye.

[76] See W. Madelung, 'Ibn al-Zubayr and the Mahdī', *Journal of Near Eastern Studies*, 40 (1981): 291–30. The expression *faqadnā* ('we lost', 'we were deprived/bereaved of') is understood by Halperin, 214, simply to mean that he perished at the Ḥarra, while Cook, 115, sees it as implying occultation.

[77] The story of what happened following the Christians' alleged taunt that only if they had the Antichrist with them would the Arabs be able to take the town, is understood by Chase Robinson as an attempt by Muslim traditionists to turn on its head 'what must have been a familiar topos', and to show that the conquest was not the work of the Antichrist but of God. He does not, however, consider the significance of the fact that it was Ibn Ṣayyād who is said to have caused the gates of the town to open. (See Chase F. Robinson, 'The Conquest of Khūzistān: a historiographical reassessment', *Bulletin of the School of Oriental and African Studies*, 67 (2004): 14–39, especially 28–9.)

[78] Cook, *Muslim Apocalyptic*, 110–11, 115–17.

indigenous, as in the cases of Riʾāb b. Zayd and Khālid b. Sinān, or resulting from contacts with Jews or Christians and their scriptures, as with Umayya b. Abī-l-Salṭ.

While the evidence that Riʾāb was regarded as, and Umayya aspired to be, a prophet is very limited, in the cases of Khālid and Ḥanẓala b. Ṣafwān their identity as prophets is central to the material about them and the truth of their prophethood is widely accepted. Although the evidence is not extensive, an argument could be made that, in spite of the doctrine of the *fatra*, over time some of those who were considered as monotheists in Arabia before Islam came to be associated with prophecy, perhaps because of their knowledge of the advent of Muhammad. Riʾāb is generally treated favourably in the tradition, to the extent that it is reported that Muhammad himself enquired about him, whereas Umayya like some other Ḥanīfs is treated as unable to accept the Prophet. Eventually there emerged figures like Ḥanẓala and Khālid who are mainly viewed as Arabian precursors of Muhammad and, in the case of Khālid, attested to be a true prophet by Muhammad himself.

One reason for the existence in the tradition of monotheistic individuals from whom these prophets emerge is evident from the material discussed here. They are necessary as witnesses to the fact that Muhammad had been foretold. That is a prominent theme already in the *Sīra* of Ibn Isḥāq.[79] The Prophet's coming was known to Christians and Jews familiar with their own scriptures, and to some Arab soothsayers who had access to elements of the truth as well as spreading falsities.

As for the tradition about the indigenous Arab monotheism distinct from Judaism and Christianity, the religion of the Ḥanīfs, at least one element in that is its witness to the fact of Abraham's introduction of monotheism into Arabia and the direct descent of Islam from it.[80]

That the prophets of the Jahiliyya developed from the theme of pre-Islamic monotheism in Arabia is probably not the whole story. Another element is clearly the need to provide names for prophets whom the Qurʾan left anonymous. That was evident in some of the material about Ḥanẓala and Khālid.

In the case of Khālid, however, the number of stories of apparently popular or folkloric origin associated with him makes it likely that he had some literary existence independent of his role as a prophet. Such themes as the destruction of the ʿAnqāʾ, the extinction of the raging fire, and possibly the story about his promise to reveal the future if his people exhumed him, seem to point to something more than the need to provide a Muslim *avant la lettre*. Perhaps

[79] Ibn Hishām, *Sīra*, 1: 204 ff. *Maʿrifaṭ al-kuhhān wa-l-aḥbār wa-l-ruhbān bi-mabʿathihi (ṣ)*.
[80] See further G. R. Hawting, *The Idea of Idolatry and the Emergence of Islam* (Cambridge: Cambridge University Press, 1999), 36–9.

he was already a figure of local or tribal legend before he became redefined as a prophet.

Umayya b. Abī-l-Salṭ also probably cannot be explained simply as a development of the idea of pre-Islamic Arab monotheism, even though the biographical material is formulaic and similar to that provided for others.

The material on others, such as Riʾāb and Ḥanẓala, is much thinner and more insubstantial, but it seems impossible to be sure whether they are merely creations of the tradition or whether some historical individual lies behind the reports.

Ibn Ṣayyād is distinct from the other prophets of the *fatra* discussed here. Not primarily connected with the idea of pre-Islamic Arabian monotheism and the foretelling of Muhammad, it seems most likely that the association of him with a claim to be a prophet has to be understood in the context of the development of early Muslim apocalyptic ideas. Again it does not seem possible to decide whether there was an historical person—or perhaps more than one—around whom the reports developed.

The traditional material on these prophets of the Jahiliyya often seems insubstantial and unconvincing as accounts of historical reality, and it is doubtful that they can help us to understand the appearance of Muhammad as a prophet. That does not, of course, mean that Muhammad did appear in a society unfamiliar with the prophetic tradition, merely that the Muslim traditional material on the Jahiliyya reflects the needs and presuppositions of those who formed early Muslim tradition rather than historical conditions in pre-Islamic inner Arabia.

BIBLIOGRAPHY

ʿAbd al-Razzāq b. Hammām al-Ṣanʿānī. *Tafsīr*, 3 vols, Maḥmūd Muḥammad ʿAbduh, ed. Beirut: Dār al-kutub al-ʿilmiyya, 1999.

Abel, Armand. 'Dadjdjāl' in *EI2*.

ʿAbū Dāʾūd, Sulaymān b. al-Ashʿath al-Sijistāni. *Sunan*, 5 vols., ʿIzzat ʿUbayd al-Daʿʿās, ed. Ḥimṣ: Muḥammad ʿAlī al-Sayyid, 1969–73.

Aghānī, see al-Iṣfahānī.

Azmeh, Aziz al-. *The Emergence of Islam in Late Antiquity: Allāh and His People.* Cambridge: Cambridge University Press, 2014.

Bauer, Thomas. 'The Relevance of Early Arabic Poetry for Qurʾanic Studies'. In Angelika Neuwirth et al., eds, *The Qurʾān in Context*, Leiden and Boston: Brill, 2010.

Bukhārī, Muḥammad b. Ismāʿīl al-. *Ṣaḥīḥ*, 5 vols, Muḥammad ʿAlī al-Quṭb, ed. Beirut: al-Maktaba al-ʿaṣriyya, 1991.

Cook, David. *Studies in Muslim Apocalyptic.* Princeton: Princeton University Press, 2002.

EI2, Encyclopaedia of Islam. 2nd edn, 12 vols, H. A. R. Gibb et al., ed. Leiden and London: Brill, 1960–2009. Online at http://referenceworks.brillonline.com.

Eickelmann, Dale. 'Musaylima: An Approach to the Social Anthropology of Seventh Century Arabia'. *Journal of the Economic and Social History of the Orient* 10 (1967): 17–52.

EQ, Encyclopaedia of the Qurʾān, 6 vols, Jane Dammen McAuliffe, ed. Leiden: Brill, 2001–06. Online at http://referenceworks.brillonline.com.

Fahd, Toufic. *La divination arabe: études religieuses, sociologiques et folkloriques sur le milieu natif de l'Islam*. Paris: Sindbad, 1987.

Fossum, Jarl E. 'The Apostle Concept in the Qurʾān and pre-Islamic Near Eastern Literature'. In Mustansir Mir, ed., *Literary Heritage of Classical Islam. Arabic and Islamic Studies in Honor of James A. Bellamy*. Princeton: Princeton University Press, 1993, 149–67.

Frank-Kamenetzky, J. *Untersuchungen über das Verhältnis der dem Umajja b. Abī s Salt zugeschriebenen Gedichte zum Qorân*. Kirchhain: Schmersow, 1911.

Friedmann, Yohanan. *Prophecy Continuous: Aspects of Aḥmadī Religious Thought and its Medieval Background*. 2nd printing. New Delhi: Oxford University Press, 2003.

Gilliot, Claude. 'Muhammad, le Coran et les "contraintes de l'histoire"'. In S. Wild, ed., *The Qurʾān as Text*. Leiden: Brill, 1996, 3–26.

Goldziher, Ignac. *Muhammedanische Studien*, vol. 2, Halle, 1890. Eng. transl. *Muslim Studies*, vol. 2, by S. M. Stern and C. R. Barber. London: Allen & Unwin, 1971.

Halperin, D. 'The Ibn Ṣayyād traditions'. *Journal of the American Oriental Society* 96 (1976): 213–25.

Hamdānī, Ḥasan b. Aḥmad Ibn al-Ḥāʾikal-. *The Antiquities of South Arabia: Being a Translation from the Arabic... of the Eighth Book of al-Hamdānī's al-Iklīl*, trans. Nabih Amin Faris. Princeton: Princeton University Press, 1938.

Hawting, Gerald. *The Idea of Idolatry and the Emergence of Islam*. Cambridge: Cambridge University Press, 1999.

Huart, Clement. 'Une nouvelle source du Qoran'. *Journal Asiatique* ser. 10 (1904): 125–67.

Ibn Abī Shayba, Abū Bakr. *Muṣannaf* 15 vols., Shaykh Mukhtār Aḥmad al-Nadawī, ed. Karachi: Idārat al-Qurʾān wal-ʿulūm al-islāmiyya, 1986.

Ibn al-Kalbī, Hishām b. Muḥammad. *Jamharat al-nasab*, in the *riwāya* of al-Sukkarī from Ibn Ḥabīb, Bājī Ḥasan, ed. Beirut: ʿĀlam al-kutub, 1982.

Ibn Durayd, Muḥammad b. al-Ḥasan, *Kitāb al-Ishtiqāq*. ʿAbd al-Salām Hārūn, ed. Baghdad: Maktabat al-Muthannā, 1979.

Ibn Hishām, ʿAbd al-Malik. *Al-Sīra al-nabawiyya*, 2 vols, Muṣṭafā al-Saqqā et al, eds. Cairo: Muṣṭafā al-Bābī al-Ḥalabī, 1955. English trans. A. Guillaume, *The Life of Muḥammad*. Oxford: Clarendon Press, 1955.

Ibn Qutayba, ʿAbd Allāh b. Muslim. *Kitāb al-Maʿārif*. Tharwa ʿUkāsha, ed. Cairo: Dār al-Maʿārif, 1969.

Ibn Shabba, Abū Zayd al-Baṣrī, *Taʾrīkh al-Madīna al-munawwara*, 4 vols, Faḥīm Muḥammad Shaltūt, ed. Beirut: Dār al-Turāth, 1410/1990.

Ibn ʿAbd al-Ḥakam, ʿAbd al-Raḥmān b. ʿAbd Allāh. *Futūḥ Miṣr wa-akhbāruhā*, Charles Torrey, ed. New Haven: Yale University Press, 1922.

Ibn ʿAbd Rabbihi, Abū ʿUmar Aḥmad b. Muḥammad, *Al-ʿIqd al-Farīd*, 9 vols, ʿAbd al-Majīd al-Ruhaynī, ed. Beirut: Dār al-kutub al-ʿilmiyya, 1404/1983.

Iṣfahānī, Abu-l-Faraj al-. *Kitāb al-Aghānī*, Iḥsān ʿAbbās et al., eds. Beirut: Dār al-Kutub al-ʻIlmīyah, 1423/2002.

Jāḥiẓ, ʿAmr b. Baḥr. *Kitāb al- Ḥayawān*, 7 vols, ʿAbd al-Salām Muḥammad Hārūn, ed. Cairo: Muṣṭafā al-Bābī al-Ḥalabī, 1938–45.

Kister, M.J. 'The Struggle against Musaylima and the Conquest of Yamama'. *Jerusalem Studies in Arabic and Islam* 27 (2002): 1–56.

Landau-Tasseron, Ella. 'Unearthing a Pre-Islamic Arabian Prophet'. *Jerusalem Studies in Arabic and Islam* 21 (1997): 42–61.

Lecker, Michael. article Ridda, in *EI2*.

Madelung, Wilferd. 'Ibn al-Zubayr and the Mahdī'. *Journal of Near Eastern Studies* 40: (1981): 291–31.

Makin, Al. 'Re-thinking Other Claimants to Prophethood: The case of Umayya b. Abī Ṣalt'. *Al-Jāmiʿah: Journal of Islamic Studies* 48 (2010): 165–90.

Maqdisī, Muṭṭahar-al. *Kitāb al-Badʾ wa-l-taʾrīkh*, 6 parts, Clement Huart, ed. Paris: Ernest Leroux, 1899–1907.

Masʿūdī, ʿAlī b. al-Ḥusayn, al-. *Murūj al-dhahab*, 7 vols. Barbier de Meynard and Pavet de Courteille, eds, revised by Ch. Pellat. Beirut: Beirut: al-Jāmi'ah al-Lubnaniyyah, 1966.

Montgomery, James. article Umayya b. Abi'l-Salṭ in *EI2*.

Morabia, A. 'L'antéchrist: s'est-il manifesté du vivant de l'envoyé d'Allah?'. *Journal Asiatique* 267 (1979): 81–94.

Muqātil b. Sulaymān, *Tafsīr*. 3 vols, Aḥmad Farīd, ed. Beirut: Dār al-Kutub al-ʻIlmīyah, 1424/2003.

Muslim b. al-Ḥajjāj al-Qushayrī. *Ṣaḥīḥ*, 5 vols, Muḥammad Fuʾād ʿAbd al-Baqī, ed. Beirut: Dār al-Fikr, 1398/1978.

Pellat, Ch., article Al-Anḳāʾ in *EI2*.

Pellat, Ch., article Ḥanẓala b. Ṣafwān in *EI2*.

Pellat, Ch., article Khālid b. Sinān in *EI2*.

Qurṭubī, Muḥammad b. Aḥmad-al. *Al-Tadhkira fī aḥwāl al-mawtā wa-umūr al-ākhira*. Cairo: Maktabat al-Kulliyyāt al-Azhariyya, 1400/1980.

Raven, Wim. 'Ibn Ṣayyād as an Islamic "Antichrist"'. In W. Brandes and F. Schmieder, eds, *Endzeiten. Eschatologie in den monotheistischen Weltreligionen*. Berlin: Walter de Gruyter, 2009, 261–91.

Robinson, Chase F. 'The Conquest of Khūzistān: A Historiographical Reassessment'. *Bulletin of the School of Oriental and African Studies* 67 (2004): 14–39.

Robinson, Neal, article Antichrist in *EQ*.

Rubin, Uri. '*Ḥanīfiyya* and Kaʿba: An Enquiry into the Arabian pre-Islamic Background of *dīn Ibrāhīm*'. *Jerusalem Studies in Arabic and Islam* 13 (1990): 85–112.

Seidentsticker, Tilman. 1996. 'The Authenticity of the Poems Ascribed to Umayya b. Abī'l-Ṣalt'. In J. R. Smart, ed., *Tradition and Modernity in Arabic Language and Literature*. Richmond, Surrey: Curzon Press, 1996, 87–101.

Shoufani, Elias. *Al-Riddah and the Muslim Conquest of Arabia*. Toronto: University of Toronto Press, 1972.

Sinai, Nicolai. 'Religious Poetry from the Quranic Milieu: Umayya b. Abī l-Salṭ on the Fate of the Thamūd'. *Bulletin of the School of Oriental and African Studies* 74 (2011): 397–416.

Suyūṭī, Jalāl al-Dīn al-. *Al-Khaṣā'iṣ al-kubrā*, 3 vols, Muḥammad Khalīl Harrās, ed. Cairo: Dār al-Kutub al-Ḥadītha, 1967.

Ṭabarī, Muḥammad b. Jarīr al-. *Ta'rīkh al-rusul wa-l-mulūk*, 3 parts, M. J. de Goeje et al., eds. Leiden: Brill, 1879–1901. English translation, 40 vols by various translators, E. Yar-Shater, ed. Albany: SUNY Press, 1985–2007.

Ṭabarī, Muḥammad b. Jarīr-al. *Tafsīr al-Ṭabarī: Jāmiʿ al-bayān ʿan ta'wīl āy al-Qur'ān*, 24 vols. Abd Allāh al-Turkī, ed. Cairo: Hajar, 2001.

Thaʿālibī, ʿAbd al-Malik b. Muḥammad al-. *Thimār al-qulūb fī-l-muḍāf wa-l-mansūb*, Ibrāhīm Muḥammad Abū-l-Faḍl, ed. Cairo: Dār al-Maʿārif, 1985.

Tirmidhī, Muḥammad b. ʿĪsā al-. *Ṣaḥīḥ*, with commentary of Ibn al-ʿArabī, 13 vols. Cairo: al-Maṭbaʿah al-Miṣrīyah bi-al-Azhar, 1931–4.

Wāqidī, Muḥammad b. ʿUmar al-. *Kitāb al-Maghāzī*, J. Marsden Jones, ed. London: Oxford University Press, 1966.

Wansbrough, John. *Quranic Studies: Sources and Methods of Scriptural Interpretation*. Oxford: Oxford University Press, 1977.

Wasserstrom, Steven. 'The Moving Finger Writes: Mughīra b. Saʿīd's Islamic Gnosis and the Myth of Its Rejection'. *History of Religions* 25 (1985–6): 1–29.

Watt, W. Montgomery, article al-Aswad in *EI2*.

Watt, W. Montgomery, article Musaylima in *EI2*.

Watt, W. Montgomery. *Muḥammad at Medina*. Oxford: Clarendon Press, 1956.

Wensinck, Arendt Jan et al. *Concordance et indices de la tradition musulmane*, 8 vols. 2nd edn. Leiden: Brill, 1992.

7

Early Medieval Christian and Muslim Attitudes to Pagan Law

A Comparison

Michael Cook

CHRISTIAN ATTITUDES

The Salic Law

As every English schoolboy once knew, Shakespeare's *Henry V* is about a young and heroic king of England who led his army to victory over the French, giving them the thrashing they deserved.[1] But why, one might ask in an age when cross-Channel brawling no longer takes the form of military campaigns, did the French deserve to be thrashed? One answer might be that they did so simply by virtue of being French. But such an answer, though it might have appealed to some of the less sophisticated members of the audience at the Globe, was not quite good enough for the Elizabethan elite. A more respectable answer was that the Valois usurper Charles VI (ruled 1380–1422) was refusing to recognize the legitimate claim of Henry V (ruled 1413–22) to be

[1] Without the help of Helmut Reimitz in early medieval European matters I could not have written this chapter; I am likewise indebted to Angela Gleason for assistance with Irish matters. On the Islamic side, I am grateful to Hossein Modarressi for numerous references and suggestions. An earlier oral form of this chapter was delivered at a conference on 'Civilizational Formation: the Carolingian and ʿAbbāsid Eras', held at Notre Dame in April 2013, under the title 'Legislation in the Early Medieval World, East and West'; my thanks to Deborah Tor for inviting me. A later version was given as one of the Merle Curti lectures at the University of Wisconsin in April 2014. A briefer treatment of the issues appears in my *Ancient Religions, Modern Politics: The Islamic Case in Comparative Perspective* (Princeton and Oxford: Princeton University Press, 2014), 271–2, 300–3, where I also touch on a couple of legal maxims attributed to pre-Islamic Arab judges.

the king of France. This sets a better tone, but unfortunately there was a fly in the ointment: a provision in the early medieval law code of the Salian Franks.

The existence of this complication meant that before the action of the play could move to France and the excitement begin, Shakespeare had to impose on his audience a long and tedious scene in which King Henry calls upon the Archbishop of Canterbury to advise him whether his claim is indeed well-founded. Hence his earnest appeal to the archbishop:

> My learnèd lord, we pray you to proceed,
> And justly and religiously unfold
> Why the law Salic that they have in France
> Or should or should not bar us in our claim.[2]

The archbishop immediately puts his finger on the problem: according to Salic law, as he paraphrases it, *In terram Salicam mulieres ne succedant.*[3] Not forgetting the less educated members of the audience, he is good enough to add a vernacular translation: 'No woman shall succeed in Salic land.'[4] This law poses a problem because Henry's claim to the French throne ran through Isabel, the French princess who had been the mother of his great-grandfather Edward III (ruled 1327–77). Obviously it is the archbishop's task to get this awkward provision out of the way. But how?

To anyone schooled in hardline monotheism of the Islamic kind, the answer is obvious: the entire Salian code is without authority because it is not revealed law. It is merely man-made law, allegedly put together by a pagan king, the early—not to say legendary—Frankish ruler Pharamond, who would have held sway, if he ever did, in the 420s.[5] And who better to make this point than a man of God such as the Archbishop of Canterbury? But that is not the move the archbishop makes; he raises no challenge to the validity of man-made law as such. Instead, he has two related points. The first is that the clause barring female succession dates only from the aftermath of the subjugation of the Saxons by Charlemagne (ruled 768–814): certain Frenchmen who stayed behind in Saxony following the conquest developed a low opinion of German women, and accordingly made a law barring them from inheriting land there. Obviously Pharamond, 'idly supposed the founder of this law', can have played no part in this. The second point is that the clause applies only to 'Salic land', which was the part of

[2] William Shakespeare, *Henry V*, Gary Taylor, ed. (Oxford: Clarendon Press, 1982), 100 (Act I, Scene 2, lines 9–12).

[3] The paraphrase is taken from Holinshed, who represents it as the 'very words' of the law (see Shakespeare, *Henry V*, 306).

[4] Shakespeare, *Henry V*, 101 (lines 38–9).

[5] For the references made by the archbishop to Pharamond see Shakespeare, *Henry V*, 101–2 (lines 37, 41, 58). For his putative date, see Colette Beaune, *The Birth of an Ideology: Myths and Symbols of Nation in Late-medieval France* (Berkeley: University of California Press, 1991), 253.

Germany in which these Frenchmen settled; the rule accordingly has no application to France:

> Then doth it well appear the Salic Law
> Was not devisèd for the realm of France.[6]

At the end of this 63-line exposition, Henry is still seeking reassurance: 'May I with right and conscience make this claim?'[7] At this point the archbishop offers an interesting addition to his main argument:

> For in the Book of Numbers it is writ,
> 'When the son dies, let the inheritance
> Descend unto the daughter.'[8]

He is of course right, subject to the constraints of blank verse; as the King James Bible was to put it a few years later, 'If a man die, and have no son, then ye shall cause his inheritance to pass unto his daughter' (Num. 27:8). So God, it turns out, had already settled the matter in His Book, and in a manner that seems to provide support for Henry's claim. Given this divine pronouncement, what, one might ask, could be the relevance of Salic law, and how could it matter what territory it purported to apply to? But this is not how Shakespeare saw things.

As one might expect, Shakespeare did not invent the centrality of the Salic law to the dispute about Henry's claim to the French throne. He simply followed his main source, the chronicle of his older contemporary Raphael Holinshed, who describes how the archbishop inveighed against 'the surmised and false feigned law Salike'.[9] And indeed the French appeal to the Salic law to rebut the English claim to the French throne goes back to the early fifteenth century, and so was fully contemporary with the reign of the historical Henry V.[10] Then and later, the French showed no embarrassment about the fact that the code was human, and not divine, legislation, or even about its alleged initial promulgation in pagan times;[11] and just as significantly, the English did not see these points as vulnerabilities in the arguments put forward by the French.

[6] Shakespeare, *Henry V*, 102 (lines 43–55). The archbishop's authority for this account is 'their own authors' (line 43). What origin the archbishop ascribes to the rest of the code is unclear and beside the point.

[7] Shakespeare, *Henry V*, 104 (line 96). [8] Shakespeare, *Henry V*, 104 (lines 98–100).

[9] See the passage from Holinshed reproduced in Shakespeare, *Henry V*, Appendix D, 306–7.

[10] See Craig Taylor, 'The Salic Law and the Valois Succession to the French Crown', *French History* 15 (2001): 359, 364. The code had only been rediscovered in the 1350s (361), and had thus played no part in the crucial succession of 1328 (360–1). See also Beaune, *Birth of an Ideology*, ch. 9.

[11] See Beaune, *Birth of an Ideology*, 251, 253, and cf. 255. Jean de Montreuil more than once makes the claim that the code was enacted before there was a Christian king in France (*Opera* (Turin: Giappichelli, 1963–86), vol. 2, 132 line 1313, 168 line 208, 274 line 268).

The law code of the Salian Franks, despite variations in wording between its various versions, does indeed contain the Salic law. Thus in one text it states that 'concerning Salic land (*terra Salica*), no portion or inheritance is for a woman but all the land belongs to members of the male sex who are brothers'.[12] Whatever may have been meant here by 'Salic land', the immediately preceding clauses make it clear that the rule was not a bar to women inheriting land in general. Moreover, its relevance to royal succession, if any, is unclear—a point that was later to prove awkward when the French made their case against the English.[13] However, we need not concern ourselves further with the substance of the Salian code; of greater interest to us is the way the code is presented in its prologue, an addition that in its longer form dates from the eighth century.[14]

This prologue opens with a strong appeal to ethnic and religious pride. We are told that 'the whole Frankish people, established by the power of God, are strong in arms, weighty in council,... brave, swift, and austere. Recently converted to the Catholic faith, they are free from heresy, rejecting barbarian rites with the help of God, keeping the faith'.[15] The process by which the code came into existence, presumably in pagan times, is described as involving both rulers and notables.[16] Then Clovis (ruled 481–511), 'king of the Franks, fiery and handsome and renowned', received Catholic baptism, after which he and two of his immediate successors 'clearly emended that which seemed less suitable' in the code.[17] Whoever esteems the Franks should live by it. Nothing here suggests that anything about the origins of the code was a source of embarrassment to Christians.

Early Medieval Attitudes Outside the Salian Code

One gets the same impression from other early Germanic law codes. The preface of the Burgundian code—a product of the reigns of King Gundobad

[12] Katherine Drew, trans., *The Laws of the Salian Franks* (Philadelphia: University of Pennsylvania Press, 1991), 122; for another version see 198, and for the Latin text of the clause in numerous versions, see Karl Eckhardt, ed., *Pactus legis Salicae* (Hanover: Hahnsche Buchhandlung, 1962), 222–3, where several versions make no reference to *terra Salica.*

[13] See Taylor, 'Salic Law', 359, 364, and Beaune, *Birth of an Ideology*, 252, on the interpolation *in regno*. François Hotman (d. 1590) argued the irrelevance of the clause in 1573, see Taylor, 'Salic Law', 375–6.

[14] See Drew, *Laws of the Salian Franks*, 241 n. 2. There is also a shorter version, thought to date from the sixth century, see 232 n. 2.

[15] Drew, *Laws of the Salian Franks*, 171–2; for the Latin text see Karl Eckhardt, ed., *Pactus legis Salicae* (Göttingen: Musterschmidt-Verlag, 1954–7), 314–15.

[16] The role of these notables is particularly prominent in the shorter version of the prologue (Drew, *Laws of the Salian Franks*, 59; Eckhardt, *Pactus legis Salicae* (Hanover), 2–3), which anticipates the ethnic but not religious pride of the longer version.

[17] Cf. also Drew, *Laws of the Salian Franks*, 142.

(ruled 473–516) and his son Sigismund (ruled 516–24)—speaks of justice as something 'through which God is pleased', and describes the provisions of the code as 'to be observed in time to come under the guidance of God'.[18] The Lombards use similar language. In the prologue to the oldest extant Lombard code, the *Edict* of Rothair (ruled 636–53) of 643, the king states that 'trusting in the mercy of Almighty God, we have perceived it necessary to improve and to reaffirm the present law, amending all earlier laws by adding that which is lacking and eliminating that which is superfluous'.[19] In 668 Grimwald (ruled 662–71) amended certain provisions of the law that seemed 'harsh and unjust'; he did so with the help of God.[20] In 713 Liutprand (ruled 712–44) was influenced to promulgate a collection of his laws 'not by his own foresight but through the wisdom and inspiration of God'; unlike his predecessors he also quoted scripture and explained that he would 'delete and add those things . . . which seem fitting to us according to the law of God'.[21] A little over thirty years later Ratchis (ruled 744–9) adopted a pious tone,[22] as did Aistulf (ruled 749–56) in 750 and 755.[23]

Such language suggests that no incompatibility was felt between divine inspiration and royal legislation the substance of which might often be of pagan origin. But this is an argument from silence, and we can do better by looking for texts that explicitly address the distinction between divine and human law.

An example is provided by Archbishop Hincmar of Rheims (d. 882). In one work he warns Christians that 'they are to be judged in the Day of Judgement not by Roman nor by Salic nor by Burgundian, but by divine and apostolic laws'.[24] But in another work, speaking of the affairs of this world, he remarks that 'kings and ministers of a republic have laws, by which they ought to rule the inhabitants of each territory'. The legislative role of Christian and even pagan kings seems clear in the continuation of this passage: he speaks of the rulings (*capitula*) of earlier Christian kings 'which they promulgated to be held

[18] Ludovicus de Salis, ed., *Leges Burgundionum* (Hanover: Hahnsche Buchhandlung, 1892), 30–1 §2, 34 following §14 = Katherine Drew, trans., *The Burgundian Code: Book of Constitutions or Law of Gundobad, Additional Enactments* (Philadelphia: University of Pennsylvania Press, 1972), 18, 21.

[19] Fridericus Bluhme, ed., *Edictus ceteraeque Langobardorum leges* (Hanover: Hahnsche Buchhandlung, 1869), 1 = Katherine Drew, trans., *The Lombard Laws* (Philadelphia: University of Pennsylvania Press, 1981), 39. For the dates of this and other Lombard legal texts, see 21.

[20] Bluhme, *Edictus*, 73 = Drew, *Lombard Laws*, 131.

[21] Bluhme, *Edictus*, 85–6, and cf. 87–8 = Drew, *Lombard Laws*, 144–5, and cf. 146–7.

[22] Bluhme, *Edictus*, 152 = Drew, *Lombard Laws*, 215.

[23] Bluhme, *Edictus*, 162, 164–5 = Drew, *Lombard Laws*, 227, 230.

[24] Hinkmar von Reims, *De divortio Lotharii regis et Theutbergae reginae*, Letha Böhringer, ed. (Hanover: Hahnsche Buchhandlung, 1992), 145.18; translation from Patrick Wormald, *The Making of English Law: King Alfred to the Twelfth Century*, vol. 1: *Legislation and Its Limits* (Oxford: Blackwell, 1999), 423.

lawfully with the general consent of their faithful men'.[25] This does not, however, mean that God has jurisdiction only in the next world. In the passage specifying the law in force on the Day of Judgement, Hincmar goes on to say that 'in a Christian kingdom, even the public laws (*leges publicae*) must be Christian', which he explains to mean that they should be 'in conformity and harmony with Christianity' (*convenientes videlicet et consonantes Christianitati*).[26] Likewise something may arise that 'is punished by custom of the gentiles more cruelly than Christian right or holy authority would rightly allow'; such a problem should be brought to the notice of the king, who 'together with those who know both laws and fear the statutes of God more than those of human laws, may so decree that both are observed where they can be, and, if not, the law of the world (*lex saeculi*) might rightly be suppressed, the justice of God preserved'.[27] In this world, then, human law is the default; but the default is to be overridden in the event of a clash with divine law. We have already seen this view adumbrated in Liutprand's resolve to 'delete and add those things . . . which seem fitting to us according to the law of God'.

The same thinking is found in the prologue to the Bavarian code, which has been dated to the eighth century.[28] We read there that the Frankish king Theodoric (ruled 511–34) 'ordered the writing down of the law of the Franks, Alamanni, and Bavarians, for each people that was subject to him, in accordance with its custom'. So far we have the default, then follows the override: 'He changed those things that were according to the custom of the pagans in accordance with the law of the Christians.' But this was not as easy as it sounds: 'Whatever Theodoric was not able to amend because of the most ancient custom of the pagans, king Childebert later made a start on it, but king Chlotar finished it.'[29] The prologue of the Bavarian code in fact propounds a

[25] Hinkmar von Reims, *De ordine palatii*, Thomas Gross and Rudolf Schieffer, ed. and trans. (Hanover: Hahnsche Buchhandlung, 1980), 46–9 lines 143–7, cited in Wormald, *Making of English Law*, 424. Again I use Wormald's translation.

[26] Hinkmar, *De divortio*, 145.20, trans. in Karl Morrison, *The Two Kingdoms: Ecclesiology in Carolingian Political Thought* (Princeton: Princeton University Press, 1964), 95; Morrison glosses 'public' as 'civil'. Note that this tract is about the efforts of a Carolingian king to divorce his wife, thus raising one of the rare issues on which Jesus made something like a legal pronouncement (Matt. 5:32, 19:6, 19:9, Mark 10:9, 11–12, Luke 16:18).

[27] Hinkmar, *De ordine palatii*, 70–3 lines 350–9, cited in Wormald, *Making of English Law*, 425, and in Harald Siems, 'Die Entwicklung von Rechtsquellen zwischen Spätantike und Mittelalter', in Theo Kölzer and Rudolf Schieffer, eds, *Von der Spätantike zum frühen Mittelalter: Kontinuitäten und Brüche, Konzeptionen und Befunde*. (Ostfildern: Jan Thorbecke, 2009), 266. Again I use Wormald's translation.

[28] For the dating see Ernst von Schwind, ed., *Lex Baiwariorum* (Hanover: Hahnsche Buchhandlung, 1926), 180–1.

[29] Von Schwind, *Lex Baiwariorum*, 201.5; see also Siems, 'Entwicklung von Rechtsquellen', 261, 265. Theodoric, Childebert (ruled 511–58), and Chlotar (ruled 511–61) were all sons of Clovis.

general theory of the derivation of ethnic law codes: 'Each people chooses its own law for itself out of [its] custom.'[30] It states this after providing a list of ethnic lawgivers and the peoples they served.[31] The list is headed by Moses for the Hebrews, followed by the lawgivers of the Greeks, the Egyptians, the Athenians, the Spartans, and the Romans. That Moses should thus appear in the same company as such heathens as Solon, Lycurgus, and Numa Pompilius is eloquent testimony to the default acceptability of pagan law. The job-description of an ethnic law-giver, it seems, is common to monotheists and pagans.

The attitude found in early Christian Ireland is no different. Thus an Old Irish text likely to date from the early eighth century gives an account of a collaboration between the poet Dubthach and St Patrick (d. *c.* 461).[32] As Dubthach maintained, 'the judgments of the men of Ireland' were in accordance with the law of nature. Moreover, 'there are many things covered in the law of nature which the law of the letter did not reach'—the 'law of the letter' being the law of the Bible. 'Dubthach expounded these to Patrick. What did not conflict with the word of God in the law of the letter... has been fastened in the canon of the judges by the church and the *filid*'—the *filid* being the poets or seers of pagan Ireland. What did not conflict with the word of God was in fact the lion's share of the pagan legal tradition: 'The whole of the law of nature was right except for the faith' and matters concerning the rights and duties of the Church. Meanwhile a Latin text perhaps of the seventh century makes ingenious use of the figure of Jethro, the Midianite father-in-law of Moses, to justify the retention of pagan law. The Bible tells us that when Jethro visited his son-in-law, he was appalled to see Moses engaged in unsustainable micromanagement. He warned Moses that he needed to delegate, telling him exactly how to do it; Moses followed his advice in full (Ex. 18:13–26). The fact that Moses accepted Jethro's counsel shows that 'if we find judgements of the heathen (*iudicia gentium*) good, which their good nature teaches them (*que natura bona illis docet*), and it is not displeasing to God, we shall keep them'.[33]

[30] Von Schwind, *Lex Baiwariorum*, 200.6 (*unaquaque gens propriam sibi ex consuetudine elegit legem*).

[31] Von Schwind, *Lex Baiwariorum*, 198.2. As indicated there, the list is borrowed from the *Etymologies* of Isidore of Seville (d. 636), see Angelo Canale, ed. and trans., *Etimologie o origini di Isidoro di Siviglia* (Turin: Unione Tipografico-Editrice Torinese, 2004), vol. 1, 386 = 387 (5.1.1–3).

[32] Donnchadh Ó Corráin et al., 'The Laws of the Irish', *Peritia* 3 (1984): 385–6; Fergus Kelly, *A Guide to Early Irish Law* (Dublin: Dublin Institute for Advanced Studies, 1988), 48; T. M. Charles-Edwards, *Early Christian Ireland* (Cambridge; New York: Cambridge University Press, 2000), 196–7 (for the date of the text, see 196 n. 58).

[33] Ludwig Bieler, ed. and trans., *The Irish Penitentials* (Dublin: Dublin Institute for Advanced Studies, 1963), 168 = 169 (for the uncertain date of the text see 8–9); Ó Corráin, 'Laws of the Irish', 392. There is some conflation with the rather different account of the reorganization found in Num. 11:11–17, 24.

This accommodating attitude to man-made law is often implied even when it is not explicit. Ecclesiastics figure in the process of legislation.[34] The Venerable Bede (d. 735) mentions the vernacular code of laws promulgated 'after the Roman manner' by King Ethelbert of Kent (ruled 560–616) in the early seventh century as one of the good things (*bona*) he did for his people.[35] A prominent Carolingian ecclesiastic who disapproved of the legal pluralism whereby every people had its own law was Bishop Agobard of Lyons (d. 840), who wrote a polemical tract against Burgundian law. But he was not concerned to abolish Burgundian law in favour of God's law; rather he sought to persuade Louis the Pious (ruled 813–40) to subject the Burgundians to Frankish law.[36] This did not, of course, mean that God's law was ignored. Kings, as we have seen, would defer to it, and they might draw on Mosaic law when compiling their own law codes. The English king Alfred (ruled 871–99) is a notable example of this.[37] But it did not prevent him from filling out his code with laws of his own devising.

Christianity and Roman Law

In taking their freedom to legislate for granted, the Germanic kings had the precedent and parallel of the Christian Roman emperors. Thus at the beginning of his account of the composition of the *Digest*, Justinian (ruled 527–65) displays the same piety, albeit in a higher rhetorical register: 'Governing under the authority of God our empire which was delivered to us by the Heavenly Majesty... we rest all our hopes in the providence of the Supreme Trinity

[34] For the Visigothic case, see Patrick Wormald, 'The *Leges Barbarorum*: Law and Ethnicity in the Post-Roman West', in Hans-Werner Goetz et al., eds, *Regna and Gentes: The Relationship between Late Antique and Early Medieval Peoples and Kingdoms in the Transformation of the Roman World* (Leiden: Brill, 2003), 38. For English examples, see F. L. Attenborough, ed. and trans., *The Laws of the Earliest English Kings* (Cambridge: Cambridge University Press, 1922), 36 = 37, where a king of Wessex legislating in the late seventh century mentions consultation with two of his bishops; Lisi Oliver, *The Beginnings of English Law* (Toronto: University of Toronto Press, 2002), 152 = 153, where an account of the laws of a contemporary king of Kent mentions the presence of an archbishop and bishop in the assembly that made the laws. Note also the 33 assembled bishops mentioned in headings of the *Pactus legis Alamannorum* and of one version of the *Lex Alamannorum* (Karl Eckhardt, ed., *Leges Alamannorum* (Hanover: Hahnsche Buchhandlung, 1966), 21, 37 col. 9; Eckhardt inclines to date the *Pactus* to the early seventh century and the *Lex* to the later seventh or early eighth, see 6, 9, and he assigns the relevant manuscript of the *Lex* to the ninth century, see 13).

[35] Siems, 'Entwicklung von Rechtsquellen', 254–5; Bede, *Ecclesiastical History of the English People*, ed. and trans. Bertram Colgrave and R. A. B. Mynors (Oxford: Clarendon Press, 1969), 150 = 151.

[36] Agobard of Lyons. 'Adversus legem Gundobadi', in L. van Acker, ed., *Agobardi Lugdunensis opera omnia.* (Turnhout: Brepols, 1981), 23 VII (*ut eos transferret ad legem Francorum*).

[37] Wormald, *Making of English Law*, 421–3; for Alfred's account of his own legislative activity, see 277.

alone.'[38] Indeed in the document confirming the *Digest*, he goes even further: 'We . . . in our accustomed manner, have resorted to the aid of the Immortal One and, invoking the Supreme Deity, have desired that God should become the author and patron of the whole work.'[39] But if God was to be the author, the work was clearly intended to be ghost-written, and there was no suggestion that God's own contribution to earlier legal literature would figure in the process. The object was to produce a digest of Roman, not Mosaic law.[40] As Justinian explains in his account of the composition of the work, 'we have found the whole extent of our laws which has come down from the foundation of the city of Rome and the days of Romulus to be so confused that it extends to an inordinate length and is beyond the comprehension of any human nature'.[41] Justinian now makes it his business to cleanse this Augean stable. It was indeed a formidable task 'to collect and amend the whole set of Roman ordinances and present the diverse books of so many authors in a single volume', and only achievable 'relying upon God'.[42] This codification of Roman law was also an exercise in legislation. As Justinian puts it at one point, 'we ascribe everything to ourselves, since it is from us that all their authority is derived';[43] for 'whatsoever is set down here, we resolve this and this alone be observed',[44] and no one is to dare 'to compare any ancient text with that which our authority has introduced'.[45] Indeed he anticipated that he himself would make new law in the future.[46] Particularly notable is the fact

[38] Justinian, *Digest*, Theodore Mommsen and Paul Krueger, eds, and Alan Watson, trans. (Philadelphia: University of Pennsylvania Press, 1985), vol. 1, xlvi. By contrast, such Christian piety is not yet in evidence in 438 in the prolegomena to the Theodosian Code (Th. Mommsen, ed., *Codex Theodosianus* (Hildesheim: Weidmann, 1990), vol. 1, 1–4 = Clyde Pharr, trans., *The Theodosian Code* (Princeton: Princeton University Press, 1952), 3–7), but has become pervasive in the prologue of the *Eclogue* of Leo III (ruled 717–41), which is adorned with quotations from the Bible (Edwin Freshfield, trans., *A Manual of Roman Law: The Ecloga* (Cambridge: Cambridge University Press, 1926), 66–70; for the Greek text and a German translation, see Ludwig Burgmann, ed. and trans., *Ecloga: das Gesetzbuch Leons III. und Konstantinos' V.* (Frankfurt am Main: Löwenklau-Gesellschaft, 1983), 160–7). Indeed the *Eclogue* is accompanied in some manuscripts by a 'synopsis of the Mosaic law' (summarized in Freshfield, *Manual*, 142–4; on this text, its relationship to the *Eclogue*, and its unclear purpose, see L. Burgmann and Sp. Troianos, 'Nomos Mosaïkos', in Dieter Simon, ed., *Fontes minores III* (Frankfurt am Main: Klostermann, 1979), 126–37, with an edition of the Greek text, 138–67).

[39] Justinian. *Digest*, vol. 1, lv.

[40] Contrast the late antique text known in modern times as the *Mosaicarum et Romanarum legum collatio*, in which passages of Pentateuchal law on a given theme are followed immediately by passages of Roman law: *Moyses dei sacerdos haec dicit: . . . . Paulus . . . dicit: . . . . Ulpianus: . . .* (M. Hyamson, ed. and trans., *Mosaicarum et Romanarum legum collatio* (London: Oxford University Press, 1913), 56 = 57; Paulus and his younger contemporary Ulpian (d. 228) were prominent Roman jurists). Unfortunately the author does not state his purpose in collating the law of the Bible and Roman law in this way (see xl).

[41] Justinian. *Digest*, vol. 1, xlvi.

[42] Justinian. *Digest*, vol. 1, xlvi, and see xlvii.

[43] Justinian, *Digest*, vol. 1, xlvii.

[44] Justinian, *Digest*, vol. 1, lxii.

[45] Justinian, *Digest*, vol. 1, lix, and see lxii.

[46] For his projected 'Novels', see Barry Nicholas, *An Introduction to Roman Law* (Oxford: Clarendon Press, 1991), 42; and cf. Justinian, *Digest*, vol. 1, lxi.

that the whole achievement met with no opposition from the custodians of the Christian tradition, the bishops and monks whose obstinacy was to frustrate all his attempts to bring order to the chaos of Christology. The Church, it seems, was content to live by Roman law.[47]

Explaining Christian Attitudes

How should we explain this accommodating attitude of Christians to human law—and indeed pagan law? Here our texts are not in general very helpful, because they tend to take it for granted that there is no problem. But we have already encountered one answer in the two Irish texts we have examined: the concept of natural law. To this we can add a Germanic parallel. A ninth-century account of the pagan Saxons remarks on the excellence of their laws for the punishment of misdeeds, and goes on to say that 'in the interest of upright morals they strove to have many useful and, according to the natural law, honourable regulations'; but for their paganism, these could have helped them on the road to salvation.[48] The idea of natural law was of course an ancient one. Zeno of Citium (d. 263 BC), the founder of the Stoic school, had believed natural law to be divine (*naturalem legem divinam esse censet*), and to have the same moral force.[49] This suggests that in spite of the diversity of human laws, there might be a significant overlap between them and natural or divine law. Three centuries later St Paul provided scriptural warrant for the adoption of the Stoic idea of natural law by Christians in just this vein, writing that 'when the Gentiles, which have not the law, do by nature (*physei*, *naturaliter*) the things contained in the law, these, having not the law, are a law unto themselves: which shew the work of the law written in their hearts,

[47] The law code of the Ripuarian Franks speaks of bishops having charters prepared *secundum legem Romanam, quam ecclesia vivit* (see Michael Moore, *A Sacred Kingdom: Bishops and the Rise of Frankish Kingship, 300–850* (Washington, DC: Catholic University of America Press, 2011), 84, 131).

[48] I quote the passage from Adam of Bremen, *History of the Archbishops of Hamburg–Bremen*, trans. Francis Tschan (New York: Columbia University Press, 2002), 10. Adam, an eleventh-century historian, attributes the account to Einhard (d. 840), see 6, 8, 11, 34; in the last of these references he speaks of Einhard's '*Gesta* of the Saxons', but no such work is known today. However, the account also occurs in a ninth-century text, the 'Translatio S. Alexandri', where it is ascribed to Rudolf of Fulda (d. 865). This text was edited by Georgius Pertz in *Monumenta Germaniae Historica, Scriptores*, vol. 2 (1829), 674–81, where our passage appears at 675.22 (*multa utilia atque secundum legem naturae honesta in morum probitate habere studuerunt*); for Rudolf's authorship see the letter of Meginhard of Fulda (674) and the marginal annotation *hucusque Rudolf* (676). I owe my knowledge of this passage to Peter Brown, *The Rise of Western Christendom: Triumph and Diversity, A.D. 200–1000* (Chichester: Wiley-Blackwell, 2013), 480.

[49] Wolfgang Kullmann, *Naturgesetz in der Vorstellung der Antike, besonders der Stoa: eine Begriffsuntersuchung* (Stuttgart: Franz Steiner, 2010), 38. The wording is Cicero's.

their conscience also bearing witness' (Rom. 2:14–15).[50] Christians duly followed this Pauline precedent. Thus Tertullian (d. *c.* 225) held that before the written law of Moses there was an unwritten law that was understood naturally (*naturaliter*); for without the justice of natural law (*lex naturalis*), how, for example, would Abraham have been reckoned the friend of God?[51] Moreover he used the notion to explain the presence of commendable elements in paganism, and held that it was given to Adam and Eve, and thus to all nations.[52] For Christian scholars in the early medieval West the idea of natural law was thus a commonplace. Isidore of Seville (d. 636) touched on the theme in his widely read *Etymologies*. He remarked that 'All laws are either divine or human; divine laws are in accord with nature, human laws with customs', and further that 'Natural law (*ius naturale*) is common to all nations.'[53] But of course such an explanation begs the question why Christianity should have been so receptive to a notion developed by pagan philosophers.

MUSLIM ATTITUDES

God's Monopoly of the Making of Law

From a Christian point of view all I have done in this chapter so far is to establish truths so obvious that they are normally taken for granted.[54] But what Christians take for granted can raise Muslim eyebrows. Thus the geographer Abū ʿUbayd al-Bakrī (d. 487/1094), after commenting on the inadequacy of Christian scripture (*muṣḥaf al-Naṣārā*) as a source of law, goes on to say that 'their Sunna is not taken from revelation (*tanzīl*) or transmission (*riwāya*) from a prophet, but rather derives entirely from their kings (*mulūk*)'.[55]

[50] For the use of the term 'nature' (*physis*) in this passage, see Horst Balz and Gerhard Schneider, eds, *Exegetical Dictionary of the New Testament* (Grand Rapids: Eerdmans, 1990–3), vol. 3, 444.

[51] Tertullian, *Adversus Iudaeos*, Hermann Tränkle, ed. (Wiesbaden: Franz Steiner, 1964), 5.17 (II 7), quoted in Kullmann, *Naturgesetz*, 124. For further instances of the idea in the works of the church fathers, see chs 12 and 13.

[52] So Jaroslav Pelikan, *The Christian Tradition: A History of the Development of Doctrine* (Chicago: University of Chicago Press, 1975–91), vol. 1, 32.

[53] Canale, *Etimologie*, vol. 1, 388 = 389 (5.2.1), 390 = 391 (5.4.1).

[54] Many of my references in this section derive from the data-base al-Maktaba al-Shāmila. I am much indebted to Usaama al-Azami for equipping me with a copy and instructing me in its use. I regret that shortage of time has prevented me delving into the Imāmī, Zaydī, and Ibāḍī sources.

[55] Abū ʿUbayd al-Bakrī, *al-Masālik waʾl-mamālik*, A. P. van Leeuwen and A. Ferré, eds (Tunis: al-Dār al-ʿArabiyya lil-Kitāb, 1992), 480–1 §809; the passage is quoted in Paul Cobb, *The Race for Paradise: An Islamic History of the Crusades* (Oxford: Oxford University Press, 2014), 12. Compare Masʿūdī (d. 345/956) on the Zanj: 'They have no religious law (*sharīʿa*) to

That the Muslim God lays claim to a monopoly of law-making is generally assumed by the Muslim scholars and would seem to be made clear in His Book. In one verse He says: 'Whosoever judges not according to what God has sent down (*man lam yaḥkum bi-mā anzala 'llāhu*)—they are the unbelievers' (Q 5:44). And soon after, He asks: 'Is it the judgment of pagandom (*ḥukm al-Jāhiliyya*) then that they are seeking? Yet who is fairer in judgment than God?' (Q 5:50).

Actually things are not quite as simple as this suggests. These verses form part of a larger polemical passage, Q 5:42–50, directed in the first instance at the Jews, who are later—from verse 46 onward—joined by the Christians. The passage has two main themes. The first is the obligation of all concerned to judge by what God has sent down, be it the Torah for the Jews, the Gospel for the Christians, or the Book (*al-Kitāb*) revealed to Muḥammad. The second theme is the way Muḥammad should respond if Jews or Christians come to him seeking judgement. In the case of Jews, at least, he has the choice of either turning away from them or giving judgement (Q 5:42); in the latter case he should judge between them—by now this includes Christians—in accordance with what God has sent down (Q 5:48–9).[56] It is therefore reasonable to ask what any of this has to do with Muslims; nothing in the passage refers directly to Muslims, or rather to purported Muslims who are or become unbelievers through their failure to implement God's law.

The exegetes are of course well aware of the Jewish, and to a lesser extent Christian, reference of the verses—they could hardly fail to be, so plain is the sense. Thus Ṭabarī (d. 310/923) says that the best view is that the verses came down regarding the unbelievers of the People of the Book; his reason is that the preceding and following verses likewise came down about them.[57] With regard to Q 5:44, there is occasional insistence that it refers *only* to non-Muslims.[58] But others say the verse refers to Muslims (*ahl al-Islām*).[59] And in any case, if we consider the wording '*whosoever* judges not according to what God has sent down', it makes sense to say that irrespective of the occasion of

which to have recourse, but rather some practices (*rusūm*) of their kings and some political traditions (*siyāsāt*) according to which they rule their subjects' (*Murūj al-dhahab*, Charles Pellat, ed. (Beirut: al-Jāmiʿa al-Lubnāniyya, 1965–74), vol. 2, 125.10 §872).

[56] One might wonder why Jews and Christians would seek judgement from Muḥammad when they already have their own scriptures; God Himself asks this question, and responds by saying that those who come to Muḥammad in this way and then turn their backs are not believers (Q 5:43).

[57] See Ṭabarī, *Tafsīr* (Beirut: Dār al-Kutub al-ʿIlmiyya, 1992), vol. 4. 597.20 in his lengthy commentary on the passage.

[58] See Ṭabarī. *Tafsīr*, vol. 4, 592 no. 12,028, where one early exegete says that the passage has nothing to do with Muslims (*laysa fī ahl al-Islām minhu shayʾ*), and 592–3 nos 12,030–1, where another maintains that it came down about non-Muslims, and not about Muslim rulers (*umarāʾ*) as his Ibāḍī interlocutors in the second tradition would have it.

[59] Ṭabarī. *Tafsīr*, vol. 4, 594.31 and 595 nos 12,043–51.

its revelation, its content would apply to all and sundry, Muslims included. This view is recorded by Ṭabarī and endorsed by him.[60] Turning to Q 5:50, Ibn Kathīr (d. 774/1373) says that it condemns whoever abandons God's law for human fancies;[61] unlike the earlier exegetes, he goes on to give two examples that fit an expansive view, one being the errors of the people of the Jahiliyya, and the other the Yāsā (Yāsaq) thrown together by Chingiz Khān and observed by his descendants. Anyone who acts in this way is an unbeliever who must be fought. Likewise the view that the verse refers to the Jews is matched by another according to which it refers to anyone who disregards God's judgement for that of the Jahiliyya.[62] And again, even if it came down with regard to the Jews, the condemnation of those seeking 'the judgment of pagandom' would surely apply also to Muslims who behaved in such a fashion; the phrase, after all, invites interpretation as a reference to the law of the pagan Arabs.[63]

Thus the principle that the only valid law is God's law can be taken as grounded in Muslim scripture. And yet the Muslim scholars recognize quite a number of the laws of Islam as having originated among the pagan Arabs.[64] How so?

Pagan Law Retained in Islamic Law: The Case of Compurgation

A straightforward example—straightforward in this respect though not in others—is compurgation (*qasāma*). Here is one account of compurgation as

[60] Ṭabarī. *Tafsīr*, vol. 4, 596.23 and 596–7 no. 12,065, where an early exegete is quoted as saying: 'It came down about the Jews, but obligates us' (*nazalat fī 'l-Yahūd, wa-hiya ʿalaynā wājiba*). For Ṭabarī's endorsement see 597.23.

[61] Ibn Kathīr, *Tafsīr* (Beirut: Dār al-Khayr, 1990–1), vol. 2, 77.4.

[62] Jaṣṣāṣ, *Aḥkām al-Qurʾān* (Beirut: Dār al-Kutub al-ʿIlmiyya, 1994), vol. 2, 554.12.

[63] Thus Ṭabarī glosses the phrase *ḥukm al-Jāhiliyya* as *aḥkām ʿabadat al-awthān min ahl al-shirk*, *Tafsīr*, vol. 4, 614.22. Note also the *shādhdh* reading *a-fa-ḥakama 'l-Jāhiliyyati* (Ibn Khālawayh, *Mukhtaṣar fī shawādhdh al-Qurʾān*, ed. G. Bergsträsser (Cairo: Maktabat al-Mutanabbī, n.d.), 39.6, describing the vocalization as entirely *maftūḥa*). This reading is adduced by Zamakhsharī (d. 538/1144) with the comment that it is as if they sought the judgement of Afʿā of Najrān—a famous judge of pagan times—or a *ḥakam* of that ilk, and wanted Muḥammad the seal of the prophets to be such a *ḥakam* (*Kashshāf*, ʿĀdil ʿAbd al-Mawjūd et al., eds (Riyadh: Maktabat al-ʿUbaykān, 1998), vol. 2, 249.8). A Shīʿite tradition quotes Muḥammad al-Bāqir (d. *c.* 118/736) exclaiming that there are two judgements, that of God and that of the Jahiliyya (*al-ḥukm ḥukmān, ḥukm Allāh wa-ḥukm al-Jāhiliyya*; he goes on to declare the judgements given by the Companion Zayd ibn Thābit on questions of inheritance to be a case of the second (Kulaynī, *Kāfī*, ed. ʿAlī Akbar al-Ghaffārī (Tehran: Dār al-Kutub al-Islāmiyya, 1362–3 sh.), vol. 7, 407.9, 407.12). For the contrast between the Sunnī and Imāmī law of inheritance that is dramatized in this tradition, see N. J. Coulson, *Succession in the Muslim Family* (Cambridge: Cambridge University Press, 1971), 131, 133.

[64] I am not concerned in this article with Muslim attitudes to legal continuity with pre-Islamic law outside Arabia. To my knowledge the question is rarely discussed in the sources; for an exception see the passage translated in Joseph Schacht, *An Introduction to Islamic law* (Oxford: Clarendon Press, 1964), 19–20.

a procedure in Islamic law: 'When a slain man is found in a quarter and it is not known who killed him, fifty men from among them, chosen by the next of kin, are required to swear: "By God, we did not kill him, and we don't know who killed him."'[65] The scholars at large—including all four Sunnī schools—accept compurgation, despite disagreement over what it involves.[66] At the same time, we know (in the sense that the Muslim scholars tell us) that compurgation was practised in pre-Islamic Arabia, though it is not portrayed as either ancient or widespread.[67] According to Ibn ʿAbbās (d. 68/687–8), 'The first compurgation that took place in the Jahiliyya was among us, the Banū Hāshim.... Abū Ṭālib came to him [the suspected killer, who is not named in this version] and said: "You have three choices: either you can pay a hundred camels for killing one of our people, or fifty of your people can swear that you didn't kill him, or if you refuse we'll kill you for him."'[68] The option chosen was the second—compurgation. We are in Mecca on the eve of the rise of Islam; Abū Ṭālib is Muḥammad's uncle.

How then did this judgement of pagandom become part of Islamic law? Here we have two well-attested traditions about the Prophet. The first is

[65] Marghīnānī, *Hidāya* (Beirut: Dār al-Kutub al-ʿIlmiyya, 1990), vols 3–4, 564.18.

[66] Ibn Rushd (al-ḥafīd), *Bidāyat al-mujtahid*, Muḥammad Muḥaysin and Shaʿbān Ismāʿīl, ed. (Cairo: Maktabat al-Kulliyāt al-Azhariyya, 1970–4), vol. 2, 460.24. He names four early authorities who rejected the institution, and states their objections in some detail (461.3); one is that it violates the principles of law because people testify to what they have not witnessed and do not know. Even for Ibn Ḥazm, who has a very long discussion of the traditions involved (*Muḥallā* (n.p.: Dār al-Fikr, n.d.), vol. 11, 64–87 nos 2148–9), the bottom line is that the Prophet invoked compurgation, and made it obligatory for us to do so (84.19).

[67] In this chapter we are not concerned to go behind the thinking of early medieval Christians and Muslims and ask whether any given law was *in fact* of pagan origin, though many may well have been. As will appear, the Muslim sources tend to present such laws as innovations of the late Jahiliyya, as here in the case of compurgation, though there are exceptions (see nn. 75, 130).

[68] Bukhārī, *Ṣaḥīḥ*, Ludolf Krehl, ed. (Leiden: Brill, 1862–1908), vol. 3, 19.8, 20.1 (*manāqib al-anṣār* 27); and see J. Wellhausen, *Reste arabischen Heidentums* (Berlin: Georg Reimer, 1897), 187–8; Johs Pedersen, *Der Eid bei den Semiten* (Strassburg: Karl J. Trübner, 1914), 180–1; Patricia Crone, 'Jāhilī and Jewish Law: The *Qasāma*', *Jerusalem Studies in Arabic and Islam* 4 (1984): 157–8. Note that this tradition is never to my knowledge cited by the jurists, and that Bukhārī himself places it in a part of his collection reserved for comic and curious traditions about the Jahiliyya, not in his treatment of compurgation as a legal topic (cf. the heading *bāb ayyām al-Jāhiliyya*, vol. 3, 16.18, and Michael Cook, 'Ibn Qutayba and the Monkeys', *Studia Islamica* 89 (1999): 62). The tradition has a moral—those who falsely swore the oath perished within a year—but it has no legal payload. It interests antiquarians, particularly those who collect 'firsts' (*awāʾil*); hence the (very different) version of the story in Abū Hilāl al-ʿAskarī, *Awāʾil*, Walīd Qaṣṣāb and Muḥammad al-Miṣrī, ed. (Riyadh: Dār al-ʿUlūm, 1981), vol. 1, 78–81 (where al-Walīd ibn al-Mughīra plays the role of judge: *fa-taḥākamū ilā ʾl-Walīd ibn al-Mughīra wa-huwa yawmaʾidhin ḥakam Quraysh*, 79.8). Ibn Qutayba in his *Maʿārif* has this version as a 'first', without the story but with the addition of a reference to the Prophet's confirmation of compurgation (ed. Tharwat ʿUkāsha (Cairo: Dār al-Maʿārif, 1981), 551.16), whence Māwardī (d. 450/1058) quotes it in his *Ḥāwī* (ed. ʿAlī Muʿawwaḍ and ʿĀdil ʿAbd al-Mawjūd (Beirut: Dār al-Kutub al-ʿIlmiyya, 1994), vol. 13, 3.22)—a rare case, but not the only one in the *Ḥāwī*, of a jurist showing a taste for antiquarian information. To my knowledge this tradition is our sole account of a case of compurgation in the Jahiliyya.

succinct: 'The Prophet confirmed (*aqarra*) compurgation as it had been (*ʿalā mā kānat ʿalayhi*) in the Jahiliyya.'[69] It is noticed by the jurists; thus Sarakhsī (d. *c.* 490/1097) quotes a version,[70] and Ibn ʿAbd al-Barr (d. 463/1071) in a legal work has a statement that echoes the wording of one form of the tradition.[71] The second tradition is a detailed story of how the Prophet proposed compurgation to resolve a case of homicide, though as it happened this compurgation never took place.[72] This tradition is widely adopted by the jurists as providing the legal basis for compurgation.[73]

Further Pagan Retentions in Islamic Law

There are a number of other aspects of Islamic law that are said to originate in the Jahiliyya but to have been 'confirmed' by Islam.[74] Here I mention some of them briefly, without attempting to identify all of them, let alone to investigate them in detail. We are told that the standard criterion for determining the sex of a hermaphrodite goes back to a pre-Islamic judge, and that the Prophet

[69] Muslim, *Ṣaḥīḥ*, ed. Muḥammad Fuʾād ʿAbd al-Bāqī (Cairo: Dār Iḥyāʾ al-Kutub al-ʿArabiyya, 1955–6), 1295 no. 1670. For a translation of another version, see Rudolph Peters, 'Murder in Khaybar: some thoughts on the origins of the *qasāma* procedure in Islamic law', *Islamic Law and Society* 9 (2002): 135; for references to occurrences of this tradition in other collections, see 135–6 n. 9. This is what Peters dubs the 'Confirmation hadith'. A weakness of this tradition in all Muslim's versions is that those who report the action of the Prophet are left anonymous.

[70] Sarakhsī, *Mabsūṭ* (Cairo: Maktabat al-Saʿāda, 1324–31), vol. 26, 107.8; compare the forms from Zuhrī noted in Muslim, *Ṣaḥīḥ*, 1295 no. 8.

[71] Ibn ʿAbd al-Barr, *Istidhkār*, ed. ʿAbd al-Muʿṭī Qalʿajī (Cairo: Dār al-Waʿy, 1993), vol. 25, 328 no. 38,437. Likewise Shāṭibī (d. 790/1388) may have this tradition in mind when he includes *qasāma* in lists of Jāhilī laws (*aḥkām*) which Islam or the Sharīʿa confirmed (*aqarrahā, aqarrat*, *Muwāfaqāt*, Mashhūr Āl Salmān, ed. (Khubar: Dār Ibn ʿAffān, 1997), vol. 2, 125.1, 524.7).

[72] This tradition is translated in Peters, 'Murder in Khaybar', 136; he dubs it the 'Khaybar murder hadith' (but note that Ibn Qutayba's 'first' is not in fact related to this tradition, cf. 150 n. 46). For references to numerous collections, including those of Bukhārī and Muslim, see 136 n. 10. See also Wellhausen, *Reste*, 188–9; Pedersen, *Eid*, 181–2.

[73] Ibn Rushd (d. 595/1198) cites it as the basis (*ʿumda*) of the position of the majority who endorse *qasāma* (*Bidāyat al-mujtahid*, vol. 2, 461.1); Māwardī begins his *kitāb al-qasāma* by quoting the tradition from Shāfiʿī (d. 204/820) (*Ḥāwī*, vol. 13, 3.4); Sarakhsī says the procedure has reached us from the Prophet, there being well-known traditions about it, among which he gives pride of place to this tradition (*Mabsūṭ*, vol. 26, 106.23); Ibn Qudāma (d. 620/1223) states that *qasāma* is based on it (*Mughnī*, ʿAbd al-Salām Shāhīn, ed. (Beirut: Dār al-Kutub al-ʿIlmiyya, 1994), vol. 8, 46.5). Those who rejected *qasāma* held that the tradition does not show the Prophet actually imposing the procedure, and can be interpreted to undermine it (Ibn Rushd, *Bidāya*, vol. 2, 461.18; the confirmation tradition is ignored here).

[74] The sources generally refer to such confirmation by using forms derived from the root *q-r-r*, usually the fourth form, less commonly the second. But for stray examples of the use of the root *b-q-y*, again in the second and fourth forms, see Ibn Ḥabīb, *Muḥabbar*, Ilse Lichtenstädter, ed. (Beirut: Dār al-Āfāq al-Jadīda, n.d.), 309.7, 319.9.

confirmed it (*qarrarahu*).[75] In the same way Islam confirmed the pre-Islamic practice of sacrificing an animal on the seventh day after the birth of a child (ʿ*aqīqa*).[76] Likewise people used to hire wet-nurses in the Jahiliyya, and the Prophet confirmed them in it.[77] They would engage in hiring and renting (*ijāra*), and again the Prophet confirmed them in it.[78] They would also punish theft by cutting off the hands of thieves; God then commanded that this should be done in Islam.[79] A pair of examples relate to blood money (*diya*). First, in the Jahiliyya blood money was payable by the blood-money group (ʿ*āqila*), and the Prophet confirmed this (*aqarrahā*) in Islam.[80] Second, the amount of the blood money for homicide was fixed as a hundred camels in the Jahiliyya, and the holy law then said the same.[81] Finally, we may add that with

[75] Sarakhsī, *Mabsūṭ*, vol. 30, 103.14 (*qarrarahu Rasūl Allāh*); and see Shāṭibī, *Muwāfaqāt*, vol. 1, 277.1 (speaking of *iqrār al-Islām*), vol. 2, 125.1 (*aqarrahā ʾl-Islām*). The judge in question, not named by Sarakhsī, is ʿĀmir ibn al-Ẓarib al-ʿAdwānī (see, e.g., Ibn Ḥabīb, *Muḥabbar*, 236.9; Ibn Qutayba, *Maʿārif*, 553.5; Ibn Hishām, *al-Sīra al-nabawiyya*, Muṣṭafā al-Saqqā et al., eds (Cairo: Muṣṭafā al-Bābī al-Ḥalabī, 1955), vols 1–2, 122.11 = A. Guillaume, trans., *The Life of Muhammad: A Translation of Ibn Isḥāq's Sīrat Rasūl Allāh* (Karachi: Oxford University Press, 1980), 51–2). The narrations of Sarakhsī and Ibn Hishām (d. 218/833) reveal that ʿĀmir owed the criterion to his daughter or slave girl. ʿĀmir is an early figure, some nine generations before Muḥammad (see Werner Caskel, *Ǧamharat an-nasab: das genealogische Werk des Hišām ibn Muḥammad al-Kalbī* (Leiden: E. J. Brill, 1966), vol. 1, Table 139 line 13; for the chronological significance of Caskel's 'lines', see 66–7).

[76] Ibn Rushd (al-jadd), *al-Bayān waʾl-taḥṣīl*, Muḥammad Ḥajjī et al., eds (Beirut: Dār al-Gharb al-Islāmī, 1984–91), vol. 3, 384.13 (*uqirrat fī ʾl-Islām*); Ibn Rushd (al-jadd), *al-Muqaddimāt al-mumahhidāt*, Muḥammad Ḥajjī et al., eds (Beirut: Dār al-Gharb al-Islāmī, 1988), vol. 1, 447.16. By contrast, an early Ḥanafī tradition describes it as a Jāhilī practice that was rejected (*rufiḍat*) with the coming of Islam (Abū Yūsuf, *Āthār*, ed. Abū ʾl-Wafā (Cairo: Maṭbaʿat al-Istiqāma, 1355), 238 no. 1054, and cf. no. 1055).

[77] Sarakhsī, *Mabsūṭ*, vol. 15, 118.17 (*aqarrahum ʿalayhi*).

[78] Sarakhsī, *Mabsūṭ*, vol. 15, 74.12 (*aqarrahum ʿalā dhālika*).

[79] Māwardī, *Ḥāwī*, vol. 13, 266.11 (*amara ʾllāhu taʿālā bihi fī ʾl-Islām*). Māwardī remarks that the first to impose this penalty was Walīd ibn al-Mughīra, a statement that clearly derives from Ibn Qutayba, *Maʿārif*, 552.2. Note that it is one of four 'firsts' ascribed by Ibn Qutayba to Walīd ibn al-Mughīra, a pagan who died when the Prophet was already middle-aged and whose son Khālid (d. 21/641–2) was to be a major figure in the Arab conquests. Here again there is no attempt to present the practice in question as of immemorial antiquity, as is confirmed by the list of Qurashīs who underwent this punishment in Jāhilī times (see Ibn Ḥabīb, *Muḥabbar*, 328.1; Ibn Ḥabīb, *Munammaq*, ed. Khwurshīd Fāriq (Hyderabad: Dār al-Maʿārif al-ʿUthmāniyya, 1964), 530.2; Hishām ibn al-Kalbī, *Mathālib al-ʿArab*, ed. Najāḥ al-Ṭāʾī (Beirut: Dār al-Hudā, 1998), 49.2).

[80] Ibn ʿAbd al-Barr, *Istdhkār*, vol. 25, 221 no. 37,826; and see Ghazzālī, *al-Mustaṣfā min ʿilm al-uṣūl* (Cairo: Maṭbaʿat Muṣṭafā Muḥammad, 1937), vol. 2, 89.26 (*qarrarahu ʾl-sharʿ*); Qarāfī, *Dhakhīra*, Muḥammad Ḥajjī et al., eds (Beirut: Dār al-Gharb al-Islāmī, 1994), vol. 12, 389.2 (*aqarrahu Rasūl Allāh*, quoting Ibn Yūnus); Shāṭibī, *Muwāfaqāt*, vol. 2, 125.1 (*aqarrahā ʾl-Islām*).

[81] Māwardī, *Ḥāwī*, vol. 12:223.7 (*jāʾa ʾl-sharʿ bihā waʾstaqarraʾl-ḥukm ʿalayhā*); similarly Ibn Rushd, *Muqaddimāt*, vol. 3, 290.16, 290.20. Here again Māwardī is quoting a 'first' from Ibn Qutayba (*Maʿārif*, 551.9). Ibn Qutayba in fact names two men as candidates for this 'first'. The first is Abū Sayyāra ʿUmayla ibn al-Aʿzal al-ʿAdwānī, who was the last to perform a certain role in the control of the Ḥajj before Islam took over (Ibn Hishām, *Sīra*, vols 1–2, 122.2 = Guillaume,

the coming of Islam the units of weight used by Quraysh in the Jahiliyya were confirmed (*uqirrat*).[82]

The two cases I now propose to discuss are not as straightforward as compurgation, and perhaps some of those just listed; they will prove of interest to us for just that reason.

Awkward Cases: The Commenda

The first is an entrepreneurial institution, the commenda (*qirāḍ*). This is a contract in which one party invests capital and the other engages in commerce; they share the profit of the enterprise.[83] The jurists frequently refer to the commenda as having been practised in the Jahiliyya and then confirmed by the Prophet in Islam.[84] And indeed there exist two traditions that have the Prophet approve it.[85] The first has him say that anyone who is burdened with maintaining three daughters is in effect a prisoner of war (*asīr*)—in other words, he is not in a position to move around to do business—and so people should help him by forming commendas with him.[86] The second tradition has the Prophet approve certain conditions that his uncle ʿAbbās used to impose when entering into a commenda contract.[87] If the Prophet approved the conditions, then by implication he must surely have approved of the institution itself. But these traditions are not found in the best collections, the first not in any, and they are ignored by many jurists.

The jurists in general thus have a problem that they do not always confront directly: there is no revealed text by which the commenda is explicitly confirmed in Islam. As Ibn Ḥazm (d. 456/1064) puts it, there is no revealed text

Life of Muhammad, 51). The second is the Prophet's grandfather ʿAbd al-Muṭṭalib. So here again, there is no reaching for antiquity.

[82] Balādhurī, *Futūḥ al-buldān*, ed. ʿAbdallāh al-Ṭabbāʿ (Beirut: Muʾassasat al-Maʿārif, 1987), 653.16. When the Prophet came to Mecca he confirmed them in their practice (*aqarrahum ʿalā dhālika*, 654.6).

[83] For a brief account see *Encyclopaedia of Islam*, 2nd edn (Leiden: E. J. Brill, 1960–2009), art. 'Ḳirāḍ' (A. L. Udovitch). As mentioned there, the words *qirāḍ* and *muḍāraba* are synonyms.

[84] Ibn ʿAbd al-Barr, *Istidhkār*, vol. 21, 119–20 no. 30,709 (*aqarrahu*); Ibn Ḥazm, *al-Iḥkām fī uṣūl al-aḥkām* (Cairo: Maṭbaʿat al-Saʿāda, 1345–7), vol. 2, 95.2 (*aqarrahu*); Ibn Ḥazm, *Muḥallā*, vol. 8, 247 no. 1367 (*aqarra*); Shāṭibī, *Muwāfaqāt*, vol. 2, 125.1 (*aqarrahā ʾl-Islām*), 524.7 (*aqarrat hādhihi ʾl-sharīʿa*); Ibn Rushd, *Bidāya*, vol. 2, 265.3 (*aqarrahu ʾl-Islām*); Sarakhsī, *Mabsūṭ*, vol. 22, 19.5 (*aqarrahum ʿala dhālika*); Marghīnānī, *Hidāya*, vols 3–4, 225.5 (*qarrarahum ʿalayhi*).

[85] Abraham Udovitch, *Partnership and profit in medieval Islam* (Princeton: Princeton University Press, 1970), 172–3, citing Sarakhsī for both and Shaybānī for the second.

[86] Sarakhsī, *Mabsūṭ*, vol. 22, 19.7. This tradition appears in other sources, but so far as I know without the mention of the commenda.

[87] Sarakhsī, *Mabsūṭ*, vol. 22, 18.8; also Māwardī, *Ḥāwī*, vol. 7, 306.1. This tradition appears in some collections, though not the most prestigious (see, e.g., Bayhaqī, *al-Sunan al-kubrā* (Hyderabad: Dāʾirat al-Maʿārif al-Niẓāmiyya, 1344–55), vol. 6, 111.18).

(*naṣṣ*) permitting it;[88] as Shāṭibī (d. 790/1388) says, it is one of a number of things practised in the Jahiliyya regarding which the revelation is silent,[89] and which are valid to this day on the basis that they were confirmed by Islam (*bāqiya ilā ʾl-ān ʿalā ḥukm iqrār al-Islām*).[90] That the commenda was confirmed by Islam is thus for such jurists a matter of consensus (*ijmāʿ*), and they accordingly stress the absence of dissenting authorities. Ibn ʿAbd al-Barr affirms that the consensus of the jurists is sufficient proof of the permissibility of the commenda,[91] and Ibn Ḥazm goes so far as to say not just that consensus is the sole proof of its permissibility, but also that if he found a single scholar who considered it abolished, he would side with him.[92] This consensus, in turn, rests on the existence of traditions from Companions of the Prophet showing that they practised or approved of the commenda.[93] Even jurists who make great play of the traditions also mention consensus. Sarakhsī says that the permissibility of the commenda is known by Sunna (i.e. through traditions) and consensus.[94] Māwardī (d. 450/1058) mentions consensus twice.[95]

The commenda is thus an interesting case for our purposes: had there existed a principle that Jāhilī law is valid unless there is specific reason to think otherwise, this would have been a good place to invoke it. The commenda is, after all, a manifestly useful institution.[96] The fact that instead the jurists speak in terms of what we might call virtual confirmation by Islam or the Prophet thus points up the absence of such a principle.

[88] Ibn Ḥazm, *Iḥkām*, vol. 2, 95.5.

[89] They are *maskūt ʿanhā*; on this argument from silence, see the subsection 'Why not argue from silence?' below.

[90] Shāṭibī, *Muwāfaqāt*, vol. 1, 276.12.

[91] Ibn ʿAbd al-Barr, *Istidhkār*, vol. 21, 119–20 no. 30,709; 121 no. 30,711; 122 no. 30,716.

[92] 'But for the consensus (*ijmāʿ*) that it is permissible thanks to the uninterrupted transmission of the ages regarding it, age after age, to the effect that the commenda (*qirāḍ*) was well-known in the Jahiliyya, and that the Prophet confirmed it (*aqarrahu*) and did not forbid it, knowing it to be widespread among Quraysh, who were merchants with no other way to make a living, we would not regard it as permitted. And were we to find a single scholar who held it to be abolished (*yaqūlu bi-ibṭālihi*), we would agree with him and adopt his view, for there is no revealed text (*naṣṣ*) showing it to be permitted' (Ibn Ḥazm, *Iḥkām*, vol. 2, 95.1). Contrast *Muḥallā*, vol. 8, 247 no. 1367, where he says that if there were any dissent, it would be ignored.

[93] See, for example, Udovitch, *Partnership*, 173; Ibn ʿAbd al-Barr, *Istidhkār*, vol. 21, 120–2 nos 1359, 1360, 30,716; and cf. Marghīnānī, *Hidāya*, vols 3–4, 225.6.

[94] Sarakhsī, *Mabsūṭ*, vol. 22, 18.7.

[95] Māwardī, *Ḥāwī*, vol. 7, 306.12, in commenting on a tradition about ʿUmar's two sons; 307.6, in an argument from analogy with the contract for the lease of agricultural land known as *musāqāt* (here he remarks that the Sunna on which *musāqāt* is based and the consensus on which *qirāḍ* is based are mutually supporting).

[96] See the passage from Sarakhsī, *Mabsūṭ*, vol. 22, 19.7 (beginning *wa-li-anna biʾl-nās ḥāja ilā hādhā ʾl-ʿaqd*), translated in Udovitch, *Partnership*, 175; also Marghīnānī, *Hidāya*, vols 3–4, 225.3, stating that the commenda is legal because of the need for it (*mashrūʿa lil-ḥāja ilayhā*).

Awkward Cases: Manumission with Effect from the Owner's Death

Another such case is the practice of declaring that one's slave will be free at one's death (*tadbīr*). Ibn Qudāma says it rests on Sunna and consensus,[97] and with such credentials we would hardly expect the institution to be a problem.

With regard to Sunna, Ibn Qudāma (620/1223) quotes a version of a widespread and well-attested tradition in which Jābir ibn ʿAbdallāh (d. 73/692–3) says that a man made such a declaration but subsequently found himself in need, so the Prophet had someone buy the slave from him.[98] But while the action taken by the Prophet in this tradition would seem to imply that he had no problem with the practice as such, it is not a direct endorsement of it.

Hence again the need felt for consensus. Thus after citing the tradition as one part of the basis of the practice, Ibn Qudāma moves on to consensus, quoting Ibn al-Mundhir (d. *c.* 318/930) to the effect that all the scholars he had memorized from agreed on its validity.[99] Meanwhile Ibn Rushd (d. 595/1198) mentions only consensus.[100] Māwardī says that the Muslims are agreed on its permissibility, and that their consensus dispenses with the need for any textual proof (*dalīl*);[101] he does of course know the Jābir tradition, and starts by quoting Shāfiʿī quoting it,[102] but unlike Ibn Qudāma he seems not to regard it as a proof-text for the practice.

Māwardī also has an interesting account of disagreement among his fellow-Shāfiʿites regarding the origin (*ibtidāʾ*) of the practice.[103] One of the views he reports is no surprise: 'It goes back to the Jahiliyya, the holy law confirmed it (*aqarrahu*) in Islam as it was in the Jahiliyya, and so it became law (*sharʿ*) through the confirmation (*iqrār*).' The other view is more arresting: 'It began in Islam through some text (*naṣṣ*) revealed about it that the Muslims put into practice, so thanks to the practice they did not need to transmit the text; thus it became law thanks to the text, while the practice became the evidence for the text [having once existed].' So where Muslim practice is uniform, but not supported by any revealed text in our possession, it seems that we are entitled to infer that it arises from a revelation now lost. Here again the practice of the Prophet's Companions is relevant. Māwardī tells us that the Muhājirūn and Anṣār did it, as did ʿĀʾisha (d. 57/678). If she did it in the lifetime of the

97 Ibn Qudāma, *Mughnī*, vol. 9, 276.3.

98 Ibn Qudāma, *Mughnī*, vol. 9, 276.4; for numerous versions of the tradition see, for example, Bayhaqī, *Sunan*, vol. 10, 308–13.

99 Ibn Qudāma, *Mughnī*, vol. 9, 276.7.

100 Ibn Rushd, *Bidāya*, vol. 2, 422.9.

101 Māwardī, *Ḥāwī*, vol. 18, 100.23.

102 Māwardī, *Ḥāwī*, vol. 18, 100.2.

103 Māwardī, *Ḥāwī*, vol. 18, 100.14.

Prophet, it must have been on his orders, and if after his death, it must have been because she knew his view.[104]

Here again, life would have been simpler if for Muslims, as for Christians, the principle had been that pagan law is acceptable unless for some specific reason it is objectionable.

Why Not Argue from Silence?

But why, one might ask, did the scholars lack such a principle? Why was it necessary for them to say that God or His Prophet had specifically endorsed an item of pagan law, and not enough for them to say that these authorities had tacitly approved it by not saying anything about it? The idea that the law can be shaped by the silence of the legislator was not alien to them: there is a tradition from the Prophet, preserved in a variety of wordings in good collections (though not the best), to the effect that there are things God commands, things He forbids, and things about which He is silent; where the last is the case, He imposes no obligation (*mā sakata ʿanhu fa-huwa mimmā ʿafā ʿanhu*).[105] Why then should this not apply to the retention of elements of pagan law? The answer would seem to be that in some limited measure it does. For the most part thinking of this kind comes in the context of a rather special case: pagan practices that remained acceptable in Islam for a brief period, up to the point at which a revelation came down and replaced them.

A case in point is the law of inheritance. As Fakhr al-Dīn al-Rāzī (d. 606/1210) tells us, when God sent Muḥammad he at first *left* his followers (*tarakahum*) to continue their Jāhilī practice, which was to give the inheritance only to warriors and deny it to women and children; but he adds that some scholars say that on the contrary, God *confirmed* them in this (*bal*

[104] Māwardī, *Ḥāwī*, vol. 18, 100.19.

[105] The wording quoted is from the version in Tirmidhī, *al-Jāmiʿ al-ṣaḥīḥ*, Aḥmad Shākir et al., eds (Cairo: Dār al-Ḥadīth, n.d.), vol. 4, 220 no. 1726 (*libās* 6). Other forms of the tradition make the point that if God is silent on something, this is not out of forgetfulness (see, for example, al-Ḥākim al-Naysābūrī, *al-Mustadrak ʿalā ʾl-Ṣaḥīḥayn* (Cairo: Dār al-Ḥaramayn, 1997), vol. 2, 442 no. 3477, quoting Q 19:64); in other words, this is a knowing silence; compare Ibn Ḥazm's defence of the commenda, where he specifies that Muḥammad *knew* the practice to be widespread among Quraysh (see n. 92). For variations on the theme note Q5:101, where the believers are instructed to 'question not concerning things which, if they were revealed to you, would vex you', and the tradition quoted by Ṭabarī in his commentary thereto in which the Prophet responds to a questioner who asks whether the pilgrimage to Mecca is obligatory every year by telling his followers to be silent with him as long as he is silent with them (*uskutū ʿannī mā sakattu ʿankum*, *Tafsīr*, vol. 5, 83–4 no. 12,809). The tradition can be used to establish that there are matters with regard to which the presumption is that they are permitted (*al-aṣl fīhā al-ibāḥa*, Ibn Ḥajar al-Haytamī, *al-Fatḥ al-mubīn bi-sharḥ al-Arbaʿīn*, Aḥmad al-Muḥammad et al., eds (Beirut: Dār al-Minhāj, 2008), 494.9, commenting on the version of the tradition included as the 30th of Nawawī's selection of 40 traditions).

qarrarahum Allāh ʿalā dhālika).[106] Jaṣṣāṣ (d. 370/981), in an extended discussion of the question, speaks mainly of confirmation,[107] but in one place he says that when Muḥammad was sent he *left* his followers (*tarakahum*) to follow existing legal rules that were not against reason,[108] and in another place he says that when Islam came the Muslims were *left* (*turikū*) as they were with regard to certain practices until these were overtaken by revelation.[109] At the same time he quotes early authorities speaking of confirmation.[110] One such authority, however, makes no mention of confirmation, and Jaṣṣāṣ links this view to a version of the silence tradition—but then immediately speaks of confirmation.[111] One thus has the impression that he does not really distinguish between the two possibilities,[112] though others, like Rāzī, undoubtedly do.

All this relates to the short term; such thinking seems to be markedly less common in the case of Jāhilī practices deemed to enjoy a continuing acceptability in Islam. But it does occur. Qāḍī Khān (d. 592/1196) rules that piercing the ears of children is in order (*lā baʾs bi-thaqb udhun al-ṭifl*) because people practised it in the Jahiliyya and the Prophet did not object to their doing so (*lam yunkir ʿalayhim dhālika*).[113] Shāṭibī speaks of Jāhilī practices that were initially validated by silence and then abrogated,[114] and then goes on to argue that these practices were indeed valid at the time, as shown by the fact that some such practices remain valid even today (*bāqiya ilā ʾl-ān ʿalā ḥukm iqrār al-Islām*).[115] But overall, it is uncommon for the jurists to apply the argument from silence to elements permanently retained from Jāhilī law. To the extent that they do, they dilute the notion of confirmation and thereby come significantly closer to Western Christian attitudes.

[106] Fakhr al-Dīn al-Rāzī, *al-Tafsīr al-kabīr* (Cairo: Dār Iḥyāʾ al-Turāth al-ʿArabī, *c.* 1934–62), vol. 9, 203.7, 203.12 (to Q4:11).

[107] As at Jaṣṣāṣ, *Aḥkām al-Qurʾān*, vol. 2, 95.1 (including also the law of marriage and divorce), 98.7, 100.28.

[108] Jaṣṣāṣ, *Aḥkām al-Qurʾān*, vol. 2, 95.18 (read *tarakahum* for *tarkihim*).

[109] Jaṣṣāṣ, *Aḥkām al-Qurʾān*, vol. 2, 95.23.

[110] Confirmation: Jaṣṣāṣ, *Aḥkām al-Qurʾān*, vol. 2, 95.3, 95.6, and cf. 96.15.

[111] Jaṣṣāṣ, *Aḥkām al-Qurʾān*, vol. 2, 95.9. In another place he speaks of Muḥammad going by the judgement of pagandom (*ḥukm al-Jāhiliyya*, 101.4).

[112] Likewise Ibn al-ʿArabī (d. 543/1148) says of a certain Jāhilī practice that at the beginning of Islam it did not constitute confirmed law about which revelation was silent (*sharʿan maskūtan ʿanhu muqarran ʿalayhi*), as if silence and confirmation were the same thing (*Aḥkām al-Qurʾān*, ed. ʿAlī al-Bajāwī (n.p.: Dār al-Fikr, 1974), vol. 1, 333.12).

[113] Qāḍī Khān, *Fatāwā* (Cairo: Maṭbaʿat Muḥammad Shāhīn, 1282), vol. 3, 416.14.

[114] Shāṭibī, *Muwāfaqāt*, vol. 1, 276.12 (*mā sukita ʿanhu fa-huwa fī maʿnā ʾl-ʿafw*).

[115] Shāṭibī, *Muwāfaqāt*, vol. 1, 277.1; one of the two examples he gives is the commenda (see n. 90). Likewise in a discussion of the silence tradition (see 274.1), he says that one might think in terms of three things, the third being *al-sukūt ʿan aʿmāl ukhidhat qablu min sharīʿat Ibrāhīm* (277.9).

Explaining Muslim Attitudes: Arabism

Why, apart from sheer inertia, should Islam appear so willing to accept legal elements of Jāhilī origin? There are at least three themes worth exploring here.

A sentiment that is plausibly present between the lines of our texts is continuing pride in the Jahiliyya as the ancestral past of the Arabs.[116] To put it bluntly, Arabs never stopped liking their Jahiliyya; indeed it could be argued that the pagan past meant more to them than it did to the Franks. Their pagan past was, of course, in some tension with the new religious dispensation, but it was too highly prized by too many Arabs to make its outright rejection a serious option. A tradition about the Prophet and his Companions nicely captures the resulting complicity of piety and pride: 'We used to sit with the Prophet and people would recite poetry and chat about matters of the Jahiliyya (*ashyāʾ min amr al-Jāhiliyya*), while the Prophet would be silent, but would sometimes smile.'[117] Such talk, the tradition is telling us, was not the kind of thing a monotheist prophet could be expected to engage in himself; but he could tolerate it in his followers—that being the message of his silence—and as his smile reveals, he was occasionally if tacitly a party to it. There was no reason why Muḥammad's later followers should seek to be more virtuous than his Companions in this respect. As a commentator on this tradition observes, it shows the permissibility of narration and conversation (*jawāz al-khabar waʾl-ḥadīth*) regarding accounts of the Jahiliyya (*akhbār al-Jāhiliyya*)—and, he generously adds, of other nations (*umam*), other that is than the Arabs.[118] But the tendency was to privilege Arab customs, particular when these were contrasted with those of the Persians. As Mālik (d. 179/795) is reported to have said, 'Kill the customs (*sunna*) of the Persians and give life to the customs of the Arabs!'[119]

The prizing of the Jahiliyya as an ancestral culture irrespective of religious rectitude led to the rise of what we might call an antiquarian literature, one that was not particularly interested in the next world, but set considerable store by the preservation of information about the doings, manners, and customs of the pre-Islamic Arabs in this world. For example, works or sections of works devoted to listing 'firsts'—statements of the form 'the first

[116] And more narrowly of Quraysh and even of the Banū Hāshim. Ibn Ḥabīb tells us that it was Quraysh who established compurgation (*wa-mimmā sannat Quraysh al-qasāma, Muḥabbar*, 335.15), while as we have seen Ibn ʿAbbās relates that 'the first compurgation that took place in the Jāhiliyya was among us, the Banū Hāshim' (see n. 68).

[117] Ibn Ḥanbal, *Musnad* (Būlāq: al-Maṭbaʿa al-Maymaniyya, 1313), vol. 5, 105.22. A variant form has the Companions laugh outright while the Prophet merely smiles (91.4). Muslim has this version (*Ṣaḥīḥ*, 463 no. 670, 1810 no. 2322); for references to other collections, see Shāṭibī, *Muwāfaqāt*, vol. 4, 443–4 n. 5.

[118] ʿIyāḍ, *Sharḥ Ṣaḥīḥ Muslim*, ed. Yaḥyā Ismāʿīl (Manṣūra: Dār al-Wafāʾ, 1998), vol. 7, 286.9.

[119] Shāṭibī, *Muwāfaqāt*, vol. 4, 114.12.

to do x was y'—have a lot to say about the Jahiliyya. Thus Ibn Qutayba (d. 276/889), in a handbook of things members of the educated elite need to know, devotes several pages to 'firsts'.[120] Here he tells us that the first to give a judgement imposing compurgation in the Jahiliyya was Walīd ibn al-Mughīra, and that the Prophet later confirmed it in Islam (*aqarrahā...fī 'l-Islām*).[121] He makes similar statements about the Jāhilī origins of such practices as the payment of a hundred camels as blood money,[122] the amputation of hands as punishment for theft,[123] the removal of one's sandals on entering the Kaʿba,[124] and the test for determining the sex of a hermaphrodite,[125] in most cases adding a reference to the continuity of the practice into Islam. Centuries later a block of six such statements appears in a massive compilation of things that bureaucrats need to know by the Egyptian bureaucrat Qalqashandī (d. 821/1418);[126] each item ends with the refrain that Islam then came and confirmed it (*thumma jāʾa 'l-Islām bi-taqrīrihi*). It is hard not to read a certain cultural pride into this emphasis on the divine endorsement of Jāhilī practices. We can detect the same pride between the lines of a chapter-heading in a work of Ibn Ḥabīb (d. 245/860): 'Those who gave judgments in the Jahiliyya that then accorded with (*wāfaqa*) the judgments of Islam (*ḥukm al-Islām*), and those who performed actions in the Jahiliyya that God then adopted (*jaʿalahu... sunnatan*) in Islam.'[127] The pride is explicit in a tribal context when an eighth-century Ṭāʾī poet boasts that it was 'one of us' who in pre-Islamic times gave judgements that were in accord with the laws of Islam.[128] The antiquarian strain of Islamic culture is not in general to be encountered in the works of the jurists and traditionists. A notable illustration of this indifference is provided by the law of inheritance established in Q 4:11, according to which a son is to receive the same share as two daughters (*lil-dhakari mithlu ḥaẓẓi 'l-unthayayn*). Nobody disputes that it was standard Jāhilī practice to exclude

[120] Ibn Qutayba, *Maʿārif*, 551–8. For the purpose of the book see 1.5.

[121] See n. 68. [122] See n. 81.

[123] See n. 79. Here the confirmation came directly from God (Q5:38), though Ibn Qutayba does not mention this.

[124] Ibn Qutayba, *Maʿārif*, 551.14. [125] Ibn Qutayba, *Maʿārif*, 553.5.

[126] Qalqashandī, *Ṣubḥ al-aʿshā* (Cairo: Wizārat al-Thaqāfa wa'l-Irshād al-Qawmī, n.d.), vol. 1, 435.8, under the heading *umūr tunsabu lil-Jāhiliyya*. For the book's emphasis on what bureaucrats need to know, see, for example, 411.17, 436.12; historical information may sometimes be required as proof of a point, or at other times be needed in order to engage in conversation with one's king or boss (412.5).

[127] Ibn Ḥabīb, *Muḥabbar*, 236.2. A later chapter-heading signals a more mixed bag: practices (*sunan*) established in the Jahiliyya of which Islam retained some and discarded others (309.7).

[128] Ibn Ḥabīb, *Muḥabbar*, 236.11 (*minnā 'lladhī ḥakama 'l-ḥukūma fa-wāfaqat/fī 'l-Jāhiliyyati sunnata 'l-Islāmī*; *ḥukūm* is presumably poetic licence for *aḥkām*, a point on which I am indebted to the comments of Andras Hamori). The poet is Adham ibn Abī 'l-Zaʿrāʾ, for whom see Caskel, *Ǧamharat an-nasab*, vol. 1, Table 254 line 29, and vol. 2, 137a; the Jāhilī judge is Dharib ibn Ḥawṭ, for whom see vol. 1, Table 254 line 27, and vol. 2, 235a.

females, assigning the inheritance only to warriors, in other words to adult males.[129] The antiquarians nevertheless tell us that this practice was not universal: a certain ʿĀmir ibn Jusham al-Yashkurī, a tribal chief known as Dhū ʾl-Majāsid, was the first to apply what was to come to be God's rule in the Jahiliyya.[130] Yet the religious scholars leave this precedent aside, thereby implying that the rule was God's innovation, rather than His confirmation of a Jāhilī precedent.[131] But by way of exception Māwardī in his law book quotes three of Ibn Qutayba's 'firsts', two of them with attribution: compurgation, hand-cutting, and the hundred-camel blood money payment.[132] Another such example of indulgence towards the traditions of the Jahiliyya is Bukhārī's placing of the tradition about the first compurgation: it comes in a section of his collection that is devoted to traditions about the Jahiliyya, and is manifestly designed more for light relief than for pious edification or legal instruction.[133] In short, while Muslims saw the culture of pre-Islamic Arabia as the Jahiliyya, for many of them it was very much *their* Jahiliyya. Like the Arabs, the Jahiliyya was ennobled by Islam.[134]

Explaining Muslim Attitudes: Divine Pragmatism

Any sensible lawgiver is a pragmatist, and God is no exception. He knows very well that it is hard to get people to change their ways, so that if their current ways are not in themselves objectionable, it makes good sense to leave them undisturbed and concentrate on the things that really have to change. So in many cases it may make sense to retain aspects of pagan law rather than upset the entire legal apple-cart. Such thinking can be seen as underlying three

[129] See, for example, Māwardī, *Ḥāwī*, vol. 8, 68.20 (*kānū fī ʾl-Jāhiliyya lā yuwarrithūna ʾl-nisāʾ waʾl-aṭfāl, wa-lā yuʿṭūna ʾl-māl illā li-man ḥamā wa-ghazā*), 69.4; Ṭabarī, *Tafsīr*, vol. 3, 616.27, 617 no. 8727, and cf. no. 8728 (to Q4:11); Jaṣṣāṣ, *Aḥkām al-Qurʾān*, vol. 2, 94.24 (to Q4:11); Rāzī, *al-Tafsīr al-kabīr*, vol. 9, 203.6 (to Q4:11). Māwardī remarks that every people (*umma*) handles inheritance according to its custom (*ʿāda*, *Ḥāwī*, vol. 8, 68.10).

[130] Ibn Ḥabīb, *Muḥabbar*, 236.15, 324.9; Hamdānī, *Iklīl*, vol. 2, Muḥammad al-Ḥiwālī, ed. (Cairo: Maṭbaʿat al-Sunna al-Muḥammadiyya, 1966), 458.6. For this ʿĀmir, see Caskel, *Ǧamharat an-nasab*, vol. 1, Table 162 line 17, and vol. 2, 159a; he is thus an early figure, some five generations before Muḥammad.

[131] Something similar seems to be the case with the prohibition of wine (Q5:90). Quite a number of people—over two dozen—are said to have forbidden it in the Jahiliyya (for lists see Ibn Ḥabīb, *Muḥabbar*, 237.2; Ibn Ḥabīb, *Munammaq*, 531.12); but so far as I am aware the jurists do not present the scriptural prohibition of wine as a confirmation of these Jāhilī precedents.

[132] For these three 'firsts' see nn. 68, 79, and 81.

[133] See n. 67. Note that the jurists could, had they so wished, have treated this tradition as a source of law in the light of the 'confirmation tradition', according to which the Prophet confirmed compurgation 'as it had been in the Jahiliyya' (see n. 69).

[134] Crone, 'Jāhilī and Jewish law', 200.

somewhat different approaches that appear in our sources, albeit mostly rather late ones.

The first is developed by Shāṭibī, and provides a certain parallel to the idea of natural law that we encountered in the Christian context, though it does not have the same status as a commonplace. His point is that ideas and practices (*maʿānī*) developed by philosophers (*ahl al-ḥikma al-falsafiyya*) and others in the absence of revelation—that is, during the inter-prophetic intervals known as *fatarāt*—are likely to be broadly on target, though falling short in matters of detail; thus divine legislation takes on the relatively limited role of perfecting the details of existing customs (*ʿādāt*).[135] 'Hence this holy law confirmed (*aqarrat*) a whole set of laws (*aḥkām*) that were current in the Jahiliyya, such as blood money, compurgation, gathering on the eve of the Sabbath (*yawm al-ʿarūba*)—that is Friday—for preaching and admonition, the commenda, the clothing of the Kaʿba, and other such practices that were highly regarded among the people of the Jahiliyya, together with good customs and fine morals (*makārim al-akhlāq*) that reason accepts (*taqbaluhā ʾl-ʿuqūl*), and there are many of them.'[136] So we are by no means to think of pagan Arab culture as rotten to the core.

The second approach is found in the law book of Sarakhsī, and doubtless elsewhere. In his accounts of two practices carried over from the Jahiliyya, namely the hiring of wet-nurses and the commenda, he explains with great clarity why people *need* the institution.[137] In other words, these are sensible institutions that meet legitimate needs.

The third approach is a certain relativism found in the writings of Shāh Walī Allāh Dihlawī (d. 1176/1762). When a prophet is sent, he has to take as his starting-point the customs of the people he is sent to. Hence a prophet 'looks into their beliefs and practices (*ʿamal*), and whichever of these are in conformity with the refinement of the soul he confirms (*yuthbituhu*) for them, and directs them towards them, while forbidding them whichever go against the refinement of the soul'.[138] The differences between cultures can be

135 Shāṭibī, *Muwāfaqāt*, vol. 2, 524.2.

136 Shāṭibī, *Muwāfaqāt*, vol. 2, 524.7. The reference to 'fine morals' echoes a tradition in which the Prophet says: 'I was sent only to perfect fine morals (*makārim al-akhlāq*)' (so the version in Bayhaqī, *Sunan*, vol. 10, 192.2).

137 For hiring wet-nurses, see Sarakhsī, *Mabsūṭ*, vol. 15, 118.19 (*biʾl-nās ilayhi ḥāja*), 118.21 (*juwwiza dhālika lil-ḥāja*). For the commenda see n. 96. Compare Marghīnānī's comment on the role of need in the legitimation of hiring and renting (*ijāra*, *Hidāya*, vols 3–4, 260.4), and Sarakhsī's remark that need is the basic principle of the law of contracts (*ḥājat al-nās aṣl fī sharʿ al-ʿuqūd*, *Mabsūṭ*, vol. 15, 75.4).

138 Walī Allāh Dihlawī, *al-Tafhīmāt al-ilāhiyya*, Ghulām Muṣṭafā al-Qāsimī, ed. (Ḥaydarābād (Sindh): Akādīmīyat al-Shāh Walī Allāh, 1967–1970), vol. 1, 92.12, in a passage translated in J. M. S. Baljon, *Religion and Thought of Shāh Walī Allāh Dihlawī, 1703–1762* (Leiden: E. J. Brill, 1986), 113. Later Baljon translates from two further passages that are relevant (172). The first is Walī Allāh Dihlawī, *Ḥujjat Allāh al-bāligha*, al-Sayyid Sābiq, ed. (Cairo: Dār al-Kutub al-Ḥadītha, n.d.), vol. 1, 248.6, 248.16 (= Marcia K. Hermansen, trans., *The Conclusive Argument*

considerable, for every people and clime has its natural disposition (*fiṭra*); that of the Indians is to find the slaughter of animals repugnant and to believe in the eternity of the universe, whereas it is the natural disposition of the Semites—Arabs and Persians—to permit the slaughter of animals and to believe in the createdness of the universe.[139] In the case of Muḥammad, his revelation was in the language of Quraysh and in conformity with their customs (*fī ʿādātihim*), and it was these customs that prepared the way for many of the laws of Islam (*kāna ʾl-muʿidd li-kathīr min al-aḥkām mā huwa fīhim*).[140] He even speaks of the need for the Sharīʿa to be in effect the 'natural religion' (*madhhab ṭabīʿī*) of the Arab and non-Arab inhabitants of the temperate climes.[141]

Explaining Muslim Attitudes: Did Jāhilī Law Have Monotheist Origins?

There is a final possibility to consider here. Could it be that Jāhilī law, or some of it at least, was in fact grounded in actual revelation? The Arabs—the northerners among them—were after all the descendants of Abraham through his son Ishmael, and they were thus born into the law of Abraham (*sharīʿat Ibrāhīm*).[142] Of course many years had passed between the time of Abraham and that of Muḥammad—more than 3,000, it is said.[143] Could it nonetheless be that a significant amount of Abrahamic law had survived among the Arabs down to Muḥammad's day? To the extent that it had survived and was adopted by Islam, the new religion would not have been confirming pagan law but rather perpetuating monotheist law. But as might be expected, opinions differed on the extent of such a survival.

Some said that in the course of this long interval the law of Abraham had disappeared.[144]

from God: Shāh Walī Allāh of Delhi's Ḥujjat Allāh al-bāligha (Leiden: E. J. Brill, 1996), 341, 342). The second is from Walī Allāh Dihlawī, *al-Fawz al-kabīr* (Karachi: Qurʾān Maḥall, 1383), 48a.12.

139 Walī Allāh, *Tafhīmāt*, vol. 1, 92.9, in the passage translated in Baljon, *Religion and Thought*, 113.

140 Walī Allāh, *Ḥujja*, vol. 2, 737.17.

141 Baljon, *Religion and Thought*, 172, paraphrasing Walī Allāh, *Ḥujja*, vol. 1, 248.6 (= Hermansen, *Conclusive Argument*, 341). Here Walī Allāh says of the Imām: *wajaba an takūna māddat sharīʿatihi mā huwa bi-manzilat al-madhhab al-ṭabīʿī li-ahl al-aqālīm al-ṣāliḥa, ʿArabihim wa-ʿAjamihim.*

142 The phrase *sunan Ibrāhīm* also appears, but is rare (Ṭabarī, *Tafsīr*, vol. 2, 303.7 (to Q2:198); Ṣaffūrī, *Nuzhat al-majālis*, ʿAbd al-Raḥīm Mārdīnī, ed. (Damascus: Dār al-Maḥabba, 1993), 451.5).

143 I take this figure from Suyūṭī, *al-Ḥāwī lil-fatāwī* (n.p.: al-Ṭibāʿa al-Munīriyya, 1352–3), vol. 2, 207.10; see also Michael Cook, *Muhammad* (Oxford and New York: Oxford University Press, 1983), 31.

144 Abū ʾl-Ḥusayn al-Baṣrī, *Muʿtamad* (Beirut: Dār al-Kutub al-ʿIlmiyya, 1983), vol. 2, 341.8 (*qad kāna ʾnqaṭaʿa naqluhā*); Fakhr al-Dīn al-Rāzī, *Maḥṣūl*, Ṭāhā al-ʿUlwānī, ed. (Riyadh: Lajnat

Others held that something of it remained. An example is the inviolability of the Meccan sanctuary for one who takes refuge in it: this, we are told by Jaṣṣāṣ, has been the law from the time of Abraham until our own day, for the Arabs in the Jahiliyya observed it in accordance with what they still retained of the law of Abraham (*ʿalā mā kāna baqiya fī aydīhim min sharīʿat Ibrāhīm*).[145] Bājī (d. 474/1081), in his commentary on Mālik's transmission of the saying of the Prophet 'I was sent to perfect good morals (*ḥusn al-akhlāq*)',[146] concedes that the Arabs were the best of people in morals (*akhlāq^{an}*) 'thanks to what they retained of earlier laws' (*bi-mā baqiya ʿindahum mimmā taqaddama min al-sharāʾiʿ qablahum*), though they had deviated from many of them through unbelief;[147] in another witness to his text we find 'thanks to what they retained of the law of Abraham' (*bi-mā baqiya ʿindahum min sharīʿat Ibrāhīm*).[148] Likewise Ibn Taymiyya (d. 728/1328) remarks that the polytheists had respect for the Kaʿba, circumambulated it, and performed the annual pilgrimage, despite what they had changed of the law of Abraham,[149] and Ibn Ḥajar al-ʿAsqalānī (d. 852/1449) speaks of the pilgrimage, circumambulation, and the like as survivals of the law of Abraham.[150] More generally, as Shāṭibī says, 'of the laws of the prophets they retained something from the law of their ancestor Abraham (*sharīʿat Ibrāhīm abīhim*)'; but he goes on to qualify this by adding that 'they altered some of them, adding and diverging', till these were rectified by Muḥammad.[151] In another passage, however, he minimizes this

al-Buḥūth, 1979–81), vol. 1, part 3, 414.4 (*qad indarasat*); and cf. Suyūṭī, *al-Ḥāwī lil-fatāwī*, vol. 2, 207.10 (*li-duthūrihā*).

[145] Jaṣṣāṣ, *Aḥkām al-Qurʾān*, vol. 1, 89.1; in another passage he includes Ishmael with Abraham (*qad kānat al-ʿArab mutamassika bi-baʿḍ sharāʾiʿ Ibrāhīm wa-Ismāʿīl*, vol. 2, 95.13). One example of the law of Ishmael would be his use of the phrase 'go to your people' (*ilḥaqī bi-ahliki*) in divorcing his first wife (Bukhārī, *Ṣaḥīḥ*, vol. 2, 344.1 (anbiyāʾ 9)). Ibn Qayyim al-Jawziyya (d. 751/1350) remarks that this tradition is explicit (*ṣarīḥ*), and that the phrase continued in use in the Jahiliyya and Islam; the Prophet did not change the usage, but rather confirmed it (*aqarrahum ʿalayhi*, *Zād al-maʿād*, Shuʿayb al-Arnaʾūṭ and ʿAbd al-Qādir al-Arnaʾūṭ, eds (Beirut: Muʾassasat al-Risāla, 1979), vol. 5, 320.8; by 'the *ḥadīth* of Ibn ʿAbbās' he means Bukhārī's tradition, see 319.10).

[146] Mālik, *Muwaṭṭaʾ*, 904 no. 8; cf. n. 136, with the more usual wording *makārim al-akhlāq*.

[147] Bājī, *Muntaqā*, ed. Muḥammad ʿAṭā (Beirut: Dār al-Kutub al-ʿIlmiyya, 1999), vol. 9, 288.18.

[148] See the quotations of the passage in Suyūṭī, *Tanwīr al-ḥawālik* (Beirut: al-Maktaba al-Thaqāfiyya, 1973), vol. 3, 97.28 and Zurqānī, *Sharḥ* of the *Muwaṭṭaʾ* of Mālik (Cairo: Maktabat al-Thaqāfa al-Dīniyya, 2003), vol. 4, 404.11. In this form the passage combines Arabism, the law of Abraham, and divine pragmatism: 'The Arabs were the best of all people in morals thanks to what they retained of the law of Abraham, though they had lost much of it through unbelief, so the Prophet was sent to perfect good morals.'

[149] ʿAbd al-Raḥmān Ibn Qāsim al-ʿĀṣimī, ed., *Majmūʿ fatāwā Shaykh al-Islām Aḥmad ibn Taymiyya* (Beirut: Muʾassasat al-Risāla, 1997), vol. 27, 256.4.

[150] Ibn Ḥajar al-ʿAsqalānī, *Fatḥ al-bārī* (Beirut: Dār Iḥyāʾ al-Turāth al-ʿArabī, 1988), vol. 8, 582.21 (*mimmā baqiya ʿindahum min sharīʿat Ibrāhīm*).

[151] Shāṭibī, *Muwāfaqāt*, vol. 2, 125.7; one expects *minhā* rather than *minhum*. The context here is the *makārim al-akhlāq* theme (see 124.3).

survival in the field of ritual: 'Of rituals (*taʿabbudāt*) valid in Islam they had only a few things taken from the religion (*milla*) of Abraham.'[152]

Some authors, however, stress the extent of the survival of the law of Abraham. Thus Yāqūt (d. 626/1229) in his entry on Mecca in his geographical dictionary has a glowing account of its people as having been quite different from the uncouth nomads (*lam yakūnū kaʾl-Aʿrāb al-ajlāf*) and holding fast to much of the law of Abraham (*mutamassikīn bi-kathīr min sharīʿat Ibrāhīm*).[153] Shāṭibī in one passage seems in line with this trend. Before Islam, he tells us, people used to distinguish marriage (*nikāḥ*) from fornication (*sifāḥ*), perform divorces, circumambulate the Kaʿba once a week, rub the Black Stone,[154] respect the holy months, wash to remove major ritual impurity, have their dead washed and enshrouded, pray over them, cut the hands of thieves, crucify highway robbers, and the like, all these being remnants of the religion of their ancestor Abraham (*baqāyā millat abīhim Ibrāhīm*) that they still retained.[155] Gentile Christians possessed no analogue to this use of Abrahamic descent.

COMPARING CHRISTIAN AND MUSLIM ATTITUDES

We have grappled with many details in the course of this chapter, but the outcome of the comparison of Christian and Muslim attitudes is not a complicated one. If we put it in terms of default and override, there is a clear contrast. On the Christian side the default is that pagan law is valid unless this default is overridden by some specific incompatibility with Christianity; whereas on the Muslim side the default is typically that pagan law is not valid unless this default is overridden by specific revealed confirmation. Another way to look at it is that the two religions share a basic assumption: unobjectionable pagan law *may* be adopted as valid law under the new religious dispensation. What they differ over is *who* is qualified to effect such adoptions. On the Christian side the answer is kings and those who are present in their assemblies, whereas on the Muslim side the answer is God and His Prophet. In both cases we find law emerging from custom; but whereas the Germanic peoples were free to *choose* their law out of their custom, the Arabs—and other Muslim peoples—were not. Or to put it differently, while God did not enjoy any monopoly as a lawmaker among the Christians, He had a real claim to one among the Muslims. Why should this

[152] Shāṭibī, *Muwāfaqāt*, vol. 2, 524.11.

[153] Yāqūt, *Muʿjam al-buldān* (Beirut: Dār Ṣādir and Dār Bayrūt, 1957), vol. 5, 184a.15.

[154] Here follow several further rituals associated with the pilgrimage that I omit.

[155] Shāṭibī, *Muwāfaqāt*, vol. 1, 277.4.

be so? We have looked at some of the intellectual mechanisms involved, but the time has perhaps come to seek a deeper level of explanation.

For this we can best go to St Augustine of Hippo (d. 430). He famously saw the situation of his fellow-Christians amid the pagans of late Roman times in terms of an opposition between two 'cities': the heavenly city (*caelestis civitas*) and the earthly city (*terrena civitas*). The Christians, of course, belonged to the heavenly city, and were accordingly strangers to the earthly city around them. But during this mortal life the two cities had a common interest: both needed the security of earthly peace (*terrena pax*). This made possible an accommodation (*concordia*) between them: 'While this heavenly city . . . goes its way as a stranger on earth, it summons citizens from all peoples (*ex omnibus gentibus*), and gathers an alien society of all languages (*in omnibus linguis*), caring naught what difference there may be in manners, laws and institutions (*quidquid in moribus legibus institutisque diversum est*) by which earthly peace is gained or maintained, abolishing and destroying nothing of the sort, nay rather preserving and following them, for however different they may be among different nations (*diversum in diversis nationibus*), they aim at one and the same end, earthly peace.' This accommodation with the ways of the earthly city was the default, but here too there was, of course, an override. Accommodation was only possible 'provided that there is no hindrance to the religion that teaches the obligation to worship one most high and true God (*unus summus et verus Deus*)'.[156] Thus the heavenly city cannot share 'laws of religion' (*religionis leges*) with the earthly city.[157] But the range of accommodation was wide, and Augustine made it clear that it extended to law: being a stranger in the earthly city, the heavenly city 'does not hesitate to obey the laws of the earthly city'.[158] We can thus see those Christians who currently find themselves on earth as a celestial diaspora, and like a good diaspora they comply so far as they can with the laws of their host societies, rather than seeking to maintain the integrity of a comprehensive law of their own.

As an account of relations between Christians and pagans in Augustine's lifetime this vision is less than persuasive; it was now the pagans who were the strangers. But it accurately summed up the long formative experience of Christianity prior to the conversion of Constantine (ruled 306–37) and the consequent emergence of Christian dominance. This early experience left an indelible mark on the religion; it is telling that Augustine should still think this

[156] Augustine, *De civitate Dei*, book 19, ch. 17, in *The City of God against the Pagans*, trans. George McCracken et al. (Cambridge, MA: Harvard University Press, 1957–72), vol. 6, 192–9; for the quotation, see 196–9 (translation slightly adapted). I owe my knowledge of this passage to Etienne Gilson, *The Christian Philosophy of Saint Augustine* (London: Victor Gollancz, 1961), 182 and 334 n. 69.

[157] Augustine, *De civitate Dei*, vol. 6, 196–7.

[158] Augustine, *De civitate Dei*, vol. 6, 194–5.

way a century after Christianity had become the sole religious beneficiary of massive imperial patronage.

The Muslims too remembered a time when they were a diaspora, exiles from Mecca taking refuge first in Ethiopia and then in Yathrib. Indeed God was at pains not to let them forget it: 'And remember when you were few and abased in the land (*mustaḍʿafūna fī ʾl-arḍ*), and were fearful that people would snatch you away' (Q 8:26). But those who were abased in the land had the promise of future dominance: 'We desired to be gracious to those that were abased in the land, and to make them rulers (*aʾimma*), and to make them the inheritors, and to establish them in the land' (Q 28:5–6).[159] Crucially, the promise quickly came true. The Muslim experience of exile was thus a transient one, and the turning of the tables had already taken place within the lifetime of the founder; from then on the state was in Muslim hands. Muslims at large were thus unlikely to see themselves as a diaspora that did not hesitate to obey the laws of its infidel hosts.

BIBLIOGRAPHY

Abū Hilāl al-ʿAskarī. *Awāʾil*, ed. Walīd Qaṣṣāb and Muḥammad al-Miṣrī. Riyadh: Dār al-ʿUlūm, 1981.

Abū ʾl-Ḥusayn al-Baṣrī. *Muʿtamad*. Beirut: Dār al-Kutub al-ʿIlmiyya, 1983.

Abū ʿUbayd al-Bakrī. *al-Masālik waʾl-mamālik*, A. P. van Leeuwen and A. Ferré, eds. Tunis: al-Dār al-ʿArabiyya lil-Kitāb, 1992.

Abū Yūsuf. *Āthār*, Abū ʾl-Wafā, ed. Cairo: Maṭbaʿat al-Istiqāma, 1355.

Adam of Bremen. *History of the Archbishops of Hamburg-Bremen*, trans. Francis Tschan. New York: Columbia University Press, 2002.

Agobard of Lyons. 'Adversus legem Gundobadi'. In L. van Acker, ed. *Agobardi Lugdunensis opera omnia*. Turnhout: Brepols, 1981.

Attenborough, F. L., ed. and trans. *The Laws of the Earliest English Kings*. Cambridge: Cambridge University Press, 1922.

Augustine. *De civitate Dei*, in *The City of God against the Pagans*, trans. George McCracken et al. Cambridge, MA: Harvard University Press, 1957–72.

Bājī. *Muntaqā*, Muḥammad ʿAṭā, ed. Beirut: Dār al-Kutub al-ʿIlmiyya, 1999.

Balādhurī. *Futūḥ al-buldān*. ʿAbdallāh al-Ṭabbāʿ, ed. Beirut: Muʾassasat al-Maʿārif, 1987.

Baljon, J. M. S. *Religion and Thought of Shāh Walī Allāh Dihlawī, 1703–1762*. Leiden: E. J. Brill, 1986.

Balz, Horst and Gerhard Schneider, eds. *Exegetical Dictionary of the New Testament*. Grand Rapids: Eerdmans, 1990–3.

Bayhaqī. *al-Sunan al-kubrā*. Hyderabad: Dāʾirat al-Maʿārif al-Niẓāmiyya, 1344–55.

[159] The verse refers to the Hebrews in bondage in Egypt, but it was soon applied in contemporary Muslim contexts.

Beaune, Colette. *The Birth of an Ideology: Myths and Symbols of Nation in Late-medieval France*. Berkeley: University of California Press, 1991.

Bede. *Ecclesiastical History of the English People*, ed. and trans. Bertram Colgrave and R. A. B. Mynors. Oxford: Clarendon Press, 1969.

Bieler, Ludwig, ed. and trans. *The Irish Penitentials*. Dublin: Dublin Institute for Advanced Studies, 1963.

Bluhme, Fridericus, ed. *Edictus ceteraeque Langobardorum leges*. Hanover: Hahnsche Buchhandlung, 1869.

Brown, Peter. *The Rise of Western Christendom: Triumph and Diversity, A.D. 200–1000*. Chichester: Wiley-Blackwell, 2013.

Bukhārī. *Ṣaḥīḥ*, ed. Ludolf Krehl. Leiden: E. J. Brill, 1862–1908.

Burgmann, L., ed. and trans. *Ecloga: das Gesetzbuch Leons III. und Konstantinos' V.* Frankfurt am Main: Löwenklau-Gesellschaft, 1983.

Burgmann, L. and Sp. Troianos. 'Nomos Mosaïkos'. In *Fontes minores III*, Dieter Simon, ed. Frankfurt am Main: Klostermann, 1979.

Canale, Angelo, ed. and trans. *Etimologie o origini di Isidoro di Siviglia*. Turin: Unione Tipografico-Editrice Torinese, 2004.

Caskel, Werner. *Ǧamharat an-nasab: das genealogische Werk des Hišām ibn Muḥammad al-Kalbī*. Leiden: E. J. Brill, 1966.

Charles-Edwards, T. M. *Early Christian Ireland*. Cambridge: Cambridge University Press, 2000.

Cobb, Paul. *The Race for Paradise: An Islamic History of the Crusades*. Oxford: Oxford University Press, 2014.

Cook, Michael. *Muhammad*. Oxford and New York: Oxford University Press, 1983.

Cook, Michael. 'Ibn Qutayba and the Monkeys'. *Studia Islamica* 89 (1999): 43–74.

Cook, Michael. *Ancient Religions, Modern Politics: The Islamic Case in Comparative Perspective*. Princeton and Oxford: Princeton University Press, 2014.

Coulson, N.J. *Succession in the Muslim Family*. Cambridge: Cambridge University Press, 1971.

Crone, Patricia. 'Jāhilī and Jewish Law: The *qasāma*'. *Jerusalem Studies in Arabic and Islam* 4 (1984): 153–201.

Drew, Katherine, trans. *The Burgundian Code: Book of Constitutions or Law of Gundobad, Additional Enactments*. Philadelphia: University of Pennsylvania Press, 1972.

Drew, Katherine, trans. *The Lombard Laws*. Philadelphia: University of Pennsylvania Press, 1981.

Drew, Katherine, trans. *The Laws of the Salian Franks*. Philadelphia: University of Pennsylvania Press, 1991.

Eckhardt, Karl, ed. *Pactus legis Salicae*. Göttingen: Musterschmidt-Verlag, 1954–7.

Eckhardt, Karl, ed. *Pactus legis Salicae*. Hanover: Hahnsche Buchhandlung, 1962.

Eckhardt, Karl, ed. *Leges Alamannorum*. Hanover: Hahnsche Buchhandlung, 1966.

Encyclopaedia of Islam, 2nd edn. Leiden: E. J. Brill, 1960–2009.

Freshfield, Edwin, trans. *A Manual of Roman Law: The Ecloga*. Cambridge: Cambridge University Press, 1926.

Ghazzālī. *al-Mustaṣfā min ʿilm al-uṣūl*. Cairo: Maṭbaʿat Muṣṭafā Muḥammad, 1937.

Gilson, Etienne. *The Christian Philosophy of Saint Augustine*. London: Victor Gollancz, 1961.

Guillaume, A., trans. *The Life of Muhammad: A Translation of Ibn Isḥāq's Sīrat Rasūl Allāh*. Karachi: Oxford University Press, 1980.

Ḥākim al-Naysābūrī, al-. *al-Mustadrak ʿalā ʾl-Ṣaḥīḥayn*. Cairo: Dār al-Ḥaramayn, 1997.

Hamdānī. *Iklīl*, vol. 2, Muḥammad al-Ḥiwālī, ed. Cairo: Maṭbaʿat al-Sunna al-Muḥammadiyya, 1966.

Hermansen, Marcia K., trans. *The Conclusive Argument from God: Shāh Walī Allāh of Delhi's Ḥujjat Allāh al-bāligha*. Leiden: E. J. Brill, 1996.

Hinkmar von Reims. *De ordine palatii*, Thomas Gross and Rudolf Schieffer, ed. and trans. Hanover: Hahnsche Buchhandlung, 1980.

Hinkmar von Reims. *De divortio Lotharii regis et Theutbergae reginae*, Letha Böhringer, ed. Hanover: Hahnsche Buchhandlung, 1992.

Hyamson, M., ed. and trans. *Mosaicarum et Romanarum legum collatio*. London: Oxford University Press, 1913.

Ibn ʿAbd al-Barr. *Istidhkār*, ʿAbd al-Muʿṭī Qalʿajī, ed. Cairo: Dār al-Waʿy, 1993.

Ibn al-ʿArabī. *Aḥkām al-Qurʾān*, ʿAlī al-Bajāwī, ed. n.p.: Dār al-Fikr, 1974.

Ibn Ḥabīb. *Munammaq*, Khwurshīd Fāriq, ed. Hyderabad: Dār al-Maʿārif al-ʿUthmāniyya, 1964.

Ibn Ḥabīb. *Muḥabbar*, Ilse Lichtenstädter, ed. Beirut: Dār al-Āfāq al-Jadīda, n.d.

Ibn Ḥajar al-ʿAsqalānī. *Fatḥ al-bārī*. Beirut: Dār Iḥyāʾ al-Turāth al-ʿArabī, 1988.

Ibn Ḥajar al-Haytamī. *al-Fatḥ al-mubīn bi-sharḥ al-Arbaʿīn*, Aḥmad al-Muḥammad et al., eds, Beirut: Dār al-Minhāj, 2008.

Ibn Ḥanbal. *Musnad*. Būlāq: al-Maṭbaʿa al-Maymaniyya, 1313.

Ibn Ḥazm. *al-Iḥkām fī uṣūl al-aḥkām*. Cairo: Maṭbaʿat al-Saʿāda, 1345–7.

Ibn Ḥazm. *Muḥallā*. n.p.: Dār al-Fikr, n.d.

Ibn Hishām. *al-Sīra al-nabawiyya*, Muṣṭafā al-Saqqā et al., eds. Cairo: Muṣṭafā al-Bābī al-Ḥalabī, 1955.

Ibn al-Kalbī, Hishām. *Mathālib al-ʿArab*, Najāḥ al-Ṭāʾī, ed. Beirut: Dār al-Hudā, 1998.

Ibn Kathīr. *Tafsīr*. Beirut: Dār al-Khayr, 1990–1.

Ibn Khālawayh. *Mukhtaṣar fī shawādhdh al-Qurʾān*, G. Bergsträsser, ed. Cairo: Maktabat al-Mutanabbī, n.d.

Ibn Qāsim al-ʿĀṣimī, ʿAbd al-Raḥmān, ed. *Majmūʿ fatāwā Shaykh al-Islām Aḥmad ibn Taymiyya*. Beirut: Muʾassasat al-Risāla, 1997.

Ibn Qayyim al-Jawziyya. *Zād al-maʿād*, Shuʿayb al-Arnaʾūṭ and ʿAbd al-Qādir al-Arnaʾūṭ, eds. Beirut: Muʾassasat al-Risāla, 1979.

Ibn Qudāma. *Mughnī*, ʿAbd al-Salām Shāhīn, ed. Beirut: Dār al-Kutub al-ʿIlmiyya, 1994.

Ibn Qutayba. *Maʿārif*, Tharwat ʿUkāsha, ed. Cairo: Dār al-Maʿārif, 1981.

Ibn Rushd (al-jadd). *al-Bayān waʾl-taḥṣīl*, Muḥammad Ḥajjī et al., eds. Beirut: Dār al-Gharb al-Islāmī, 1984–91.

Ibn Rushd (al-jadd). *al-Muqaddimāt al-mumahhidāt*, Muḥammad Ḥajjī et al., eds. Beirut: Dār al-Gharb al-Islāmī, 1988.

Ibn Rushd (al-ḥafīd). *Bidāyat al-mujtahid*, Muḥammad Muḥaysin and Shaʿbān Ismāʿīl, eds. Cairo: Maktabat al-Kulliyāt al-Azhariyya, 1970–4.

ʿIyāḍ. *Sharḥ Ṣaḥīḥ Muslim*, Yaḥyā Ismāʿīl, ed. Manṣūra: Dār al-Wafāʾ, 1998.

Jaṣṣāṣ. *Aḥkām al-Qurʾān*. Beirut: Dār al-Kutub al-ʿIlmiyya, 1994.

Justinian. *Digest*, Theodore Mommsen and Paul Krueger, eds, and trans. Alan Watson. Philadelphia: University of Pennsylvania Press, 1985.
Kelly, Fergus. *A Guide to Early Irish Law*. Dublin: Dublin Institute for Advanced Studies, 1988.
Kulaynī. *Kāfī*, ʿAlī Akbar al-Ghaffārī, ed. Tehran: Dār al-Kutub al-Islāmiyya, 1362–3 sh.
Kullmann, Wolfgang. *Naturgesetz in der Vorstellung der Antike, besonders der Stoa: eine Begriffsuntersuchung*. Stuttgart: Franz Steiner, 2010.
Marghīnānī. *Hidāya*. Beirut: Dār al-Kutub al-ʿIlmiyya, 1990.
Masʿūdī. *Murūj al-dhahab*, Charles Pellat, ed. Beirut: al-Jāmiʿa al-Lubnāniyya, 1965–74.
Māwardī. *Ḥāwī*, ʿAlī Muʿawwaḍ and ʿĀdil ʿAbd al-Mawjūd, eds. Beirut: Dār al-Kutub al-ʿIlmiyya, 1994.
Mommsen, Th., ed. *Codex Theodosianus*. Hildesheim: Weidmann, 1990.
Montreuil, Jean de. *Opera*. Turin: Giappichelli, 1963–86.
Moore, Michael. *A Sacred Kingdom: Bishops and the Rise of Frankish Kingship, 300–850*. Washington, DC: Catholic University of America Press, 2011.
Morrison, Karl. *The Two Kingdoms: Ecclesiology in Carolingian Political Thought*. Princeton: Princeton University Press, 1964.
Muslim. *Ṣaḥīḥ*, Muḥammad Fuʾād ʿAbd al-Bāqī, ed. Cairo: Dār Iḥyāʾ al-Kutub al-ʿArabiyya, 1955–6.
Nicholas, Barry. *An Introduction to Roman Law*. Oxford: Clarendon Press, 1991.
Ó Corráin, Donnchadh et al. 'The Laws of the Irish', *Peritia* 3 (1984): 382–438.
Oliver, Lisi. *The Beginnings of English Law*. Toronto: University of Toronto Press, 2002.
Pedersen, Johs. *Der Eid bei den Semiten*. Strassburg: Karl J. Trübner, 1914.
Pelikan, Jaroslav. *The Christian Tradition: A History of the Development of Doctrine*. Chicago: University of Chicago Press, 1975–91.
Peters, Rudolph. 'Murder in Khaybar: Some Thoughts on the Origins of the *Qasāma* Procedure in Islamic Law'. *Islamic Law and Society* 9 (2002): 132–67.
Pharr, Clyde, trans. *The Theodosian Code*. Princeton: Princeton University Press, 1952.
Qāḍī Khān. *Fatāwā*. Cairo: Maṭbaʿat Muḥammad Shāhīn, 1282.
Qalqashandī. *Ṣubḥ al-aʿshā*. Cairo: Wizārat al-Thaqāfa waʾl-Irshād al-Qawmī, n.d.
Qarāfī. *Dhakhīra*, Muḥammad Ḥajjī et al., eds. Beirut: Dār al-Gharb al-Islāmī, 1994.
Rāzī, Fakhr al-Dīn al-. *al-Tafsīr al-kabīr*. Cairo: Dār Iḥyāʾ al-Turāth al-ʿArabī, *c.* 1934–62.
Rāzī, Fakhr al-Dīn al-. *Maḥṣūl*, Ṭāhā al-ʿUlwānī, ed. Riyadh: Lajnat al-Buḥūth, 1979–81.
Rudolf of Fulda, 'Translatio S. Alexandri', in Georgius Pertz, ed., *Monumenta Germaniae Historica, Scriptores*, vol. 2, Impensis Bibliopolii Hahniani, Hanover (1829): 674–81.
Ṣaffūrī. *Nuzhat al-majālis*, ʿAbd al-Raḥīm Mārdīnī, ed. Damascus: Dār al-Maḥabba, 1993.
Salis, Ludovicus de, ed. *Leges Burgundionum*. Hanover: Hahnsche Buchhandlung, 1892.
Sarakhsī. *Mabsūṭ*. Cairo: Maktabat al-Saʿāda, 1324–31.
Schacht, Joseph. *An Introduction to Islamic Law*. Oxford: Clarendon Press, 1964.
Schwind, Ernst von, ed. *Lex Baiwariorum*. Hanover: Hahnsche Buchhandlung, 1926.

Shakespeare, William. *Henry V*, Gary Taylor, ed. Oxford: Clarendon Press, 1982.

Shāṭibī. *Muwāfaqāt*, Mashhūr Āl Salmān, ed. Khubar: Dār Ibn ʿAffān, 1997.

Siems, Harald. 'Die Entwicklung von Rechtsquellen zwischen Spätantike und Mittelalter'. In Theo Kölzer and Rudolf Schieffer, eds, *Von der Spätantike zum frühen Mittelalter: Kontinuitäten und Brüche, Konzeptionen und Befunde*. Ostfildern: Jan Thorbecke, 2009.

Suyūṭī. *Tanwīr al-ḥawālik*. Beirut: al-Maktaba al-Thaqāfiyya, 1973.

Suyūṭī. *al-Ḥāwī lil-fatāwī*. n.p.: al-Ṭibāʿa al-Munīriyya, 1352–3.

Ṭabarī. *Tafsīr*. Beirut: Dār al-Kutub al-ʿIlmiyya, 1992.

Taylor, Craig. 'The Salic Law and the Valois Succession to the French Crown'. *French History* 15 (2001): 358–77.

Tertullian. *Adversus Iudaeos*, Hermann Tränkle, ed. Wiesbaden: Franz Steiner, 1964.

Tirmidhī. *al-Jāmiʿ al-ṣaḥīḥ*, Aḥmad Shākir et al., eds. Cairo: Dār al-Ḥadīth, n.d.

Udovitch, Abraham. *Partnership and Profit in Medieval Islam*. Princeton: Princeton University Press, 1970.

Walī Allāh Dihlawī. *al-Fawz al-kabīr*. Karachi: Qurʾān Maḥall, 1383.

Walī Allāh Dihlawī. *al-Tafhīmāt al-ilāhiyya*, Ghulām Muṣṭafā al-Qāsimī, ed. Ḥaydarābād (Sindh): Akādīmīyat al-Shāh Walī Allāh, 1967–70.

Walī Allāh Dihlawī. *Ḥujjat Allāh al-bāligha*, al-Sayyid Sābiq, ed. Cairo: Dār al-Kutub al-Ḥadītha, n.d.

Wellhausen, J. *Reste arabischen Heidentums*. Berlin: Georg Reimer, 1897.

Wormald, Patrick. *The Making of English Law: King Alfred to the Twelfth Century*, vol. 1: *Legislation and Its Limits*. Oxford: Blackwell, 1999.

Wormald, Patrick. 'The *Leges Barbarorum*: Law and Ethnicity in the Post-Roman West'. In Hans-Werner Goetz et al., eds, *Regna and Gentes: The Relationship between Late Antique and Early Medieval Peoples and Kingdoms in the Transformation of the Roman World*. Leiden: Brill, 2003.

Yāqūt. *Muʿjam al-buldān*. Beirut: Dār Ṣādir and Dār Bayrūt, 1957.

Zamakhsharī. *Kashshāf*, ʿĀdil ʿAbd al-Mawjūd et al., eds. Riyadh: Maktabat al-ʿUbaykān, 1998.

Zurqānī. *Sharḥ* of the *Muwaṭṭaʾ* of Mālik. Cairo: Maktabat al-Thaqāfa al-Dīniyya, 2003.

8

Remarks on Monotheism in Ancient South Arabia

Iwona Gajda

The South Arabian civilisation developed in the early first millennium BCE and flourished for centuries until its decline shortly before the rise of Islam. Several South Arabian kingdoms dominated a territory corresponding roughly to that of modern Yemen.

From the fourth century on, the kings of Ḥimyar, having unified the ancient kingdoms of South Arabia, launched military expeditions to the north. In the second half of the fifth and at the beginning of the sixth century CE, Ḥimyar controlled the powerful tribe confederation of Maʿadd in central Arabia as several Ḥimyarite inscriptions engraved on rocks in Naǧd prove.

Since the fourth century CE at the latest, some Jews and Christians were present in South Arabia. The Ḥimyarite kings adopted monotheism in the second half of the fourth century. They probably meant to reinforce the unity of their kingdom, still heterogeneous, as the population worshipped traditional deities associated with local powers, ancient kingdoms, and large tribes. The cult of one God venerated by the whole population might have been seen as a potential unifying factor. The temples of ancient gods were thus abandoned and from this time on, all inscriptions with very few exceptions addressed the one God named Raḥmānān or Ilān/Ilahān. Several texts are certainly Jewish, mentioning Israel and using specific Jewish religious formulas, whereas the majority simply invokes God. No royal inscription is clearly Jewish, but we know that king Yūsuf, who attempted a coup around 523, was a Jew as the inscriptions of his army chief and external sources report. During the Ethiopian domination, around 530–70, Christian inscriptions invoke God by the same name: Raḥmānān or Ilān.

The nature of South Arabian monotheism has been subject to vivid discussion since the very discovery of the first inscriptions. Could it be simply qualified as Judaism? Yet no rabbinic source reports the existence of a Jewish kingdom in South Arabia. Could this monotheism belong to a branch of non-orthodox Judaism considered heretical by the Jewish religious authorities in Palestine, as some of its traits suggest? Or could those monotheists be considered as Godfearers? Or did they profess a monotheism influenced by Judaism? This could explain the silence of the rabbinic sources. Some new documents allow us to give a more nuanced picture.

SEVERAL HYPOTHESES ON THE MONOTHEISM OF PRE-ISLAMIC SOUTH ARABIA

A lot has been said about monotheism in Ancient South Arabia; however, in the light of several recent publications, additional remarks are in order. Until recently the conversion of the Ḥimyarite kingdom to monotheism was considered abrupt and total. It was assumed that at the end of the fourth century CE the Ḥimyarite sovereigns suddenly abandoned their ancestral beliefs, and adopted monotheism which the entire population also followed.

The nature of this dominant religion has been much discussed since the very first discovery of inscriptions invoking the one god. The initial hypothesis that these inscriptions were Christian was soon rejected, giving way to the notion that they are more generally of monotheistic or specifically of Jewish provenance. Thus views on the nature of the dominant religion vary. Some researchers have qualified it as Judaism,[1] whereas A. F. L. Beeston considered Ḥimyarite monotheism more neutrally and used the term 'Raḥmanism' to describe it.[2] Abraham G. Lundin maintained that Jewish communities lived in South Arabia while the population was superficially converted to Judaism.[3] According to Christian Robin, Ḥimyar converted to Judaism principally for political reasons, but this choice did not result in a total conversion except for a small part of the population.[4]

[1] For instance Christian Robin, 'Judaïsme et christianisme en Arabie du sud d'après les sources épigraphiques et archéologiques'. *Proceedings of the Seminar for Arabian Studies* 10 (1980): 85–96.

[2] Beeston, 'Himyarite monotheism'. A. M. Abdalla et al., eds, *Studies in the History of Arabia*, vol. II: *Pre-Islamic Arabia, Proceedings of the Second International Symposium on Studies in the History of Arabia, April 1979, King Saud University* (Riyadh: King Saud University Press—formerly Riyadh University, 1984), 149–54; Beeston, 'Judaism and Christianity in Pre-Islamic Yemen'. In Joseph Chelhod et al., *L'Arabie du Sud. Histoire et civilisation, 1. Le peuple yéménite et ses racines* (Islam d'hier et d'aujourd'hui 21) (Paris: Maisonneuve et Larose, 1984), 271–8.

[3] Abraham Lundin, 'The Jewish Communities in Yemen during the 4th–6th Centuries (according to epigraphic material)', in Ephraim Isaac and Yosef Tobi, eds, *Judaeo-Yemenite Studies, Proceedings of the Second International Congress* (Princeton: Princeton University, 1999), 17–25.

[4] Christian Julien Robin, 'Le judaïsme de Ḥimyar', *Arabia* 1 (2003): 154; Robin, 'Quel judaïsme en Arabie ?', in Christian Julien Robin, ed., *Le judaïsme de l'Arabie antique*, Actes du

Indeed, Jewish communities existed in South Arabia and the dominant monotheism was strongly influenced by Judaism, but the fact that the sovereigns never officially declared their belief as Judaism (except for king Yūsuf in the sixth century) is certainly significant. It can be assumed that it was a conscious political choice to adopt a kind of neutral monotheism acceptable to many people who abandoned their ancestral beliefs and venerated one god.[5] The fact that the adepts of Judaism consider themselves as a part of the people of Israel and are not supposed to belong to other tribes could prevent the inhabitants of South Arabia from adhering to Judaism. Nevertheless, they could have accepted more easily the adoption of a monotheism inspired of Judaism but giving them the possibility of keeping their old traditions and preserving their ancestral tribal system.

NEW DATA

Recent research sheds light on our understanding of monotheism in South Arabia. To begin with, the conversion to monotheism does not seem total and abrupt. Several inscriptions on wood, dated by Peter Stein to the monotheistic period, most of them to the fifth century CE, contain invocations to dhū-Samawī, the god of the tribe of Amīr, living in the northern part of the country, between the region of the modern Jawf and Nağrān, and also invocations to the gods ʿAthtar and Almaqah; some texts mention also personal theophoric names composed with the divine name of Dhū-Samawī.[6] Peter Stein has noted that these invocations and theophoric names prove the survival of the ancient polytheistic cults among the common people in South Arabia, after the establishment of monotheism as the dominant religion in the second half of the fourth century CE. Indeed, some invocations of the traditional deities in the texts on wooden sticks reveal that the polytheistic cults survived for some time,

Colloque de Jérusalem, février 2006 (Judaïsme ancien et origines du christianisme 3; Turnhout: Brepols, 2015), 297–329.

[5] Iwona Gajda, *Le royaume de Ḥimyar à l'époque monothéiste. L'histoire de l'Arabie du Sud ancienne de la fin du IVe siècle de l'ère chrétienne jusqu'à l'avènement de l'islam* (Paris: l'Académie des Inscriptions et Belles-Lettres, 2009), 223–52; Gajda, 'Quel monothéisme en Arabie du Sud ancienne?', in Joëlle Beaucamp, Françoise Briquel-Chatonnet, and Christian Julien Robin, eds, *Juifs et chrétiens en Arabie aux Ve et VIe siècles: Regards croisés sur les sources* (Monographies 32. Le Massacre de Najrân II; Paris: Centre de recherche d'histoire et civilisation de Byzance), 107–20.

[6] Peter Stein, 'Monotheismus oder religiöse Vielfalt? Ḏū-Samāwī, die Stammesgottheit der ʾAmir, im 5. Jh. n. Chr.', in Werner Arnold, Michael Jursa, Walter W. Müller, and Stephan Prochazka, eds, *Philologisches und Historisches zwischen Anatolien und Sokotra. Analecta Semitica In Memoriam Alexander Sima* (Wiesbaden: Harrassowitz, 2009), 339–50.

to some extent, mostly among the common people, even if the cults were no longer celebrated in the temples of these deities.

Furthermore, some new South Arabian inscriptions confirm the existence of monotheistic cults, Judaism and Christianity, which were reported already in the first half of the fourth century CE by a Roman source, Philostorgius.[7] Philostorgius described the Christian mission of Theophilos the Indian sent by the Emperor Constantius II to Ethiopia and South Arabia, probably between 339 and 344. In South Arabia, the mission received support from the local king, whose name is not given, who agreed to help to construct churches for merchants in the capital and in two major cities. According to Philostorgius, the local people worshipped at that time Helios and Selene and many Jews were present at the royal court.[8]

Now also local epigraphic sources confirm the existence of monotheism at that time, in the southern part of the country (see the inscriptions Buraʿ al-Aʿlā 1 and 2).[9]

Recently published inscriptions afford us an opportunity to reassess the nature of the official religion. For example, the rock inscription MS Šiǧāʿ 1 was discovered by Mohammed Ali Al-Salami some 40 km north-east of Ṣanʿāʾ, at the Naqīl Šiǧāʿ (the Šiǧāʿ Pass), on the ancient road leading from Ṣanʿāʾ to Mārib.[10] The author of this inscription, King Abīkarib Asʿad, probably accompanied by his brother and/or son(s), commemorated an ibex hunt in the surrounding mountains. The inscription could date to the year 539 of the Ḥimyarite era (that is 429 CE); however, we cannot be certain, given the fragmentary context. King Abīkarib Asʿad invoked the 'Lord of Heaven' (*m(r)ʾ s¹myn)*. The editor of the text noted that another hunt had been organized at the Šiǧāʿ Pass a few centuries before by the Sabaean king Dhamarʿalī Dhāriḥ son of Karibʾil Watar, who reigned in the first century CE. It is noteworthy that the hunt of Dhamarʿalī Dhāriḥ was clearly a ritual hunt practised for the gods ʿAthtar and *Krwm* (this is known from the inscription Ry 544/3–4: *ywm ṣyd ṣyd ʿṯtr w-Krwm*). The inscription of Abīkarib Asʿad, line 15, where the one god is mentioned, is fragmentary:

]m(r)ʾ s¹myn s¹bʿ mʾtm wṯny ʾlfn wqdmy ḏn (ḫ)[rfn
]Lord of Heaven two thousand seven hundred and before this y[ear...

In spite of this fragmentary context, it seems that the divine name is directly connected to the number of hunted animals, probably ibexes as they are the

[7] Joseph Bidez. ed., *Philostorgius, Kirchengeschichte* (Die griechischen christlichen Schriftsteller der ersten Jahrhunderte) (Leipzig: Hinrichs, 1913).

[8] Ibid., III 4–6, 32–6.

[9] For the inscriptions Buraʿ al-Aʿlā 1 & 2, see Fahmī Aghbarī, 'Nuqūš sabaʾiyya ǧadīda taḥtawī ʿalā aqdam naqsh tawḥīdī muʾarraḫ', *Raydān* 8 (2013): 167–83.

[10] Mohammed Ali Al-Salami, *Sabäische Inschriften aus dem Ḫawlān* (Jenaer Beiträge zum Vorderen Orient 7; Wiesbaden: Harrassowitz, 2011).

only animals mentioned in this text. The syntax of this fragmentary phrase lets us suppose that 2,700 ibexes were either hunted for the Lord of Heaven or sacrificed to the Lord of Heaven. The other interpretation of this fragment could be '[with the help of] the Lord of Heaven [they have hunted?] two thousand seven hundred . . . ' but this seems less probable as one would expect the religious invocation at the end of the text. It seems rather that the inscription relates to a ritual hunt and is a continuation of an ancient tradition.

Of course not all the texts reporting a hunt in ancient South Arabia refer to a ritual hunt. Alexander Sima has shown that only a small proportion of the inscriptions can be considered as referring to a ritual hunt. Most of them are very ancient and date back to the seventh century BCE. The only one more recent is precisely the inscription of the King Dhamarʿalī Dhāriḥ from the Šiǧāʿ Pass, mentioned above.[11] It is possible that Abīkarib Asʿad wanted to restore an ancient tradition.

Should the proposed interpretation of the inscription as either a ritual hunt in honour of the Lord of Heaven or a sacrifice of the hunted animals to the Lord of Heaven be correct, we ought to consider the conformity of each of these supposed acts with the religion of King Abīkarib Asʿad. According to the laws of Judaism, neither of these acts is permitted, as they are incompatible with the prescriptions of the Torah. However, this does not necessarily mean that King Abīkarib Asʿad did not profess Judaism. In cases of conversion to a new religion, the ancient tradition is often preserved, sometimes for generations. And this ritual hunt was visibly an important and solemn royal tradition.

NEW STUDIES AND RECONSIDERATIONS

Inscriptions on Wood and Religious Beliefs in the Last Centuries before Islam: Clarification

In his publication of the texts on wood containing invocations to the god dhū-Samawī and also to ʿAthtar and Almaqah, Peter Stein postulates that the official adoption of monotheism in South Arabia was no real end of polytheism and that monotheism influenced by Judaism and later by Christianity had the same position as the traditional polytheistic cults practised by the common people.[12] His postulate, however, is problematic. In fact, the majority (almost all) of the monumental and solemn inscriptions of that time (from the end of

[11] Alexander Sima, 'Die Jagd im antiken Südarabien', *Die Welt des Orients* 31 (2001): 84–109.

[12] Stein, 'Monotheismus oder religiöse Vielfalt? Ḏū-Samāwī, die Stammesgottheit der ʾAmir, im 5. Jh. n. Chr.', 347–8.

the fourth until the sixth century CE), inscriptions which contain any religious formula, are either clearly Jewish, influenced by Judaism or vaguely monotheistic, and in the sixth century several inscriptions are clearly Christian. Of over one hundred monumental inscriptions of that period only two could testify of polytheistic cults. In contrast, almost all the polytheistic invocations (seven known in total) and theophoric names (two) appear in the inscriptions on wood, reflecting everyday life and emanating from the common people. These texts belong to different categories and it is impossible to consider them on the same level. Moreover, in this period the proportion of polytheistic texts is very small. From the end of the fourth century on, there were no dedications to the traditional gods and the polytheistic temples were abandoned. Thus it seems difficult to describe this situation as one of religious multiplicity ('religiose Vielfalt'). Rather, it seems that after the conversion of the whole kingdom of Ḥimyar to monotheism and the abandonment of polytheistic temples by the end of the fourth century CE, some traditional cults survived for a certain time, especially among ordinary people in South Arabia.

For comparison, we can look at the history of the Roman Empire. After Christianity had been imposed in Rome as an official religion and paganism banned by Theodosius, the traditional cults were still practised, often in secret, mostly by the common people. Several laws were promulgated forbidding pagan cults and feasts during the fifth century.

Inscriptions in Hebrew or in Sabaic Attesting to Rabbinic Judaism in South Arabia

Several inscriptions from Yemen and Palestine attest Jewish communities living in Yemen at the latest from the fourth century CE on. Two of these inscriptions prove the existence of rabbinic Judaism in ancient South Arabia. The inscription DJE 23, in Hebrew, records priestly courses called *mishmarot*, in service of the Temple in Jerusalem.[13] All the priests originate from Galilee: the name of every priest is accompanied by the name of his town or village. The second inscription, Ḥaṣī 1, in Sabaic, is a decree of a local lord who accorded plots for a Jewish cemetery where no gentiles were to be buried. As the recent thorough study of Yosef Tobi demonstrates, the use of several

[13] The inscription was published by Rainer Degen, 'Die hebräische Inschrift DJE 23 aus dem Jemen', in Rainer Degen, Walter W. Müller, and Wolfgang Röllig, eds, *Neue Ephemeris für Semitische Epigraphik* (Wiesbaden 2, 111–16, pl. IX, no. 31, 1974), and more recently studied by Maria Gorea, 'Les classes sacerdotales (*mišmārôt*) de l'inscription juive de Bayt Ḥāḍir (Yémen)', in Christian Julien Robin, ed., *Le judaïsme de l'Arabie antique*, 297–329.

precise terms, loanwords from Hebrew or Aramaic, proves that the person who wrote the text knew Jewish law very well.[14]

Problems of Interpretation of Some Jewish Inscriptions in Sabaic

The interpretation of some expressions in other inscriptions, visibly Jewish, is sometimes problematic.

- In inscription CIH 543, the authors display this invocation:

> *[b]rk w-tbrk s*^{1}*m Rḥmnn ḏ-b-s*^{1}*myn w-Ys*^{3}*rʾl w-ʾlh-hmw Rb-Yhd ḏ-hrdʾ ʿbd-hmw S*^{2}*hrm w-ʾm-hw Bdm w-hs*^{2}*kt-hw S*^{2}*ms*^{1}*m w-ʾwld-hmy. . . .*

This could be rendered as follows:

> 'Blessed and praised be the name of Raḥmānān who is in Heaven and Israel (Yisrāʾīl) and their God, Lord of Jews (*Rb-Yhd*) who helped Shahrum, his mother Buddum, his wife Shamsum and their children. . . . '

The root *brk*, 'to bless, praise', is a loanword from Hebrew or Aramaic. However, the divine name Rab-Yahūd, 'Lord of Jews', is not known in Hebrew or Aramaic. Rab-Yahūd is described as 'their god' (*ʾlh-hmw*); the possessive pronoun seems to refer to the community of Israel. In this curious invocation apparently two gods are distinguished: Raḥmānān and the 'Lord of Jews'.

Another inscription, Ry 515, written during the siege of Najrān by two chiefs of the army of the Jewish king Yūsuf in 623 of the Ḥimyarite Era (probably around 523 AD), closes with an invocation to *Rb-hwd b-Rḥmnn*: 'Lord of Jews by / with (?) Raḥmānān'. Again two gods or two divine names are distinguished, unless the second one should be considered as qualifying the first, which is difficult to support for reasons of syntax.

In one of the three major inscriptions from the siege of Najrān, Ja 1028/12, a similar formula appears: *Rb-hd b-Mḥmd*: 'Lord of Jews by / with (?) the Praised'.

In the invocations in the inscriptions Ry 515 and Ja 1028, the two names of God (*Rb-hwd b-Rḥmnn* and *Rb-hd b-Mḥmd*) are linked by the preposition *b-*, which is usually rendered as 'in, with, by' ('Lord of Jews by / with (?) Raḥmānān' and 'Lord of Jews by / with (?) the Praised'). Thus the two gods seem to be one entity.

These invocations, especially the first one, show that their authors, seemingly Jews, distinguish two gods. How could that be explained?

[14] Yosef Yuval Tobi, 'The Jewish Community in Ḥaṣī, South Yemen, in the Light of its Makrab Ṣūrīʾēl and Cemetery', in Christian Julien Robin, ed., *Le judaïsme de l'Arabie antique*, 373–85.

Perhaps they believed in the one god, Raḥmānān, common to all the monotheists of South Arabia, and also in the God of Jews. They could have distinguished these two gods.[15] Or they could have identified these two gods in some form of syncretism. This is only supposition. According to this hypothesis, the god called Raḥmānān would not have been considered exclusively as the Lord of Jews. This is for instance the case in several Christian inscriptions from the sixth century whose authors call God Raḥmānān.[16] There were probably other worshippers of the one God, called Raḥmānān or Ilān/Ilahān, in South Arabia, but they were not considered as Jews by the Jews.

CONCLUSIONS

The conversion from polytheism to monotheism and its adoption as dominant religion do not seem so abrupt as was thought before. It appears that the change was gradual and that the process started in the first half of the fourth century CE, even if the Ḥimyarite kings probably decided to impose monotheism only in the second half of the fourth century.

Furthermore, the conversion to monotheism and the abandonment of the ancestral cults does not seem to have been total. Even if the sovereigns, nobles, and the majority of the population adopted monotheism, the ancient polytheistic cults survived, at least for a certain time, among the common people.

The Jews present in South Arabia were in part Jews from Palestine, respecting the precepts of the Torah according to the laws of rabbinic Judaism, but there were also others, possibly adepts of different forms of Judaism, considered as heretics by the rabbinic authorities, and proselytes of whom we do not know much (it is quite probable that some of them were also devotees of the forms of Judaism regarded as heresies by the rabbinic authorities).

The question of the nature of monotheism in ancient South Arabia remains open, but, thanks to recent discoveries and studies, some aspects become clearer, even if the general picture of the religious situation appears more complex than researchers had imagined a few decades ago.

Monotheism influenced by Judaism was dominant. It seems that this official religion was deliberately neutral. While the nobles adopted monotheism, in some cases Judaism, pagan cults survived to some extent. The official religion was influenced by Judaism but does not seem to have been a form of Judaism acceptable to the rabbinic authorities. This hypothesis could explain why Judaism in ancient South Arabia (and more generally in Arabia) is completely ignored by the Jewish sources.

[15] Robin, *Le judaïsme de l'Arabie antique*, 54–5, has recently postulated a similar hypothesis.

[16] CIH 541, Ry 506, Ja 547 + Ja 546 + Ja 544 + Ja 545.

The nature of the dominant religion is unclear. Was it a kind of Judaism considered heretical by the rabbinic authorities or monotheism influenced by Judaism, perhaps a vague 'Ḥimyarite monotheism'? Or was it another form of Judaism, a kind of free interpretation of this religion by the Ḥimyarites who adopted some general ideas from Judaism but did not respect all the strict prescriptions of the Torah? This is possible. It is certain that the Jews of the Diaspora lived in Yemen, even if it is not easy to estimate their number. Could the inhabitants of South Arabia be compared to the Godfearers (*theosebeis*) from Palestine or other regions?[17] The definition of the Godfearers (*theosebeis*) is itself problematic, as this term could also be applied to Jews, proselytes or sympathisers with Judaism. It is therefore better to avoid such a comparison in South Arabia.

New discoveries could explain how the inhabitants of Southern Arabia understood their monotheism(s), which were without any doubt strongly influenced by Judaism and probably quite heterodox. Among the South Arabian monotheists there were Jews, Jewish proselytes and more neutral monotheists (and also some Christians, especially in the sixth century). They seem to have venerated the one God, whose exact nature could perhaps have been understood in some different ways, but He had mostly the same name.

The monotheism in South Arabia, whatever its exact nature, was imposed by the Ḥimyarite kings for political reasons. These sovereigns manifestly wanted to reinforce the unity of their kingdom. They stayed neutral, proposing a cult of one god in whom everybody could recognize his god.

BIBLIOGRAPHY

Sigla of inscriptions

For inscriptions published before 1982 refer to the *Sabaic Dictionary.*
Buraʿ al-Aʿlā 1 & 2: cf. al-Aghbarī 2013.

Bibliographic references

Aghbarī, Fahmī al-. 'Nuqūš saba'iyya ğadīda taḥtawī ʿalā aqdam naqsh tawḥīdī mu'arraḫ'. *Raydān* 8 (2013): 167–83.

Beeston, A. F. L. 'Himyarite Monotheism'. In A. M. Abdalla et al., eds. *Studies in the History of Arabia*, vol. II: *Pre-Islamic Arabia. Proceedings of the Second International Symposium on Studies in the History of Arabia, April 1979, King Saud University.* Riyadh: King Saud University Press, formerly Riyadh University, 1984, 149–54.

Beeston, A. F. L. 'Judaism and Christianity in Pre-Islamic Yemen'. In Joseph Chelhod et al., *L'Arabie du Sud. Histoire et civilisation,* 1. *Le peuple yéménite et ses racines* (Islam d'hier et d'aujourd'hui 21). Paris: Maisonneuve et Larose, 1984, 271–8.

[17] See for instance Joyce Reynolds and Robert Tannenbaum, *Jews and God-Fearers at Aphrodisias* (Cambridge: Cambridge University Press: 1987).

Beeston, A. F. L., M. A.Ghul, Walter W. Müller, and J. Ryckmans, eds. *Sabaic Dictionary* (English–French–Arabic). (Publication of the University of Sanaa, YAR.) Louvain-la-Neuve-Beyrouth: Peeters-Librairie du Liban, 1982.

Bidez, Joseph, ed. *Philostorgius, Kirchengeschichte* (Die griechischen christlichen Schriftsteller der ersten Jahrhunderte). Leipzig: Hinrichs, 1913. 2nd edn, F. Winkelmann, ed. Berlin: Akademie-Verlag, 1972.

Degen, Rainer. 'Die hebräische Inschrift DJE 23 aus dem Jemen'. In Rainer Degen, Walter W. Müller, and Wolfgang Röllig, eds. *Neue Ephemeris für Semitische Epigraphik*, 2, Wiesbaden: Harrassowitz, 1974, 111–16, pl. IX, no. 31.

Gajda, Iwona. *Le royaume de Ḥimyar à l'époque monothéiste. L'histoire de l'Arabie du Sud ancienne de la fin du* IV*e siècle de l'ère chrétienne jusqu'à l'avènement de l'islam.* Paris: Mémoires de l'Académie des Inscriptions et Belles-Lettres, 2009.

Gajda, Iwona. 'Quel monothéisme en Arabie du Sud ancienne?' In Joëlle Beaucamp, Françoise Briquel-Chatonnet, and Christian Julien Robin, eds. *Juifs et chrétiens en Arabie aux* V*e et* VI*e siècles. Regards croisés sur les sources.* Monographies 32. Le Massacre de Najrân II. Paris: Centre de recherche d'histoire et civilisation de Byzance, 2010, 107–20.

Gorea, Maria. 'Les classes sacerdotales (*mišmārôt*) de l'inscription juive de Bayt Ḥāḍir (Yémen)'. In Christian Julien Robin, ed., *Le judaïsme de l'Arabie antique.* Actes du Colloque de Jérusalem (février 2006), Judaïsme ancien et origines du christianisme 3. Turnhout: Brepols, 2015, 297–329.

Lundin, Abraham G. 'The Jewish Communities in Yemen during the 4th–6th Centuries (according to epigraphic material)'. In Ephraim Isaac et Yosef Tobi, eds, *Judaeo-Yemenite Studies, Proceedings of the Second International Congress*, Princeton: Princeton University, 1999.

Salami, Mohammed Ali al-. *Sabäische Inschriften aus dem Ḫawlān* (Jenaer Beiträge zum Vorderen Orient 7). Wiesbaden: Harrassowitz, 2011.

Reynolds, Joyce and Tannenbaum, Robert. *Jews and God-Fearers at Aphrodisias.* Cambridge: Cambridge University Press, 1987.

Robin, Christian. 'Judaïsme et christianisme en Arabie du sud d'après les sources épigraphiques et archéologiques'. *Proceedings of the Seminar for Arabian Studies* 10 (1980): 85–96.

Robin, Christian. 'Le judaïsme de Ḥimyar'. *Arabia* 1 (2003): 97–172.

Robin, Christian. 'Quel judaïsme en Arabie?'. In Christian Julien Robin, ed., *Le judaïsme de l'Arabie antique.* Actes du Colloque de Jérusalem (février 2006), Judaïsme ancien et origines du christianisme 3. Turnhout: Brepols, 2015, 297–329.

Sima, Alexander. 'Die Jagd im antiken Südarabien'. *Die Welt des Orients* 31 (2001): 84–109.

Stein, Peter. 'Monotheismus oder religiöse Vielfalt? Ḏū-Samāwī, die Stammesgottheit der ʾAmir, im 5. Jh. n. Chr.'. In Werner Arnold, Michael Jursa, Walter W. Müller, and Stephan Prochazka, eds. *Philologisches und Historisches zwischen Anatolien und Sokotra. Analecta Semitica in Memoriam Alexander Sima.* Wiesbaden: Harrassowitz, 2009, 339–50.

Tobi, Yosef Yuval. 'The Jewish community in Ḥaṣī, South Yemen, in the Light of its Makrab Ṣūrīʾēl and Cemetery'. In Christian Julien Robin, ed., *Le judaïsme de l'Arabie antique.* Actes du Colloque de Jérusalem (février 2006), Judaïsme ancien et origines du christianisme 3. Turnhout: Brepols, 2015, 373–85.

Index

Aaron 123–4, 123–4n16, 124n18, 126–7, 126n29
ʿAbdallāh b. Salām 157
Abīkarib Asʿad, inscription concerning the hunt of 250–1
Abraham 49, 92, 143n13, 155, 171n22, 173, 197, 208
appropriation of by Jews and Christians 182
intercession of for his Arab progeny 177–8
and Isaac (the Abrahamic sacrifice) 179–81
law of 238–40, 239n148
pilgrimage of to Mecca 181
prayer of 181–2
relationship of with Muhammad 182–3
Abū Bakr 91n76
Abū al-Ḥasan al-Ḥarallī 27
Abu Sahlieh, Sami Aldeeb 12
Abū Ṭālib 226
Abū ʿUbayd al-Bakrī 223, 223–4n55
Abu Zayd, Nasr Hamid 169–70n17
ʿĀd b. Iram 190
Agobard of Lyons 220
ahl al-kitāb (scriptural people) 178
Ahrens, Karl 9
aḥzāb 158
ʿĀʾisha 134, 231
Aistulf 217
Akedah 180, 180n34, 183
Alcorani Textus Universus Arabbicè et Latinè (Maracci) 8
Alfred (king of England) 220
Ali, Kecia 45
alladhīna fī qulūbihim maraḍun (those in whose hearts is sickness) 74, 74n21
alladhīna ūtū l-kitāb (those who have been given the Scripture) 74, 74n21
Allohistorians/Allohistory 20, 28–30
problems concerning the scholarship of 29–30
Almaqah 249, 251
Amari, Michele 11
ʿĀmir ibn Jusham al-Yashkurī 236
ʿĀmir ibn al-Ẓarib al-ʿAdwānī 228n75
Anṣār 231
ʿAnsī, al-Aswad b. Kaʿb al- 193
Ancient West Arabian (Rabin) 41
Andrae, Tor 9, 15
angels 141–3, 141n4, 143n13, 143n18, 156
as intercessors 142
as the 'sons of God' 141–2
Aphrodisias 151
Arabs 161, 234–5, 239
God's revelation to 156
morality of 239n148
ṭayyāye 'Arabs' 29
see also pagan Arabs
Aramaic language 21–2
Archbishop of Canterbury 214–15, 215n6
Armenian language 22
asbāb al-nuzūl (the occasions of revelation) 26, 32, 69, 70, 168
Ashbah waʾl-naẓaʾir, al- 48
aslama, derivatives of 84n51
Associators (*al-mushrikūn*) 89, 89n72, 95n88, 96–103, 99n97, 141, 143–5, 155n79
conflict with 89, 89n72, 90–6, 95n88, 96–103
conversion/repentance of 93, 100, 101, 102
hostility of toward believers 159
and the phrase 'God and His Messenger are quit (*barīʾ*) of the Associators' 90–1, 92, 92n79
and the 'Sword verse' 96–7, 100, 103
treaties/covenants with 93, 95–6, 97nn90–2, 99, 100–1
warfare against during the sacred months 93–4, 94n83, 95, 95n88, 100
ʿAthtar 249, 250, 251
Augustine, St 241–2
Azaiez, Mehdi 50
Azmeh, Aziz al- 37, 168–9, 191, 194, 198–9

Badawi, El Said 38
Badawi, Emran El- 23
Banū Hāshim 226, 234n116
Barlas, Asma 45
bashar (skin, mankind) 73–4n18
Bathsheba 129–30
Bauer, Karen 45
Bauer, Thomas 40
Bavarian code 218–19
al-Bayḍāwī 25
Bede 220
Beeston, A. F. L. 248
Before and After Muhammad (Fowden) 31
Beilegen (parallel phrases) 33, 38, 48

believers 155–8, 155n79
  hostility toward the Jews and the *mushrikūn* 159
Bell, Richard 9, 12, 47, 50, 52, 89n70, 91, 98n94, 99n97
  on the early verses of Surah 9 98, 99n97, 100, 100n101, 101n102, 102
  Sinai's criticism of concerning secondary additions to the Qurʾan 72–3, 72–3n12
  translation of the Qurʾan by 17–18
Bergsträsser, Gotthelf 11, 12, 32
Bible, the 183–4
  canonical shape of the prophetic books of 76
  and the concept of promise in 173
  patristic readings of Old Testament texts based on Paul's theology 171–2
  reading of not reserved to Jews and Christians 182
  use of by Muslim scholars 27
  See also Qurʾan, biblical tradition in
biblical history, and counter-history 172–3
Biblische Erzählungen im Koran, Die (Speyer) 14
Biqāʿī, al- 17, 27
Birkeland, Harris 15, 16
Blachère, Régis 12, 14, 50, 52
Blois, François de 86, 160
blood money, payment of 228, 235, 236, 237
Bobzin, Hartmut 129n42
Brèves, François Savary de 7
Brown, Peter 31, 167
Bultmann, Rudolf 18, 19
  concern of with *Gemeindebildung* (formation of the community) 49
Burgundian code 216–17, 220
Busse, Heribert 47, 171, 171n22

Calder, Norman 104
Capitolina 151n55
Charlemagne 214
Charles VI 213
Childebert 218
Chingiz Khān 225
Chlotar 218
Christians (*naṣārā*)/Christianity 18, 141, 142, 144, 146, 152, 153n70, 154, 159, 160, 208, 224n56
  Gentile Christians 155, 161, 240
  hermeneutic experience of in the later surahs 179
  and individual monotheists (*ḥanīfs*) 187
  and interfaith marriage 87–8, 88n68
  and Roman law 220–2
  in South Arabia 247, 250, 251–2
  see also Jewish Christians/Christianity; pagan law, Christian attitudes toward
Clovis 216
Commodian 152
Companions of the Prophet 230, 231, 234, 234n117
Concordantiae Corani arabicae (Flügel) 8
Conrad, Lawrence 31
Constantine 241
Constantius II 250
'Constitution of Medina' 93n81
Contre-discours coranique, Le (Azaiez) 50
Cook, David 207
Cook, Michael 1, 3, 28, 29n33, 34
Cornelius 150
Corpus Coranicum project 19, 32
Crone, Patricia 1, 2, 28, 29n33, 37, 86
Culte des bétyles et les processions religieuses chez les Arabes préislamiques, Le (Lammens) 10
Cuypers, Michel 43, 44, 78, 78n33
Cyril of Alexandria 151–2

David, King 129–30
De Origine et compositione Surarum qoranicarum ipsiusque Qorani (Nöldeke) 11
Death of the Prophet (Shoemaker) 29
Der Koran als Text der Spätantike 48
Déroche, François 34, 35
Dhamarʿalī Dhāriḥ, inscription concerning the hunt of 250, 251
Dhū al-Qarnayn 24
Dhū Samawī 251
Dibelius, Martin 49
Didascalia 23–4
Digest (Justinian) 220–2
divine teaching/instruction 172
Donner, Fred 29, 49
Dubthach 219
Dundes, Alan 48
Dutton, Yasin 35

Edict of Rothair 217
Edward III 214
Eickelmann, Dale 192
Einleitung in den Koran (Weil) 10–11
Emergence of Islam in Late Antiquity, The: Allah and His People(al-Azmeh) 37
Encyclopaedia of the Quran 19, 38, 51
Enlightenment, the 165
Ephrem of Nisibis 180
Erpenius, Thomas 7
Ethelbert of Kent 220
Ethiopic language 22

Eusebius, on the distinction between Hebrews (pre-Mosaic Israelites) and Jews 154
Extra-Peninsulists *see* Allohistorians/ Allohistory

Fahd, Toufic 10, 37, 41
Fakhr al-Dīn al-Rāzī 121n5, 232–3
Farahi, Hamiduddin 42
Farrin, Raymond 43, 104
fasting 76
Fedeli, Alba 35
Festin, Le. Une lecture de la sourate al-Mâ'ida (Cuypers) 43
Flügel, Gustav 8
food prohibitions, Christian and Jewish 86, 86–7n61, 87n62, 152, 153
Foreign Vocabulary of the Qur'an (Jeffery) 38
Formgeschichte (Form-History) 17–19, 49
Fossum, Jarl 190
Fowden, Garth 31
Freytag, Georg Wilhelm Friedrich 8
Friedenreich, David M. 86, 87n63
Friedmann, Yohanan 195, 200
From Empire to Commonwealth (Fowden) 31
Fück, Johann 15, 16
Fudge, Bruce 104

Gajda, Iwona 1, 3
Geiger, Abraham 8–9, 24, 27, 51, 125, 170–1
Georgian language 22
Geschichte des Korantextes, Die (The History of the Qur'anic Text [Bergsträsser]) 11
Geschichte des Qorans (Nöldeke and Schwally) 11, 12, 13, 14, 39, 51, 72, 168
Gilliot, Claude 50, 52
God-fearers 146–54, 150n53, 255
- in Arabia 152, 153–4
- attestations of in the Bible 147
- as Gentiles attracted to Jewish ways (*theosebeis*) 147, 152, 154
- Greek sources concerning 146
- and Jews 148–50
- Josephus's claims concerning 147–8, 148n40
- Latin sources concerning 148
- literary evidence for Gentile God-fearers 150–1
- mention of in the Acts of the Apostles 147, 150
- in rabbinic writings 146
- as surviving the triumph of Christianity 151–2, 151–2n61
- and worshippers of *theos hypsistos* (God the highest) 150, 150n51
- *see also* Muhammad the Prophet/ Messenger, and the God-fearer hypothesis

Goitein, Fritz 9
Goldziher, Ignaz 12, 13, 14, 17, 51, 201n50
Golius, Jacob 7
Goudarzi, Mohsen 35
Graham, William 15
Gregory of Nazianzus 150
Griffith, Sidney 23, 47, 171
Gross, Markus 28
Gundobad, Burgundian king 216–17
Gwynne, Rosalind 50

ḥadīths 27, 198
Ḥafṣa 134
Hagarism (Cook and Crone) 28–9
Haleem, Abdel 38, 50
Halperin, D. 206, 206n71
Haman 36, 171
Hamdānī, al- 190, 200
Hammer-Purgstall, Joseph von 38
Ḥanẓala b. Ṣafwān 189, 190–1, 200–1, 202, 208, 209
Hassan, Riffat 45
Hawting, Gerald 1, 3
Helena 149
Helios 250
Henry V 213–14, 215
Henry V (Shakespeare) 213, 214, 215
Hibri, Aziza 45
Hidayatullah, Ayesha 46
Hilali, Asma 35
Ḥimyarite kingdom 247, 248, 253
Hincmar of Rheims 217–18
Hirschfeld, Hartwig 9, 128, 128nn36–7
Historical Jesus movement 15
Holinshed, Raphael 215
Horace 148
Horowitz, Josef 9, 47
Hoyland, Robert 30
Hūd 189
Hypsistarians 150

Iblīs, fall of 22
Ibn ʿAbbās 135, 226
Ibn ʿAbd al-Barr 227, 230
Ibn Ḥabīb 198, 235
Ibn Ḥajar al-ʿAsqalānī 239
Ibn Ḥazm 27, 229–30, 232n105
Ibn Hishām 12, 198
Ibn Isḥāq 192, 198, 208
Ibn al-Jawzī 126
Ibn al-Kalbī 195
Ibn Kathīr 225
Ibn Masʿūd 32
Ibn al-Mundhir 231
Ibn Qudāma 231

Ibn Qutayba 198, 227n72, 236
on the four 'firsts' 228n79, 228–9n81
Ibn Rushd 227n73, 231
Ibn Ṣayyād (Ibn Ṣā'id) 191, 204–7, 206n72
claim of to be a prophet 204–5, 205nn66–7
confrontations of with Muhammad 204–5
as the personification of the Antichrist (*al-Dajjāl*) 204, 206–7, 206–7n75
Ibn Taymiyya 239
Ibn Wathīma, ʿUmāra 122
Iklīl (al-Hamdānī) 190
ʿilm al-makkī wa-l-madanī 168
infanticide 141
inheritance, Islamic law concerning 232–3, 235–6, 236n129
innahā la-iḥdā l-kubar (it is one of the gravest matters) 75
Institute of Ismaili Studies 19
International Qurʾanic Studies Association (IQSA) 19
Introduction to the Qurʾan (Bell) 14–15
Isaac 179–81
Ishmael 153, 197
law of 239n145
Ishmaelites 152–3, 155n74
Iṣlāḥī, Amīn Aḥsan 42
Islamic historians, training of 31
Isrāʾīliyyāt 27
istiqsām, practice of by means of arrows 79–80, 80n39
Itqān fi ʿulum al-Qurʾan, al-(al-Suyūṭī) 8, 11, 52
Izates 147n26, 148, 149
Izutso, Toshihiko 16

Jābir ibn ʿAbdallāh 231
Jahiliyya 226, 226n67, 227, 237
aspects of Islamic law originating in 227–32, 235, 235n127, 236
ear-piercing of children in 233
ennobling of by Islam 236
errors of the people in 225
possible monotheistic origins of Jāhilī law 238–40
practice of hiring wet nurses in 228, 237, 237n137
prizing of as an ancestral culture 234–5
prophets in 189–91, 207–9
prophets in identified as monotheists 195–9, 203, 208
Jāḥiẓ 202–3
Jāmiʿal-bayān fi taʾ wīl āy al-Qurʾān (al-Ṭabarī) 13
Jaṣṣāṣ 233, 239
Jeffery, Arthur 13, 14, 15, 38
Jerusalem 176
Jerusalem Temple (*al-masjid al-aqṣā*) 176–7, 179–80
association of with Golgatha 180
as erected by the father-son synergy of God and Christ 180
Jesus Christ 126n26, 157, 159, 180, 187
and dietary food laws 86–7n61
followers of 160
Jethro 152, 219
Jewish Christians/Christianity 36–7, 157–8, 160, 161
and the elders (*zeqenim*) of 159–60
Jews 141, 142, 145n22, 146, 147, 152, 153n70, 154, 158–9, 187, 224n56
of Akmoneia 149
in Arabia 155, 155n74, 247, 248–9
and God-fearers 148–50, 151, 155
hermeneutic experience of in the later surahs 179
of Medina 178–9
opposition of to the concept of the resurrection 144
and proselytization 148, 148–9n42
John of Damascus 166
Jomier, Jacques 16
Jones, Alan 50
Joseph 128
Josephus 149, 150n53, 151
claims of concerning God-fearers 147–8, 148n40
Journal of the International Qurʾanic Studies Association 19
Journal of Qurʾanic Studies 19
Jubbāʾī, al- 17
Judaism 18, 88n68, 149, 186, 193, 208
influence of on monotheism in South Arabia 248, 250, 251–2, 254–5
problems concerning Jewish inscriptions in Sabaic 253–4
and proselytization 148–9n42
rabbinic Judaism in South Arabia 252–3
Juvenal 148, 150n51

Kaʿba, establishment of 181
kalām al-ʿarab 26
Kandil, Lamia 41
Katsch, Avraham 9
Ketton, Robert 7
Khālid b. Sinān al-ʿAbsī 189, 191, 191n14, 201–4, 208–9
burial story of 202, 202n56, 203n62
contested nature of his prophethood 202–3, 203n60
meeting of his daughter with Muhammad 202, 203

recognition of by Muhammad as a prophet 201–2
role of in killing the *ʿanqāʾ* 202
Khalidi, Tarif 50
Khaṭīb, ʿAbd al-Laṭīf al- 34
Kister, M. J. 193
Kitāb al-Aghānī 195, 196, 197
Klamroth, Martin 39
Kommentar und Konkordanz (Paret) 32–3, 38, 48
Koren, Judith 28, 29
kuhhān (soothsayers of pre-Islamic Arabia) 5

Landau-Tasseron, Ella 201, 203
Late Antiquity 20, 30–2
Arabian Late Antiquity 168
as the epistemic space of the Qurʾan's genesis 167–70
as an essentially Christian epoch 165
expansion of monotheistic religions during 168, 183–4
hermeneutics of (typology versus literality) 170–3
see also Qurʾan, biblical tradition in
law
of Abraham 238–40, 239n148
of Ishmael 239n145
Islamic law as 'confirmed' by Islam and Muhammad 227–8, 227n74, 232–3, 235, 235n123, 236n133
the law of inheritance 232–3, 235–6, 236n129
Mosaic law 220
natural law 222–3, 237
possible monotheistic origins of Jāhilī law 238–40
and the role of ecclesiastics in English law 220
Roman law and Christianity 220–2, 222n47
Salic law 213–16, 215n10
see also pagan law, Christian attitudes toward; pagan law, Muslim attitudes toward
Leben Muhammeds nach Muhammed Ibn Ishak, Das (Wüstenfeld) 8
Leben und die Lehre des Mohammad, nach bisher größtenteils unbenutzten Quellen Das (Sprenger) 11
Lex Mahumet pseudoprophete (Ketton) 7
Lexicon Arabico-Latinum (Freytag) 8
Lexicon Arabico-Latinum (Golius) 7
Life of Adam and Eve 22
Linear B 21
Liutprand 217
Logic, Rhetoric and Legal Reasoning in the Qurʾan: God's Arguments(Gwynne) 50
Lüling, Günter 4, 24
Lundin, Abraham G. 248
Luxenberg, Christoph 4, 5, 24, 28, 29
on the Christian influence on the Qurʾan 20–2
mistaken proposals of 22–3
plausible general ideas of 22
on the Qurʾan as written in a mixed Arabic-Aramaic language 22

McAuliffe, Jane 16
McElwain, Thomas 39
Makin, Al 190, 196n33
Makram, ʿAbd al-ʿĀl Sālim 34
Mālik 234, 239
Maqāmāt (al-Ḥarīrī) 38
Maracci, Ludovigo 8
Māriya the Copt 34
marriage, interfaith 87–8, 88n68
Marshall, David 47
Marxen, Willi 49
Mary 49
Masri, Ghassan El- 40
'masters of the fire' (*aṣḥāb al-nār*) 74
al-Masʿūdī 200
Materials for the History of the Text of the Qurʾan (Jeffery) 13
Māwardī 228–9n81, 230, 236
on manumission 231–2
Mecca 146, 146n23, 173, 239
as a new Jerusalem 181, 183
rise in the status of 177–8
Yāqūt's description of the people of 240
Medinensische Einschübe in mekkanischen Suren (Nagel) 33
Melchert, Christopher 34
Mir, Mustansir 38, 42
Miriam 126–7, 126n29
modernity 165
monasticism 160
monotheism 143, 149n47, 153, 155, 165, 188, 214
Arabian monotheism 173, 189, 208
expansion of monotheistic religions during Late Antiquity 168
the God of monotheism (Allāh or al-Raḥmān) 4, 193, 194
individual monotheists (*ḥanīfs*) 187, 197, 203, 208
monotheists in the Jahiliyya identified as prophets 195–9, 203, 208
possible monotheistic origins of Jāhilī law 238–40
see also monotheism, in ancient South Arabia; monotheistic community (Muslim); pagan Arabs, as monotheists

monotheism, in ancient South Arabia 247–8, 254–5
hypothesis concerning 248–9
new data concerning 249–51
studies of inscriptions concerning 251–4
survival of polytheism after the establishment of monotheism 249–50
monotheistic community (Muslim) 168, 175, 176, 178
challenges faced by 172–3
intellectual development within 169
and the Jews of Medina 178–9
as a liturgical community 174
new identity of as an Abrahamic faith 182–3
the Qur'an as the property of 169–70
Moses 49, 83, 83n49, 152, 155, 172, 187, 219
accusations against as being a sorcerer 126n26
exodus narrative of as a punitive narrative 177
typology of 176–7
see also Q33:69, exegesis of
Moses in the Qur'an and Islamic Exegesis (Wheeler) 16
Muhammad the Prophet/Messenger 196, 196n31, 197–8, 224n56, 234, 239
and compurgation (*qasāma*) 225–7, 227n69, 227n71, 227n73, 235
confrontations of with Ibn Ṣayyād 204–5, 205nn66–7
and the 'Constitution of Medina' 93n81
family life of as reflected in the Qur'an (Q 66:1–5 and 24:11ff) and later traditions 133–5
Farewell Pilgrimage of 81, 91n76
and the God-fearer hypothesis 155–61
and the golden bracelets 193, 193n20
as a heretical Christian 7
influence of in the Yemen 193
instructions of on the insertion of new passages into existing surahs 76–7
and knowledge of the 'Night of Power' (*laylat al-qadr*) 193, 193n19
'Meccan' period of 69, 175
Medinese surahs of 158–9
opponents of 140, 187
as a polemicist 140
prophecy of the thirty antichrists by 193
prophetic mission of 47, 170, 172, 175
psychology of 15
relationship of with Abraham 182–3
revelation of 238
self-identification of as a prophet 192–3
on the sins of the Jews 158–9
tradition of prophecy associated with 186–7
travel of to the Jerusalem Temple 176–7
wives of and the accusations against them 134–5
and Zayd's former wife 129–31, 129n42, 131n49, 133
see also Companions of the Prophet
'Muhammad's Pilgrimage Proclamation' (Bell) 89n70, 91, 91–2n77, 98n94
Muhammedanische Studien (Goldziher) 12
Mujāhid, al- 52
Müller, David Heinrich 39, 51
Müller, Friedrun R. 40
Mu'minūn 'Believers' 29
Musaylima 192, 192n16, 194–5, 194n23
activity of as a prophet before Muhammad 193–4
activity of in the Yamāmah 193, 194
contact of with Muhammad 194–5
as *raḥmān al-Yamāma* 194, 194n25
Muslims 7, 14–16, 23, 29, 157, 160, 161, 206, 206n72, 224–5, 224n58, 233, 236
and the exile from Mecca 242
and interfaith marriage 88n68
and manumission 231–2
modern Muslims 26
see also monotheistic community (Muslim); pagan law, Muslim attitudes toward

Nagel, Tilman 33, 51
Nasr, Shady 34
Nero 148, 149
Neskhāna 24
Neuwirth, Angelika 1, 2, 16, 19, 32, 33, 41, 48
on coincidences between qur'anic passages and the Psalms 36
and the composition of the Meccan surahs 51
on the liturgical aspects of the Qur'an 49
on the polyphonic characteristics of the Qur'an 50
on qur'anic descriptions of ruins 40
Nevo, Yehuda D. 28, 29
New Biblicists/New Biblicism 20–8
advances made by 27–8
criticism of 27
opposition of between New Biblicists and their opponents 26–7
on the pre-modern commentaries on the Qur'an 25
primary arguments of concerning Western study of the Qur'an 26
New Textualists 32–6
'Night of Power' (*laylat al-qadr*) 193
Niyār b. Rabīʿa 191, 191n14

Niẓām al-Qurʾān (Farahi) 42
Noah 36, 47
Nöldeke, Theodor 11, 12, 14, 32, 33, 41, 51, 52, 168
chronology of the surahs by 39
on qurʾanic language 37–8

Ohlig, Karl-Heinz 28
olives/olive harvesting 146n23
One True God (Stark) 149n47
Orientalism 5
Orientalists, nineteenth-century, interest of in qurʾanic rhyme and rhythm 38–9

pagan Arabs 140–6, 160–1
beliefs concerning the resurrection 143–4
biblical knowledge of 145–6, 154–5
as monotheists 142–3
as polytheists 141
and the religious milieu surrounding the Messenger 140–1
pagan law, Christian attitudes toward 222–3, 226n67
comparison of Christian and Muslim attitudes 240–2
early medieval attitudes 216–20
and Roman law 220–2
and Salic law 213–16
pagan law, Muslim attitudes toward 226n67
and Arabism 234–6
and the argument from silence 232–3, 232n105, 233n112, 233n115
comparison of Muslim and Christian attitudes 240–2
and divine pragmatism 236–8
God's monopoly of the making of law 223–5
and the possible monotheist origins of *Jāhilī* law 238–40
retention of pagan law in Islamic law 227–9
retention of pagan law in Islamic law (the case of the commenda [*qirāḍ*]) 229–30, 230n92, 232n105
retention of pagan law in Islamic law (the case of compurgation [*qasāma*]) 225–7, 226n67, 227n69, 227n71, 227n73
retention of pagan law in Islamic law (the case of manumission) 231–2
Palestine 152, 254, 255
Paret, Rudi 14, 15, 16, 32–3, 38, 48, 50
Patrick, St 219
Paul, St 147, 171, 222
Paul of Samosata 143n18
People of the Book 157n82, 158–9, 161
Peters, Rudolph 227n69
Pharamond 214
Pharaoh 126, 171, 177
Philostorgius 250
Phoenicia 152
poetry 234
Arabic poetry 168, 174–5
biblical poetry 51, 172
qurʾanic rhyme and rhythm 38–41
Ur-poetry of the Semites 39, 51
Pohlmann, Karl-Friedrich 49, 76n28, 77
Pola 148, 151–2n61
Pollock, Sheldon 169
Poppaea 148, 149, 149n45
pork 86, 87n62
avoidance of 152, 153
promotion of the consumption of by Christian authorities 86n55
prophets/prophecy 186–7, 237–8
biblical tradition of 187, 188–9, 190, 198
of the *fatra* (the time between Jesus and Muhammad) 187–8, 187n4, 200–4
pre-Islamic 'Arabian prophets' 187, 189, 190–1, 190n10
prophets in the Jahiliyya 189–91, 207–9
prophets in the Jahiliyya identified as monotheists 195–9, 203, 208
Ridda prophets 190, 191–5
terms used in connection with 186
see also *individually listed prophets*
Puin, Elisabeth 35
Puin, Gerard 28
pre-Islamic Arab religion, as 'tribal humanism' 10
presbyters/priests (*qissīsūn*) 159, 160

Q 33:69, exegesis of
and the alleged deformity of Moses 121–2, 122n8, 122n11
Christian parallels to 120
classical interpretations of 121–6, 121n5, 131n49, 131–2n51
compared to Q 61:5 121
contextual reading of 129–31
and the death of Aaron 123–4, 123–4n16, 124n18
immediate literary context of 128–31
and the *ʿinda* or *ʿabdan* reading of 132–3, 132nn52–3
introduction to 120
and Korah and Moses 124–5, 125n19, 125n21
and the link to Numbers 12 126–8, 133, 135
and Moses speaking to the rock to bring forth water 122–3, 122–3n12
variant reading of attributed to Ibn Masʿūd 131–3

Qāḍī Khān 233
Qalqashandī 235
qirā'āt, study of in Islamic literature 34
Qummī, ʿAlī b. Ibrāhīm al- 134
Qur'an 2–3, 154–61, 183–4, 186–7
  'Arabian prophets' of 187, 189, 190–1, 190n10
  background traditions in the formation of (Jewish, Christian, pre-Islamic pagan) 4–5, 10
  as a collective work 49–50
  competition for a work on the history of (1858) 11
  composition of and *Formgeschichte* (Form-History) 17–19, 49
  concordances of 52
  controversy concerning Jewish versus Christian tradition of 9–10
  cultural milieu of 169
  debates concerning the proper framework for the interpretation of 4–6
  early use of the word '*qur'ān*' 174
  as an epigonal text 166
  expense involved in producing early copies of 34
  as a 'flat text' 166
  fragmentary copies of 35–6
  lesser deities condemned in 141
  literary character of 167–8
  location of in world history 165–7
  multiple chronological layers in the same qur'anic passage 160n94
  orality and the canonization of 48–9
  poetry in 38–41, 172
  polemics and the misreading of 166
  principal subgenres of 168
  progress made in the history of 33–4
  as the 'property' of a community 169–70, 169–70n19
  'punishment stories' in 47
  qur'anic texts that resemble pre-Islamic *sajʿ* 41
  relation of to Christian texts and traditions 5
  ring-compositional approach to 42–4, 76, 104
  sources of 36–7
  textual growth of during the lifetime of the Prophet 76–7
  see also Qur'an, biblical tradition in; Qur'an, surahs of; qur'anic studies; Surah 5; Surah 9
Qur'an, biblical tradition in 173–5
  eclipsing the biblical tradition (the new mythopoiesis) 178–82
  penetrating the biblical tradition 175–8
Qur'an, surahs of 38, 172, 179
  chronology of 33, 39
  division of 32
  early Meccan surahs and the *illā* clauses 99n99
  examples of later expansion of (Q 73:20 and Q 74:31) 73–5, 77n32, 75n23
  identification of secondary additions to a given surah 70–2
  Meccan or Medinan settings of 69–70
  Medinan insertions in later Meccan surahs 75, 75n24
  Muhammad and the insertion of new passages into existing surahs 76–7
  order of 32
  resemblance of to biblical Psalms 174–5
  the structure of long surahs and ring-theory 42–4, 76
  surahs of the Middle Meccan period 175–6
  see also *individually listed surahs*
Qur'anic Christians (McAuliffe) 16
qur'anic studies 165–7
  beginnings of modern Western qur'anic studies 8–14
  biblical elements evident in 24–5
  book series devoted to 19–20
  contemporary growth of 6
  critical introductions to the Qur'an 10–11
  explosion of interest in 19–20
  five periods of 6
  focus of on the Syriac language 23–4
  from the early nineteenth century to the Second World War 8, 14–17
  future of 50–2
  and the Islamic commentarial tradition 25
  in the middle ages 7
  pagan influence studies 10
  qur'anic codicology 34–5
  of qur'anic language and style 37–41
  of qur'anic rhyme and rhythm 38–41
  on the role of *sajʿ* in the Qur'an 41
  on the series of oaths that open qur'anic surahs 41
  shift toward the Christian influence on the Qur'an 24
  similarity of to biblical studies 20
  in the sixteenth century 7–8
  three primary fields of enquiry in 7
  typology studies 47–8, 170–3, 183
  and the weakness of Western scholarship concerning the Arabic language 51–2
  see also Allohistorians/Allohistory; Late Antiquity; New Biblicists/New Biblicism; New Textualists; Q 33:69, exegesis of; qur'anic studies, feminist
qur'anic studies, feminist 44–7

construction of a feminist reading of the Qur'an 45–6
hermeneutical techniques of 46–7
political nature of 45
problematic texts for feminists 46
Qur'anic Studies (Wansbrough) 18, 28, 49
'Qur'an's Theopoetic Manifesto, The' (El-Masri) 40
Quraysh 234n116, 238

Rabb, Intisar 35
Rabin, Chaim 41
Rab-Yahūd 253
Rahman, Fazlur 16
Raḥmānān (Ilān/Ilahān) 247, 253, 254
Ratchis 217
Reste arabischen Heidentums (Wellhausen) 10
Review of Qur'anic Research (online site of the IQSA) 19
Reynolds, Gabriel Said 23, 33
Reynolds, J. 151
Ri'āb b. Zayd 189, 195–6, 197, 199, 203, 208, 209
association of with the Arabian soothsaying tradition 196
association of with Christianity 196
Richter, Gustav 38
Richtungen der Islamischen Koranauslegung, Die(Goldziher) 13, 14, 51
Riddah prophets *see* prophets/prophecy
Rippin, Andrew 16, 51, 104
Robin, Christian 248
Robinson, Neal 44, 77–8n32
Rodwell, John Medows 12
Rubin, Uri 197
Rückert, Friedrich 38

Sacy, Antoine Sylvestre de 8
Sadeghi, Behnam 33, 35
Ṣafī b. Ṣayyād 206
Ṣafiyya bint Ḥuyayy b. Akhṭab 134–5
Ṣafwān al-ʿAbsī 200
Salami, Mohammed Ali Al- 250
Saleh, Walid 104
Ṣāliḥ 189, 199
Sammlung des Qorans, Die (The Collection of the Qur'an [Schwally]) 11
Ṣanʿāʾ Palimpsest 35
saqar (fire of hell) 73–4, 73n16, 73–4n18, 75
Saracens 152, 153n69
Sarakhsī 230, 237
Scaliger, Joseph Justus 7
Schapiro, Israel 9
Schultens, Albert 7
Schwally, Friedrich 11, 72
Sciallac, Victor (Naṣrallāh Shalaq al-ʿĀqūrī) 7
Scriptural Polemics (Sirry) 50
Sectarian Milieu, The (Wansbrough) 18
Seeing Islam as Others Saw It (Hoyland) 30
Segovia, Carlos A. 36, 49
Seidensticker, Tilman 198
Selene 250
Sells, Michael 40
'Semitic rhetoric', theory of 43
Severa, Julia 149, 152
Shah, Mustafa 34
Shāṭibī 230, 237, 240
Shoemaker, Stephen 28, 29
Shuʿayb 189, 190
Sigismund, Burgundian king 217
Silverstein, Adam 36, 171
Sima, Alexander 251
Sinai, Nicolai 1–2, 19, 49, 199
Sionita, Gabriel (Jibrāʾīl al-Ṣahyūnī) 7
Sīra (Ibn Ishāq) 208
Sīrah (Ibn Hishām) 12, 27
Sīrah of the Prophet 33, 52
Sirry, Mun'im 50
Sleepers of Ephesus 22
Sokomos 153
Solomon 147, 171
Sozomen 152–3, 154
Speyer, Heinrich 9, 14, 16, 24
Spitaler, Anton 12, 32
Sprenger, Aloys 8, 11
Stark, Rodney 149n47
Stefanidis, Emmanuelle 33
Stein, Peter 249, 251–2
Stewart, Devin J. 1, 41, 47, 49
Stroumsa, Guy 176
Studien zur Komposition der mekkanischen Suren (Neuwirth) 33, 40
Suetonius 148
Sulaymān, Muqātil 52
Surah 577–89, 77–8n32
conclusions concerning 103–5
as a farewell speech 83, 83n49
on food exchange and intermarriage 88, 88n68
function of segment D as a 'wrap-up' unit 83, 83n48
mean verse length of 82, 82n44
penultimate segment of (5:3D) 80–2
prohibitions mentioned in 79–80, 83, 83nn46–7, 84–5, 86–7, 87n62
Q 5:3 79–84, 79n34
Q 5:4 84–5
Q 5:5 (relations of with the 'People of the Scripture') 85–9, 86–7n61
subdivision of 78

Surah (*cont.*)
use of the verbal noun *islām* (submission) in 83–4
verbal recurrences in 78n33
verse 3, 4, and 5 of as inserted at a secondary stage 78–9
the *yas'alūnaka* formula in 84, 84n52, 85n54
see also *Sūrat al-Mā'idah*
Surah 989–103 *passim*
analysis of the *barā'a* and the *adhān* in 98–103, 98n94
the *barā'a* declaration in 91
chronological order of the *barā'a* and the *adhān* in 102–3, 102n105
commentary on Q 9:1–16 90–6
conclusions concerning 103–5
and conflict with the Associators (*al-mushrikūn*) 89, 89n72, 90–6, 95n88, 96–103
and the content of the *adhān* made on the day of the pilgrimage 92
on the 'hypocrites' (*al-munāfiqūn*) 89
literary growth of the opening section of 96–103
the *naskh* (abrogation) approach to 97–8
opening section of 89–90, 91n76
pre-modern Islamic exegetical responses to the difficulties of 97–8
relationship between the 'sacred months' and the four-month grace period in 93–5, 94n83, 94n85, 94–5n86, 95nn87–8, 96n89
Sword Verse of 96–7, 100, 103
thematic subdivision of 90
traditional names of (*Barā'a* or *al-Tawba*) 89, 89n71, 90–1, 90n74
see also Bell, Richard, on the early verses of Surah 9; 'Muhammad's Pilgrimage Proclamation' (Bell)
surahs *see* Qur'an, surahs of
Sūrat al-Baqarah 42, 43
Sūrat Āl ʿImrān 42, 179
Sūrat al-Kahf 22, 24
Sūrat al-Mā'idah 42, 44 *see also* Surah 5
Sūrat Maryam 22
Sūrat al-Qamar 42, 47
Sūrat al-Qāriʿah 42
Sūrat al-Shuʿarā' 47
Sūrat al-Tawbah. See Surah 9
Sūrat al-Tīn 42
Sūrat al-Zilzāl 42
Sūs, siege of 206, 207, 207n77
al-Suyūṭī 52
synagogues
openness of 148, 148n41
single mention of in the Qur'an 155
synoptic Gospels 18, 49
Synoptische Tradition, Die (Bultmann) 18
Syriac language 21–2
Syriac dictionaries 21
Syriac Milieu of the Qur'an: The Recasting of Biblical Narratives (Witztum) 23–4

Ṭabarī, al- 16, 17, 25, 26, 52, 81, 90n73, 206n72
on '*istiqsām* by arrows' 80n39
on verses regarding unbelievers 224–5, 224n58, 225n63
Ṭabrisī, al- 17, 126
Tadabbur-i Qur'ān (Iṣlāḥī) 42
tafsīr (qur'anic exegesis) 13, 27, 46, 52
debates concerning interpretations found in 25–6
focus of in pre-modern Islamic scholarship 16
on matters of general usage 26
progress made in studies of 16–17
scholarly studies of 15–16, 27
Ṭā'if 196
Tannenbaum, R. 151
ṭayyāye 'Arabs' 29
Thaʿlabī, al- 17
Thamūd 199
Theodoric 218
Theophilos 250
Toorawa, Shawkat 39, 41
Torah, the 4, 124n18, 159, 175, 179, 181, 182
food laws of 86–7n61
Torrey, Charles Cutler 9
typology 47–8, 170–3
of Moses 176–7
and parallelization 172
reflecting typology 182–3

Ubayy b. Kaʿb 32, 160
Über den Ursprung des Qorans (On the Origin of the Qur'an [Schwally]) 11
ʿUmar, Aḥmad Mukhtār 34
Umayya b. Abī-l-Salṭ 190, 191, 196–8, 196nn32–3, 197nn34–5, 203, 208
authenticity of the verses attributed to him 198–9, 198n40
Umayyads 206, 207
Untersuchungen zur Reimprosa im Koran (F. R. Müller) 40
Urchristentum im Rahmen der antiken Religionen, Das (Bultmann) 18
Uzayr 159

Ventris, Michael 21
Verbal Idioms in the Qur'an (Mir) 38
verse-counting traditions 32

Volkssprache und Schriftsprache im alten Arabien 39–40
Vollers, Karl 39–40, 51, 92n79

Wadud, Amina 45
Walīd ibn al-Mughīra 235
Wansbrough, John 17, 18–19, 28, 29, 47
Waraqa b. Nawfal 188, 196, 197, 203
Was hat Mohammed aus dem Judenthume aufgenommen ('What Did Muhammad Take Over from Judaism?' [Geiger]) 8–9
Watt, W. Montgomery 10, 14, 16, 47, 194
Weil, Gustav 13, 32
Welch, Alford 47, 48, 49, 51
Wellhausen, Julius 9, 10, 37, 41
wet nurses 228, 237, 237n137
Wheeler, Brannon 16
Widengren, G. 190
Wild, Stefan 32
wine, prohibition of 236n131
Witztum, Joseph 1, 2, 23, 24
  criticism of Wansbrough 49
Wujūh waʾl-naẓāʾir, al- 48
Wüstenfeld, Heinrich Ferdinand 8

Yāqūt 240
Yūsuf 247, 253

Zahniser, Matthias 43
  on the concept of compositional 'hinges' 77–8n32
zakāt, paying of 155, 155n79
Zamakhsharī, al- 17, 25
Zammit, Martin 38
Zellentin, Holger 23, 37, 86
  on Jewish and Muslim dietary laws 86–7n61, 87n63
Zeno of Citium 222
Zwettler, Michael 47, 48